977. What was the profession of Hitler's mistress, Eva Braun? **978.** During the Civil War, how many states fought for the Union; how many for the Confederacy? **979.** What two nations were involved in a year-long conflict that was popularly known as the Pastry War? **980.** What president ordered the integration of American armed forces? **981.** What famous American signed the Treaty of Kanagawa? **982.** Adolf Hitler called his country home Eagle's Nest. What name did Winston Churchill give to his? **983.** What American billionaire flew to airlift 28 tons of medicine and Christmas gifts to American POWs in North Vietnam in 1969? **984.** Charles de Gaulle served as ghost-writer of the book *The Soldier* for what famous World War I military hero? **985.** How does Lockheed manufacture of the Trident missile, transmit data from its Sunnyvale, California headquarters to its plant thirty miles away in Santa Cruz? **986.** During whose presidency was the U.S. War Dept. replaced by the Defense Dept.? **987.** What famous American patriot served as a rear admiral in the Russian navy? **988.** What actress obtained a patent as co-inventor of a radar-controlled system to direct torpedoes at moving ships? **989.** When the city of Khartoum was under siege in 1884, who organized the 1,500-flotilla of troops and supplies that came to its rescue? **990.** Where was the Battle of Bunker Hill actually fought in June 1775? **991.** What was the Age of Reason? **992.** What American military leader said, "Lafayette, we are here" and on what occasion? **993.** What physical ailment is said to have contributed to Napolean's defeat at Waterloo? **994.** What war was the first to have authorized film coverage? **995.** "GI Joe" won the Dickins Medal for saving a thousand British soldiers from a bombing attack in Italy during World War II. Who was he and what's the Dickins Medal? **996.** In 1969 the Navy spent $375,000 on an "aerodynamic analysis of the self-suspended flare." What was the study's

977. What was the profession of Hitler's mistress, Eva Braun? 978. During the Civil War, how many states fought for the Union; how many for the Confederacy? 979. What two nations were involved in a year-long conflict that was popularly known as the Pastry War? 980. What president ordered the integration of American armed forces? 981. What famous American signed the Treaty of Kanagawa? 982. Adolf Hitler called his country home Eagle's Nest. What name did Winston Churchill give to his? 983. What American billionaire offered to airlift 28 tons of medicine and Christmas gifts to American POWs in North Vietnam in 1969? 984. Charles de Gaulle served as ghost-writer of the book The Soldier for what famous World War I military hero? 985. How does Lockheed, manufacturer of the Trident missile, transmit data from its Sunnyvale, California headquarters to its plant thirty miles away in Santa Cruz? 986. During whose presidency was the U.S. War Dept. replaced by the Defense Dept.? 987. What famous American patriot served as a rear admiral in the Russian navy? 988. What actress obtained a patent as co-inventor of a radar-controlled system to direct torpedoes at moving ships? 989. When the British garrison at Khartoum was under siege in 1884, who organized the 1,500-flotilla of troops and supplies that came to its rescue? 990. Where was the Battle of Bunker Hill actually fought in June 1775? 991. What was the Axis alliance known as? 992. What American military leader said, "Lafayette, we are here," and on what occasion? 993. What physical ailment is said to have contributed to Napolean's defeat at Waterloo? 994. What war was the first to have authorized film coverage? 995. "GI Joe" won the Dickins Medal for saving a thousand British soldiers from a bombing attack in Italy during World War II. Who was he and what's the Dickins Medal? 996. In 1969 the Navy spent $375,000 on an "aerodynamic analysis of the self-suspended flare." What was the study's

By Marsha Kranes,
Fred Worth and
Steve Tamerius

Edited by
Michael Driscoll

BLACK DOG
& LEVENTHAL
PUBLISHERS
NEW YORK

Published by
Black Dog & Leventhal Publishers, Inc.
151 West 19th Street
New York, NY 10011

Distributed by
Workman Publishing Company
708 Broadway
New York, NY 10003

Designed by Sabrina Bowers

Manufactured in the United States of America

ISBN-10:1-57912-086-5
ISBN-13:978-1-57912-086-3

j k l m n o p q r

Library of Congress Cataloging-in-Publication Data
Kranes, Marsha
        5087 trivia questions & answers / by Marsha Kranes, Fred Worth
& Steve Tamerius ; edited by Michael Driscoll
        p. cm.
        ISBN 1-57912-086-5
        1. Questions and answers. I. Worth, Fred L. II. Tamerius, Steve
D. III. Driscoll, Michael, 1973- IV. Title. V. Title: 5087 trivia questions
and answers
AG195.K74 1999
031.02--dc21   99-39874
                                                    CIP

Contents

Arts, Comics & Literature

Questions

1. What do P. G. Wodehouse, Ezra Pound and William Joyce have in common?

2. What was the first published Sherlock Holmes story written by Sir Arthur Conan Doyle?

3. Who was Clark Kent's high school sweetheart?

4. What is the name of Dr. Seuss's egg-hatching elephant?

5. George G. Moppet was the father of what comic strip character?

6. John Clayton Jr. was the childhood name of what well-known fictional character?

7. What one word was intentionally left out of the movie version of Mario Puzo's novel, "The Godfather," even though this word was the working title of the book?

8. Ernest Hemingway once wrote that a man must do four things in his life to demonstrate his manhood. What were they?

9. What is the name of the poem which appears on the pedestal of the Statue of Liberty?

Answers

1. *They all made broadcasts for the enemy during World War II.*

2. *A Study In Scarlet, in 1887.*

3. *Lana Lang.*

4. *Horton.*

5. *Little Lulu.*

6. *Tarzan, whose title was Lord Greystoke.*

7. *"Mafia."*

8. *Plant a tree, fight a bull, write a book, and have a son.*

9. *"The New Colossus," by Emma Lazarus.*

10. In the comic strips, what was the name of Mandrake the Magician's giant partner?

11. *Men Against the Sea* and *Pitcairn's Island* were two sequels to what famous novel?

12. What novel contains the longest sentence in literature?

13. Where did Samuel Clemens get the idea for his pseudonym, Mark Twain?

14. In what comic strip would you have found an animal called the "Schmoo"?

15. What couple live next door to Dagwood and Blondie Bumstead in "Blondie"?

16. What is the only novel to top the best-seller lists for two consecutive years?

17. What classic gothic novel of 1818 was subtitled, *The Modern Prometheus?*

18. Who was the Lone Ranger's great grand-nephew?

19. Psychologist William Moulton Marston, inventor of the polygraph, or lie detector, also created a famous comic book heroine. Who was she?

20. The Max Fleischer cartoon character, Betty Boop, was based on which real-life actress?

21. "Last night I dreamt I went to Manderley again," was the first line of what Daphne du Maurier novel?

22. What is the actual title of Leonardo da Vinci's "Mona Lisa"?

23. Who did cartoonist Milton Caniff use as his inspiration for the Dragon Lady, in his "Terry and the Pirates" comic strip?

24. In Henry Wadsworth Longfellow's famous poem, *Hiawatha*, what was the name of Hiawatha's wife?

10. *Lothar.*

11. Mutiny On The Bounty *(Charles Nordoff and James Norman Hall co-wrote all three novels).*

12. Les Miserables, *by Victor Hugo, with 823 words.*

13. *It was the river call used by boatmen on the Mississippi to signify two fathoms of water.*

14. Li'l Abner. *The Schmoo gave milk, laid eggs and tasted similar to chicken or steak.*

15. *Herb and Tootsie Woodley.*

16. Jonathan Livingston Seagull, *by Richard Bach, in 1972 and 1973.*

17. Frankenstein, *by Mary Wollstonecraft Shelley.*

18. *The Green Hornet. The relationship was as follows: John Reid (the Lone Ranger) had a brother named Dan Reid, who had a son named Dan Jr., who had a son named Henry Reid, who had a son named Britt Reid (the Green Hornet).*

19. *Wonder Woman.*

20. *Helen Kane, known as the boop-boop-a-doop girl.*

21. Rebecca.

22. La Gioconda.

23. *Joan Crawford.*

24. *Minnehaha.*

25. Puddleburg was the hometown of what cartoon character?

26. "The temperature hit ninety degrees the day she arrived" was the opening line of one of the best-selling novels ever. What was it?

27. Who was the first writer to incorporate himself?

28. Tess Truehcart is the wife of what comic strip character?

29. What is the native country of Agatha Christie's detective Hercule Poirot?

30. What was the hometown of Sgt. Snorkel in *Beetle Bailey*?

31. In the Robin Hood stories, what was the real name of Little John?

32. What was Scarlett O'Hara's real first name?

33. Most of us are familiar with the faces of Dr. B. H. McKeeby and Nan Wood, but who are they and where have we seen them?

34. In the *Little Orphan Annie* comic strip, what was the name of Daddy Warbucks's giant bodyguard who wore a turban?

35. *The Last Of The Really Great Whangdoodles and Mandy* are children's books written by what well-known Oscar-winning actress?

36. Under what assumed name did Oscar Wilde live out the last three years of his life, in France?

37. By what pseudonym is writer Frederick Dannay Manfred Bennington Lee better known?

38. What was the name of the pig leader in George Orwell's *Animal Farm*?

39. What was the name of the girlfriend of Felix the Cat?

40. To whom did Herman Mclville dedicate his novel, *Moby Dick*?

25. Woody Woodpecker.

26. The Valley of the Dolls *by Jacqueline Susann.*

27. Edgar Rice Burroughs, the creator of Tarzan, who became a corporation in 1923.

28. Dick Tracy.

29. Belgium.

30. Pork Corners, Kansas.

31. John Little.

32. Katie.

33. The farmer and his wife in Grant Wood's classic painting, American Gothic

34. Punjab.

35. Julie Andrews.

36. Sebastian Melmoth.

37. Ellery Queen.

38. Napoleon.

39. Phyllis.

40. Nathaniel Hawthorne.

41. What comic strip character was named after heavyweight boxing champion James J. Jeffries

42. What was Juliet's last name, in Shakespeare's *Romeo and Juliet*?

43. *The Terror of the Monster* was an early title for a best-selling novel which inspired one of the highest-grossing movies of the mid-70's. Under what name did it eventually terrify the reading and filmgoing public.

44. *The Emerald City* was the working title of which classic novel?

45. What was the name of the gang that was always trying to steal Scrooge McDuck's money in the comics?

46. What famous writer named a dull-witted character in one of his plays Moron, introducing the word into the vocabulary?

47. What famous American poet penned the oft-quoted line "Into each life some rain must fall"?

48. Who is the only named dog to appear in a Shakespearean play?

49. What was strange about the watch worn by the Mad Hatter in the Lewis Carroll classic *Alice's Adventures in Wonderland*?

50. What was the favorite cocktail of Ian Fleming, creator of suave superspy James Bond?

51. What famous American writer's gravestone epitaph is this last line from one of his novels: "So we beat on, boats against the current, borne back ceaselessly into the past"?

52. To what famous architect do we attribute the dictum "Less is more"?

53. What unusual use did writer D. H. Lawrence make of his favorite horse, Aaron, after it died?

54. What popular comic strip has a concerto named in its honor by a contemporary composer?

41. Jeff, of Mutt and Jeff.

42. Capulet.

43. Jaws, *by Peter Benchley.*

44. The Wonderful Wizard of Oz, *by L. Frank Baum.*

45. The Beagle Boys.

46. Molière. The play was La Princesse d'Elide.

47. Henry Wadsworth Longfellow. The line is from his poem The Rainy Day, *written in 1842.*

48. Crab. The play is The Two Gentlemen of Verona. *Dogs are mentioned, but not by name, in several other Shakespearean plays.*

49. As Alice observed: "It tells the day of the month but doesn't tell what o'clock it is."

50. Pink gin—not Bond's famous vodka martini (shaken, not stirred).

51. F. Scott Fitzgerald's. The line quoted is from The Great Gatsby.

52. Ludwig Mies van der Rohe.

53. He had the hide made into a duffel bag.

54. Peanuts. The concerto is by Ellen Taaffe Zwilich.

55. What famous British poet and playwright had an m—for "murderer"—branded on his left thumb?

56. What famous character in literature was inspired by an Augustinian monk named Alonso Quixado.

57. What was popular author Louis L'Amour's real name?

58. The title of what poetic drama by Robert Browning was used to name a Kentucky town?

59. How many years did Robinson Crusoe spend shipwrecked on his island?

60. What did L. Frank Baum, author of *The Wonderful Wizard* of *Oz*, call his home in Hollywood?

61. What famous American poet was a West Point cadet for two weeks, but was forced to leave after failing arithmetic and grammar?

62. What is the real name of the evil Batman comic strip character known as the Riddler?

63. What were the names of the brothers Karamozov in the novel by Feodor Dostoevsky?

64. What exotic city was featured in *National Geographic* magazine's first photo story in 1905?

65. What was the name of Dick and Jane's baby sister in elementary school primers of old?

66. What was mystery writer Dashiell Hammett's first name?

67. How many exclamation points did author Tom Wolfe use in his blockbuster bestseller *The Bonfire of the Vanities?*

68. What is the literary source of the F. Scott Fitzgerald book title *Tender Is the Night?*

55. *Ben Jonson, for killing an actor in a duel in 1598. Jonson escaped the gallows by pleading benefit of clergy and forfeiting all his goods and chattels.*

56. Don Quixote. *Quixado was writer Miguel de Cervantes's great-uncle by marriage.*

57. *Louis LaMoore.*

58. Pippa Passes. *The name was suggested by a schoolteacher in 1915. Browning's play gave us the line: "God's in his heaven—/All's right with the world."*

59. *24.*

60. *Ozcot.*

61. *Carl Sandburg, in 1899. One of his classmates was general-to-be Douglas MacArthur.*

62. *E. Nigma. The E. is for Edward.*

63. *Dmitri (or Mitya), Ivan (or Vanya), Alexei (or Alyosha) and Smerdyakov.*

64. *Lhasa, Tibet.*

65. *Sally.*

66. *Samuel, or Sam—as in Sam Spade, his famous detective.*

67. *2,343.*

68. *Keats' poem* Ode to a Nightingale.

69. What well-known writer appeared in the 1981 movie *Ragtime* as Stanford White, the celebrated architect who was shot to death in the sensational *Girl in the Red Velvet Swing* murder?

70. What did Jughead, the buddy of comic strip character Archie, become when he grew up, according to a 1990 TV movie about the two Riverdale High School grads?

71. What was the name of the dog that was with Rip Van Winkle when he fell asleep for 20 years?

72. What was Dr. Frankenstein's first name in the famous novel by Mary Wollstonecraft Shelley?

73. What cartoon character's "racy lifestyle" once led to a ban on his comic books in youth club libraries in Helsinki, Finland?

74. How many references are there to crying in Tammy Faye Bakker's two books, *I Gotta Be Me* and *Run to the Roar* ?

75. What was the title of Harpo Marx's 1985 autobiography?

76. What famous artist's first name means welcome in his native tongue?

77. What was the name of the cat Alice left behind when she fell down the rabbit hole in *Alice's Adventures in Wonderland* by Lewis Carroll?

78. What was Rembrandt's last name?

79. What American novel was the first to sell over one million copies?

80. What comic strip character was the first to grow up and age in the strip?

81. What is the name of the gypsy girl the hunchback Quasimodo falls in love with in Victor Hugo's *The Hunchback of Notre Dame* ?

69. *Norman Mailer.*

70. *A psychiatrist—known by his given name, Forsythe, rather than Jughead.*

71. *Wolf.*

72. *Victor.*

73. *Donald Duck's, in 1978. His questionable behavior included a 50-year engagement to Daisy Duck; the uncertain parentage of his nephews, Huey, Dewey and Louie; and his regular appearance in a sailor suit that failed to cover his feathery behind.*

74. *60.*

75. *The zany, but silent Marx brother called his book* Harpo Speaks!

76. *Benvenuto Cellini's.*

77. *Dinah.*

78. *Van Ryn (or van Rijn).*

79. Uncle Tom's Cabin, *or,* Life Among the Lowly, *by Harriet Beecher Stowe, which was published in 1852.*

80. *Skeezix, who first appeared in the* Gasoline Alley *comic strip as a baby left on bachelor Walt Wallet's doorstep.*

81. *Esmeralda.*

ARTS, COMICS & LITERATURE—QUESTIONS 19

82. What was the ransom paid for the release of yeoman Geoffrey Chaucer after he was captured by the French in 1359 during the Hundred Years' War?

83. What famous American writer worked as an entertainer aboard a Swedish ocean liner cruising the Caribbean before being drafted to serve in World War II?

84. To whom did Helen Keller dedicate her autobiography, *The Story of My Life?*

85. What did famed architect Frank Lloyd Wright reply when an important client called to complain that water on the roof of his newly completed house was leaking onto a dinner guest?

86. What famous book begins: "Chug, chug, chug. Puff, puff, puff"?

87. What was the name of Don Quixote's worn-out old horse?

88. What were the first names of L'il Abner Yokum's parents in the popular Al Capp comic strip?

89. How many husbands did the Wife of Bath have, as reported in *Chaucer's Canterbury Tales?*

90. What were the first names of Robert Louis Stevenson's Dr. Jekyll and Mr. Hyde?

91. In what unusual way did writer Nathan Weinstein follow publisher Horace Greeley's advice to "Go west, young man"?

92. What was the name of the she-ape that rescued the infant Tarzan and raised him to be Lord of the Apes?

93. In what best-selling book did an author offer acknowledgment to a friend who later killed him?

94. What Pulitzer and Nobel Prize-winning American novelist worked on the screenplays of the movies *The Road to Glory, Gunga , To Have and Have Not* and *The Big Sleep?*

82. £16—about $4,800 in today's currency.

83. J. D. Salinger.

84. To inventor Alexander Graham Bell, who helped direct her education and considered himself, first and foremost, a teacher of the deaf.

85. "Tell him to move his chair."

86. The children's book The Little Engine That Could," by Watty Piper.

87. Rosinante. Sidekick Sancho Panza's donkey was called Dapple.

88. Mammy was Pansy; Pappy, Lucifer.

89. Five.

90. The good doctor was Henry; the evil Mr. Hyde, Edward.

91. He changed his last name to West—and became famous as Nathanael West, author of "Miss Lonelyhearts" and "The Day of the Locust."

92. Kala.

93. "The Complete Scarsdale Medical Diet," in which Dr. Herman Tarnower thanked his friend Jean Harris.

94. William Faulkner.

95. What is the origin of the expression "Cowabunga!"—the war cry of the Teenage Mutant Ninja Turtles?

96. How many times did Ernest Hemingway revise the last page of *A Farewell to Arms*?

97. What is the name of the elementary school attended by Lucy, Linus and Charlie Brown in Charles Schulz's *Peanuts* comic strip?

98. How many syllables are there in a Japanese haiku poem?

99. In Lewis Carroll's poem *The Hunting of the Snark*, what did the elusive, troublesome snark turn into to fool hunters?

100. In the novel *Shoeless Joe*—upon which the 1989 hit movie *Field of Dreams* was based—what real-life American writer was "kidnapped" by the hero, Iowa farmer Ray Kinsella?

101. What unflattering observation did poet Dylan Thomas make about writer T. S. Eliot's name?

102. In the original L. Frank Baum story *The Wonderful Wizard of Oz*, what color were Dorothy's slippers?

103. What was art-world guru Andy Warhol's name at birth?

104. What phrase did French impressionist artist Paul Cezanne teach his pet parrot to say over and over again?

105. What was the maiden name of Blondie Bumstead, the comic-strip wife of hapless Dagwood Bumstead?

106. Whose autobiography is entitled *The Wheel of Fortune*?

107. What famous comic strip character was inspired by the 1936 Henry Fonda film *Trail of the Lonesome Pine*?

108. What was the original name of the orphan created in 1924 by cartoonist Harold Gray in the comic strip we know as *Little Orphan Annie*?

109. In what comic strip did the onomatopoeia "ZAP" originate?

95. *It was the greeting exchanged by Buffalo Bob Smith and Chief Thunderthud on the "Howdy Doody" TV show in the 1950s. Its use spread through the "Gidget" surfer movies, and later the "Peanuts" comic strip.*

96. *39 times.*

97. *Birchwood.*

98. *17, arranged in 3 lines of 5, 7 and 5 syllables.*

99. *A boojum.*

100. *The reclusive J. D. Salinger. Because Salinger threatened to sue, he was replaced in the film by a fictitious writer named Terence Mann, who was portrayed by James Earl Jones.*

101. *Backward—but for one misplaced letter—it would spell toilets.*

102. *Silver.*

103. *Andrew Warhola.*

104. *"Cezanne is a great painter!"*

105. *Boopadoop. In the early days of the Chic Young cartoon "Blondie," she was a gold-digging flapper trailed by rich suitors, one of whom was playboy Dagwood.*

106. *The answer is not Vanna White, who was only eight years old when the book was published in 1965. Its author was French singer Edith Piaf.*

107. *Al Capp's Li'l Abner. Fonda played a backwoods mountaineer in the movie.*

108. *Otto. Gray was advised to "put a skirt on the kid and call it 'Little Orphan Annie'" by Chicago Tribune publisher Joseph Patterson.*

109. *In Buck Rogers, in 1929. Cartoonist Philip Francis Nowlan used it to describe the sound of Buck's paralyzing ray gun.*

110. Why was Clark Kent—alias Superman—rejected for military service during World War II?

111. What is the native language of English playwright Tom Stoppard, author of *Rosencrantz and Guildenstern Are Dead*, *Travesties* and *The Real Thing*?

112. What was Captain Queeg's first name and rank in the 1951 novel—and later movie—*The Caine Mutiny*?

113. Under what name did Italian artist Jocopo Robusti gain world renown?

114. What title did Russian author Leo Tolstoy originally give to the novel we know as *War and Peace*?

115. What classic adventure story did author William Styron reject when he was a reader for McGraw-Hill—a mistake he had his narrator, Stingo, repeat in his novel *Sophie's Choice*?

116. Vincent Van Gogh's painting *Sunflowers* was sold at auction for $39.9 million in 1987. How much did that come to per sunflower?

117. What famous character in English literature made his debut in *Beeton's Christmas Annual* in 1887?

118. How many medals and ribbons were awarded to comic strip hero Steve Canyon during his 41 years in the Air Force?

119. What was the title of the detective story by stripteaser Gypsy Rose Lee, published in 1941?

120. What headgear is named after the title character of a Robert Burns poem?

121. What is the last line of the Thomas Hood poem that begins:
No sun—no moon!
No morn—no noon
No dawn—no dusk—no proper time of day.

122. How many names did Andy Warhol, the gossipy guru of the avant garde, drop in his diaries, which were published in 1989?.

110. *He failed the eye test portion of the Army physical. Because of his X-ray vision, he inadvertently read an eye chart in another room.*

111. *Czech. He was born Thomas Straussler in Zlin, Czechoslovakia, 1937. Stoppard is the name of the British Army officer his mother married in 1946.*

112. *First name, Philip; rank, lieutenant commander.*

113. *Tintorette. Robusti's nickname—Italian for "little dyer"—was bestowed on him because his father was a dyer, or tintore, of silk.*

114. All's Well That Ends Well.

115. Kon-Tiki *by Thor Heyerdahl.*

116. *$2.66 million. There are 15 sunflowers in the painting.*

117. *Sherlock Holmes. His first published exploit was* A Study in Scarlet, *for which Sir Arthur Conan Doyle was paid £25.*

118. *21—that's 13 medals and 8 ribbons. They're on display at Ohio State University, the alma mater of both Canyon and his creator, Milton Caniff*

119. The G-String Murders. *The book, ghost-written by Craig Rice, is about two striptease queens murdered with their own G-strings.*

120. *The tam-o'-shanter, or tam.*

121. *"November!" The poem's title is* No!

122. *According to "Fame" magazine, exactly 2,809—or more than three per page in the 807-page book.*

123. What Pulitzer Prize-winning novelist worked as a hod carrier, wheeling 100-pound barrows of concrete along scaffolding, during construction of New York's Madison Square Garden in the 1920s?

124. In what play does the title character have a son named Swiss Cheese?

125. How many grandchildren did artist Grandma Moses have?

126. In the early James Bond books, Agent 007 packed a Walther PPK. What weapon replaced it in his later appearances?

127. In what state was playwright Tennessee Williams born?

128. Who said "Nothing is so much to be feared as fear"?

129. What was the name of Elizabeth Barrett Browning's pet golden cocker spaniel?

130. What famous novel provided the basic story line for Francis Ford Coppola's 1979 Vietnam War film epic, *Apocalypse Now?*

131. What famous British literary figure wrote under the pseudonym S.P.A.M.?

132. What do the initials P. G. stand for in writer P. G. Wodehouse's name?

133. What 804-page book by a little-known zoologist became a best-seller in 1948 despite a reviewer's description of it as "so turgid, so repetitive, so full of nearly meaningless tables, that it will only be read by specialists..."?

134. Alexandra Ripley was paid $4.94 million in 1988 as an advance for the sequel to *Gone With the Wind*. What was Margaret Mitchell's advance for the best-selling, Pulitzer Prize-winning original?

135. In what language was the first complete Bible in America printed?

123. *John Steinbeck.*

124. Mother Courage and Her Children *by Bertolt Brecht.*

125. *11.*

126. *A German-made, 9-millimeter, Heckler and Koch semi-automatic pistol.*

127. *In Mississippi, as Thomas Lanier Williams. He took the name Tennessee after his father's home state.*

128. *Henry David Thoreau, in his 14-volume* Journal, *published posthumously in 1906.*

129. *Flush.*

130. The Heart of Darkness *by Joseph Conrad, published in 1902 and set in Africa.*

131. *Satirist Jonathan Swift. It was one of a series of pseudonyms he used—others were Isaac Bickerstaff, Martinus Scribberus, T. Tinker, Dr. Andrew Tripe and Simon Wagstaff.*

132. *Pelham Grenville.*

133. *The* Kinsey Report *by Alfred C. Kinsey, published as* Sexual Behavior in the Human Male.

134. *$500.*

135. *That of the Algonquin Indians of Massachusetts. It was translated into their language by the Rev. John Eliot and published in 1663.*

136. What famous American writer wrote a fictional biography of Joan of Arc that was published anonymously in *Harper's* magazine?

137. What was the title of Mae West's 1959 autobiography?

138. How many copies did Doubleday run off the presses in its first printing of Bill Cosby's 1987 book *Time Flies?*

139. Why did 70-year-old Miguel Ramirez sue writer Ernest Hemingway?

140. Complete this Biblical quotation: "It is easier for a camel to go through the eye of a needle, than..."

141. What is unusual about the 50,100-word novel *Gadsby*, written by Ernest Vincent Wright in 1937?

142. What words did Lewis Carroll combine to come up with the term "chortle" in *Through a Looking-Glass?*

143. What literary animals "dined on mince, and slices of quince, which they ate with a runcible spoon"? And just what is a runcible spoon?

144. Who wrote, "Oh, East is East, and West is West, and never the twain shall meet"?

145. Who was the subject of the 1968 biography *Always on Sunday?*

146. Where did mystery writer Agatha Christie acquire her extensive knowledge of poisons?

147. What was Truman Capote's last name before he was adopted by his stepfather?

148. What book knocked Henry Kissinger's *White House Years* out of first place on the best-seller list in November 1979?

149. Shakespeare wrote that "brevity is the soul of wit." What did noted wit Dorothy Parker say it was?

136. *Mark Twain, in 1896. It was called* Personal Recollections of Joan of Arc *and written under the pseudonym of* The Sieur Louis de Conte, *page and secretary to Joan of Arc* **137.** Goodness Had Nothing to Do With It.

138. *1.5 million.*

139. *The Cuban fisherman claimed Hemingway stole his story, the Pulitzer Prize-winning* The Old Man and the Sea. *The suit was thrown out.*

140. *"...for a rich man to enter into the kingdom of God." The words are those of Jesus, from Matthew 19:24.*

141. *It doesn't contain a single letter "e"—the most frequently used letter in the English alphabet. Wright made sure he didn't use it by tying down the "e" bar on his typewriter.*

142. *Chuckle and snort.*

143. *The Owl and the Pussy-Cat did the dining in the poem of the same name by Edward Lear. A runcible spoon is a three-pronged fork that's curved like a spoon and has a cutting edge.*

144. *Rudyard Kipling, in "The Ballad of East and West."*

145. *Ed Sullivan.*

146. *In a hospital dispensary—where she worked during World War I.*

147. *Persons.*

148. *"Aunt Erma's Cope Book," by Erma Bombeck.*

149. *"The soul of lingerie."*

150. The title of what artist's painting was used to name the Blue Rider (Blaue Reiter) school of German expressionist painters?

151. Who wrote the poem *The Pied Piper of Hamelin?*

152. By what pseudonym is novelist David John Moore Cornwell best known?

153. By what score was Mudville defeated in Ernest Thayer's classic poem *Casey at the Bat?*

154. For what career was Western writer Zane Grey trained?

155. What American literary classic was published in Russian 50 years ago under the title *Volshebnik Izumrudnovo Goroda?*

156. What famous play served as the inspiration for the 1956 science-fiction film *Forbidden Planet?*

157. What is the name of the town in which Thornton Wilder's Pulitzer Prize-winning play *Our Town* takes place?

158. What famous writer is believed to have made the first reference to tennis in English literature?

159. How much was poet John Milton paid for his epic poem *Paradise Lost,* which was first published in 1667

160. In *Gulliver's Travels,* what was a professor at the Grand Academy in Lagado busily trying to extract from cucumbers?

161. What was the first name of supercapitalist war profiteer "Daddy" Warbucks in the *Little Orphan Annie* cartoon series?

162. What play opens with "Now is the winter of our discontent"?

163. What was the title of the biography of Thomas Crapper, the British sanitary engineer who invented the modern flush toilet in 1878?

164. What second career did nineteenth-century literary giants Nathaniel Hawthorne and William Dean Howells have in common?

150. *Russian Wassily Kandinsky.*

151. *Robert Browning, in 1842.*

152. *John Le Carré, which translated from the French means John the Square.*

153. *The score was 4 to 2.*

154. *Dentistry.*

155. The Wonderful Wizard of Oz.

156. *Shakespeare's* The Tempest.

157. *Grover's Corners, New Hampshire.*

158. *Geoffrey Chaucer, in 1380, when he wrote of "playen racket to and fro" in* Troilus and Criseyde.

159. *Ten pounds—five down and another five pounds when all 1,300 copies in the first printing were sold. After Milton's death, his widow gave up all future claims for an additional eight pounds.*

160. *Sunbeams.*

161. *Oliver.*

162. *Shakespeare's "The Tragedy of King Richard III."*

163. Flushed with Pride: The Story of Thomas Crapper.

164. *Both were diplomats: Hawthorne wrote a campaign biography of Franklin Pierce, earning himself the consul post in Liverpool; Howells' campaign biography of Abraham Lincoln won him the consul post in Venice.*

165. Who wrote the story upon which Alfred Hitchcock based his 1963 suspense film *The Birds*?

166. What famous American writer was granted a patent for a best-selling book that contained no words?

167. Where will you find a 24-foot-long, 3,500-pound aluminum lipstick tube mounted on a caterpillar tractor tread?

168. What foreign government did Rex Stout's fictional Sleuth Nero Wolfe serve as a secret agent when he was a young man?

169. What famous American writer called a volume of his short stories *Rolling Stones*?

170. What was the name of the life-saving pet mongoose in *The Jungle Book by Rudyard Kipling*?

171. What controversial painting caused an uproar at the New York Armory Show in 1913?

172. What are the four ghosts in Charles Dickens' *A Christmas Carol*?

173. What writer worked as a Pinkerton detective on cases involving movie comic Fatty Arbuckle and gambler Nicky Arnstein?

174. What book was Mark David Chapman carrying with him when he killed John Lennon on 12/8/80?

175. What writer was expelled from West Point for showing up for public parade wearing only a white belt and gloves?

176. What was the working title of Joseph Heller's best-selling *Catch 22*?

177. What Frenchman wrote about two fantastic space odysseys— one to the moon and one to the sun—more than 200 years before Jules Verne?

178. What kind of tree was Betty Smith referring to in her book "A Tree Grows in Brooklyn"?

165. *Daphne du Maurier, best known for* Rebecca.

166. *Mark Twain. It was a* Self-Pasting Scrapbook *containing blank pages coated with a gum veneer.*

167. *On the Yale University campus in New Haven, Connecticut—it's a sculpture donated by pop artist Claes Oldenburg.*

168. *Austria.*

169. *O. Henry (William Sydney Porter), in 1913. Earlier, he had founded a humorous weekly called* The Rolling Stone.

170. *Rikki-Tikki-Tavi.*

171. Nude Descending a Staircase No. 2, *by Marcel Duchamp.*

172. *The ghosts of Christmas Past, Christmas Present, Christmas Yet to Come, and Jacob Marley (Scrooge's partner).*

173. *Dashiell Hammett.*

174. J. D. Salinger's Catcher in the Rye.

175. *Edgar Allan Poe.*

176. Catch 18. *The title was changed because of the Leon Uris novel,* Mila 18, *published the same year, 1961.*

177. *Cyrano de Bergerac.*

178. *An ailanthus, known as "the tree of heaven."*

179. What nineteenth-century American literary classic was labeled "downright socialistic" and banned from U.S. Information Service libraries in 1954?

180. Who wrote:
> "Twinkle Twinkle little bat!
> How I wonder what you're at!
> Up above the world you fly!
> Like a tea tray in the sky!"

181. What great American writer ran rum because he couldn't sell his work?

182. Who was Little Lulu's boy companion in the comic strip created by Marjorie Henderson?

183. What major British literary figure served two years at hard labor after being found guilty of homosexuality?

184. What special commission did a French baron give to artists Georges Braque, Marc Chagall, Salvatore Dali, and Andy Warhol?

185. Sherlock Holmes' sidekick, Dr. Watson, suffered a war-time bullet wound. Where was it?

186. Dorothy Parker wrote:
> "Men seldom make passes
> At girls who wear glasses."
> Did she?

187. What was Huck Finn's remedy for warts?

188. What book was once banned by the Eldon, Missouri library because it contained 39 "objectionable" words?

189. William Sidney Porter, whom we know as O. Henry, spent some time in Honduras. What was he doing there?

190. What do mystery writers Gordon Ashe, Michael Halliday, J. J. Marric, and Kyle Hunt have in common?

191. What was *Jazz Age* writer F. Scott Fitzgerald's full name?

179. Walden, *by Henry David Thoreau.*

180. *Lewis Carroll, in* Alice in Wonderland. *It was sung by the Mad Hatter.*

181. *William Faulkner, creator of Yoknapatawpha County and two-time Pulitzer Prize winner for fiction (*A Fable *and* The Reivers*).*

182. *Tubby.*

183. *Oscar Wilde, who wrote* De Profundis *during his imprisonment.*

184. *Designing wine labels for Mouton Rothschild. The baron was Philippe de Rothschild.*

185. *On his shoulder, according to* A Study in Scarlet; *in the leg, according to* The Sign of Four.

186. *Yes.*

187. *Swinging a dead cat in a graveyard at midnight.*

188. *The American Heritage Dictionary.*

189. *Fleeing prosecution on embezzlement charges. When he returned to the U.S., he served time in jail—where he began writing the adventure stories that made him famous.*

190. *They're all the same man, John Creasey, who used 26 pseudonyms for his 600-plus books.*

191. *Francis Scott Key Fitzgerald. He was a distant relative of the man who wrote our national anthem.*

192. *Tattered Tom* and *Ragged Dick* were the heroes and titles of books written by what nineteenth century American author?

193. What are the names of Popeye's four nephews?

194. What writer-friend nicknamed T. S. Eliot "Old Possum"?

195. What American writer, while a war correspondent, is credited with capturing a town single-handedly during the Spanish-American War?

196. What cartoon character said, "The trouble with the rat race is there is never a finish line"?

197. What visual impairment do some experts believe influenced the styles of artists El Greco and Modigliani?

198. *All the King's Men* by Robert Penn Warren is a roman à clef about what American political figure?

199. What famous writer had several butterflies named after him?

200. In the novel *Futility*, published in 1898—fourteen years before the sinking of the Titanic—an "unsinkable" luxury liner was lost after hitting an iceberg on its maiden voyage. What was the ship's name?

201. What was the house in the background of Grant Wood's classic painting *American Gothic*?

202. Who wrote:
> "There was a little girl
> Who had a little curl
> Right in the middle of her forehead"?

203. What was the name of Frances Hodgson Burnett's character Little Lord Fauntleroy?

204. What was the first daily comic strip published in the U.S.?

205. What fellow artist did French impressionist Paul Gauguin refer to as "the little green chemist"?

192. *Horatio Alger, who wrote more than 100 rags-to-riches success stories about hardworking and honest young men.*

193. *Pipeye, Peepeye, Pupeye, and Poopeye.*

194. *Ezra Pound.*

195. *Stephen Crane. The town was Juana Diáz in Puerto Rico; the resistance was nonexistent.*

196. *Dagwood in the* Blondie *strip.*

197. *Astigmatism.*

198. *Louisiana governor and senator Huey Long.*

199. Lolita *author Vladimir Nabokov, who was also a lepidopterist.*

200. *The Titan. It was the creation of writer Morgan Robertson.*

201. *A brothel in Eldon, Iowa.*

202. *Henry Wadsworth Longfellow, in his 1883 poem* There Was a Little Girl.

203. *Cedric Errol.*

204. Mr. Mutt *by H.C. (Bud) Fisher, later called* Mutt and Jeff. *The strip first appeared in the San Francisco Chronicle in 1907.*

205. *Pointillist Georges Seurat.*

206. What skill won people high office in the land of Lilliput in Jonathan Swift's *Gulliver's Travels*?

207. When Goofy first appeared in a Mickey Mouse cartoon, what was his name?

208. What did Clark Kent's adoptive mother, Martha, use to make his Superman costume?

209. How many knights could be seated around King Arthur's Round Table?

210. Abstract expressionist painter Arshile Gorky plagiarized the work of sculptor Henri Gaudier-Brzeska, but it wasn't art that he copied. What was it?

211. What were Cinderella's slippers made of in Frenchman Charles Perrault's original version of the fairy tale classic?

212. In the cartoon *Hazel*, what is the name of the Baxter family cat?

213. William Shakespeare left his wife his second-best bed and willed the bulk of his estate to his two daughters. What were their names?

214. Where was Snoopy born in Charles Schulz' popular *Peanuts* comic strip?

215. Whose fortune was estimated at $1 multiplijillion, 9 obsquatumatillion?

216. In which of his plays did William Shakespeare include the stage direction "Exit, pursued by a bear"?

217. What was the name of the cat featured with Dick, Jane and their dog spot in the old school primer *Now We Read*?

218. The first western novel of what popular author was entitled *Hopalong Cassidy and the Riders of High Rock*?

206. *Rope dancing.*

207. *Dippy Dawg. He was renamed when he began costarring with Mickey in the mid-1930s.*

208. *The swaddling clothes that protected him on his rocket journey from Krypton to Earth.*

209. *The Round Table accommodated one hundred and fifty knights.*

210. *The sculptor's love letters.*

211. *Fur. The slippers became glass when the story was translated into English and pantoufle en vair (fur slipper) was mistaken for en verre (glass).*

212. *Mostly, because she is mostly Siamese.*

213. *Susanna and Judith.*

214. *At the Daisy Hill Puppy Farm.*

215. *Scrooge McDuck, Donald Duck's uncle.*

216. The Winter's Tale *(Act III, Scene iii).*

217. *Puff.*

218. *Louis L'Amour, using the pseudonym Tex Burns in 1951.*

219. How many years after American expatriate Henry Miller's *Tropic of Cancer* was published in France did the novel become legal in the United States?

220. What does "rubaiyat" mean—as in the famous *Ruaiyat of Omar Khayyam?*

221. In the Disney version of *Snow White and the Seven Dwarfs*, the wicked Queen falls off a precipice and dies. How does she meet her end in the original Grimm brothers fairy tale?

222. What bizarre theory about Dr. Watson did mystery writer Rex Stout, an ardent Sherlock Holmes fan, once suggest to fellow members of the Baker Street Irregulars?

223. In H.G. Wells's science-fiction classic *War of the Worlds*, how did the Martian invaders get to Earth?

224. What best-selling author opened the first Saab auto dealership in the United States?

225. What was the inspiration for the title of the long-running TV mystery series *Murder, She Wrote* starring Angela Lansbury?

226. What is the first name of mystery writer Georges Simenon's celebrated Inspector Maigret?

227. What book was the best-seller of the year in America in 1794?

228. According to Howland Owl, the scienterrific genius of the *Pogo* comic strip, what would you get if you crossed a geranium plant and a baby yew tree?

229. To whom did writer John le Carré dedicate his 1991 spy thriller *The Secret Pilgrim?*

230. What are the names of Shakespeare's *Two Gentlemen of Verona?*

231. What was the name of Tarzan's pet chimpanzee in Edgar Rice Burroughs's books about the King of the Apes?

219. 27. *Published in France in 1934 with a dust jacket cautioning booksellers not to display it in their shop windows, the book was banned in the U.S. until 1961 on the grounds of obscenity.*

220. *Quatrains.*

221. *She was condemned to dance in red-hot iron shoes until she died.*

222. *That Watson was a woman.*

223. *They were shot to Earth in giant projectiles.*

224. *Kurt Vonnegut.*

225. *The 1961 movie* Murder She Said, *which was based on the Agatha Christie mystery "4:50 from Paddington."*

226. *Jules.*

227. *Benjamin Franklin's* Autobiography, *which had been published in England the year before—three years after his death.*

228. *A yew-ranium bush.*

229. *To actor Alec Guinness, who portrayed spymaster George Smiley in the TV versions of le Carré's earlier books* Tinker, Tailor, Soldier, Spy *and* Smiley's People.

230. *Valentine and Proteus.*

231. *Nkima. The chimp was renamed Cheeta for Johnny Weissmuller's film debut as* Tarzan the Ape Man *in 1932.*

232. Which is the only Shakespearean play to include a mention of America?

233. What was on the ceiling of the Vatican's Sistine Chapel before Michelangelo painted his famous fresco?

234. What famous writer claimed she did most of the plotting for her books while sitting in a bathtub munching on apples?

235. What famous nineteenth-century French novelist published a plagiarized nonfiction work under the pseudonym Bombet and, when the plagiarism was discovered, defended the nonexistent Bombet in letters signed by an equally nonexistent Bombet Jr.?

236. What kind of ship was the *U.S.S. Caine* in Herman Wouk's 1952 Pulitzer Prize-winning novel, *The Caine Mutiny*?

237. In what year was George Orwell's chilling political satire *Nineteen Eighty-four* published?

238. What was the title of the 1960 autobiography of the very first Fuller Brush man, Alfred Fuller?

239. In what writer's work did author Cicily Isabel Fairfield Andrews find her famous pseudonym—Rebecca West?

240. What famous artist designed shirts, hats, ashtrays, stamps, brandy bottles, coat hangers, bathing suits, crystal ware, tapestries and playing cards—among other things?

241. How many books with "rags to riches" success stories did Horatio Alger write?

242. What was the name of the seaport hometown of comic strip hero Popeye the Sailor?

243. What is the only building in the Western Hemisphere designed by famed British architect Sir Christopher Wren?

244. What is the Greek meaning of Utopia—the name of the perfect island society created by Sir Thomas More in his book of the same name?

232. The Comedy of Errors *(Act III, Scene ii).*

233. Silver stars on a plain blue field.

234. Agatha Christie.

235. Stendhal, who is best known for his novels The Red and the Black *and* The Charterhouse of Parma. *For his plagiarized work,* The Lives of Haydn, Mozart, and Metastasio, *he lifted from two biographies and a eulogy.*

236. A minesweeper.

237. In 1949.

238. A Foot in the Door.

239. Henrik Ibsen's. Rebecca West is the name of the strong-willed heroine in his play Rosmersholm.

240. Surrealist Salvador Dali.

241. 119.

242. Sweetwater.

243. The Wren Building at the College of William and Mary in Williamsburg, Virginia. It is the oldest academic building still in use in the United States.

244. It means nowhere, from the Greek ou, *meaning "not," and* topos, *meaning "a place."*

245. What Alfred Hitchcock movie title is drawn from Shake-speare's *Hamlet*?

246. Who was Sir Galahad's father?

247. What was the name of French writer Alexandre Dumas' palatial home in Paris?

248. What piece of tableware is upset in Leonardo da Vinci's famous painting of the Last Supper?

249. What was the estate tax paid to the French government by Pablo Picasso's heirs after the artist died in 1973 at age 91?

250. In the Ernest Hemingway classic *The Old Man and the Sea*, what famous athlete does the old man say he would like to take fishing?

251. What is the name of the principal city in Hell—"the high capital of Satan and his peers"—in John Milton's epic poem *Paradise Lost*?

252. What did writer Edgar Allan Poe and rock n' roller Jerry Lee Lewis have in common in their choice of wives?

253. Who was the inspiration for the popular sixteenth-century nursery rhyme *Little Miss Muffet*?

254. What was Goldilocks's name when the hungry little girl was first introduced in the famous children's fairy tale *The Three Little Bears* over a hundred years ago?

255. What were the names of Scarlett O'Hara's sisters in the Margaret Mitchell classic *Gone With the Wind*?

256. In May 1969 *Esquire* magazine featured a story about the decline of the American avant-garde. How was this illustrated on its cover?

257. What architect designed the Gateway Arch in St. Louis?

258. To whom did Abraham Lincoln say: "Is this the little woman whose book made such a war?"

245. *The 1959 thriller,* North by Northwest, *in which Cary Grant feigns madness. The title is taken from Hamlet's words: "I am but mad north-north-west; when the wind is southerly, I know a hawk from a handsaw.*

246. *Sir Lancelot.*

247. *Monte-Cristo, after his famous novel* The Count of Monte Cristo.

248. *A salt cellar near Judas Iscariot.*

249. *They paid $78.5 million. The value of the artwork, properties and investments he left was estimated for tax purposes at $312 million, but in reality they were worth well over $1 billion.*

250. The Great DiMaggio.

251. *Pandemonium.*

252. *Each married a 13-year-old cousin.*

253. *Patience Muffet, the daughter of the poem's creator, Dr. Thomas Muffet, an entomologist who wrote about spiders more often than he did about his little girl.*

254. *Silver Hair. From that she became Golden Hair, and finally Goldilocks.*

255. *Her two younger sisters were Careen, for Caroline Irene, and Suellen, for Susan Elinor.*

256. *By a picture of Andy Warhol drowning in a can of Campbell's tomato soup.*

257. *Eero Saarinen.*

258. *Harriet Beecher Stowe, author of* Uncle Tom's Cabin.

259. What French writer used Alcofribas Nasier—an anagram of his real name—as a pseudonym?

260. What was Dr. Frankenstein's first name in the Mary Shelley horror classic?

261. How many kinds of kisses are described in the Kama Sutra, the classical Indian text on eroticism?

262. Who attended the Mad Hatter's tea party in Lewis Carroll's Alice's Adventures in Wonderland?

263. What name did artist Doménikos TheotokÛpoulos sign on his paintings?

264. What twentieth-century English writer used the words hook, line and sinker in the titles of a three-book espionage series?

265. What American novelist's great-grandfather wrote a book in response to Harriet Beecher Stowe's *Uncle Tom's Cabin?*

266. What was the first painting by an American obtained by the world-famous Louvre Museum in Paris?

267. What famous writer was the as-told-to author of The Autobiography of Malcolm X?

268. What was the name of the ocean liner that provided the setting for Katherine Anne Porter's novel *A Ship of Fools?*

269. What famous author wrote the short story *Dry September* in 1931 and the novel Light in August in 1932?

270. What world-famous artist painted the historic Civil War sea battle between the Union sloop Kearsage and the Confederacy's corvette Alabama?

271. What popular table game does William Shakespeare have Cleopatra play in *Antony and Cleopatra?*

272. In Herman Melville's famous novel Moby Dick, what was Captain Ahab's peg leg made from?

259. *Francois Rabelais. He used the pseudonym for his satirical works.*

260. *Victor.*

261. *20.*

262. *The Mad Hatter, the March Hare, the Dormouse and Alice.*

263. *El Greco, which means "the Greek."*

264. *Len Deighton. The books were* Spy Hook, Spy Line and Spy Sinker.

265. *William Faulkner's great-grandfather William Clark Falkner (the family's original name). The book was entitled The Little Brick Church. The older Falkner also wrote a romantic novel, The White Rose of Memphis, and a book about his travels, Rapid Ramblings in Europe.*

266. *James Abbott McNeill Whistler's portrait of his elderly mother, formally known as Arrangement in* Grey and Black, No. 1: The Artist's Mother, *and popularly known as* Whistler's Mother.

267. *Alex Haley, best known for his 1976 epic Roots.*

268. *The Vera. It sailed from Veracruz, Mexico, to Bremerhaven, Germany.*

269. *William Faulkner.*

270. *French artist Edouard Manet. The battle, fought in French waters outside Cherbourg harbor on June 15, 1864, was watched from shore and small boats by more than 15,000 people—one of them, Manet. The naval engagement ended with the sinking of the Alabama, which had defeated more than 60 Union ships in prior battles.*

271. *Billiards.*

272. *The ivory from the jawbone of a whale. Ahab's leg had been snapped off during an encounter with the whale Moby Dick.*

273. What is the chief oil in the oil paints used by artists?

274. What Shakespearean character was based on a London doctor who served as Queen Elizabeth I's chief physician—until he was arrested and hanged for conspiring to kill her?

275. Hamlet—with 1,530 lines— is the longest speaking part in all of Shakespeare's plays. What is the second longest?

276. What popular American comic strip is known as Radishes in Denmark?

277. What happened to the parents of Batman's sidekick, Robin, a.k.a. Dick Grayson?

278. For what famous writer was the drink known as the Brandy Alexander named?

279. What was the name of the broken-down, partially blind old horse Ichabod Crane rode in Washington Irving's *Legend of Sleepy Hollow*?

280. What famous poet was known to his close friends by the nickname Junkets?

281. All told, how many novels did the Bronte sisters—Anne, Charlotte and Emily—write?

282. What was Jeeves's first name in humorist P. G. Wodehouse's stories about Bertie Wooster and his resourceful valet?

283. In the folk tale about Rumpelstiltskin, how long did it take the miller's daughter to guess his name?

284. What famous English writer, while living in Vermont, invented snow golf—painting his golf balls red so he could find them?

285. What is the name of Babar the Elephant's wife?

286. Who owned the land on Walden Pond, where Henry David Thoreau built a cabin and wrote the essays that became his book Walden, or Life in the Woods?

273. *Linseed oil—made from the seed of the flax plant, Linum usitatissimum.*

274. *Shylock, the money-lender in The Merchant of Venice. The doctor's name was Roderigo Lopez.*

275. Richard III, *with 1,164 lines.*

276. Peanuts.

277. *The Boy Wonder's parents—circus performers known as The Flying Graysons—died in a trapeze accident.*

278. *Alexander Woollcott, drama and literary critic and Algonquin Round Table regular.*

279. *Gunpowder.*

280. *John Keats.*

281. *Seven. Emily wrote one,* Wuthering Heights; *Anne wrote two,* Agnes Grey and The Tenant of Wildfell Hall; *and Charlotte wrote four,* Jane Eyre, The Professor, Villette, *and* Shirley.

282. *Reginald.*

283. *Three days.*

284. *Rudyard Kipling.*

285. *Celeste.*

286. *Ralph Waldo Emerson.*

287. What was Gulliver's first name in Jonathan Swift's *Gulliver's Travels?*

288. What famous American poet wrote the line that provided the title for the 1942 Bette Davis film *Now Voyager?*

289. What environmentally correct gesture did publisher Harper San Francisco make in 1990 in conjunction with its publication of the book 2 Minutes a Day for a Greener Planet?

290. What popular children's book was written by Ian Fleming, creator of British secret agent James Bond?

291. What early American writer used the pen names Geoffrey Crayon and Jonathan Oldstyle?

292. What famous entertainer wrote the bestsellers *The Man in Black* in 1975 and *Man in White* in 1986?

293. What is the title of the 1989 biography of cartoonist Charles Schulz?

294. What did the letters in the magic word SHAZAM represent in the Captain Marvel comics?

295. In what famous novel did physicist Murray Gell-Mann find the word quark—which he used to name the basic building block of matter in the early 1960s?

296. What famous American poet wrote: "My candle burns at both ends;/It will not last the night"?

297. What popular comic strip featured a character named Appassionata Von Climax?

298. How many sonnets did William Shakespeare write?

299. What river did artist Emanuel Leutze use as a model for the Delaware when he painted his famous historical work "Washington Crossing the Delaware" in 1851?

287. Lemuel.

288. Walt Whitman. In his two-line poem The Untold Want, *in* Leaves of Grass, *he wrote: "Now voyager sail thou forth to seek and find." The movie was based on the novel* Now Voyager *by Olive Higgins Prouty.*

289. It planted 1,000 trees to replace those used in producing the book.

290. Chitty Chitty Bang Bang, the Magical Car.

291. Washington Irving.

292. Country singer Johnny Cash. Black *is an autobiography;* White, *a novel about the apostle Saint Paul.*

293. Good Grief. It was written by Rheta Grimsley Johnson.

294. Solomon's wisdom, Hercules' strength, Atlas' s stamina, Zeus' s power, Achilles' courage, and Mercury's speed.

295. In James Joyce's Finnegan's Wake.

296. Edna St. Vincent Millay. The lines are from her poem First Fig.

297. Li'l Abner.

298. 154.

299. The Rhine. Leutze was in his native Germany when he painted it.

300. What famous rock star returned a $5 million advance on his memoirs, explaining that he "couldn't remember" significant details of his own life?

301. In *Mad* magazine's spoofs of Superman, what names were used for the Man of Steel and his newspaperman alter ego?

302. What did Robert Browning use to wean and cure his wife, Elizabeth Barrett Browning, from her addiction to laudanum?

303. Whose painting of a sunset gave the Impressionist school of art its name?

304. What two great writers died on the same day—April 23, 1616?

305. What American novelist was challenged to a duel and beaten by a woman he later married?

306. Whose autobiography is entitled *What's It All About?*

307. What sexually explicit novel banned as obscene in the U.S. and England for 30 years—was originally called Tenderness by its author?

308. What novel is set in the year 632AF (for After Ford)?

309. What famous novel is set in Thornfield Hall?

310. Whose life story is told in the 1974 biography *Shooting Star?*

311. Who wrote the popular children's poem *The Pied Piper of Hamelin* ?

312. What was the medical specialty of Sherlock Holme's creator, Arthur Conan Doyle?

313. What sinister fictional killer was introduced to movie audiences in the 1986 film *Manhunter?*

314. What was the name of the Indian chief referred to in the title of James Fenimore Cooper's 1826 novel *The Last of the Mohicans?*

300. *Mick Jagger.*

301. *Superduperman and Clark Bent. Lois Lane was Lois Pain.*

302. *Chianti.*

303. *Claude Monet's. The painting was called "Impression: Sunrise." The first use of the term Impressionist came in 1874 in a satirical article ridiculing Monet and his artist friends.*

304. *Shakespeare and Cervantes.*

305. *Jack London. His duel with Charmian Kittredge was with foils, face masks and breast plates.*

306. *Actor Michael Caine. The book title was taken from the first line in the title song of Caine's first big movie, Alfie. The line is: "What's it all about, Alfie?"*

307. *Lawrence's Lady Chatterley's Lover. Before it was given its final name, it also was known as John Thomas and Lady Jane.*

308. Brave New World, *by Aldous Huxley.*

309. *Charlotte Bronte's* Jane Eyre.

310. *John Wayne's.*

311. *Robert Browning.*

312. *He was an ophthalmologist or eye doctor.*

313. *Hannibal Lecter, whom most moviegoers became acquainted with in the 1991 Academy Award-winning film* Silence of the Lambs. *Both films were based on Thomas Harris's novel* Red Dragon.

314. *Uncas.*

315. What book begins, "He came into the world in the middle of the thicket, in one of those little, hidden forest glades which seems to be entirely open, but are really screened in on all sides"?

316. What future playwright was expelled from Princeton University by Woodrow Wilson when the American president-to-be was president of the university?

317. What famous writer is credited with originating the expression "rain cats and dogs"?

318. What did artist Pablo Picasso reply when he was asked to name his favorite among all his paintings?

319. What unusual message was attached to all copies of Henry Miller's sex-packed novel *Tropic of Cancer* when it was first offered for sale in France in 1934?

320. On orders from Pope Pius IV, what did Italian artist Daniele de Volterra add to Michelangelo's Last Judgment on the west wall of the Sistine Chapel in the mid-sixteenth century.

321. What famous writer gave us the line, "Polly put the kettle on, we'll all have tea"?

322. According to Shakespeare, what was England's Henry VIII doing on the night his daughter, future Queen Elizabeth I, was born?

323. What satiric fifth-century B.C. play introduced the classic comedy team of the tall, thin, insulting straight man and the short, fat buffoon?

324. In Jonathan Swift's *Gulliver's Travels*, why were Lilliputian heretics known as Big-Enders?

325. What writer originated the phrase "Do not count your chickens before they are hatched" in a story about a farmer's daughter?

326. Who is the subject of the biography *Poison Pen*, published in 1991?

315. Bambi, *by Felix Salten.*

316. Eugene O'Neill. He was expelled for throwing a bottle of beer through Wilson's office window.

317. Jonathan Swift, in A Complete Collection of Polite and Ingenious Conversation, *which he originally had published under the pseudonym Simon Wagstaff, Esquire.*

318. "The next one."

319. A warning to book dealers—on a removable band—not to display the controversial novel in their shop windows.

320. Loincloths, to cover up the nudity that shocked church officials. The commission earned the artist the nickname Il Braghettone, "the breeches maker."

321. Charles Dickens, in Barnaby Rudge.

322. Playing cards. The game was primero, an early form of poker.

323. Lysistrata, *by Aristophanes.*

324. They believed eggs should be broken at the big end—as opposed to the traditionalist Little-Enders, who broke their eggs at the little end.

325. Aesop, in his story The Milkmaid and Her Pail.

326. Kitty Kelley, author of unauthorized biographies of Jacqueline Kennedy Onassis, Elizabeth Taylor, Frank Sinatra and Nancy Reagan.

327. Who serves as Dante's guide through Hell and Purgatory in his masterpiece *The Divine Comedy*?

328. The house of what famous Greek poet was the only home spared by Alexander the Great when he invaded and destroyed the city of Thebes in 335 B.C.?

329. How many self-portraits did Rembrandt paint?

330. The name of what Texas town came close to being changed in the late 1950s because of a controversial best-selling novel?

331. Who immortalized the world of American finance with a painting entitled *The New Orleans Cotton Exchange*?

332. What was the first career-girl comic strip?

333. What English literary classic was inspired by the adventures of Scottish pirate Andrew Selkirk?

334. What is the only sculpture on which Michelangelo is believed to have carved his name?

335. Did science fiction writer Jules Verne—who told of trips around the world and to the moon—ever fly?

336. What was the first book to vanish from the Association of American Publishers' display at the Moscow Book Fair in September 1985?

337. In the Nero Wolfe mysteries, what did Archie keep in his closet?

338. What was the name of Smilin' Jack's buddy in the comic strip about the dashing aviator?

339. Whose autobiography was entitled, *R.S.V.P.*?

340. What great writer, shortly before his death at age 90, successfully defended himself against senility charges by reading his latest work in court?

327. *The Roman poet Virgil.*

328. *Pindar.*

329. *Almost 100—that are known.*

330. *Lolita. The novel was* Lolita, *by Vladimir Nabokov. After much debate, the citizens of the small southeast Texas town decided to keep the name adopted by their forefathers in honor of early settler Lolita Reese.*

331. *French impressionist Edgar Degas. He did a painting of the exchange during an 1872-73 visit to New Orleans, where his uncle and two brothers were in the cotton business.*

332. Winnie Winkle, *by Martin Branner, which made its debut in 1920.*

333. Robinson Crusoe. *Daniel Defoe wrote the tale after hearing the story of Selkirk's four and a half years on uninhabited Juan Fernandez Island off the coast of Chile.*

334. *The Pieta. He reportedly did it after overhearing someone mistakenly attribute it to sculptor Christoforo Solari.*

335. *Yes, once. He made a balloon ascension in 1873.*

336. Jane Fonda's Workout Book. *The second was the Sears, Roebuck and Company catalog.*

337. *A bottle of rye, for the times when he was particularly frustrated with Nero Wolfe.*

338. *Downwind.*

339. *Professional party-giver Elsa Maxwell's.*

340. *Sophocles. The work was* Oedipus at Colonus.

341. *Lolly Willowes,* a novel about a spinster who realizes her vocation as a witch, won what unique honor when it was published in 1926?

342. How many lovers are named in Casanova's memoirs, *Story of My Life,* first published in their complete form in the early 1960s?

343. Who drew the first cartoon published in an American newspaper?

344. What famous American's 1952 autobiography is entitled *From Under My Hat* ?

345. Somerset Maugham's 1919 novel *The Moon and Sixpence* is a roman à clef about what great French artist?

346. What is the origin of the phrase, "United we stand, divided we fall"?

347. The first Encyclopedia Britannica, published in 1771, devoted its first volume to "A" and "B." How many additional volumes did it take to cover "C" through "Z"?

348. Whose marriage in March 1952 was featured in a "Life" magazine cover story?

349. The work of what famous French artist hung upside down in the Museum of Modern Art in New York for 47 days before someone realized it?

350. What comic-strip character started out in 1932 as a middle-aged woman who sold apples on street corners?

351. Who use the pen names Acton, Ellis and Currer Bell?

352. What book did Aristotle Onassis keep on his desk in his multimillion-dollar yacht Christina?

353. Who wrote the first modern ghost story in the English language?

341. The book, by British author Sylvia Townsend Warner, was the first offering of the Book-of-the-Month Club.

342. Though he boasted about seducing thousands, the great lover named only 116.

343. Benjamin Franklin. His drawing of a severed snake—each piece representing one of the colonies—appeared with the motto "Unite or Die" in the Pennsylvania Gazette *on May 9, 1754.*

344. Hedda Hopper's—she was known for her exotic hats and juicy Hollywood gossip.

345. Paul Gauguin.

346. Aesop's fables. It's from The Four Oxen and the Lion, *written in the sixth century B.C.*

347. Only two.

348. Comic strip characters Daisy Mae Scragg and Li'l Abner of Dogpatch. Marryin' Sam performed the ceremony for $1.35, ending their 17-year courtship.

349. Henri Matisse, in 1961. The painting was Le Bateau.

350. "Mary Worth," who was originally known as "Apple Mary."

351. Anne, Emily and Charlotte Bronte.

352. A copy of J. Paul Getty's How to be Rich.

353. Daniel Defoe. It was True Relation of the Apparition of One Mrs. Veal.

354. What American literary classic was made into a film called *I Married a Doctor*?

355. Who designed the red, yellow and dark blue Renaissance uniform worn by the Swiss Guard at the Vatican?

356. Who wrote: "All animals are equal, but some animals are more equal than others"?

357. How many paintings did Flemish Dutch artits Vincent Van Gogh sell during his lifetime?

358. Where did writer Ian Fleming find the name James Bond for his hero-spy?

359. Whose autobiography, published in 1977, is called *Grinding It Out*?

360. What book was the first submitted to a publisher as a typewritten manuscript?

361. In the *Mad Magazine* parody of the *Archie* comic book, what name was given to the teenage hero?

362. How little was Stuart Little, the mouse born into an otherwise human family in the E. B. White children's fantasy?

363. What famous American writer created the Cisco Kid?

364. Writer Kay Thompson's goddaughter provided the inspiration for her books about Eloise, the mischievous little girl who lived at the Plaza Hotel in New York. Who was she?

365. In Jules Verne's 1865 book *From Earth to the Moon,* three men are blasted to the moon by cannon. Their speed of departure has proven to be the earth's escape velocity. What is it?

366. Who were Miss Marple's next door neighbors in the Agatha Christie mysteries about the sleuthing senior citizen from St. Mary Mead?

367. Whom did Olive Oyl go out with before she met Popeye?

354. Main Street, *by Sinclair Lewis. Producer Jack Warner reportedly claimed that nobody would go to see "a picture about a street."*

355. Michelangelo. It's one of several costumes worn by the Gendarmeria Pontifica.

356. George Orwell in Animal Farm.

357. Only one.

358. On a coffee-table book, Birds of the West Indies, *by ornithologist James Bond.*

359. Ray Kroc's. He was the traveling salesman behind McDonald's franchising empire.

360. Mark Twain's The Adventures of Tom Sawyer. *The year was 1876; the typewriter, a Remington.*

361. Starchie. In the "Mad" parody, which appeared in June 1954 and cost 10 cents, Starchie ended up in jail for running a high school protection racket.

362. He was two inches high and slept in a bed made from a cigarette box and four clothespins.

363. *O.Henry, in his short story,* The Caballero's Way.

364. Liza Minnelli.

365. Seven miles a second. (Escape velocity is the minimum speed required to escape a planet's pull.)

366. Dr. Haydock and Miss Harnell.

367. Ham Gravy.

368. What British writer and noted wit claimed "America had often been discovered before Columbus, but it had always been hushed up"?

369. In the poem *Jabberwocky* in the *Alice in Wonderland* sequel *Through the Looking Glass,* what words did author Lewis Carroll combine to create the nonsense word slithy?

370. What novel provided the story line for the 1975 Robert Redford-Faye Dunaway movie *Three Days of the Condor?*

371. What famous American novelist has written several mysteries under the pen name Edgar Box?

372. What was the name of Joe and Frank Hardy's maiden aunt—and detective Fenton Hardy's sister—in the popular book series for boys?

373. What does Don Quixote's sidekick Sancho Panza's last name mean in Spanish?

374. What name did cartoonist Al Capp give the hero in his *Li'l Abner* parody of *Gone With the Wind?*

375. In the *Alley Oop* comic strip, who was the king of Moo?

376. The novel *Ulysses* takes place in Dublin on one day—June 16, 1904. What significance did that day have for writer James Joyce?

377. What do the initials J. D. stand for in author J. D. Salinger's name?

378. Who wrote, "A good education is the next best thing to a pushy mother"?

379. What first name did author Margaret Mitchell originally give her *Gone With the Wind* heroine, Scarlett O'Hara?

380. What does Rex Stout's cerebral sleuth Nero Wolfe do for exercise?

368. *Oscar Wilde.*

369. *Slimy and lithe.*

370. Six Days of the Condor, *by James Grady.*

371. *Gore Vidal.*

372. *Aunt Gertrude.*

373. *Panza means "paunch."*

374. *Wreck Butler.*

375. *King Guzzle.*

376. *It was the day of his first date with Nora Barnacle, the woman he eventually married.*

377. *Jerome David.*

378. *Charles Schulz, in* Peanuts.

379. *Pansy.*

380. *He plays javelins—darts as we know it—for 15 minutes a day.*

381. What American literary figure wrote his daughter: "Worry about cleanliness, courage, efficiency and horsemanship, but don't worry about the past, the future, boys, mosquitoes and popular opinion"?

382. Writer Robert Benchley demanded a stuntman's fee for his performance in the 1941 film comedy *Bedtime Story*. What was his "stunt"?

383. Who was the subject of the Auguste Rodin sculpture *The Thinker*?

384. What famous writer fought to ban Mark Twain's *Huckleberry Finn* from the public library, claiming it was inappropriate for "our pure-minded lads and lassies"?

385. How did writer L. Frank Baum pick Oz for the name of the fantasyland in his *Wizard of Oz* stories?

386. What is unusual about Mona Lisa's eyebrows in the famous Leonardo da Vinci painting?

387. Pinocchio had two pets. What were they and what were their names?

388. What was the name of Popeye's ship?

389. Pop artist Andy Warhol once declared that everyone would be famous for how long?

390. In what field is the Hugo Award given?

391. What popular American writer coined the word nerd?

392. What is the literal translation of Dada—the name given to the anti-traditionalist art movement begun in 1916?

393. In Spain, kids call them Pitufo; in Germany, Schlumpf. What do American kids call them?

394. What was the name of the last book written by Amelia Earhart?

381. Scott Fitzgerald.

382. He drank 13 glasses of milk.

383. The poet Dante.

384. Little Women author Louisa May Alcott.

385. He spotted a file cabinet marked O-Z while he was making up the story for his children and their friends.

386. She has none.

387. A cat named Figaro and a goldfish named Cleo.

388. The Olive, in honor of his longtime girlfriend.

389. 15 minutes.

390. Science fiction writing. The award was named for Hugo Gernsback, the "father of science fiction."

391. Dr. Seuss—whose real name was Theodor Seuss Geisel.

392. It means "hobby horse" in French. The name was chosen at random from a dictionary.

393. Smurfs.

394. Last Flight. It was published after she disappeared in the central Pacific in 1937 while attempting an around-the-world flight. Her husband, publisher George Putnam, put it together using her letters, diary entries, charts, cables, and phone conversations.

395. Before settling on the name Tiny Tim for Bob Cratchit's crippled son in his book *A Christmas Carol*, what three alliterative names did Charles Dickens consider?

396. Why is the well-known chrome-and-leather chair designed by German-born architect Ludwig Mies van der Rohe called the Barcelona chair?

397. What famous writer bragged that he gave his talent to his work and saved his genius for his life?

398. What famous artist shocked the art world in 1919 by painting a mustache, eyebrows and a beard on a reproduction of the Mona Lisa and submitting it to a Paris art show?

399. What was the name of the orange-and-white kitten in the classic children's books that featured Dick and Jane and their dog Spot?

400. What title did William Burroughs intend to give his controversial, scatological book *Naked Lunch*?

401. What famous artist in 1953 erased an original abstract expressionist drawing by Willem de Kooning— with his consent— and then framed it and exhibited it as an original work of his own?

402. How did Madrid's famous art museum come to be named the Prado?

403. What famous American writer claimed that a brand of cigarettes was named after him?

404. Under what title do we know the book that was originally published as *Murder in the Calais Coach*?

405. What art form is known as xylography?

406. Where did the name Winnie, for Winnie the Pooh, come from?

407. What first name did Arthur Conan Doyle give to him famous detective before he came up with Sherlock?

395. *Little Larry, Puny Pete and Small Sam.*

396. *He created it for the International Exposition in Barcelona in 1929, to go in the German pavilion, which he also designed.*

397. *Oscar Wilde.*

398. *Marcel Duchamp.*

399. Puff. *The book series was called Now We Read.*

400. Naked Lust. *Its name was changed by accident. Fellow Beat Generation writer Allen Ginsberg misread Burroughs' handwriting, and the wrong title stuck.*

401. *Robert Rauschenberg. He called the work* Erased de Kooning.

402. *It was named for the meadow, or prado, that once surrounded it.*

403. *Truman Capote. The brand, True.*

404. *Agatha Christie's* Murder on the Orient Express. *The name was not changed until several editions had been printed.*

405. *Wood engraving. In Greek xylon means "wood," and graphe means "writing" or "drawing."*

406. *From a bear named Winnie in the London Zoo. The animal had been born in Winnipeg, Canada, and was brought to London in 1914 as the mascot of a Canadian regiment.*

407. *Sherringford. The name was used in a short story Doyle wrote in 1886. Holmes's sidekick in the story was called Ormond Sacker—soon to be renamed Thomas Watson.*

408. What famous American author's grandfather was the model for Oliver Wendell Holmes' poem *The Last Leaf*, about an aged survivor of the Boston Tea Party?

409. What cultural phenomena did psychiatrist Fredric Wertheim link to juvenile delinquency in his 1954 book *Seduction of the Innocent?*

410. What artist had his wife pose for the face of Christ in his painting of the Last Supper?

411. Where was the sprawling family estate of early American novelist James Fenimore Cooper?

412. The novella Pal Joey by John O'Hara consists of a series of letters written by nightclub singer Pal Joey—to whom?

413. To whom did French painter Edgar Degas write, "Most women paint as though they are trimming hats....Not you"?

414. What was the name of the parrot that taught Dr. Dolittle to talk to the animals?

415. What French novelist inadvertently provided actress Ruth Davis with her stage name, Bette Davis?

416. Who is the subject of the unauthorized 1997 biography entitled *The Good, the Bad and the Very Ugly?*

417. What famous author wrote under the pen names Thomas Jefferson Snodgrass, Sergeant Fathom and W. Apaminondas Adrastus Blab before switching to the name with which he gained fame?

418. What famous woman entrepreneur provided the money to help artist Marc Chagall and his wife flee the Nazis and move to New York City in 1941?

419. When *The Joy of Cooking* was revised and republished in 1997, it contained 4,500 recipes. How many were in the original Joy, self-published by Irma Rombauer in 1931?

408. *Herman Melville's grandfather, Major Thomas Melvill. (Melvill was the original spelling of the family name.)*

409. *Comic books. His book led to Senate hearings and the establishment of the Comics Code Authority, which banned "all scenes of horror, excessive bloodshed, gory or gruesome crimes, depravity, lust, sadism [and] masochism."*

410. *Spanish surrealist Salvador Dali. The title of the painting is* Sacrament of the Last Supper.

411. *In Cooperstown, New York—it was the setting of his Leather Stocking Tales and is today the home of the Baseball Hall of Fame. William Cooper, the writer's father and one of the wealthiest landowners of his time, purchased the Cooperstown site in 1785.*

412. *Pal Ted, a bandleader.*

413. *American artist and Degas disciple Mary Cassatt.*

414. *Polynesia. The doctor's other pets in the popular series of children's books by Hugh Lofting were his duck, Dab Dab; his owl, Too Too; his baby pig, Gub Gub; his monkey, Chee Chee; and his dog, Jib.*

415. *Honorè de Balzac. Davis took her stage name from the title of his 1840 novel Cousin Bette.*

416. *Clint Eastwood. The bio was written by his ex-girlfriend Sondra Locke.*

417. *Samuel Clemens, who finally settled on the name Mark Twain.*

418. *Cosmetics queen Helena Rubinstein.*

419. *1,195. The original sold for $3; the new edition, the sixth, was priced at $30.*

420. Which book did Americans rate as their favorite—second only to the Bible in 1900?

421. What famous French dramatist, as a 20-year-old, served Louis XIII as valet-tapissier du roi—maker of the king's bed?

422. What famous novel opens with the line: "Once upon a time and a very good time it was there was a moocow coming down along the road..."?

423. What famous artist served as a war correspondent for *Harper's Weekly* magazine during the Civil War?

424. What American artist named most of his 17 children after famous artists—including Rembrandt, Titian, Rubens and Raphael?

425. How many of Shakespeare's heroines disguise themselves as males?

426. The first published drawings of what famous children's book author-illustrator appeared in a physics text entitled *Atomics for the Millions*?

427. In the book *Gone With the Wind,* how many months actually pass during Melanie's pregnancy?

Bonus Trivia

428. Poet Henry Wadsworth Longfellow was the first American to have plumbing installed in his house, in 1840.

420. *The Sears Roebuck catalog.*

421. *Molière.*

422. A Portrait of the Artist as a Young Man *by James Joyce.*

423. *Winslow Homer. As an artist-reporter for the magazine, he covered a number of campaigns with the Union Army.*

424. *Charles Wilson Peale. The four children named all achieved prominence as artists.*

425. *Five—Rosalind in* As You Like It; *Julia in* Two Gentlemen of Verona; *Portia in* The Merchant of Venice; *Viola in* Twelfth Night; *Imogen in* Cymbeline.

426. *Maurice Sendak. The text was written by one of his high-school teachers, who Sendak said gave him a passing grade and small fee for his illustrations.*

427. *21—based on the battles mentioned. When this was pointed out to author Margaret Mitchell, she reportedly replied that a Southerner's pace is slower than that of a Yankee.*

Sports & Games

Questions

429. What sport was the first to be filmed—and who filmed it?

430. What souvenir did New York Giant linebacker Lawrence Taylor request from a referee after he played his last game in January 1994?

431. How many games did Chicago Bears running back Walter Payton miss during his 13-year National Football League career?

432. What is the distance between bases on a Little League baseball field?

433. What was the first sport in which women were invited to compete at the Olympics?

434. What card game gave us the term bilk?

435. What college once had 22 members of the Phi Beta Kappa honor society on its football team?

436. How wide and high are the netted goals in ice hockey? How about field hockey?

Answers

429. *The sport was boxing; the man who did the filming, Thomas A. Edison; the year, 1894. Edison filmed a boxing match between Jack Cushing and Mike Leonard in a studio on the grounds of his laboratory complex in West Orange, New Jersey.*

430. *The referee's yellow flag. Taylor said he felt he deserved it because the refs "throw it against me often enough."*

431. *Only one. He carried the ball more often (3,838 times) for more yards (16,726) and scored more rushing touchdowns (110) than anyone else.*

432. *60 feet. In the major leagues, the distance is 90 feet.*

433. *Tennis, at the 1900 games in Paris. Charlotte Cooper of Great Britain was the first gold medalist.*

434. *Cribbage. Bilk, a variant of balk, originally meant "to defraud an opposing player of points through sharp, sly tactics." It now means "to cheat."*

435. *Dartmouth, in 1925.*

436. *Ice, 6 feet wide and 4 feet high; field, 4 yards wide and 7 feet high.*

437. How many home runs did baseball great Ty Cobb hit in the three World Series in which he played?

438. What career did Hawaiian swimming and surfing star Duke Kahanamoku pursue after playing Polynesian chiefs in Hollywood movies?

439. In cross-country bike racing, what do the initials BMX represent?

440. Under what name did Dr. Joshua Pim of Great Britain enter and win the Wimbledon tennis tournament in 1893?

441. In 1939, what famous American athlete starred on UCLA's undefeated football team and was the top scorer in the Pacific Coast Conference for basketball?

442. Which popular sport did Joe Sobek invent at the Greenwich, Connecticut, YMCA in 1950?

443. In blackjack, players try to get cards that add up to 21, and no higher. What is the count sought in baccarat?

444. Who was the first Olympic gold medalist to win a professional world boxing title?

445. What sports activity was originally known in England as "plank-gliding"?

446. Which was the first sport to have its top players named to an All-American team?

447. What was golfing great Ben Hogan's famous reply when he was asked how to improve one's game?

448. How many world records did swimmer Mark Spitz set when he won seven gold medals at the 1972 Olympics?

449. After retiring as a player, with what team did baseball great Babe Ruth spend one year as a coach?

437. *None. Cobb's overall World Series batting average—for 1907, 1908 and 1909—was .262. His team, the Detroit Tigers, lost the first two to the Chicago Cubs, the third to the Pittsburgh Pirates.*

438. *Kahanamoku, the inventor of windsurfing, was sheriff of Honolulu for 20 years.*

439. *Bicycle moto x (cross).*

440. *Mr. X. Because he feared that revealing his true identity would hurt his medical practice, Pim entered under the mystery name.*

441. *Jackie Robinson, who later gained national fame playing professional baseball. At UCLA, he earned letters in baseball, basketball, football and track.*

442. *Racquetball. Sobek designed a "strung paddle racquet" and handle, and combined the rules of squash and handball, to create the game he called "paddle rackets."*

443. *Nine.*

444. *Floyd Patterson, who won the Olympic gold medal as a middleweight in 1952, and the world championship as a heavyweight in 1956.*

445. *Waterskiing. The first recorded mention of the sport in England was in 1914.*

446. *Football, in 1889. The idea originated with famed football authority Walter Camp, who picked 36 All-American teams until his death in 1925.*

447. *"Hit the ball closer to the hole."*

448. *Seven—one in each of the races in which he competed.*

449. *The Brooklyn Dodgers in 1938.*

450. Which property represented as a railroad on the Monopoly game board was not actually a railroad?

451. In what year's Olympics were electric timing devices and a public-address system used for the first time?

452. What is the maximum weight permitted for calves in rodeo calf-roping competition?

453. How many different types of figure eights does the International Skating Union recognize in competition?

454. What Baseball Hall of Fame pitcher hit a home run in his first major league at-bat—and never hit another?

455. What baseball player hit the only home run of his 22-year major league career off his own brother?

456. What 1921 sporting event took up all of the first 13 pages of The New York Times—except for a little space on the front page devoted to the formal end of World War I?

457. In the National Football League, how many footballs is the home team required to provide for each game?

458. Brooks Robinson and Carl Yastrzemski hold the major league baseball record for playing the greatest number of seasons with the same team. How many years did they play—and with what teams?

459. How much liquid can the 27-inch-high silver America's Cup hold?

460. Why is the site of a boxing match called a ring when it's square?

461. In the very first Boston Marathon, 15 runners competed. How many finished?

462. How long is the average pool cue?

450. *Short Line. It was a bus company.*

451. *In 1912, in Stockholm*

452. *350 pounds. The minimum is 200 pounds.*

453. *48.*

454. *New York Giant knuckleballer Hoyt Wilhelm, in 1952.*

455. *Joe Niekro in 1976. Niekro, a pitcher with the Houston Astros, hit a four-bagger off his brother Phil, who was pitching for the Atlanta Braves. Houston won the game, 4-3.*

456. *The July 2nd heavyweight championship bout between Jack Dempsey and George Carpentier, the first fight to gross over $1 million in gate receipts. Dempsey won in a fourth-round knockout.*

457. *24—although from 8 to 12 are usually used.*

458. *23 years. Third baseman Robinson played with the Baltimore Orioles from 1955 to 1977; Carl Yastrzemski, outfielder/first baseman, played with the Boston Red Sox from 1961 to 1983.*

459. *None. It's bottomless.*

460. *Boxing rings were originally circular.*

461. *10.*

462. *57 inches.*

463. Under the rules outlined in the charter of the International Olympic Committee, how much pure gold must there be in each gold medal awarded to first-place winners?

464. What professional ice hockey star didn't hang up his skates until he was 52?

465. What is the state sport of Alaska?

466. Who was the first athlete to hit a major league home run and make a professional football touchdown in the same week?

467. Who was the famous great-great-great-grandfather of San Francisco 49er quarterback Steve Young?

468. Who was the first professional athlete to win championship rings in two major sports?

469. How long and wide is the balance beam used in Olympic gymnastic competition?

470. What sport besides football did famed fullback Jim Brown compete and excel in while he attended Syracuse University in the mid 1950s?

471. How much did a one-minute TV spot cost advertisers on the first Super Bowl broadcast in 1967?

472. How many of the four Grand Slam trophies in tennis are gold; how many are silver?

473. What pitcher made it into the Baseball Hall of Fame with a 28-31 major league win-loss record?

474. Who was the first sports great to have his number retired by his team?

475. How many points did Chicago Cardinals fullback Ernie Nevers rack up in a 1929 game to set the highest single-game scoring mark in National Football League history?

463. *At least 6 grams. Silver medals must be at least .925 sterling silver. There are no rules regarding the purity of bronze medals. All medals must be 60 millimeters in diameter and 3 millimeters thick.*

464. *Gordie Howe, who played in 1,687 games in the National Hockey League.*

465. *Dog-mushing.*

466. *Jim Thorpe, in 1917. He did it a second time in 1919. Deion Sanders was the second athlete to accomplish the feat—70 years later, in 1989.*

467. *Mormon leader Brigham Young.*

468. *Gene Conley. He pitched for the Milwaukee Braves team that won the 1957 World Series, and was on the Boston Celtic teams that won National Basketball Association championships in 1959, 1960 and 1961.*

469. *Length, 16 feet 3 inches; width, 4 inches.*

470. *Lacrosse. He made All-American.*

471. *$85,000. It now costs well over $1 million for a half-minute spot.*

472. *Only the Wimbledon trophy is gold; the others—for the U.S. Open, the French Open and the Australian Open—are silver.*

473. *The legendary Satchel Paige, who played pro ball for 22 years— reportedly winning more than 2,000 of the 2,500 games he pitched—before he joined the majors in 1949 at age 42.*

474. *Lou Gehrig. The New York Yankees retired his No. 4 from play on July 4, 1939.*

475. *40—which accounted for all his team's points in its 40-6 Thanksgiving Day victory over the Chicago Bears. Nevers scored six touchdowns and kicked four extra points.*

476. What is the standard width of a bowling alley—gutters not included?

477. What is par on the longest golf hole in the world—the 909-yard 7th hole at Japan's Sano Course at the Satsuki Golf Club?

478. What was Babe Ruth's won-lost record as a big-league pitcher?

479. Within what range must the water temperature be in competitive swimming events at the Olympics?

480. Why did Roberta Gibb Bingay wear a hooded sweatshirt to disguise her appearance when she ran in the Boston Marathon in 1966?

481. What subject did football legend Knute Rockne teach at Notre Dame before he was named head coach of the Fighting Irish in 1918?

482. In tennis, what is the difference—in width—between a singles court and a doubles court?

483. What was the fitting name of the first miniature golf course in the United States?

484. What is the given name of football coach Weeb Ewbank, the only coach to win championships in both the National and American Football Leagues?

485. In 1974, what sport banned all lefties—except those who had already been playing—from competing in sanctioned matches in the U.S.?

486. Why was world champion swimmer Eleanor Holm disqualified from competing in the 1936 Olympics in Berlin?

487. For how many years was the instant replay rule in effect in the National Football League?

488. What is the only track and field event for which a world record has never been set in Olympic competition?

476. *41½ inches, with a tolerance of plus or minus a half-inch permitted.*

477. *Seven.*

478. *94-46.*

479. *Between 78° and 80° Fahrenheit (25.5° to 26.6° Celsius).*

480. *Women were banned from the race until 1972. Bingay, of San Diego, California, was the first woman to complete the race. Her time—unofficial because she was an illegal participant—was 3 hours 20 minutes.*

481. *Chemistry.*

482. *9 feet. A singles court is 27 feet across. A 4½-foot-wide alley is added to each side for a doubles court, making it 36 feet across.*

483. *The Tom Thumb Golf Course. It was built in 1929 in Chattanooga, Tennessee, by John Garnet Carter.*

484. *Wilbur. The nickname Weeb originated with a younger brother's mispronunciation of his name.*

485. *Polo. The rule was imposed by the U.S. Polo Association to prevent collisions between lefties and righties.*

486. *"For sipping champagne with officials" en route to the competition.*

487. *Six—from 1986 to 1992.*

488. *The discus throw.*

489. What American sister and brother won the mixed doubles tennis championship at Wimbledon in 1980?

490. What was unique about the two no-hitters pitched by Cincinnati Red southpaw John Vandermeer?

491. In tennis, what is a golden set?

492. When American Eric Heiden swept all five men's speed-skating events at the 1980 Winter Olympics, his waist size was 32 inches. What did his thighs measure?

493. What popular sport was known in ancient Germany as Heidenwerfen?

494. In what sport is a stimpmeter used, and what does it measure?

495. In the game of Monopoly, how much is a player awarded for drawing the Community Chest card that announces, "You have just won second prize in a beauty contest"?

496. What basketball player racked up the greatest number of personal fouls during his professional career?

497. What major league baseball team was featured in the 1951 film Angels in the Outfield, starring Paul Douglas and Janet Leigh?

498. In what game do you find taws, bowlers, reelers and monnies?

499. What is the greatest distance the Olympic torch ever has been carried within a single country?

500. How many numbered sections is a standard roulette wheel divided into?

501. Who was the first professional football player to run for more than 2,000 yards in a season?

502. In gambling, what is an ambsace?

489. *Tracy and John Austin.*

490. *They were consecutive—and the only no-hitters he ever threw. Vandermeer blanked both the Boston Braves and the Brooklyn Dodgers in June 1938. He's in the record books as the only pitcher in major league history to throw back-to-back no-hitters.*

491. *A set for which the score is 6-0, with the winner not losing a single point.*

492. *A muscular 29 inches according to published reports; 27 inches according to Heiden.*

493. *Bowling. Heidenwerfen means "strike down the heathens."*

494. *It's used in golf to measure the speed of the greens on a golf course. It's named for Ed Stimpson, the man who developed it in 1935.*

495. *$10.*

496. *Kareem Abdul-Jabbar—with 4,657. Other career records he holds include number of minutes played (57,446), points scored (38,387), and field goals scored (15,837). He played from 1969 to 1989.*

497. *The Pittsburgh Pirates. (When President Eisenhower was in office, he told an interviewer it was his favorite movie.)*

498. *Marbles. They're all slang for shooter marbles. Target marbles are known as ducks, stickers, dibs, hoodles, kimmies, immies, commies and mibs.*

499. *11,222 miles—in Canada. The torch was carried from St. John's to Calgary for the 1988 Winter Olympics. Of the 11,222 miles, 5,088 were covered by foot, 4,419 by aircraft and ferry, 1,712 by snowmobile, and 3 by dogsled.*

500. *In the United States, 38; in Europe, 37. In the U.S., sections of the wheel are numbered 1 through 36, 0 and 00. In Europe, there's no 00.*

501. *O.J Simpson, who racked up 2,003 yards for Buffalo in 1973, breaking the previous record of 1,863 yards set 10 years earlier by Jim Brown.*

502. *Double aces—the lowest throw at dice. In general use, the term means bad luck.*

503. How many baseball gloves can be made from one cow?

504. How far must the left and right field fences be from home plate in a major league baseball park?

505. What was the first U.S. city to host the Olympics?

506. Under what name did boxing great Walter Smith enjoy a 25-year ring career, winning both the welterweight and middleweight championship titles?

507. Who was the heaviest heavyweight boxer to compete in a title fight?

508. Who was baseball's first Rookie of the Year?

509. What is the average lifespan of an NBA basketball—in bounces?

510. Why did the Cincinnati Reds baseball team send an autographed second-base bag to cowboy movie star Roy Rogers?

511. Wood from what tree is used in making the bats used in major league baseball?

512. What tennis breakthrough was made by Lili de Alvarez on center court at Wimbledon in 1931?

513. What now-standard riding practice did turn-of-the-century jockey Tod Sloan popularize in horse racing?

514. To whom is the Lady Byng trophy awarded annually?

515. What baseball legend hit Yankee Stadium's first two World Series home runs?

516. Where was the Rose Bowl played in 1942—the only time it wasn't played in Pasadena, California?

503. Five.

504. 325 feet. The minimum distance was set in 1959.

505. St. Louis, Missouri—in 1904.

506. "Sugar Ray" Robinson. Born Walter Smith, he started boxing when he was too young to legally enter the ring—so he used the fight card of an older friend, Ray Robinson. He stuck with the name; a sportswriter added "Sugar" some years later.

507. Italy's Primo Carnera, who tipped the scales at 270 pounds when he successfully defended his title against 184-pound Tommy Loughran in March 1934. Carnera lost the title three months later to Max Baer, whom he outweighed 263¼ to 209½.

508. Brooklyn Dodger great Jackie Robinson, who was given the award in 1947. Forty years later, it was officially renamed the Jackie Robinson Award, although it's still widely called Rookie of the Year.

509. 10,000—according to the manufacturer, Spalding.

510. The red-brick tenement that was his boyhood home once stood on the site of second base at Cincinnati's Riverfront Stadium.

511. Ash.

512. She wore shorts—she was the first woman to do so at Wimbledon.

513. The "monkey crouch" position—knees tucked under chin, upper body lying along the horse's neck.

514. To the National Hockey League player who combines the highest degree of sportsmanship and gentlemanly behavior with a high standard of playing ability. Lady Byng was the wife of the governor-general of Canada when the award was first given in 1925.

515. Casey Stengel—in the 1923 World Series when he was playing for the New York Giants. The homers were hit in games one and three, the only two games the Giants won in the series.

516. In Durham, North Carolina. The reason: Pearl Harbor had been bombed less than a month earlier, and there were fears that California would be next.

517. Who was the only two-time winner of the Heisman Trophy?

518. Basketball star Kareem Abdul-Jabbar and singer Frank Sinatra had what in common?

519. Who was the first athlete to high jump over seven feet?

520. What future politician scored the only touchdown for Harvard when they played Yale in 1955?

521. Who was the only member of the College Football Hall of Fame to receive an Oscar?

522. Who was the only major league baseball player to have a brand of cigarettes named after him?

523. In 1999, who became only the fifth man to win all four major tennis tournaments-Wimbleton, the U.S Open, the Austrialian Open and the French Open-completing a career Grand Slam?

524. In 1927, when Babe Ruth hit his 60 home runs, two of those home runs were hit off a pitcher who was later elected to the Pro Football Hall of Fame. Who was this multi-talented individual?

525. Who was scheduled to be the next batter when Bobby Thomson hit his famous home run in the 1951 National League play-offs, winning the pennant for the New York Giants?

526. Who were the only three men to play for both the Milwaukee Braves and Milwaukee Brewers?

527. The legendary race horse, Man O'War, lost the only race of his illustrious career on August 13, 1919. To whom did "Big Red" lose?

528. "Daredevil Jack" is the title of a 1920 movie serial starring which heavyweight boxer?

529. What Cleveland Indians shortstop stopped Joe DiMaggio's record consecutive hitting streak at 56 games by snaring Joe's potential hit in the eighth inning of a night game July 17, 1941?

530. Who are the only brothers to hit All-Star game home runs?

517. *Archie Griffin of Ohio State, who won the award in both 1974 and 1975.*

518. *They both weighed 13 pounds when born.*

519. *The American, Charlie Dumas, in 1956.*

520. *Edward M. Kennedy.*

521. *Irvine (Cotton) Warburton, who won the Best Film Editing award for "Mary Poppins," in 1964 and was an All-American at the University of Southern California.*

522. *Ty Cobb.*

523. *Andre Agassi. He was also the first to do it on three surfces (the French Open's clay, Wimbledon's grass and the concrete of the United States Open and the Austrialian Open). The four previous Grand Slam winners-Don Budge, Fred Perry, Rod Laver and Roy Emerson-won the French Open when it was still played on grass.*

524. *Ernie Nevers, who played baseball for the St. Louis Browns in 1926, '27 and '28; and football for the Duluth Eskimos in 1926 and '27, and the Chicago Cardinals in 1929, '30 and '31.*

525. *Rookie Willie Mays.*

526. *Hank Aaron, Phil Roof, and Felipe Alou.*

527. *To a horse named Upset, who at odds of 8-to-1, forced Man O'War into second place in the Sanford Memorial Stakes in Saratoga.*

528. *Jack Dempsey.*

529. *Lou Boudreau.*

530. *Joe and Vince DiMaggio. Joe hit his in 1939 for the American League and Vince reciprocated in 1943 for the National League.*

531. What was the occupation of Joseph Cooper, the man with whom Billy Martin had the confrontation that cost him his job as manager of the New York Yankees in 1979?

532. Fred Cox, former Minnesota Viking kicker, holds the patent on what athletic toy?

533. Who was the first woman to ride in the Kentucky Derby?

534. Mickey Mantle wore number 7 throughout most of his career with the New York Yankees. What number did he wear as a rookie?

535. Who was the only man in major league history to bat over .400 during his official rookie season?

536. What former heavyweight boxing champion was rejected for the role of Apollo Creed in the 1976 film, *Rocky*, because he made Sylvester Stallone look too small?

537. Who, in 1954, was named *Sports Illustrated* magazine's first Sportsman of the Year?

538. Who was the first major league pitcher to be selected Most Valuable Player and win the Cy Young award in the same year?

539. Who was the only American to win a gold medal at the 1968 Winter Olympics?

540. Where would the 1940 Olympic Games have been held if World War II had not intervened?

541. Of what Colorado mining town was heavyweight boxing champion Jack Dempsey a native?

542. In the game of jacks, how many prongs are there are on each jack?

543. How many possible hands can a player be dealt in a game of bridge?

544. What are the odds against hitting the jackpot on a slot machine?

531. A marshmallow salesman.

532. The Nerf Ball.

533. Diane Crump, on May 2, 1970.

534. Number 6.

535. Shoeless Joe Jackson, who hit .408 for the Cleveland Indians in 1911.

536. Ken Norton.

537. Roger Bannister, who broke the four-minute mile.

538. Don Newcombe, with the Brooklyn Dodgers, in 1956.

539. Figure skater Peggy Fleming.

540. Tokyo, Japan.

541. Manassa—thus his nickname, the Manassa Mauler, coined by Damon Runyon.

542. Six.*543.* Over 600 billion—635,013,559,599 to be exact.

544. 889 to 1.

545. How many clues were there in the first crossword puzzle published in the United States?

546. How many bills does each player get at the beginning of a game of Monopoly?

547. How many dots are there on a pair of dice?

548. How did the French dice game known as hazards come to be called craps in the United States?

549. What popular board game did New Yorker Alfred Butta invent in 1931—and finally find someone to market in 1948?

550. What game featured ghosts named Inky, Blinky, Pinky and Clyde?

551. How many bedrooms are there in the detective board game Clue?

552. Who won five of the United States' six gold medals at the 1980 Winter Olympics at Lake Placid—becoming the first athlete in history to win five gold medals at a Winter Olympics?

553. How many Olympic gold medals in swimming did aquatic movie star Esther Williams win?

554. What is the meaning of basketball great Shaquille Rashaun O'Neal's given Islamic name?

555. In what major league ballpark was a pitcher charged with a balk when the wind blew him off the mound during an All-Star game?

556. How much is a tennis ball supposed to weigh?

557. In boxing, what is the top weight allowed a flyweight?

558. According to ancient chronicles, why were trainers required to be nude at the original Olympics?

559. In what sport do players scrummage?

545. *32. The puzzle appeared in the* New York World *in December 1913.*

546. *27. The bills add up to $1,500 (five $1s, $5s and $10s; two $50s, $100s and $500s; and six $20s).*

547. *42.*

548. *The game was introduced to the U.S. in New Orleans by a Creole in 1813—when the nickname for a Creole man was Johnny Crapaud. At first, the game was referred to as Crapaud's game, and later as craps.*

549. *Scrabble.*

550. *The Pac-Man video arcade game.*

551. *None. There's a ballroom billiard room, conservatory, dining room, kitchen, library, lounge, study and hall.*

552. *Skater Eric Heiden.*

553. *None. In 1940, the year in which she was to compete, the Olympic games scheduled for Finland were canceled because of World War II.*

554. *"Little Warrior." O'Neal is 7 feet 1 inch tall.*

555. *Candlestick Park, home of the San Francisco Giants, in 1961. The pitcher, Stu Miller of the Giants, ended up credited with the National League's 5-4 win. An All-Star record of 7 errors were committed during the 10-inning game.*

556. *Between 2 and 2¹⁄₁₆ ounces.*

557. *112 pounds.*

558. *To enforce the ban on women at the competition. The nude requirement for trainers went into effect after a mother attended the men-only event unnoticed, disguised as her son's trainer, until her robe fell open when she leaped over a barrier to congratulate him for winning.*

559. *English rugby. The term—used for the battle for possession of the ball—was changed to scrimmage and adopted by American football in 1880. Both scrimmage and scrummage are early versions of the word skirmish.*

560. How many times does a sprinter, running at top speed, make contact with the ground during a 100-meter (328-foot) race?

561. What error record did New York Yankee pitcher Tommy John set in a 1988 baseball game against the Milwaukee Brewers?

562. How many players are on a hurling team?

563. Who was the first sports figure to be featured on the covers of *Time, Sports Illustrated, Newsweek* and *U.S. News and World Report* on the same day?

564. How thick is a regulation ice hockey puck?

565. Who was the first American golfer to break 60 on 18 holes in a major tournament

566. How long did the longest wrestling match in Olympic history last?

567. What happens at a golf tournament when a competitor signs his card and it has the wrong score?

568. When Harvard and Yale competed in the first U.S. intercollegiate athletic contest, what was the event?

569. What is the only major sport created in the United States that did not have roots in another sport?

570. What is the world's fastest racquet sport?

571. How many of the 271 events at the 1996 Summer Olympics in Atlanta were open to both male and female competitors?

572. In the jargon of archery, what is a Robin Hood?

573. Who was the first major league baseball player to win a batting title in three different decades?

560. *Approximately 40.*

561. *He made three errors in a single play. He bobbled a slow roller and threw too late to get the batter at first base, his throw was wild and went into right field, then he cut off the throw to home plate and made a second wild throw. Despite all this, the Yankees won the game 16-3 and John had only four errors for the season.*

562. *15.*

563. *Basketball great Magic Johnson, on February 12, 1996—when he returned to the Los Angeles Lakers.*

564. *1 inch. It's 3 inches in diameter.*

565. *Sam Snead, who shot a 59 (31 out, 28 in), 11 strokes under par, in the 1959 Greenbrier Open at White Sulphur Springs, West Virginia. The competition has since been renamed the Sam Snead Festival Golf Tournament.*

566. *11 hours and 40 minutes. The match, a Greco-Roman middleweight bout at the 1912 Olympics, was between Estonian Martin Klein and Finn Alfred Asikainen. Klein won, but was too exhausted to compete in the final. He ended up with the silver medal; Asikainen with the bronze.*

567. *If the score on the card is lower than his actual score, he's disqualified. It it's higher, it replaces his score.*

568. *A boat race, in 1852.*

569. *Basketball.*

570. *Badminton. Shuttlecock speeds approach 200 mph.*

571. *11—mixed doubles badminton, four classes of yachting and all the equestrian events. Of the remaining events, 165 were for men only, and 95 for women only.*

572. *When the tip and shaft of an arrow is fired deep into the end of an arrow already in the bull's-eye.*

573. *George Brett, of the Kansas City Royals. Third baseman Brett won the title with a .333 average in 1976, a .390 average in 1980 and a .329 average in 1990.*

574. Who is the shortest player to lead the National Basketball Association in rebounding?

575. In 1988, Christa Rothenburger-Luding of East Germany became the only Olympic competitor to earn medals in winter and summer games of the same year. What events did she win?

576. What annual sports event was introduced in 1933 as an adjunct to the Chicago World's Fair?

577. In horseracing, what's a walkover?

578. What first name was shared by baseball managers Birdie Tebbetts and Sparky Anderson?

579. In 1996, how much of the $12.9 million earned by basketball oddball Dennis Rodman was compensation for playing for the Chicago Bulls?

580. How did Ernie Shore of the Boston Red Sox get to pitch the only perfect game thrown by a reliever?

581. How many players compete on an equestrian polo team? How about a water polo team?

582. To boost his chances of retrieving a home-run ball, what baseball-loving movie star paid $6,537 for several hundred seats behind the left-field fence for a 1996 game at Anaheim Stadium?

583. What item found in the pocket of pitcher Tom Seaver's New York Mets game jacket—worn from 1967 through 1969—brought $440 at auction?

584. What professional ice hockey star didn't hang up his skates until he was 52—and had played in 2,421 games?

585. What immodest two-word statement is on basketball great Michael Jordan's Illinois vanity license plate?

586. Why were there two kickoffs at the start of the second half of Superbowl I?

574. *Charles Barkley, at 6 foot 5 inches. He led in rebounding, with a 14.6 per game average for the 1986-87 season, when he was with the Philadelphia 76ers.*

575. *Speed skating (gold and silver medals) and cycling (silver medal). Her feat cannot be duplicated because winter and summer games are now held in different years.*

576. *Baseball's All-Star Game. The first All-Star Game was played at Comiskey Park. The American League, managed by Connie Mack, defeated the National League, managed by John McGraw, 4-2.*

577. *A race in which a horse is uncontested and simply has to walk the course to win. Spectacular Bid won the 1980 Woodward Stakes at Belmont Raceway in a walkover.*

578. *George.*

579. *$3.9 million. Most of his earnings came from endorsements, and some came from his best-selling book, Bad as I Wanna Be.*

580. *Starting pitcher Babe Ruth was thrown out of the 1917 game for cussing out the umpire after throwing four balls to the lead-off batter. Shore took over on the mound and retired the next 27 batters.*

581. *Equestrian, 4; water, 7.*

582. *Charlie Sheen, who attended the game with three friends. They came up empty-handed—no homers were hit their way.*

583. *A toothpick.*

584. *Gordie Howe. He played for 32 seasons—26 in the National Hockey League and six in the World Hockey Association—racking up 1,071 goals, 1,518 assists and 2,418 penalty minutes.*

585. *RARE AIR.*

586. *NBC was running a commercial and missed the first kickoff. Officials nullified the play and had the half start over again. The 1967 game ended with the Green Bay Packers beating the Kansas City Chiefs, 35-10.*

587. What two baseball players were named rookie of the year in 1964—the first time African-Americans won the coveted award in both leagues?

588. In what sport does competition generally take place on a triangular race course?

589. Who was tennis star Monica Seles playing in the 1993 Citizen's Cup Tournament in Hamburg, Germany, when she was stabbed in the back by a spectator?

590. What baseball era ended in 1894 with the retirement of infielder Jeremiah Denny, who had played with the Indianapolis Hoosiers and Louisville Colonels?

591. In bowling, what is the difference between the headpin and the kingpin?

592. What boxing great has been credited with inventing the left hook?

593. Who belted 43 home runs in 1973—matching Baseball Hall of Famer Roger Hornsby's record for the most home runs by a second baseman in one season?

594. Professional teams playing in St. Louis include the Blues (hockey) and the Cardinals (baseball). What big league sports teams has the city had and lost since World War II?

595. American horse racing's top three contests—the Kentucky Derby, the Preakness and the Belmont Stakes—are known as the Triple Crown. What are the three big races exclusively for fillies called?

596. What regulation about fighters' footwear is included in the 12 Marquis of Queensberry Rules, which have governed boxing for over 100 years?

597. With what football team did the huddle originate?

598. Saint Lydwina is the patron saint of what sport?

587. Richie Allen, third baseman for the Philadelphia Phillies, won in the National League; Tony Oliva, outfielder for the Minnesota Twins, won in the American League.

588. Sailing.

589. Magdalena Maleeva. The spectator wanted fellow German Steffi Graf to win the tournament—but she lost the final to Arantxa Sanchez Vicario.

590. The era of bare-handed fielding.

591. The headpin is pin number one, located at the head of the triangle of pins; the kingpin is pin number five, located in the center of all the other pins. Some bowlers and dictionaries mistakenly use both terms for the number one pin.

592. James "Gentleman Jim" Corbett—who came up with the powerful punch in 1889 after suffering two broken knuckles in a heavyweight bout.

593. Manager-to-be Davey Johnson, who was with the Atlanta Braves at the time.

594. The Browns (baseball); the Hawks (basketball); and the Cardinals (football).

595. The Triple Tiara—they are the Acorn, the Mother Goose and the Coaching Club-American Oaks.

596. "No shoes or boots with springs allowed."

597. With the deaf Gallaudet College team, in the 1890s. Members of the Washington, D.C., team went into a huddle to hide the hand signals they were using during a game against another deaf team.

598. Ice skating.

599. What was the championship seed-spitting distance set by John Wilkinson at the "11th Annual Watermelon Thump" held in Luling, Texas, in 1980?

600. What hockey first was achieved by Clarence "Taffy" Abel of the New York Rangers in 1929?

601. With what game did the expression "knuckle down" originate?

602. What action did temperamental relief pitcher Pedro Borbon take when the Cincinnati Reds traded him to the San Francisco Giants in 1979?

603. What National Football League team had its start as the Boston Braves in 1932?

604. What TV newsman was part of the Lancia car racing team that competed in the 1959 Sebring 12-hour race?

605. Ty Cobb's first name was Tyrus. What was the first name of that other baseball great Cy Young?

606. What are the periods of play in a polo match called?

607. Who coined the slogan, "You can't tell the players without a scorecard"?

608. What was boxing great Rocky Marciano's nickname for his deadly right hand?

609. What defensive end was named to the Pro Bowl squad in all but one of his 15 years in the game—a National Football League record?

610. "Lefty" historically has been the most common nickname in baseball. What were the real first names of Hall of Fame southpaws Lefty Grove and Lefty Gomez?

611. What great ballplayer played first base in high school and had pitched only one season in college when he was given a bonus to pitch in the major leagues?

599. *65 feet 4 inches.*

600. *He was the first American-born player to be on a Stanley Cup team.*

601. *Marbles—players put fist (knuckles) to the ground for their best shots.*

602. *He put a voodoo curse on the Reds.*

603. *The Washington Redskins. The team became the Boston Redskins a year later, and moved to Washington in 1937.*

604. *Walter Cronkite.*

605. *Denton. He was nicknamed Cy—for Cyclone—because of the destruction wrought by his famous fastball.*

606. *Chukkers. In U.S. competition there are six of them in a normal game, each seven and a half minutes long.*

607. *Baseball's first professional concessionaire, Harry M. Stevens, who used it when he started hawking ballpark programs in Columbus, Ohio, in the 1880s.*

608. *Suzi-Q.*

609. *Merlin Olsen, who played with the L.A. Rams. Olsen, now a sportscaster and actor, was bypassed for the Pro Bowl squad in 1976—his last season.*

610. *Robert and Vernon, respectively.*

611. *Sandy Koufax, who was 19 in 1954 when the Brooklyn Dodgers signed him up with a $14,000 bonus and an annual salary of $6,000.*

612. What baseball-playing brothers came in first and second in the race for the National League batting title in 1966?

613. Where were the first outdoor miniature golf courses in the United States built?

614. What fruit did early Greek Olympians eat for their health and sometimes even wear as medals?

615. What was baseball great Babe Ruth's response when he was asked why he deserved a higher salary than President Herbert Hoover?

616. What country established the modern tradition of having the Olympic torch carried from Greece to the site of the international games?

617. How long did England's Roger Bannister, the first athlete to run the long-elusive four-minute mile, hold the world title in the event?

618. Whose tennis serve was the fastest ever recorded?

619. What was the average weight of the legendary Four Horsemen—the gridiron greats who played for Notre Dame under Knute Rockne in 1924?

620. Basketball great Kareem Abdul-Jabbar wore number 33 during his 20-year career because it was the number of his favorite football player. Can you name that player?

621. Famed boxer Jack Dempsey was named after what American president?

622. Who was the only major league baseball player to hit a home run to win the seventh game of a World Series?

623. What was baseball great Stan Musial's advice to those trying to hit a spitball?

624. In what sport is a battledore used?

612. *The Alou brothers, Matty and Felipe. Matty's batting average with the Pittsburgh Pirates was .342; Felipe's average with the Atlanta Braves was .327.*

613. *On rooftops in New York City—in 1926.*

614. *Figs.*

615. *"Why not? I had a better year." Ruth's salary at the time (1931) was $80,000; Hoover's, $75,000.*

616. *Germany, in 1936—when the Olympics were held in Berlin.*

617. *For 46 days. Bannister's record of 3:59.4, set on May 6, 1954, was broken by Australia's John Landy, who hit the tape at 3:58.0 on June 21, 1954.*

618. *Bill Tilden's. It was measured at 163.6 miles per hour in 1931.*

619. *159 pounds. The breakdown: fullback Elmer Layden, 162; halfback Don Miller, 160; halfback James Crowley, 159; and quarterback Harry Stuhldreher, 155.*

620. *Former New York Giants running back Mel Triplett.*

621. *William Henry Harrison. The "Manassa Mauler" was named William Harrison Dempsey at birth.*

622. *Bill Mazeroski, who clinched the 1960 series for the Pittsburgh Pirates with his homer off Ralph Terry of the New York Yankees.*

623. *"Hit it on the dry side."*

624. *In badminton—it's the racket used to hit the shuttlecock. Originally the game was known as battledore and shuttlecock.*

625. How many times did the "Father of Baseball," Abner Doubleday, mention that sport in his 67 diaries?

626. How many players are there on a men's lacrosse team?

627. Who was the only rookie in baseball history to be honored as rookie of the year and most valuable player in the same season?

628. What baseball team introduced the sacrifice bunt, the squeeze play, the hit-and-run play, and double-steal?

629. Why did baseball manager Hal Lanier order all television sets removed from the Houston Astros clubhouse in 1986?

630. Who was the first black athlete to carry the American flag in the opening procession of the Olympics?

631. How much did premier jockey Eddie Arcaro earn in purses during his 30-year career?

632. In golfing slang, what is a Dolly Parton?

633. In 1950, baseball commissioner Ford Frick ordered New York Giant second baseman Eddie Stanky to stop performing "the Stanky maneuver." What was it?

634. What famous sports commentator announced his first major league baseball game without ever having seen one before?

635. The Kentucky Derby is named for its home state; the Belmont Stakes for its founder, August Belmont. How did the Preakness get its name?

636. What was the greatest number of home runs hit in a single season by baseball's "Georgia Peach," Ty Cobb?

637. What hard-hitting football great once said: "I wouldn't ever set out to hurt anybody deliberately unless it was, you know, important. Like a league game or something."

638. What well-known baseball pitcher is descended from a Hessian mercenary who fought for the British in the American Revolution?

625. *Not once.*

626. *Ten—three defensemen, three midfield players, three attackmen, and a goalkeeper.*

627. *Outfielder Fred Lynn, in 1975, when he helped the Boston Red Sox capture the American League pennant by batting .331.*

628. *The Baltimore Orioles—before the turn of the century.*

629. *The players were skipping infield practice to watch "Wheel of Fortune."*

630. *Decathlon champion Rafer Johnson, in Rome in 1960.*

631. *Exactly $30,039,543—of which his share was approximately 10 percent.*

632. *A putt on an especially hilly green. It's also known as a roller coaster.*

633. *Jumping up and down and waving wildly to distract batters. As one baseball executive said of Stanky: "He cannot hit, he cannot throw, and he cannot outrun his grandmother. But if there's a way to beat the other team, he'll find it."*

634. *Red Barber, in 1934 for the Cincinnati Reds.*

635. *From the colt that won the first stakes race ever held at Maryland's Pimlico Race Course.*

636. *12.*

637. *Hall of Fame linebacker Dick Butkus, who helped the Chicago Bears earn the title "monsters of the midway" in the late 1960s and early '70s.*

638. *Orel Hershiser, whose first name is Slavic for "eagle."*

639. How many points did basketball great Kareem Abdul-Jabbar score during his 20-season career?

640. Why was Russian pentathlon star Boris Onischenko disqualified for cheating at the 1976 Olympics in Montreal?

641. What was the name of the only National Football League team playing in Pennsylvania in 1943?

642. What is the width of a football field?

643. How big a cut did baseball's Gary Carter take in his base pay when he signed with the San Francisco Giants in 1990 after being dropped as a catcher by the New York Mets?

644. What was basketball great Wilt Chamberlain's record high for points scored in one half?

645. What sport has a sex allowance?

646. The New York Jets were beating the Oakland Raiders 32-29 with 75 seconds of play to go in November 1968 when the game was pre-empted by the children's classic "Heidi." What was the final score?

647. How did baseball superstar Leroy "Satchel" Paige get his nickname?

648. What is the diameter of the cup on a standard golf course putting green?

649. How old was boxer Archie Moore in 1952 when he won the light-heavyweight championship?

650. What does basketball great Kareem Abdul-Jabbar's name mean in English?

651. What two baseball-playing brothers hit home runs in the same World Series game?

652. What left-handed British head of state competed at Wimbledon—and lost in a first-round doubles match?

639. *A record 38,387—or 44,149 if you're counting playoffs.*

640. *He was caught using a rigged épée in the fencing competition. It had an electronic device in its handle that caused a "hit" to be registered on the electronic scoreboard when none had been made.*

641. *The Steagles—the Pittsburgh Steelers and Philadelphia Eagles merged during World War II when many players were serving overseas.*

642. *53⅓ yards.*

643. *Almost $2 million—he went from $2.2 million to $250,000.*

644. *He scored 59 points in one half; his game high was 100.*

645. *Thoroughbred horse racing. It's the number of pounds below the minimum—usually three to five pounds—that fillies are permitted to carry when running against males.*

646. *The Raiders won, 43-32, after making two last-minute touchdowns.*

647. *From his size-14 shoes, which were "as big as satchels."*

648. *Exactly 4¼ inches.*

649. *He was 39—and he held the NBA title from 1952 to 1961.*

650. *Generous Servant of Allah.*

651. *The Boyers, Ken and Clete, third basemen for the St. Louis Cardinals and New York Yankees, respectively. Their homers came in the seventh game of the 1964 Series.*

652. *King George VI—father of Queen Elizabeth II—in 1926 when he was the Duke of York.*

653. How many tiles are there in a game of dominoes?

654. What was the controversial name of the French yacht that competed in the 1987 America's Cup race?

655. What famous boxer once said: "I was never knocked out. I've been unconscious, but it's always been on my feet"?

656. Who was the first designated hitter in major league baseball history?

657. What was long-time Philadelphia Athletics baseball manager Connie Mack's name before he shortened it to fit on the scoreboard?

658. How did basketball get its name?

659. The Indianapolis 500 was begun in 1911. When was the first time the winning race car exceeded 100 mph?

660. What popular actor was part owner of the racehorse that placed third in the 1980 Kentucky Derby?

661. What sport did novelist Joyce Carol Oates write a book about?

662. Walter Alston, manager of the Brooklyn and L.A. Dodgers, appeared in only one major league game as a player. For what team did he go to bat and how did he do?

663. What are the odds of getting four of a kind in a five-card deal in poker?

664. What is the maximum length and thickness permitted for a major league baseball bat?

665. What two sports have telltales—and what are they?

666. What did tennis star Gussie Moran wear in a tournament in Egypt nine months after she stunned the staid Wimbledon crowd by wearing white lace-fringed panties?

653. *There are 28.*

654. *French Kiss.*

655. *Floyd Patterson, world heavyweight champion from 1956 to 1959 and from 1960 to 1962.*

656. *Ron Blomberg of the New York Yankees. He drew a bases-loaded walk from Red Sox pitcher Luis Tiant in his historic April 6, 1973 at-bat at Boston's Fenway Park.*

657. *Cornelius McGillicuddy.*

658. *From the half-bushel peach baskets used as targets by the sport's originator, James A. Naismith, in the first game in December 1891.*

659. *In 1925, when Peter De Paolo averaged 101.13 mph in an 8-cylinder Duesenberg Special.*

660. *Jack ("Quincy" and "Oscar Madison") Klugman. The horse was named Jaklin Klugman.*

661. *Boxing. The book, published in 1987, is called "On Boxing."*

662. *In his sole at-bat for the 1936 St. Louis Cardinals, Alston struck out.*

663. *The odds are 4,164 to 1.*

664. *Length, 42 inches; thickness, 2¾ inches.*

665. *Squash and sailing. In squash, it is the narrow 17-inch-high metal strip the ball must clear on the front wall. In sailing, it's a small piece of cloth or yarn attached to the shroud or backstay to indicate the relative direction of the wind.*

666. *Black shorts. She explained that she made the change because she had gained 13 pounds and her white tennis attire no longer fit.*

667. What is the maximum a horseshoe may weigh in the game of horseshoes?

668. Whom did Casey Stengel advise, "Kid, you're too small. You ought to go out and shine shoes"?

669. How long is a standard six-foot-wide shuffleboard court?

670. What is the average life span of a baseball—in pitches—in the major leagues?

671. How tall is former Dallas Cowboy defensive end Ed "Too Tall" Jones?

672. What major league pitcher was ordered to stop wearing hair curlers on the field during practice?

673. In the National Hockey League, how many members of a team are permitted to suit up for a game?

674. What former major league baseball player is the younger brother of tennis great Billie Jean King?

675. How many feathers are there on a standard badminton shuttlecock?

676. Who was the first woman to serve as grand marshal of the Tournament of Roses parade, first held in 1890?

677. What TV western star was once the highest paid, highest scoring professional lacrosse player in Canadian history?

678. How many pieces does each player start with in a chess game?

679. What sport was banned in Scotland in 1457 by King James II, and why?

680. What boxers competed in the first prize fight with a $1 million gate?

681. In what event did Dr. Benjamin Spock compete in the 1924 Paris Olympics?

667. *The maximum is 2½ pounds. Those worn by horses vary, with thoroughbred racehorses wearing 4-ounce aluminum shoes and pleasure horses wearing 12-ounce steel shoes.*

668. *Phil Rizzuto, who went on to play with the New York Yankees as a shortstop under Stengel and later became the Yankees' broadcaster. Casey made the remark while he was managing the Brooklyn Dodgers.*

669. *It's 52 feet long.*

670. *Five.*

671. *He's 6 feet 9 inches tall.*

672. *Dock Ellis of the Pittsburgh Pirates, in 1973.*

673. *Twenty.*

674. *Randy Moffitt, who pitched for the San Francisco Giants and the Toronto Blue Jays.*

675. *Between 14 and 16, each from 2½ to 2¾ inches long, from its tip to the top of the shuttlecock's cork base.*

676. *Humorist and syndicated columnist Erma Bombeck, in 1986.*

677. *Jay Silverheels—Tonto on "The Lone Ranger."*

678. *Sixteen—a king, a queen, two knights, two bishops, two castles, and eight pawns.*

679. *Golf—he claimed it distracted people from the archery practice needed for national defense.*

680. *Heavyweights Jack Dempsey and George Carpentier. Dempsey won the 1921 bout, billed as "The Fight of the Century," with a fourth round knockout.*

681. *Rowing. He won a gold medal as a member of the Yale team.*

682. How did poker's Dead Man's Hand—a pair of aces and a pair of eights—get its name?

683. What West Point cadet's football career came to an abrupt halt when he injured his knee tackling Jim Thorpe, who was playing for the Carlisle Indian School?

684. In 1882, who knocked out Paddy Ryan to become the last bareknuckle world's heavyweight boxing champion?

685. What pitcher's career spanned the greatest number of years—twenty-five seasons?

686. What are the three one-eyed face cards in a desk of cards?

687. What is the name of golfer Jack Nicklaus's international real-estate conglomerate?

688. Participants in the 1960 Olympics were asked what question concerning their early childhoods on an official questionnaire?

689. What Olympic requirement was waived for Princess Anne when she competed as an equestrian in the 1976 summer games in Montreal?

690. What does the O. J. in football star O. J. Simpson's name stand for?

691. In what game did William Shakespeare play against Henry Wadsworth Longfellow?

692. What St. Louis Cardinal pitchers won two games each to clinch the 1934 World Series against the Detroit Tigers?

693. What two-time Wimbledon champion became the first tennis millionaire in 1971?

694. Who were the swimming stars in Billy Rose's "Aquacade" at the 1939 New York World's Fair?

695. On what team did basketball greats Oscar Robertson, Jerry West, and John Havlicek play together?

682. *It was the hand held by Wild Bill Hickok when he was gunned down.*

683. *Dwight D. Eisenhower, left halfback on the losing team. Score: 27 to 6.*

684. *John L. Sullivan.*

685. *James L. Kaat, who retired in 1983.*

686. *The king of diamonds, the jack of spades, and the jack of hearts.*

687. *Golden Bear, Inc.—inspired by his golf circuit nickname, Golden Bear.*

688. *They were asked if they had been bottle- or breast-fed.*

689. *She was the only female competitor not given a chromosome (sex) test.*

690. *Orenthal James.*

691. *Football—in 1935, Notre Dame's Shakespeare faced Northwestern's Longfellow. Longfellow's team won, 14 to 7.*

692. *Brothers Dizzy and Daffy Dean.*

693. *Australian Rod Laver.*

694. *American Olympic gold medal winners Johnny Weissmuller, Eleanor Holm, and Gertrude Ederle, the first woman to swim across the English Channel.*

695. *The winning 1960 U.S. Olympic basketball team.*

696. In what sport did sailor Alvin "Shipwreck" Kelly rise to the top?

697. What game did the Duchess of Windsor teach TV interviewer Edward R. Murrow to play on "Person to Person"?

698. What American ballet star was a boxing champion in college?

699. Who asked: "Sin tax? Are them jokers down in Washington puttin' a tax on that, too?"

700. What number did baseball legend Ty Cobb wear?

701. Where are all baseballs used in the U.S. major leagues manufactured?

702. What is the origin of the winning term "checkmate" in chess?

703. What two college teams played the first football game in the U.S.?

704. What boxing champion-to-be was disqualified in the 1952 Olympic heavyweight finals for "inactivity in the ring"?

705. Outfielder Pete Gray played with the St. Louis Browns in 1945 despite a serious handicap. What was it?

706. What did the French Boxing Federation ban in an official edict in 1924?

707. What famous football coach had every member of his team take dancing lessons "to develop a sense of rhythm essential in the timing of shift plays"?

708. In bowling, what term describes the split in which the 5 and 10 pins are left standing?

709. How long was Muhammad Ali exiled from boxing for refusing to enter military service during the war in Vietnam?

710. What football teams were playing when TV made its first use of the instant replay 30 years ago?

696. *Flagpole sitting. He traveled the country setting records. His best time was 49 days; his lifetime total was 20,613 hours.*

697. *Jacks.*

698. *Edward Villella.*

699. *Baseball great turned sportscaster Dizzy Dean, when told that his syntax greatly distressed educators.*

700. *None. He played before numbers were used.*

701. *In Haiti, where cheap labor is used to handstitch the leather cover on each 369-yard roll of woolen yarn and cotton string. (The Rawlings Sporting Goods Co.'s exclusive contract expired in 1986.)*

702. *The Arabic phrase "shah mat," literally "the king is dead."*

703. *Princeton and Rutgers. Rutgers won the 1869 contest, 6 to 4.*

704. *Sweden's Ingemar Johansson. He was presented with the silver medal thirty years later.*

705. *He had only one arm.*

706. *The fighters' practice of kissing one another at the end of their bouts.*

707. *Notre Dame's Knute Rockne, in 1923.*

708. *Woolworth.*

709. *For 3½ years, from April 1967 to October 1970, when he returned to the ring and knocked out Jerry Quarry.*

710. *Army and Navy. The play shown was a touchdown by Army quarterback Carl "Rollie" Stichweh.*

711. What popular sport was called Sphairistikè when it was introduced in England in 1873?

712. How many pentagonal patches are there on a soccer ball?

713. What two well-known hockey figures teamed up to pay $451,000 for a rare Honus Wagner baseball card in 1991?

714. In golfing slang, what is a Volkswagen?

715. Who was the last major league baseball player to get on base more than 50 percent of the time during a season with at least 400 at-bats?

716. How much did CBS pay for the United States TV broadcast rights to the 1994 Winter Olympics in Lillehammer, Norway?

717. After what popular TV actor of the 1960s was football-baseball star Bo Jackson named?

718. What change did Charlie O. Finley, the colorful former owner of the Oakland Athletics, try but fail to make in the ball used in our national pastime?

719. Who holds the basketball record for the most free throws made in a game?

720. What message was on the T-shirt worn by New York Yankee pitcher Gaylord Perry—who was nicknamed the Great Expectorator—on the day he won his 300th game?

721. What famous American boxer was named Arnold Raymond Cream at birth?

722. What unusual—and quite revolutionary—track and field event was officially recognized by the Physical Culture and Sports Commission of Communist China in 1956?

723. What now standard boxing equipment did ringside newspaper-telegraph operator Stanley Taylor invent in a bid to upgrade the sport?

711. *Th modern game of tennis. Its creator was Major Walter C. Wingfield. Sphairistikè is a Greek word that means "to play."*

712. *12. They're usually black. The white patches are hexagons.*

713. *Wayne Gretzky and Los Angeles Kings owner Bruce McNall.*

714. *An awkward or bad shot that turns out well.*

715. *New York Yankee Mickey Mantle, in 1957, when his on-base average was .515. The Boston Red Sox's Ted Williams holds the record for the best on-base average ever, .551, achieved in 1941.*

716. *$300 million—$57 million more than it paid for the rights to broadcast the 1992 games held in Albertville, France.*

717. *Vince Edwards. Jackson, whose given name is Vincent Edward, was named after the actor who appeared in the title role on the "Ben Casey" show. The nickname Bo is a shortened version of Boar—the moniker Jackson's brother gave him when he was eight because he was as tough as a wild boar.*

718. *He wanted baseballs to be yellow.*

719. *Bob Cousy of the Boston Celtics, who made 30 of 32 free-throw attempts in a 1953 four-overtime playoff game against the Syracuse Nationals. Although he racked up 50 points, the Celtics lost 111-105.*

720. *"300 wins is nothing to spit at." The win came in May 1982. Perry retired the following year with a career record of 314 wins and 265 losses.*

721. *Jersey Joe Walcott.*

722. *The hand-grenade throw.*

723. *The protective cup. Taylor had seen too many losing boxers turn the tide of their bouts with low blows.*

724. Who was the first relief pitcher elected to baseball's Hall of Fame?

725. What is the maximum circumference of a standard bowling ball?

726. What was the name of the only horse to beat Man O'War in his incredible 21-race career?

727. What happens in major league baseball if an outfielder catches a fly ball with his hat instead of his glove?

728. Before wooden tees were introduced in the late 1920s, what did golfers use to elevate the ball for driving?

729. What famous American tennis player's father boxed for Iran in the 1948 and 1952 Olympics?

730. When they play trictrac in France, what game are they playing?

731. Who was the first black to play major league baseball with an American League team?

732. What did Japan's century-old Nintendo company manufacture before it made its mark in the world of computer games?

733. The winner of the Kentucky Derby is blanketed with roses. What flowers are used to adorn the winners of the Belmont Stakes and the Preakness?

734. What sport is named for the country estate of the English duke whose house guests helped devise and popularize it?

735. How many wickets and wooden stakes are used in playing tournament croquet?

736. Name the seven baseball greats who share the distinction of having been voted "most valuable player" three times.

737. What is unusual about the names boxer George Foreman has given his five sons?

724. *Right-handed knuckleball specialist Hoyt Wilhelm, in 1985.*

725. *27 inches—or 27.002 inches, to be exact.*

726. *Upset.*

727. *The batter gets three bases.*

728. *A small mound of sand.*

729. *Andre Agassi's Armenian-born father, Emmanuel Agassi, better known as Mike.*

730. *Backgammon.*

731. *Larry Doby, who joined the Cleveland Indians in July 1947—11 weeks after Jackie Robinson broke the major league color barrier by joining the Brooklyn Dodgers.*

732. *Playing cards.*

733. *At Belmont, white carnations are traditional. At the Preakness, yellow daisies are dabbed with black shoe polish to look like black-eyed Susans—the Maryland state flower, which doesn't bloom until a month after the big race.*

734. *Badminton. It was during a house party on a rainy day in 1873 at the Duke of Beaufort's home in Gloucestershire, that guests picked up the battledores and shuttlecock used in a children's game and began playing over a cord stretched across a hall.*

735. *Six wickets and one stake.*

736. *Jimmy Foxx, Joe DiMaggio, Stan Musial, Yogi Berra, Roy Campanella, Mickey Mantle and Mike Schmidt.*

737. *All are named George.*

738. How many sides are there on the grip of a standard tennis racket?

739. What vessels were used when the first regattas were held in the seventeenth century?

740. How many field goals and how many free throws did basketball great Wilt "The Stilt" Chamberlain make in his famous 100-point game in 1962?

741. By what name was Dimitrios Synodinos better known in the sporting world?

742. In what country did the card game canasta originate?

743. In what city did basketball's barnstorming Harlem Globetrotters get their start?

744. When the New York Knickerbockers became the first baseball club to adopt an official uniform in 1849, what did team members wear on their heads?

745. What was sports great Jesse Owens's real given name?

746. What is the name of the cookbook that Boston Red Sox third baseman Wade Boggs co-authored with his wife, Debbie, in 1984?

747. In golf, what is an albatross?

748. What were the first American and National League baseball teams to draw over one million fans in a season?

749. How many hits did the "Yankee Clipper," Joe DiMaggio, get during his 56-game batting streak in 1941?

750. In the earliest days of baseball, how many balls were required for a batter to draw a walk?

751. In bowling alley slang, what's a turkey?

752. When you hit a tennis ball, how much time does it spend in contact with your tennis racket?

738. *Eight.*

739. *Gondolas. The regattas were held on the Grand Canal in Venice.*

740. *Chamberlain, playing for the Philadelphia Warriors, scored 36 field goals and 28 free throws against the New York Knickerbockers in that historic game.*

741. *Jimmy "the Greek" Snyder—the famous Las Vegas oddsmaker.*

742. *In Uruguay, in the 1940s.*

743. *In Chicago—home of team organizer Abe Saperstein.*

744. *Straw hats. The rest of the uniform consisted of blue woolen pantaloons and white flannel shirts.*

745. *James Cleveland. He was known by his initials, J.C., until he was nine, when a teacher mistakenly called him Jesse—and a new nickname was born.*

746. *"Fowl Tips." It's a chicken cookbook. Boggs says he eats chicken every day.*

747. *Three under par—which also is known as a double eagle.*

748. *For the American League, the New York Yankees—1,289,422 in 1920; for the National League, the Chicago Cubs—1,159,168 in 1927.*

749. *He got 91 hits, knocked in 55 runs and reached home himself 56 times. Of his 91 hits, 56 were singles, 16 were doubles, 4 were triples and 15 were homers.*

750. *Nine. The number was reduced little by little until 1889, when it became four.*

751. *Three strikes in a row. The term dates back to the late 1800s, when bowling alley owners presented live turkeys around Thanksgiving and Christmas to the first member of a team to score three consecutive strikes.*

752. *$\frac{1}{1,000}$ second.*

753. What is the minimum weight permitted for a baseball in the major leagues?

754. What was the name of the very first video game?

755. What did pentathlon and decathlon winner Jim Thorpe reply when Sweden's King Gustav V called him "the greatest athlete in the world" as he presented him with his gold medals at the 1912 Olympics?

756. What does zugzwang describe in the game of chess?

757. What was the original meaning of bogey—the golf term that now indicates one stroke over par?

758. Who was on the mound for the Brooklyn Dodgers when Yankee righthander Don Larsen pitched his perfect game in the 1956 World Series?

759. What dubious first did discus thrower Danuta Rosani of Poland achieve at the 1976 Olympics in Montreal?

760. Who was the first tennis player from an Iron Curtain country to win the United States Open?

761. According to the rules in effect at the first intercollegiate baseball game ever played—back in 1859—the first team to score 65 runs would be the winner. How long did the game last?

762. What are the five events in the modern Olympic pentathlon?

763. Under what weather conditions does a baseball travel farthest?

764. Who was the first driver to cover a mile in less than a minute in a gas-powered automobile?

765. In 1988 the Chicago Cubs became the last major league team to get lights for night baseball. What team was next to last?

766. In 1896 in Athens, Greece, Harvard student James B. Connolly became the first gold medal winner in modern Olympic history. What was his event?

753. *The minimum is 5 ounces. (The maximum weight allowed is 5¼ ounces.)*

754. *Pong—which was introduced in 1972 by Noel Bushnell, who soon after created Atari.*

755. *"Thanks, King." Thorpe, who was later disqualified for alleged professionalism, was posthumously restored to the roster of Olympic champions in 1982.*

756. *A situation in which all possible moves are to the player's disadvantage.*

757. *It originally meant par—and still does in Great Britain.*

758. *Sal Maglie, who allowed only five hits in the 2-0 Dodger loss.*

759. *She failed the test for anabolic steroids and became the first Olympic athlete to be disqualified for taking drugs.*

760. *Romanian Ilie Nastase, in 1972.*

761. *It went 26 innings, or "rounds," with Amherst beating Williams 66-32.*

762. *The 5,000-meter cross-country horseback ride, 300-meter swim, 4,000-meter cross-country run, foil fencing and pistol shooting.*

763. *When it is hot and humid—because the air is less dense than when it is cold and dry.*

764. *Legendary race car driver Barney Oldfield in 1903. He did the mile in 59.6 seconds in a Ford 999.*

765. *The Detroit Tigers, 40 years earlier.*

766. *The hop, step and jump, now known as the triple jump. Connolly went a distance of 45 feet.*

767. What are the usual dimensions of the professional boxing ring?

768. What baseball team got its name because of a second baseman named Louis Bierbauer?

769. In how many World Series did Babe Ruth play during his 22-year baseball career?

770. What was the final score of the $100,000, winner-take-all "Battle of the Sexes" tennis match between Billy Jean King and Bobby Riggs at the Houston Astrodome in 1973?

771. Who was the first American sports figure to earn $1 million during his career?

772. What are the ten events in the grueling Olympic decathlon competition?

773. How many homeruns did Mark McGwire hit in 1998—the year he broke Roger Maris's longstanding record?

774. Who directed the opening ceremonies at the 1960 Winter Olympics in Squaw Valley, California?

775. What is the distance from foul line to head pin on a bowling lane?

776. How many rounds did John L. Sullivan and Jake Kilrain go in America's last professional bare-knuckle heavyweight boxing bout?

777. How many fingers did Mordecai "Three Finger" Brown, the great right-handed Chicago Cub pitcher, have?

778. In modern day camel racing in Abu Dhabi, in the United Arab Emirates, what is used to keep jockeys on their mounts?

779. Who was the only tennis player to win the U.S. Open on three different surfaces—grass and clay at Forest Hills and hardcourt at Flushing Meadows?

780. Who was the first female athlete to appear in a Wheaties "Breakfast of Champions" television commercial?

767. *The professional ring is generally 20 feet square (although the size may vary from 16 to 24 feet square).*

768. *The Pittsburgh Pirates. The team—which had gone through a variety of names including the Alleghenies, Potato Bugs, Zulus and Smoked Italians— earned the name by "pirating" Bierbauer away from the Philadelphia Athletics.*

769. *Ten, with his team winning seven of them.*

770. *King (age 29) beat Riggs (age 55) in three sets, 6-4, 6-3, 6-3.*

771. *Heavyweight boxer John L. Sullivan.*

772. *The 100-meter, 400-meter and 1,500-meter races, the long jump, 16-pound shot put, high jump, 110-meter high hurdles, discus throw, pole vault and javelin throw.*

773. *70—nine more than Maris hit in 1961*

774. *Walt Disney.*

775. *Sixty feet.*

776. *The 1889 bout went 75 rounds—with Bat Masterson serving as timekeeper for loser Kilrain.*

777. *Nine and a half. He was missing the top half of his right index finger.*

778. *Velcro. It has replaced rope.*

779. *Jimmy Connors.*

780. *Pint-sized gymnast Mary Lou Retton, shortly after her gold medal triumph at the 1984 Summer Olympics.*

781. Where did the home run hit by Pittsburgh Pirate Hall of Famer Willie Stargell land in the 1965 All-Star baseball game in Minnesota?

782. Name the tallest shortstop in the history of major league baseball.

783. What physical deformity did American Kristi Yamaguchi, winner of a 1992 Olympic gold medal in figure-skating, have at birth and later overcome?

784. What was sports great Jim Thorpe's batting average during his 289-game career as a major league baseball player?

785. How many World Series championships did the New York Yankees win while baseball great Joe DiMaggio was on the team?

786. What union did players on basketball's Harlem Globetrotters become affiliated with in 1974?

787. In amateur boxing, how many cloth-wrapped strands of rope are required along the four sides of the boxing ring?

788. In golfing circles, what is a snowman?

789. How were numbers assigned when members of the 1929 New York Yankees became the first baseball players to have them on their uniforms?

790. What are the odds that a professional golfer will get a hole-in-one?

791. Which member of the legendary Tinker-to-Evers-to-Chance double-play team was the first to be elected to the Baseball Hall of Fame?

792. What ice-skating spin is named for Olympic gold medalist Dorothy Hamill?

793. What famous baseball player's older brother was runner-up to Jesse Owens in the 200-meter race at the 1936 Olympic Games in Berlin?

781. *Inside a tuba in the right field bullpen—where a marching band was practicing.*

782. *Cal Ripken Jr., of the Baltimore Orioles. His height is 6 feet 4.*

783. *Clubfeet—which were treated with corrective shoes.*

784. *Thorpe played the outfield in the National League from 1913 to 1919, when he went into football.*

785. *9—of the 10 he played in.*

786. *They joined a local of the Service Employees Union, which represents janitors, vendors, stagehands and others who work in arenas.*

787. *Four.*

788. *A score of 8 for a hole or 88 for a round. The name is derived from the number 8's resemblance to a snowman.*

789. *According to their position in the batting lineup. No. 1 was centerfielder Earl Combs, who batted first; No. 2, third baseman Mark Koenig, who batted second; No. 3, rightfielder Babe Ruth, who batted third; No. 4, first baseman Lou Gehrig, who batted fourth; and so on down the line.*

790. *One in 15,000.*

791. *They were elected as a unit in 1946. The three Chicago Cub infielders were Joe Tinker, Johnny Evers and Frank Chance.*

792. *Hamill's camel.*

793. *Jackie Robinson's. His brother Mack's time was 21.1 seconds to Owens's 20.7.*

794. What international sports competition is named for former president George Bush's grandfather?

795. What song did members of the "miracle" New York Mets baseball team sing on the Ed Sullivan TV show after they won the 1969 World Series?

796. In speed skating, what do the competitors wear to indicate which lane they start in?

797. What popular sport does the Fédération Internationale des Quilleurs (FIQ) oversee?

798. What American baseball team introduced the "high five"?

799. What sport—in its primitive form—gave us the word melee?

800. What major change was made in 1967 in the uniforms worn by major league baseball players?

801. How many home runs did Mickey Mantle hit in 1961, the year his New York Yankee teammate Roger Maris hit a then-record-setting 61?

802. What key word was eliminated from the Olympic Charter in 1971?

803. How many more career wins did major league pitcher Gaylord Perry have than his older brother Jim Perry?

804. In professional ice hockey, what is the maximum length permitted for the blade of a hockey stick?

805. What is the standard pitching distance in the game of horseshoes?

806. What did Boston Red Sox slugger Ted Williams do in his last major league at-bat in September 1960?

794. *Amateur golf's Walker Cup. It was named in honor of George Herbert Walker Bush's grandfather, George Herbert Walker, after he donated the tournament trophy for the first competition in 1922.*

795. *"You've Gotta Have Heart" from the musical Damn Yankees.*

796. *Colored armbands. White is worn by the skater starting in the inner lane; red by the skater starting in the outer lane. The skaters change lanes after each circuit of the track.*

797. *Bowling.*

798. *The Los Angeles Dodgers. Outfielder Glenn Burke is credited with originating it in 1977.*

799. *Soccer. In French, melée means "a confused mass," which was what the playing field looked like in Europe in the Middle Ages when towns competed using teams of up to a hundred players, with the goals a half-mile or so apart.*

800. *The fabric was switched from flannel to double knit.*

801. *54.*

802. *Amateur.*

803. *99. Gaylord had 314 wins; Jim, 215.*

804. *For all players except the goaltender, the blade is limited to 12½ inches in length; for a goaltender, it can be up to 15½ inches long.*

805. *40 feet for men; 30 feet for women and juniors.*

806. *He hit a home run off Baltimore's Jack Fisher. It was his 521st homer.*

807. A German named Hermann Ratjen claims the Nazis forced him to masquerade as a woman and compete in the women's high jump at the 1936 Olympics. How did "Dora Ratjen" rank in the event?

808. What two pitchers were baseball's first free agents?

809. What football player was the recipient of the biggest Super Bowl ring ever made?

810. In the 1992 America's Cup competition, what was the significance of the letters ENZA on the sails of the New Zealand yacht?

811. On the Professional Golf Association tour, how much time are players allotted for each shot?

812. What football teams were on the field in the 1977 film *Black Sunday*?

813. What teams competed in the first football Superbowl in 1967?

814. Who is the only man elected to both the Baseball and Football Halls of Fame?

815. Who was the youngest golfer to win the Masters Tournament?

816. What does the small printed label on the back of all National Football League helmets say?

817. Where does catgut—used in stringed instruments, surgical sutures and tennis rackets—come from?

818. Who said, "Show me a good loser and I'll show you a loser"?

819. Who played basketball with the Boston Celtics, hockey with the Boston Bruins, football with the Detroit Lions and soccer with the Tampa Bay Rowdies?

820. How high is a tennis ball supposed to bounce when it's dropped on concrete from a height of 100 inches?

807. Fourth.

808. Andy Messersmith and Dave McNally, in 1976.

809. Defensive tackle William "The Refrigerator" Perry of the Chicago Bears in 1986. The ring was a size 23.

810. They stood for Eat New Zealand Apples. The New Zealand Apple and Pear Marketing Board was a sponsor of New Zealand's entry in the prestigious regatta.

811. They get 45 seconds per shot—with a $500 fine after 4 violations in a round; an additional $1,000 fine after 8 violations; a two-stroke penalty after 10; and disqualification from the tournament for 12.

812. The Dallas Cowboys and the Pittsburgh Steelers. The game shown is Super Bowl X at the Orange Bowl, won by the Steelers, 21-17.

813. The Green Bay Packers and the Kansas City Chiefs. The Packers won the game, 35-10.

814. Cal Hubbard, the tackle for the Green Bay Packers and New York Giants who became an American League umpire after his retirement from football.

815. Tiger Woods, at the age of 21 in 1997. He won by a margin of twelve strokes—another Master's record.

816. It warns players. in 72 words, not to use the helmet "to butt, ram or spear an opposing player."

817. The intestines of sheep, horses and several other animals—but not from cats. Some believe the word is a shortened form of cattlegut.

818. Former Ohio State football coach Woody Hayes, who was fired for being a bad loser and attacking a Clemson player who intercepted a pass in the closing moments of the 1978 Gator Bowl. Ohio lost, 17-15.

819. Amateur athlete and professional writer George Plimpton.

820. Between 53 and 58 inches, measured from the bottom of the ball, according to the U.S. Lawn Tennis Association. The concrete surface should be a minimum of 4 inches thick.

821. Who was the first seven-footer to play professional basketball?

822. What did the umpires rule when Dave Kingman, batting for the Oakland Athletics in May 1984, smashed a ball 180 feet up into the fabric ceiling of the Minnesota Twins' Metrodome?

823. Who received the first perfect score ever—a 10—in Olympic gymnastic competition?

824. How much do the gloves worn by professional boxers weight. How about Golden Glovers?

825. Why is tennis scored 15, 30, 40 rather than the more traditional 1 point, 2 points, 3 points of other sports?

826. Who threw baseball's last legal spitball?

827. What American multimillionaire was knocked out during a sparring match with world heavyweight champion Jack Dempsey in the 1920s?

828. What baseball card is considered the most valuable?

829. Why was baseball great Charles Dillon Stengel nicknamed Casey?

830. How long does a cowboy have to hang on in a rodeo bull-riding competition?

831. In what direction—clockwise or counterclockwise—do horses race in Europe?

832. What do baseball fans have Reuben Berman to thank for?

833. Four players on the first New York Mets team became major-league managers. Name them.

834. How many characters are the names of registered thoroughbred horses limited to in the United States?

835. What baseball player said, "Some people give their bodies to science, I give mine to baseball"?

821. *Ralph (Sky) Siewert, who played with the St. Louis Bombers and Toronto Huskies. In his 21 games he scored a total of 20 points.*

822. *They called it a ground-rule double. The ball was removed from the ceiling and is now on display at the Baseball Hall of Fame.*

823. *Nadia Comaneci of Romania, in the 1976 Olympics. She was 14 years old at the time.*

824. *Professionals, 8 ounces; Golden Glovers, 10 ounces.*

825. *In its early days as an indoor sport, a tennis game's score was kept by moving the hands of a clock to 15, 30 and 45. Later, for reasons now obscure, the 45 became 40.*

826. *Hall of Famer Burleigh Grimes, for the New York Yankees in 1934. Although the pitch had been outlawed 14 years earlier, those already throwing it were permitted to continue.*

827. *Paul Getty.*

828. *The 1910 Piedmont cigarette card of Honus Wagner. The great Pittsburgh Pirate shortstop was a strict Southern Baptist who disapproved of smoking and asked that his card be discontinued. Only 20 are known to exist.*

829. *His hometown was Kansas City—which led first to the nickname K.C. and then to Casey.*

830. *Eight seconds. The same is true for bareback-bronc and saddle-bronc events.*

831. *Clockwise. In the United States they race counterclockwise.*

832. *His 1921 lawsuit against the New York Giants, which established a fan's right to keep a baseball hit into the stands.*

833. *Gil Hodges, Don Zimmer, Roger Craig and Jim Marshall were the four future managers on Casey Stengel's 1962 Mets.*

834. *Eighteen (including spaces).*

835. *Ron Hunt—who was hit by a record-setting 243 pitches during his career.*

836. What former baseball player, winner of the prestigious jewel-studded Hickok Belt as 1962's Professional Athlete of the Year, lost a court battle with the Internal Revenue Service after claiming the belt as non-taxable income?

837. While visiting Russia in the early 1970s, Phil Esposito and other North American hockey stars removed what they thought was an electronic bugging device from the floor of their Moscow hotel room. What happened?

838. In baseball, how wide is home plate?

839. In 1979 what golfers competed in the first sudden-death playoff in the history of the Masters Tournament?

840. What pitcher was baseball's first 200-game winner?

841. Which Triple Crown race is the shortest?

842. What are the six weapons available in the game of Clue?

843. When Pete Rose of the Cincinnati Reds broke baseball great Ty Cobb's 4,191-hit record on September 11, 1985, what famous ex-slugger said, "If I'd a hit that many singles, I'd a wore a dress"?

844. What baseball star was the first Little Leaguer voted Most Valuable Player of the Year in the big leagues?

845. What horses did jockey Eddie Arcaro ride to the winner's circle in his two Triple Crown victories?

846. How did the game of ninepins, brought to the U.S. by the Dutch in the 1600s, get changed to ten-pins, the popular bowling game of today?

847. Who threw New York Giant Bobby Thomson the pennant-winning home-run pitch in the 1951 National League playoffs?

848. In professional golf, how many clubs is a player limited to during a round?

836. *Los Angeles Dodger shortstop Maury Wills, who was honored for stealing 104 bases.*

837. *They detached the chandelier in the room below and it went crashing to the floor.*

838. *Seventeen inches.*

839. *Frank "Fuzzy" Zoeller Jr., Tom Watson and Ed Sneed. Zoeller won.*

840. *Hall of Famer Albert G. Spalding, a founder, captain, manager and eventual owner of the Chicago White Stockings (now the Cubs) and the man who started the sporting goods company that still bears his name.*

841. *The Preakness, at 1³⁄₁₆ miles. The Kentucky Derby is 1¼ miles; the Belmont, 1½.*

842. *A knife, a rope, a candlestick, a lead pipe, a revolver and a wrench.*

843. *Mickey Mantle.*

844. *The Philadelphia Phillies' slugging infielder Mike Schmidt, in 1980. He won again in 1981.*

845. *Whirlaway in 1941; Citation in 1948.*

846. *Ninepins was outlawed by New York and Connecticut in the 1840s because of heavy gambling. Since the ban didn't forbid bowling in general, a tenth pin was added to circumvent the law.*

847. *Ralph Branca of the Brooklyn Dodgers, wearing number 13. He gave up the three-run homer in the bottom of the ninth after relieving Don Newcombe.*

848. *Fourteen.*

849. What was the game of softball originally called when its rules were written down in Minneapolis in 1895?

850. What sports hall of fame is located in Ishpeming, Michigan?

851. What was unusual about Stanley Steamer, a five-year-old gelding that lost its one-and-only harness race at Florida's Pompano Park in 1974?

852. What baseball great frowned on exercise, saying, "I believe in training by rising gently up and down from the bench"?

853. Who was known as La Tulipe Noire in France, Il Re in Italy, O Vasilas in Greece and El Peligor in Chile?

854. How tall was 7-foot-2 Kareem Abdul-Jabbar at birth?

855. Among card players, what is a pone?

856. What was the World Series batting average of Shoeless Joe Jackson, one of the eight Chicago White Sox players convicted of accepting bribes to throw the 1919 world championship to the Cincinnati Reds?

857. What professional sport did Dave DeBusschere play before he decided to devote full attention to his basketball career in 1964?

858. Together, baseball-playing brothers Hank and Tommy Aaron hit 768 home runs. How many were Tommy's?

859. Who was the first heavyweight champion in history to lose his title and then regain it?

860. Why was Kansas City Royal slugger George Brett issued a driver's license in 1985 without being required to take a vision test?

861. What is Muhammad Ali's CB (citizens band) handle?

862. Why is nineteenth-century pitcher William Arthur "Candy" Cummings—who had a two-year, 21-22 win-loss record in the major leagues—in the Baseball Hall of Fame?

849. *Kitten ball. It became known as softball in 1926.*

850. *Skiing.*

851. *It was a zebra.*

852. *Hall of Fame pitcher Satchel Paige.*

853. *Brazilian soccer great Pele—who was born Edson Arantes de Nascimento.*

854. *Just a bit taller than the average newborn at 22½ inches, but he weighed a hefty 12 pounds 11 ounces.*

855. *The person who sits to the dealer's right.*

856. *He had the highest average in the series, .375, as well as a perfect fielding record.*

857. *Baseball. He pitched for the Chicago White Sox for two seasons, earning a 3-4 record and a 2.90 ERA in 36 games.*

858. *Thirteen.*

859. *American Floyd Patterson, who lost to Swede Ingemar Johansson in 1959 and then beat him to win the title back a year later.*

860. *According to a Kansas official, "If he can hit .350, we figured he could see."*

861. *Big Bopper.*

862. *He is credited with inventing the curveball in 1866. He got the idea while throwing clam shells on a Brooklyn, New York, beach.*

863. Why was the marathon, originally 26 miles long, increased by 385 yards in 1908?

864. Who was the last baseball player to have a season's batting average over .400?

865. How many games did the longest Wimbledon men's singles match on record last?

866. What unique player restriction is in effect in both polo and jai alai?

867. What was the winning speed when automobile designer Ray Harroun won the first Indianapolis 500 in 1911?

868. What baseball team was the first to introduce numbers as a permanent part of their players' uniforms?

869. What team always marches last in the opening procession of the Olympics?

870. Whose bat was San Francisco Giant slugger Willie Mays using when he slammed four home runs in a single game in April 1961?

871. Who said, "It took me 17 years to get 3,000 hits in baseball. I did it in one afternoon on the golf course"?

872. What football gear did Miami Dolphin running back Woody Bennett introduce and market in 1983?

873. Where can you find the world's largest collection of baseball cards—more than 200,000?

874. What famous American sports figure served as director of physical fitness for the Navy during World War II?

875. What colors were chosen for the five Olympic rings and why?

863. So that the race would finish in front of King Edward VII's royal box in the Olympic Stadium in London.

864. Boston Red Sox slugger Ted Williams, in 1941. His average was .406.

865. It went 112 games, with Pancho Gonzalez beating Charlie Pasarell 22-24, 1-6, 16-14, 6-3, 11-9. It took place in 1969—two years before the tie-breaker was introduced to the game.

866. Left-handers are barred from competition.

867. He averaged 74.59 miles per hour in his Marmon Wasp, the only single-seater in the race and the first car to have a rearview mirror.

868. The New York Yankees, in 1929.

869. The team representing the host nation.

870. Teammate Joe Amalfitano's.

871. Hank Aaron.

872. A lightweight padded girdle to cushion blows.

873. At the prestigious Metropolitan Museum of Art in New York City.

874. Undefeated world heavyweight boxing champion Gene Tunney.

875. The rings are blue, red, yellow, black and green. They were chosen because at least one of them appears in the flag of every nation in the world.

876. What was the bonus paid to players on the Chicago Bears for their 23-21 victory over the New York Giants in the first NFL East-West championship game in 1933?

877. What is the maximum weight permitted for a bowling ball?

878. On her record-breaking English Channel crossing in August 1926, how many miles did Gertrude Ederle have to swim to cover the 21-mile distance between Cape Gris-Nez and Dover?

879. What is the origin of the word furlong—used in horse racing to describe a distance of ⅛ mile?

880. What sport do we have to thank for the phrase "red herring"?

881. How did the axel—the difficult figure-skating jump-turn—get its name?

882. Where did the divining board game "Ouija" get its name?

883. What do the British call the game we know as checkers?

884. What popular game gave us the word "debut"?

885. In mountain-biking slang, what's a snakebite?

886. Members of what football team recorded the rap song "Super Bowl Shuffle" in November 1985—and went on to win Super Bowl XX two months later?

887. Who was the first Japanese-born player in major league baseball in the United States?

888. Which are the most frequently landed-upon properties in the game of Monopoly?

889. How many basic dives are listed on the official Olympic dive chart?

876. *They received $210.34 each, plus a free overcoat if they scored a touchdown. The losers received $140.22 each.*

877. *Sixteen pounds.*

878. *Thirty-five, because of rough seas. Nevertheless she bettered the world record by an hour and 59 minutes making the crossing in 14 hours and 31 minutes.*

879. *It dates back to the days when a race was a furrow long—the length of a plowed field.*

880. *Fox-hunting. In seventeenth-century England, anti-hunt advocates would draw smelly, dried smoked herring across a fox's path to throw the pursuing hounds off the scent.*

881. *It's named for the Norwegian skater who invented it, Axel Paulsen.*

882. *From the French and German words for "yes"—oui and ja.*

883. *Draughts.*

884. *Billiards. Debut is derived from the French word debuter—to make the first stroke in billiards, to lead off.*

885. *A flat tire caused by hitting a hard object, resulting in the wheel rim piercing the inner tube, creating a two-hole puncture that resembles a snakebite.*

886. *The Chicago Bears.*

887. *Masanori Murakami. He pitched for the San Francisco Giants in 1964 and 1965, compiling a 5-1 record with nine saves. Thirty years later, Hideo Nomo joined the Los Angeles Dodgers as the second Japanese-born major leaguer and was named National League rookie of the year.*

888. *The four railroads—B & O, Reading, Shortline and Pennsylvania. A survey by Parker Brothers, the manufacturer, found that the odds are 64 percent that a player will land on one of the four in a single trip around the game board. The least landed-on properties—with 24 percent odds—are the dark purple-colored Mediterranean and Baltic avenues.*

889. *87—with 348 variations based on body position (straight, pike, tuck or free).*

890. What ancient sport gave us the phrase "turning point"?

891. What U.S. city was the first to have a team in the National Hockey League?

892. How many record-setting times was Don Baylor hit by a pitch during his 9 years as a major league baseball player?

893. What did Minnesota Twins players rub for good luck during the 1987 World Series?

894. What baseball great has had his uniform number retired by three teams?

895. How many points did the Denver Nuggets pile up in the 1983 game in which star Kiki Vandeweghe scored his career high of 51 points?

896. What is the maximum height allowed for a fence in equestrian horse-jumping competitions?

897. In 1904 William K. Vanderbilt II created the Vanderbilt Cup for auto racing; for what did Harold S. Vanderbilt establish a Vanderbilt Cup in 1928?

898. What system was used instead of rounds when boxing matches were introduced at the 23rd ancient Olympiad in 776 B.C.?

899. What team's baseball cap did Tom Selleck often wear in his title role in TV's *Magnum, P.I.*?

900. What is the meaning of TWIsM, the name of basketball great Shaquille O'Neals' record label and line of clothing?

901. What major league baseball player retired in 1980 after playing in five different decades?

902. Who was the first American Leaguer to hit four consecutive home runs in one game?

890. *Chariot racing. Turning points were the places where chariot drivers turned at each end of a stadium.*

891. *Boston, in 1924. The league was organized in 1917 with Canadian teams.*

892. *267.*

893. *Teammate Kirby Puckett's shaved head. The Twins defeated the St. Louis Cardinals, 4 games to 3, in the series.*

894. *Nolan Ryan, who pitched a record seven no-hitters during his career. His number, 34, has been retired by the California (Anaheim) Angels, the Texas Rangers and the Houston Astros.*

895. *Denver scored 184 and lost by two points to the Detroit Pistons in triple overtime. The December 13, 1983, contest was the highest-scoring game in NBA history.*

896. *5.6 feet.*

897. *Contract bridge.*

898. *None. Competitors boxed until one man either dropped or raised a fist, conceding defeat. There were no breaks or segments.*

899. *The Detroit Tigers. Selleck is a rabid Tigers fan.*

900. *It stands for "The world is mine," the slogan O'Neal has tattooed on his right biceps—encircling a globe held in the palm of a massive hand.*

901. *Outfielder Minnie Minoso, who started out with the Cleveland Indians in 1949, and ended his career as a pinch hitter for the Chicago White Sox.*

902. *Lou Gehrig, on June 3, 1932. Gehrig, playing for the New York Yankees, hit four-baggers in the first, fourth, fifth and seventh innings against Philadelphia. The Yankees won, 20-13.*

903. What is the fist size—in inches—of James "Big Cat" Williams, the 6-foot-7, 340-pound right tackle of the Chicago Bears?

904. How many bases do major league teams usually have ready for a regular-season game—home plate not included?

905. For what sport did Col. Meriwether Lewis Clark, Jr., develop most of the rules in the United States?

906. In the game of craps, what does the slang term "Little Phoebe" refer to?

907. In the 1950s, grass on golf putting greens was generally mowed to a height of one-quarter inch. What is the average grass height today?

908. What are Blue Professor, Bottle Imp, General Hooker, Tango Triumph, Walla Walls and Rat-Faced McDougal?

909. What baseball great holds the record for winning the greatest number of league batting titles?

910. Who was the only golfer to win three of the four major men's professional tournaments in the same year?

911. For what sport did baseball pitching great Sandy Koufax win a college athletic scholarship?

912. What did archers at the ancient Olympic Games use as targets?

913. What basketball great has been selected for more NBA All-Star teams than any other player?

914. Who was the first catcher in major league baseball history to win the Rookie of the Year award?

915. With what sport did the word "stymie" originate?

916. To what section did the Hollywood Wax Museum move boxer Mike Tyson's figure after his infamous 1997 ear-biting attack on Evander Holyfield?

903. *14½ inches. His biceps are 21 inches; neck, 23; waist, 44; chest, 54.*

904. *Nine.*

905. *Horse racing. He founded Churchill Downs, where the first Kentucky Derby was held in 1875.*

906. *A throw of 5 on the dice.*

907. *One-eighth of an inch. The height has gotten progressively lower through the years.*

908. *Flies used in trout fishing.*

909. *Ty Cobb—with 12 titles.*

910. *Ben Hogan, who won the U.S. Open, the Masters and the British Open in 1953. (The fourth major tournament is the PGA championship.)*

911. *Basketball. He tried out for the University of Cincinnati baseball team only after he learned that it was going on a trip to New Orleans.*

912. *Tethered doves.*

913. *Kareem Abdul-Jabbar. The former Los Angeles Laker was named to 19 All-Star teams.*

914. *Johnny Bench of the Cincinnati Reds, in 1968.*

915. *Golf. To be stymied meant to find an opponent's ball between your ball and the hole on the green. Until 1952, when the rules of golf were changed, the ball had to remain where it was, blocking yours, so that you had to loft your ball to reach the hole.*

916. *The Chamber of Horrors—he was relocated alongside Hannibal Lecter. Tyson's figure was originally in the museum's Sports Hall of Fame.*

917. Baseball fan Robert Heuer won $2,250,000 in the New York State lottery in 1987 with the numbers of his favorite players— DiMaggio, Ford, Mays, Marichal, Stengel and McCovey. What were his winning numbers?

918. To a competitive swimmer, what does the abbreviation d.p.s. mean?

919. What nonstandard item of football clothing did one-time New York Jet quarterback Joe Namath donate to Planet Hollywood?

920. How many cows does it take to make the 22,000 footballs used per season by the teams in the National Football League?

Bonus Trivia

921. The oldest individual to win a medal in the Olympics was Oscar Swahn, who won a silver medal in shooting for Sweden in 1920. He was 72.

922. John Heisman—whose name is commemorated by the award given to college football's best player, the Heisman Trophy—was the coach at Georgia Tech when they set a college football record on October 7, 1916: they slaughtered Cumberland, 222 to 0.

923. The oldest driver in the 1979 Le Mans 24-hour race was actor Paul Newman.

924. ABC-TV's "Monday Night Football" premiered in September, 1970. Its three original commentators were Keith Jackson, Don Meredith and Howard Cosell.

925. Boog Powell, former first baseman for the Baltimore Orioles, was the first baseball player to appear in both the Little League World Series (for Lakeland, Florida) and the Major League World Series.

917. *5, 16, 24, 27, 37 and 44, respectively.*

918. *Distance per stroke.*

919. *The pantyhose he wore on the playing field on chilly days.*

920. *3,000.*

War & the Military

Questions

926. What was the only U.S. battleship to be present at both the Japanese attack on Pearl Harbor, on December 7, 1941, and at the D-Day invasion, on June 6, 1944?

927. What organization has the motto, "Peace Is Our Profession"?

928. How were the height and width of modern American battleships originally determined?

929. What was the first U.S. Navy ship named in honor of a black person?

930. What was the name of the Japanese destroyer that sank PT-109, commanded by Lt. John F. Kennedy, on August 2, 1943?

931. The 7th Earl of Cardigan led the charge of the Light Brigade during the Crimean War. What was the name of the British commander who ordered the ill-fated attack?

932. After German flying ace Manfred von Richthofen was killed in action in World War I, who became commander of his "Flying Circus" fighter squadron?

Answers

926. *The* U.S.S. Nevada.

927. *The U.S. Air Force Strategic Air Command (SAC).*

928. *The ships had to be able to go beneath the Brooklyn Bridge and through the Panama Canal.*

929. *The* U.S.S. Harmon, *named after Leonard Roy Harmon, a mess attendant who was killed at Guadalcanal on July 25, 1943.*

930. *Amigiri.*

931. *Lord Raglan. Both men are better remembered for fashions they introduced during the war—Cardigan for the woolen jacket he designed for his troops, and Raglan for the unique sleeves on the coat he wore.*

932. *Hermann Goering, who went on to become one of Adolf Hitler's closest associates.*

933. What type of aircraft was used to drop bombs in the first German air raids on London in 1915?

934. What is the meaning of the Comanche phrase posah-tai-vo, the term Indian code-talkers in the Army Signal Corps used on the battlefield during World War II to refer to Adolf Hitler?

935. In 1996, which country's army became the last in the world to disband its carrier pigeon service?

936. What were the code names for the five beachheads invaded by the Allies on D-Day, June 6, 1944?

937. What message was transmitted to the French resistance during World War II with the first line of the Paul Verlaine poem *Autumn Song*?

938. In World War II American army slang, what was a GI Moe?

939. Which of the U.S. service academies was the first to admit women?

940. How many times did the nuclear submarine USS Triton surface during its historic 1960 underwater circumnavigation of the globe?

941. In what war was the color khaki first used for uniforms?

942. How many crewmembers and officers were required to run the Britannia, Great Britain's 412-foot royal yacht?

943. Where is Yalta—the city where President Franklin D. Roosevelt met with Russia's Joseph Stalin and England's Winston Churchill in 1945 to plan the final defeat of Nazi Germany?

944. Who was issued ID number 01 when the U.S. military started issuing dog tags in 1918?

945. What animal did the Carthaginians use to defeat the Romans at sea during the third century B.C.?

946. Who was the first to use the term "atomic bomb"?

933. *A zeppelin.*

934. *Crazy white man.*

935. *Switzerland's. Its army owned 7,000 pigeons and had another 23,000 privately owned birds on standby in case of a national emergency. The pigeon service was disbanded in hopes of saving money and instituting a more modern communications system.*

936. *Utah, Omaha, Gold, Juno and Sword.*

937. *That the D-Day landings were about to begin. The line from Verlaine was: "The long sobs/Of the violins of autumnÖ"*

938. *An army mule.*

939. *The Coast Guard Academy, in July 1976.*

940. *Twice—once to remove a sick crew member, and once to pay tribute to Ferdinand Magellan on the island of Mactan in the Philippines, where the explorer was killed in 1521 during his circumnavigation of the globe.*

941. *The Afghan War in 1880—the color was considered good camouflage.*

942. *Crew, 230; officers, 20. The yacht, christened by Queen Elizabeth II in 1953 and decommissioned in 1997 was costing $18.5 million a year to operate.*

943. *In the Crimea, in the Soviet Union.*

944. *General John J. Pershing.*

945. *Snakes. The Carthaginians catapulted earthenware pots of poisonous snakes onto the decks of the Roman ships.*

946. *Science fiction writer H.G. Wells, in the story* The World Set Free, *written in 1914.*

947. What was the cause of the brief undeclared war that broke out between Honduras and El Salvador in July 1969?

948. What did the famous backstage mother of actress Ginger Rogers do during World War I?

949. How did wartime conservation efforts affect the Oscars handed out at Academy Award ceremonies during World War II?

950. Soldiers of what nation do not have to salute officers and are paid overtime for KP and other undesirable assignments?

951. How did Napoleon Bonaparte finance his invasion of Russia in 1812?

952. What bathtub-bathing edict did England's King George VI issue for Buckingham Palace and Windsor Castle to cut down on the use of fuel during World War II?

953. When World War II ended in 1945, how many enlisted men and women were in the nation's armed services?

954. What is a military contractor referring to when talking about a "manually powered fastener-driving impact device"?

955. For what expenditure did the tiny European principality of Andorra allocate its entire national defense budget of $5 twenty years ago?

956. What utensil were British sailors forbidden to use until the very late nineteenth century because it was considered both unmanly and harmful to discipline?

957. Who beat out Frank Sinatra as the favorite singer of American servicemen in Europe in a poll taken during World War II?

958. As a young naval officer serving in World War II, what famous American set up the only hamburger stand in the South Pacific?

959. In a military contract, what item is referred to as a "portable, hand-held communications inscriber"?

947. El Salvador's victory over Honduras in the three-game World Cup soccer play-off. The war is known as the Soccer War.

948. Lela Rogers was a Marine sergeant.

949. They were made out of wood—gilded wood, of course. After the war, they were replaced by real Oscars.

950. The Netherlands, whose army was fully unionized in the 1960s.

951. With counterfeit money. After printing it at a factory he set up in Paris, he used it to purchase military supplies.

952. He decreed that tubs could be filled with no more than five inches of water—and had lines painted at the five-inch level to make the depth of his commitment clear.

953. Almost eleven million (10,795,775).

954. A hammer.

955. For bullets (blanks), for ceremonial salutes to guest dignitaries.

956. The fork.

957. Country singer Ray Acuff. During the war, correspondent Ernie Pyle wrote of a Japanese attack that was preceded by the battle cry: "To hell with Roosevelt! To hell with Babe Ruth! To hell with Roy Acuff!"

958. President-to-be Richard M. Nixon, who was a Navy lieutenant at the time. At Nixon's Snack Shack, he served free hamburgers and Australian beer to flight crews.

959. A pencil.

960. How long did the Battle of Waterloo last?

961. When during World War II did Russia declare war on Japan?

962. How many oarsmen were carried aboard triremes—the fast-moving warships that helped the Greeks rule the Mediterranean during the fifth century B.C.?

963. How many pounds of feed were consumed daily by the 5,000 horses that pulled the artillery for Napoleon's Army of the North in 1815?

964. For whom was Italian dictator Benito Mussolini named?

965. How many inmates were liberated from the Bastille after it was stormed by an angry mob on July 14, 1789, at the start of the French Revolution?

966. How did the Dutch in Amsterdam mobilize to defeat the invading Spanish during the winter of 1572-73?

967. What did the real Butch Cassidy do after escaping to Bolivia with his partner-in-crime, the Sundance Kid?

968. What problem in expressing themselves did Aristotle, Sir Isaac Newton, Moses and Charles Darwin have in common?

969. Where did Adolf Hitler's sister-in-law work during World War II?

970. Who was the first American congressman to don a uniform following the Japanese attack on Pearl Harbor on December 7, 1941?

971. The U.S. government entered the nuclear arms race in 1940 when it issued a grant for research into an atomic bomb. How much was allocated?

972. What famous former public figure commanded the squadron of torpedo boats in which John F. Kennedy served as a skipper during World War II?

960. *About nine and a half hours.*

961. *On August 8, 1945—two days after the U.S. bombed Hiroshima.*

962. *170—they were seated at banks of 31, 27 and 27 oars on each side of the ship.*

963. *10,000 pounds—or 50 tons. That comes to 20 pounds per horse.*

964. *Mexican liberator Benito Juarez.*

965. *Seven.*

966. *The ice-locked Dutch routed the Spanish on skates.*

967. *Cassidy, whose real name was Robert LeRoy Parker, reportedly returned to the U.S. and went into the adding machine manufacturing business.*

968. *They all stuttered.*

969. *For British War Relief in New York City. Bridget Hitler was the Irish-born wife of Hitler's older half-brother, Alois.*

970. *President-to-be Lyndon Johnson, who served in the Navy.*

971. *$6,000.*

972. *John N. Mitchell, who went on to become U.S. attorney general in the Nixon administration.*

973. Why did U.S. secret agents abandon plans—approved by President Franklin D. Roosevelt—to drop live bats from airplanes to frighten the Japanese during World War II?

974. What unsung role did William Dawes and Samuel Prescott play in American history?

975. Why was infantryman (and actor-to-be) James Arness picked to go first when the troops aboard his landing craft splashed ashore during the Allied attack at Anzio during World War II?

976. How much money in U.S. humanitarian aid did the Nicaraguan contras spend on deodorant in 1985 and 1986?

977. What was the profession of Hitler's mistress, Eva Braun?

978. During the Civil War, how many states fought for the Union; how many for the Confederacy?

979. What two nations were involved in a year-long conflict that was popularly known as the Pastry War?

980. What president ordered the integration of America's armed forces?

981. What famous American signed the Treaty of Kanagawa?

982. Adolf Hitler called his country home Eagle's Nest. What name did Winston Churchill give to his?

983. What American billionaire tried to airlift 28 tons of medicine and Christmas gifts to American POWs in North Vietnam in 1969?

984. Charles de Gaulle served as ghost-writer of the book "The Soldier" for what famous World War I military hero?

985. How does Lockheed, manufacturer of the Trident missile, transmit data from its Sunnyvale, California, headquarters to its plant thirty miles away in Santa Cruz?

986. During whose presidency was the U.S. War Dept. replaced by the Defense Dept.?

973. *The bats froze at high altitudes, before they could be released.*

974. *They accompanied Paul Revere on his celebrated midnight ride to warn their countrymen that "the British are coming."*

975. *At 6 feet 6, he was the tallest man in his outfit—and his commanding officer wanted to know just how deep the water was.*

976. *$5,760—the expenditure was approved by the State Department's Nicaraguan Humanitarian Assistance Office.*

977. *Photographer's assistant.*

978. *For the Union, 23; for the Confederacy, 11.*

979. *France and Mexico, in 1838. It was triggered by Mexico's refusal to pay for damage done by Mexican army officers to a restaurant run by a French pastry chef in Tacubaya, now a section of Mexico City.*

980. *Harry S. Truman, in 1948.*

981. *Commodore Matthew C. Perry, on March 31, 1854. The treaty opened Japan to western trade.*

982. *Cosy Pig, although it was formally known as Chartwell.*

983. *Ross Perot.*

984. *Marshal Philippe Pétain, whose 1945 death sentence for collaboration during WWII was commuted by de Gaulle to life imprisonment.*

985. *By carrier pigeon.*

986. *Harry S. Truman's, in 1947.*

987. What famous American patriot served as a rear admiral in the Russian navy?

988. What actress obtained a patent as co-inventor of a radar-controlled system to direct torpedoes at moving ships?

989. When the British garrison at Khartoum was under siege in 1884, who organized the 1,500-boat flotilla of troops and supplies that came to its rescue?

990. Where was the Battle of Bunker Hill actually fought in June 1775?

991. What was the Allies' password on D-Day?

992. What American military leader said, "Lafayette we are here," and on what occasion?

993. What physical ailment is said to have contributed to Napoleon's defeat at Waterloo?

994. What war was the first to have authorized film coverage?

995. "GI Joe" won the Dickins Medal for saving a thousand British solders from a bombing attack in Italy during World War II. Who was he and what's the Dickins Medal?

996. In 1969 the Navy spent $375,000 on an "aerodynamic analysis of the self-suspended flare." What was the study's conclusion?

997. Why did Caedwalla, King of Gwynedd (north Wales), order his soldiers to wear leeks fastened to their helmets when they battled the troops of King Edwin of Northumbria in 632 A.D.?

998. During World War I, what famous American directed U.S. Navy research in torpedo mechanisms and anti-submarine devices?

999. What sport had been played on the court at Stagg Field in Chicago that was converted into the Manhattan Project laboratory where scientists achieved the first self-sustaining nuclear chain reaction in history?

987. *John Paul Jones, who won several naval victories in Russian encounters with the Turks in 1788.*

988. *Hedy Lamarr. Her co-inventor was composer George Antheil.*

989. *The travel agency Thomas Cook & Son, for a fee of $15 million.*

990. *On Breed's Hill, southeast of Bunker Hill.*

991. *"Mickey Mouse."*

992. *Gen. Black Jack Pershing, arriving in France in 1917 after the U.S. entered WWI.*

993. *Hemorrhoids, which prevented him from surveying the battlefield on horseback.*

994. *The Boer War (1899-1902).*

995. *He was a pigeon, one of thirty-one WWII pigeons to receive Britain's "Animal Victoria Cross."*

996. *The Frisbee isn't feasible as military hardware.*

997. *So he could tell his men from the enemy. Caedwalla was victorious, Edwin was slain, and the leek later became the national emblem of Wales.*

998. *Thomas Edison, who served as head of the Naval Consulting Board.*

999. *Squash.*

1000. What military firsts were achieved by Benjamin O. Davis Sr. and Benjamin O. Davis Jr.?

1001. What actor has attained the highest U.S. military rank in history for an entertainer?

1002. Before the U.S. Navy adopted the standard 21-gun salute in 1841, how many blasts did its warships fire when they sailed into foreign ports?

1003. What was a tenth-century Chinese alchemist trying to discover when he accidentally produced gunpowder?

1004. On what side did British-born newspaperman-explorer Henry Morton Stanley (of "Dr. Livingston, I presume" fame) fight in the American Civil War?

1005. What rank did Russian czar Peter the Great give himself in the Russian Army?

1006. In the military world, what is EGADS?

1007. Who was Andrea Doria—the person for whom the famous passenger ship was named?

1008. You may remember the Alamo, but do you know what the word means in Spanish?

1009. What did the Marquis de Lafayette, America's Revolutionary War ally, name his only son?

1010. Who were Michael Strank, Harlon H. Block, Franklin R. Sousley, Ira Hayes, Rene Gagnon and John H. Bradley, and how have they been memorialized?

1011. Why was actor Paul Newman disqualified from the Navy's pilot-training program during World War II?

1012. What was the name of the barbaric German tribe that overran Gaul, Spain and North Africa and sacked Rome in the fifth century?

1000. In 1940, Davis Sr. became the first black general in U.S. Army history; in 1954, his son Davis Jr. became the first black general in U.S. Air Force history.

1001. James Stewart, who rose to the rank of brigadier general in the U.S. Air Force Reserve.

1002. One for each state in the Union.

1003. A formula for immortality.

1004. Both. He first joined the Confederate Army, but after being captured at Shiloh, he enlisted in the Union Navy to avoid imprisonment.

1005. None. He served as a common soldier in the artillery.

1006. The signal used when it's necessary to destroy a missile in flight. EGADS is an acronym for Electronic Ground Automatic Destruct System.

1007. He was a sixteenth-century Genoese admiral who was known as the "Father of Peace" and the "Liberator of Genoa."

1008. Cottonwood.

1009. George Washington Lafayette.

1010. They were the six servicemen who raised the American flag on Mount Suribachi on Iwo Jima during World War II—and who are memorialized in the dramatic 78-foot-high Iwo Jima Monument in Arlington, Virginia.

1011. Newman's dazzling blue eyes are colorblind.

1012. The Vandals.

1013. Lt. Col. George Armstrong Custer paid a $127.80 premium for a life insurance policy in 1874, two years before the Battle of Little Bighorn. How much was his coverage?

1014. By what name did Chief Crazy Horse know the Little Bighorn River, the scene of Custer's last stand?

1015. At a 1986 auction, what was the winning bid for two arrows from the Battle of Little Bighorn?

1016. What state was the setting of the Battle of the Little Bighorn, where George Armstrong Custer made his infamous last stand?

1017. What was George Armstrong Custer's rank when he was killed at Little Bighorn in 1876?

1018. Who fired the first Union shot of the Civil War?

1019. What nation was the first to use frogmen in warfare?

1020. What did the U.S. military name in honor of American physiologist Ancel Keys?

1021. What major Japanese company made the famous Zero fighter plane during World War II?

1022. How long—in days—did the 1991 Persian Gulf War last?

1023. Translated from Pentagon doublespeak, what is a "combat emplacement evacuator"?

1024. The site of what state capital was given to the Marquis de Lafayette for his services during the Revolutionary War?

1025. When Adolf Hitler declared himself ruler of the Third Reich, what did he view as Germany's first and second reichs?

1026. To celebrate the patriots' success in getting the British to evacuate Boston on this day in 1776, Gen. George Washington chose "Boston" as his army's password of the day. What did he pick as the proper response?

1013. *It was for $5,000.*

1014. *The Greasy Grass River.*

1015. *$17,000.*

1016. *Montana.*

1017. *Lieutenant Colonel.*

1018. *Gen. Abner Doubleday, in 1861, at Fort Sumter. He is the same Abner Doubleday who is often incorrectly given credit for inventing baseball.*

1019. *Italy, in December 1941, against the British in the Mediterranean. Three frogmen disabled the British battleships Valiant and Queen Elizabeth, as well as a tanker and a destroyer, in Alexandria harbor.*

1020. *The K ration—the small packet of food, containing all the essential nutrients, that served as emergency rations for soldiers in the field.*

1021. *Mitsubishi. The company now known for its cars, TVs and hundreds of other products, was prohibited from producing aircraft for seven years after the war.*

1022. *42 days from January 16 to February 27.*

1023. *A shovel.*

1024. *Tallahassee, Florida. Lafayette never occupied the then-wilderness site, but one of the city's early residents was a nephew of Napoleon Bonaparte, Prince Napoleon Achille Murat, who married a grandniece of George Washington.*

1025. *The first was the Holy Roman Empire of Charlemagne; the second was Bismarck's united Germany, declared in 1871 and known as the German Empire.*

1026. *St. Patrick.*

1027. What childhood name was shared by Gen. George A. Custer and Chief Crazy Horse, the Oglala Sioux leader he faced at the Battle of the Little Bighorn?

1028. How long did it take Napoleon to send a message from Rome to Paris—almost 700 miles—using a semaphore system to signal from mountaintop to mountaintop?

1029. The walls of what structure—made entirely of natural material—stand up better to modern artillery than a concrete barricade, according to tests conducted by the Swedish army?

1030. What film was based on the Civil War exploits of the 54th Massachusetts Infantry Regiment?

1031. Where did Napoleon Bonaparte bid farewell to his imperial guard in 1814?

1032. In World War II Navy slang, what was an airdale?

1033. What was the daily ration of hard liquor for soldiers in the Continental Army during the Revolutionary War?

1034. During World War II, what wearing apparel were American women encouraged to turn in for use in making parachutes?

1035. What army did the Greeks defeat at the battle of Marathon in 490 B.C.?

1036. How many members of Lt. Col. George Armstrong Custer's family were killed at the Battle of Little Big Horn?

1037. A pin-up photo of what actress adorned the first test bomb dropped on Bikini atoll in the Marshall Islands in July 1946?

1038. What European country—the last surviving monarchy of the Holy Roman Empire—hasn't had an army since 1868?

1039. What was the name of Japanese propagandist Tokyo Rose's World War II radio show for U.S. servicemen in the Pacific?

1027. *Curly.*

1028. *Four hours.*

1029. *The igloo. Not only do its walls absorb an artillery blast, but they are almost invisible from the air and can't be spotted by the infrared sensors that guide today's missiles.*

1030. *Glory. The 54th was one of two black regiments formed by Massachusetts in 1862. Massachusetts was the first state to have blacks in its organized militia.*

1031. *In the courtyard at Fontainebleau Palace—which is now known as the Adieux Courtyard. In French, adieux means "farewell."*

1032. *A naval aviation recruit.*

1033. *Four ounces—when available.*

1034. *Their nylon stockings—which were melted down and turned into parachute fabric.*

1035. *The Persian army. The marathon race commemorates the run a Greek courier made from the battlefield to Athens to deliver news of the victory before collapsing and dying of exhaustion.*

1036. *Five, counting Custer. Those who died with him were his half-brothers, Tom and Boston; a nephew, Harry Armstrong Reed; and a brother-in-law, James Calhoun.*

1037. *Rita Hayworth.*

1038. *Liechtenstein.*

1039. *Zero Hour.*

1040. Why did the British Broadcasting Company (BBC) play the opening bars of Beethoven's Fifth Symphony in all its broadcasts to Europe during World War II?

1041. What was the name of General Robert E. Lee's favorite horse before he bought it for $175 and rechristened it Traveller?

1042. Before going into battle, what did the notorious pirate Blackbeard put under his tricorn to frighten those he was attacking?

1043. What were the names of the horses ridden by Napoleon Bonaparte and the Duke of Wellington at the Battle of Waterloo?

1044. What bird's name has been given to the U.S. Marine tilt-rotor transport that takes off and lands like a helicopter, but flies like an airplane?

1045. What were the Q-ships put to sea by the United States and Britain during World War I?

1046. Who lead the U.S. marine detachment that captured abolitionist John Brown following his 1859 raid on the federal arsenal at Harper's Ferry?

1047. What was the full name of the V-2 rocket developed by Wernher von Braun for the Germans during World War II?

1048. What was the only southern town to remain in Union hands throughout the Civil War?

1049. Who was the führer of Germany when World War II ended?

1050. In the event of a nuclear holocaust, what artifact did architect Frank Lloyd Wright believe would be excavated in great quantity from the ruins of twentieth-century civilization?

1051. What entertainer sold more U.S. war bonds than anyone else during World War II?

1040. *Because its familiar "dah-dah-dah-DAAAAH" opening is the same as Morse code for the letter v (dot-dot-dot-dash)—the symbol adopted for "victory."*

1041. *Jeff Davis.*

1042. *Slow-burning fuses that would wreath his head in black smoke.*

1043. *Napoleon rode the white stallion Marengo; Wellington, the chestnut Copenhagen. Both men named their mounts after famous battle sites where they had been victorious.*

1044. *Osprey. The aircraft is also known as the V-22.*

1045. *They were heavily armed warships camouflaged as harmless merchant vessels, which were used to lure German U-boats to their destruction. When a German submarine surfaced to attack (saving its torpedoes for armed vessels), the Q-ship dropped its dummy bulwarks and opened fire.*

1046. *Robert E. Lee, then a colonel.*

1047. *Vergeltungswaffe Zwei—Revenge Weapon Two.*

1048. *Key West, Florida, the southernmost city in the continental United States.*

1049. *Grand Admiral Karl Doenitz. Hitler appointed Doenitz before taking his own life a week before the Nazi surrender.*

1050. *The vitreous china toilet bowl.*

1051. *Kate "God Bless America" Smith. She sold $600 million worth.*

1052. What American actor was given the British Distinguished Service Cross for commanding a flotilla of raiding craft for Admiral Louis Mountbatten's commandos during World War II

1053. What great military leader was an accomplished yo-yo player?

1054. Who was Emil R. Goldfus of Brooklyn, New York?

1055. What was the first war in which soldiers wore machine-made uniforms?

1056. At the Battle of the Marne in 1914, how were French reinforcements rushed from Paris to the front in order to help fend off the advancing Germans?

1057. Who signed Major Clark Gable's army discharge papers in 1944?

1058. How did the army of Persian king Xerxes I cross the Hellespont—the strait between Europe and Asia—in 480 B.C.?

1059. Who was the youngest U.S. Army officer ever to be promoted to general?

1060. How many stars were on the American flag during the Spanish-American War in 1898?

1061. For what did General John J. "Black Jack" Pershing win a Pulitzer Prize in 1932?

1062. Following the British defeat at Dunkirk in June 1940, who made the stirring broadcast vowing that "we shall fight in the fields and in the streets...we shall never surrender"?

1063. What was the inspiration for the name Rough Riders—the name of the elite fighting unit Theodore Roosevelt organized for the Spanish-American War?

1064. How many years did Hyman Rickover, the man credited with propelling the Navy into the nuclear age, serve on active duty÷

1052. *Douglas Fairbanks Jr.*

1053. *Napoleon's nemesis, the Duke of Wellington. At the time, the yo-yo was known as a bandalore.*

1054. *Colonel Rudolf Abel, the Soviet intelligence agent convicted of spying in 1957, who was exchanged for downed American U-2 reconnaissance pilot Francis Gary Powers in 1962.*

1055. *The American Civil War.*

1056. *In commandeered Renault taxis. Each cabbie was paid a 27-percent tip on top of his metered fare.*

1057. *President-to-be Ronald Reagan, then a captain.*

1058. *On two bridges of boats. Alexander the Great duplicated the feat 146 years later.*

1059. *George Custer, a graduate of West Point, who became a general at age 23—14 years before his infamous battle of Little Big Horn.*

1060. *Forty-five. The five states not yet admitted to the Union and not represented on the flag were Oklahoma, New Mexico, Arizona, Alaska and Hawaii.*

1061. *History, for his book* My Experiences in the World War.

1062. *British actor Norman Shelley. He sounded just like Winston Churchill and read the address so that the prime minister could deal with pressing matters of state.*

1063. *The Rough Riders Hotel in Medora, North Dakota, where Roosevelt had tried ranching.*

1064. *Sixty—he was forced to retire at age 82 by President Ronald Reagan.*

1065. Who were the two servicemen who carried the American flag as Jeanette MacDonald sang the national anthem at the wartime Oscar awards ceremony in 1943?

1066. How many volumes made up the Pentagon Papers, the Defense Department's study of U.S. involvement in the Vietnam War?

1067. How did the MiG, the famous Soviet jet fighter, get its name?

1068. What did Dutch-born German spy Mata Hari wear to her firing squad execution in October 1917?

1069. In Air Force slang, what is the meaning of the term "laundry bag"?

1070. How many pushups do young female recruits have to do in two minutes to pass U.S. Army basic training? How about their male counterparts?

1071. What was the first enemy fighting ship captured by the U.S. Navy after the War of 1812?

1072. What is the meaning of the U.S. Coast Guard motto, *semper paratus*?

1073. What Revolutionary War figure laid the cornerstone of the Bunker Hill Monument on June 17, 1825—the 50th anniversary of the famous battle?

1074. How many masts are on the *U.S.S. Constitution*, the historic square-rigged flagship of the U.S. Navy popularly known as "Old Ironsides"?

1075. What insect served as Napoleon Bonaparte's official emblem?

1076. Where would a soldier wear a havelock?

1077. In which state is the Wyoming Battle Monument located?

1065. *Marine private Tyrone Power and Army private Alan Ladd.*

1066. *Forty-seven—they included 3,000 pages of text, 4,000 pages of documents and weighed 60 pounds.*

1067. *From the names of the plane's designers, Artem Mikoyan and Mikhail I. Gurevich.*

1068. *Black—black velvet, fur-trimmed cape; black silk stockings; black kid gloves; and large floppy black hat with a black silk ribbon.*

1069. *It's a parachute.*

1070. *Women, a minimum of 17; men, a minimum of 40.*

1071. *The U-505, a World War II German submarine. It was captured in the Atlantic off the coast of French West Africa in 1944 and is now on exhibit at the Museum of Science and Industry in Chicago.*

1072. *Always prepared.*

1073. *The Marquis de Lafayette, who was visiting the U.S. at the time. Daniel Webster made the key address.*

1074. *Three. The warship, first launched in 1797, was restored at a cost of $12 million and is now on exhibit in Boston.*

1075. *The bumblebee.*

1076. *On his head, in the desert. It's the light cloth covering, attached to a military cap, that protects the back of a soldier's neck from the sun. It was named for Sir Henry Havelock, a British officer who served in India.*

1077. *In Pennsylvania. The monument commemorates a July 1778 Revolutionary War battle in which a group of Loyalists and Indians massacred settlers in Wyoming Valley in northeastern Pennsylvania.*

1078. What auto maker built the first armored tanks used by U.S. troops in battle?

1079. What baseball Hall of Famer was court-martialed for refusing to take a seat in the back of a U.S. Army bus?

1080. What future U.S. Army general participated in the 1912 Olympics in Stockholm, Sweden?

1081. Which controversial hero graduated at the bottom of his West Point class in 1861?

1082. What twentieth-century American general had a grandfather who was a Confederate brigadier general in the Civil War, and a great-great-great-grandfather who was a general in the Revolutionary War?

1083. What was the name of Adolf Hitler's favorite dog—the Alsatian he used to make sure his cyanide capsules were lethal?

1078. *Renault. The French-made tanks first saw service in the Battle of St. Mihiel on September 12, 1918. No American-made tanks were used in World War I.*

1079. *Jackie Robinson, in 1944, while a second lieutenant. He was acquitted.*

1080. *George S. Patton, who was a contestant in the pentathlon.*

1081. *Gen. George Armstrong Custer.*

1082. *George S. Patton.*

1083. *Blondi. Hitler used the cyanide to commit suicide after seeing that it worked on Blondi.*

1084. What was the name of ventriloquist Edgar Bergen's female dummy?

1085. What actress was the high-school girlfriend of Judge Joseph A. Wapner of TV's *The People's Court*?

1086. Who turned down the role of Columbo before Peter Falk was signed up for the TV detective series?

1087. What TV newsman lived with a tribe of headhunters for a month after bailing out of a crippled military plane in the Himalayas during World War II?

1088. What TV personality had four skywriting planes draw a three-mile-wide Valentine's Day heart for his wife?

1089. What is the name of Oscar the Grouch's pet worm on TV's *Street Street* ?

1090. Two members of TV's *A Team* had names with initials— B.A. Baracus and H.M. Murdock. What do the initials represent?

1091. Why does Mr. Spock of TV's *Star Trek* have green skin?

Answers

1084. *Effie Klinker.*

1085. *Lana Turner.*

1086. *Bing Crosby.*

1087. *Eric Sevareid.*

1088. *Garry Moore. The heart was pierced by a six-mile-long arrow and had the names "Garry & Nell"—written inside.*

1089. *Slimey.*

1090. *B.A. is for Bad Attitude; H.M., for Howling Mad.*

1091. *Because of traces of nickel and copper in his blood.*

1092. On whose 1932 talk and variety show did comedian Jack Benny make his radio debut?

1093. What was the radio show *Inner Sanctum* originally called?"

1094. What famous family comedy act started on the road to success as the Six Mascots, featuring brothers Leonard, Adolph, Julius, Milton, mother Minnie and aunt Hannah?

1095. How old was Clark Kent when he landed his job at the *Daily Planet* on the *Superman* TV series starring George Reeves?

1096. "You rang?" were the only words spoken by Lurch, the 7-foot-tall butler on TV's *The Addams Family*. What other TV sitcom character also popularized the phrase?

1097. What was the TV soap opera *One Life To Live* originally going to be called?

1098. On TV's *The Honeymooners*, who earned more money—bus driver Ralph Kramden or sewer worker Ed Norton?

1099. What was the first name of Lieutenant Columbo, portrayed on TV by Peter Falk?

1100. Who wrote "Johnny's Theme," the signature music of Johnny Carson's *Tonight Show?*

1101. What were the names of Woody Woodpecker's niece and nephew?

1102. What was the biggest jackpot ever won on TV's *The $64,000 Question?*

1103. Who was the television clown whose nose blinked the message *CBS Presents* and whose bald head proclaimed *The Big Top* from July 1950 to September 1957?

1104. Who was the first black entertainer to star in a dramatic TV series?

1092. *Ed Sullivan's. Others first heard on the radio on Sullivan's show included Irving Berlin and George M. Cohan.*

1093. The Squeaky Door.

1094. *The Marx brothers. Leonard later became Chico; Adolph, Harpo; Julius, Groucho; and Milton, Gummo.*

1095. *He was 25.*

1096. *Maynard G. Krebs on* The Many Loves of Dobie Gillis.

1097. Between Heaven and Hell. *The title was rejected as too racy by ABC-TV executives before its debut in July 1968.*

1098. *Their weekly pay was the same—$62.*

1099. *Phillip.*

1100. *Paul Anka, with Johnny Carson.*

1101. *Splinter was his niece; Knothead, his nephew.*

1102. *Three times $64,000—for a total of $192,000. The winner, a 10-year-old fifth-grader named Robert Strom, hit the jackpot on April 16, 1957.*

1103. *Johnny Carson's announcer-sidekick Ed McMahon.*

1104. *Bill Cosby, in* I Spy *in 1965.*

1105. What are the names of the two old codgers who wisecrack from their box seats on *The Muppet Show* ?

1106. What was Johnny Carson's famous reply when a reporter asked what he would like his epitaph to be?

1107. What 1949 television program was the very first coast-to-coast network show?

1108. What great American tried to stump the celebrity panel on TV's *Masquerade Party* by showing up in a penguin costume?

1109. Who played Beau Maverick on the TV Western comedy series *Maverick* ?

1110. Where did *M*A*S*H* army surgeon Hawkeye Pierce hail from?

1111. What did *Candid Camera* creator Alan Funt do before he started catching people off-guard with his hidden camera?

1112. In real life—and in TV script—who was married at the Byram River Beagle Club in Greenwich, Connecticut?

1113. What four actresses played Sid Caesar's wife during his run on *Your Show of Shows* ?

1114. What was the waist size of the Ralph Kramden bus driver's uniform that Jackie Gleason gave to R.A.L.P.H. (Royal Association for the Longevity & Preservation of the Honeymooners)?

1115. Who provided Superman's radio voice in the 1940s?

1116. How many plumes were on the tail of the original NBC peacock?

1117. What were the only words spoken by Clarabell the Clown on *The Howdy Doody Show* ?

1118. What popular television and movie actor served as senior director of news and special events for ABC-TV before launching his career as a performer?

1105. *Statler and Waldorf.*

1106. *"I'll be right back."*

1107. Kukla, Fan and Ollie.

1108. *Explorer Richard E. Byrd, who made the first flights over both the North and South Poles and established the* Little America *base in Antarctica.*

1109. *Roger Moore.*

1110. *Crab Apple Cove, Maine.*

1111. *He caught people off-guard with a hidden microphone on a successful radio show called* Candid Microphone.

1112. *Lucille Ball and Desi Arnaz.*

1113. *Imogene Coca, Nanette Fabray, Janet Blair and Gisele Mackenzie.*

1114. *It was 49¾ inches.*

1115. *TV emcee Bud Collyer, who also supplied the Man of Steel's voice for the animated television series in 1966.*

1116. *Eleven.*

1117. *"Good bye kids," on the 2,343rd-and-last episode of the popular kiddie show on September 30, 1960.*

1118. *Telly Savalas.*

1119. To what tribe did Jay Silverheels, who played Tonto on TV's *The Lone Ranger,* belong?

1120. What was the address of Big Bird's nest on TV's *Sesame Street?*

1121. How many fingers does Mickey Mouse have on each hand?

1122. Who portrayed Elvis Presley in the 1981 made-for-TV film *Elvis and the Beauty Queen?*

1123. What subject was actor Errol Flynn questioned about when he appeared as a contestant on the mid-1950s TV quiz show *The Big Surprise?*

1124. What popular stand-up comic turned down the role of Trapper John McIntyre in the TV sitcom *M*A*S*H* before Wayne Rogers signed on for the part?

1125. How many opening monologues did Johnny Carson deliver during his 30 years as host of *The Tonight Show?*

1126. What television personality appeared as a kiss-and-tell lothario who is murdered in the 1992 Perry Mason TV episode entitled *The Case of the Reckless Romeo* ?

1127. What American TV personality, while an art student in Italy, appeared as a dancing meatball in an Italian TV commercial and also was in the food orgy scene in Fellini's *Satyricon?*

1128. What was the number of the mobile hospital unit Hawkeye Pierce and Hot Lips Houlihan belonged to on TV's *M*A*S*H* ?

1129. What comic strip character did Gary Burghoff play off-Broadway before he became known to moviegoers and TV viewers as Corporal Radar O'Reilly of *M*A*S*H* ?

1130. On what early 1950s children's TV show did acting unknowns and future *Odd Couple* Tony Randall and Jack Klugman meet?

1131. What was the name of the church to which comedian Flip Wilson's character Reverend Leroy belonged?

1119. *Mohawk. He was born on the Six Nations Indian Reservation in Ontario, Canada.*

1120. *123½ Sesame Street.*

1121. *Four.*

1122. *Don Johnson.*

1123. *Sailing. Flynn won $30,000.*

1124. *Robert Klein.*

1125. *4,531.*

1126. *Tabloid TV star Geraldo Rivera.*

1127. *Fitness guru Richard Simmons.*

1128. *The 4077.*

1129. *He played Charlie Brown in the musical* You're a Good Man, Charlie Brown, *in 1967.*

1130. Captain Video and His Video Rangers.

1131. *The Church of What's Happening Now.*

1132. What was the name of the horse-ghost buddy of cartoon character Casper, the Friendly Ghost?

1133. What role did Art Carney play in Jackie Gleason's very first *Honeymooners* sketch?

1134. Who was the first mystery guest to appear on the TV quiz show *What's My Line* in 1950?

1135. In the TV sitcom *Mork and Mindy*, how far from Earth was Ork, Mork's home planet?

1136. What TV sitcom family lived at 1313 Mockingbird Lane?

1137. What was the theme song Jack Benny played off-key on his violin?

1138. What character actress provides the voice of mother Marge on TV's animated sitcom *The Simpsons* ?

1139. What is the only radio station in the United States with call letters that spell out the name of its home city?

1140. What famous American won $15,000 on the TV quiz show *Name That Tune* ? Hint: One of the 25 songs he named correctly was "Far Away Places."

1141. Who portrayed a wacky housewife in a 1948 radio series called *My Favorite Husband*?

1142. What car did TV's Archie Bunker recall fondly in "Those Were the Days," the theme song of the sitcom *All in the Family* ?

1143. What actress, as a 12-year-old, won $32,000, on TV's *$64,000* Challenge" and later admitted she had been given the answers in advance?

1144. What was the name Walt Disney originally proposed for Mickey Mouse?

1145. What famous Hollywood star turned down the role of Marshal Matt Dillon on TV's *Gunsmoke* before James Arness was offered the part?

1132. *Nightmare.*

1133. *A policeman—it was a minor role. The sketch was part of a 1950 Cavalcade of Stars show.*

1134. *Yankee shortstop Phil Rizzuto.*

1135. *60 bleems—or 60 billion light-years.*

1136. *The Munsters.*

1137. *"Love in Bloom."*

1138. *Julie Kavner—who first came to the attention of TV audiences as Brenda Morgenstern, the awkward kid sister on "Rhoda."*

1139. *WACO in Waco, Texas.*

1140. *Former Ohio senator and astronaut John Glenn, who was a Marine major at the time.*

1141. *Lucille Ball, who is best known as the wacky housewife on TV's "I Love Lucy."*

1142. *The LaSalle. He sang, "Gee our old LaSalle ran great."*

1143. *Patty Duke, in 1958, shortly before she won acclaim for her portrayal of Helen Keller in "The Miracle Worker" on Broadway.*

1144. *Mortimer.*

1145. *John Wayne—who recommended his little-known actor-friend Arness for the role.*

1146. On what TV show did Robert Guillaume first portray the sharp-witted, sharp-tongued butler Benson?

1147. Who was the host of television's first telethon, which raised $1.1 million for cancer research?

1148. Who was the last mystery guest on the long-running TV show *What's My Line* when it went off the air in September 1967?

1149. What innovative TV show brought us the first joint Chinese-American television production?

1150. Who played Kato, the faithful Philippine valet-chauffeur, on the TV show *The Green Hornet*?

1151. What actress was featured in the TV horror films *Satan's School for Girls*, *Killer Bees*, *Death Cruise* and *Death Scream* during the 1970s?

1152. Who portrayed Arnold Ziffel on *Green Acres*, the late 1960s TV sitcom that starred Eddie Albert and Eva Gabor?

1153. What building on Maxwell Street in Chicago should be familiar to most prime-time TV viewers?

1154. What famous person was interviewed in his pajamas on Ed Murrow's *Person to Person* TV show in 1959?

1155. What clever telegram message convinced a reluctant William F. Buckley Jr. to make a cameo TV appearance on Rowan and Martin's *Laugh-In*?

1156. How did Larry Gelbart, the brilliant writer behind TV's *M*A*S*H* and Hollywood's *Tootsie*, get his start in show biz at age 16?

1157. TV talk show host and entrepreneur Merv Griffin sold his privately held entertainment company, Merv Griffin Enterprises, in 1986 for a reported $250 million. Who bought it?

1146. On Soap, *in 1977, two years before the spinoff series "Benson."*

1147. Mr. Television, *Milton Berle, in 1949.*

1148. The show's moderator, John Charles Daly.

1149. Sesame Street, *in 1983. The show that resulted was "Big Bird in China."*

1150. Bruce Lee, before he became a kung fu movie star.

1151. Kate Jackson.

1152. A pig named Arnold.

1153. The former Maxwell Street police station, now headquarters for Chicago's vice squad. It's the setting of the exterior shots of the Hill Street stationhouse on Hill Street Blues.

1154. Cuban dictator Fidel Castro, who had just seized power.

1155. Buckley was asked, "Would you be on the show if we flew you on a plane with two right wings?"

1156. Through his father, who was comedian Danny Thomas' barber. Gelbart wrote his fist gags for Thomas, who delivered them on the Fanny Brice radio show.

1157. The Coca-Cola Company. Among the firm's holdings were the popular TV game shows Wheel of Fortune *and* Jeopardy, *both of which were created by Griffin.*

1158. In the TV sitcom *All in the Family*, what did Edith Bunker claim Archie told her as he carried her over the threshold after their marriage?

1159. What did TV comic Red Skelton claim is the longest word?

1160. What TV series appeared opposite Judy Garland's musical variety show in 1963 and knocked the popular singer off the air after only one season?

1161. What was the name of the short-lived spin-off of TV's popular *Columbo* show, which featured Peter Falk as the rumpled, cigar-smoking sleuth?

1162. How many cases did Perry Mason lose in the nine seasons Raymond Bur appeared on TV as the ace defense lawyer?

1163. Whom did Mary Hartman's father, George Shumway, look like after an accident forced him to undergo plastic surgery on the satirical TV soap opera *Mary Hartman, Mary Hartman*?

1164. What was the first name of mild-mannered bespectacled Mr. Peepers in the 1950s TV sitcom of that name starring Wally Cox?

1165. What musical instrument did Fibber McGee keep in his cluttered hall closet at 79 Wistful Vista on the popular radio show *Fibber McGee and Molly*?

1166. Who was the only person ever shown smoking a cigar on *The Camel News Caravan*, the early TV news show sponsored by Camel cigarettes and starring John Cameron Swayze?

1167. What childhood word game was the inspiration for TV's very popular *Wheel of Fortune*?

1168. What TV performer was described in 1955 by the Russian newspaper *Izvestia* as "a symbol of the American way of life...necessary in order that the average American should not look into reports on rising taxes and decreasing pay."?

1158. *"Watch your head dingbat, or you'll knock your brains out."*

1159. *The one that follows the announcement, "And now a word from our sponsor."*

1160. *Bonanza. Garland's hour-long show appeared on CBS Sundays at 9 P.M. from September 1963 to March 1964.*

1161. Mrs. Columbo. *The show, aired in 1979, starred Kate Mulgrew as Kate Columbo. Before it went off the air it went through two name changes—to* Kate the Detective *and* Kate Loves a Mystery—*and* Mrs. Columbo *became* Ms. Callahan.

1162. *Only one—but he later proved his client innocent and caught the guilty party.*

1163. *Actor Tab Hunter.*

1164. *Robinson.*

1165. *A mandolin.*

1166. *Winston Churchill.*

1167. *Hangman.*

1168. *Celebrity chimpanzee J. Fred Muggs, mascot of* The Today Show.

1169. What was the year and model of comedian Jack Benny's oft-mentioned automobile?

1170. On what TV show did comic Robin Williams first appear as the alien Mork?

1171. In what century does the 1979 film *Star Trek: The Motion Picture take place?*

1172. What was the address of the Bellamy family's London townhouse in the TV series *Upstairs, Downstairs?*

1173. What were the names of the three sons in the TV sitcom *My Three Sons*, which featured Fred MacMurray as widower Steve Douglas?

1174. What did the acronym UNCLE stand for on the TV spy series *The Man from U.N.C.L.E.*, starring Robert Vaughn and David McCallum?

1175. Who was the only cast member of the movie *M*A*S*H* to appear as a regular in the popular TV version.

1176. What is the meaning of kemo sabe—the words Tonto used to address the Lone Ranger?

1177. What town in the Ozarks was home to the Clampett clan on TV's *Beverly Hillbillies* ?

1178. Who was featured as comedian Jimmy Durante's sidekick on his popular radio show from 1943 to 1948?

1179. What hours are considered prime time on television?

1180. What famous entertainer was offered the role of Archie Bunker in the TV pilot for *All in the Family* before Carroll O'Connor was signed for the role?

1181. What was the name of Baby Snooks' baby brother in the popular radio show that starred Fanny Brice?

1182. Who starred in the title role of TV's kiddie space program *Rod Brown of the Rocket Rangers* in 1953?

1169. *It was a 1924 Maxwell.*

1170. *On "Happy Days"—in a dream of Richie Cunningham's.*

1171. *The twenty-third century.*

1172. *165 Eaton Place.*

1173. *Chip, Mike and Robbie in the show's first five years. When Mike married and moved away, Chip's orphaned buddy, Ernie, was adopted to keep the show's title valid.*

1174. *United Network Command for Law Enforcement.*

1175. *Gary Burghoff, who appeared as Corporal Radar O'Reilly in both.*

1176. *Trusty scout.*

1177. *Hooterville, which served as the setting for the spinoff series* Petticoat Junction *and* Green Acres.

1178. *Garry Moore.*

1179. *From 8 to 11 P.M. weekdays and Saturdays; from 7 to 11 P.M. on Sundays.*

1180. *Mickey Rooney.*

1181. *Robespierre.*

1182. *Actor Cliff Robertson.*

1183. What was the first opera written especially for television?

1184. How did the TV sitcom *Sanford and Son* get its name?

1185. What first in radio history occurred on December 24, 1906, thanks to electrical engineer Reginald Fessenden?

1186. What sitcom was the most popular show on television in 1963?

1187. Under what name did show biz entrepreneur Merv Griffin originally try to sell the TV game show we know as *Jeopardy* ?

1188. What actor seen munching a carrot in a movie inspired cartoonist Bob Clampett to create Bugs Bunny?

1189. Which of TV's *Golden Girls* was the oldest—Beatrice Arthur (Dorothy), Estelle Getty (Sophia), Rue McClanahan (Blanche) or Betty White (Rose)?

1190. What actress's unpublished home telephone number did comedienne Joan Rivers give out on national TV in 1986 when she was hosting *The Late Show Starring Joan Rivers* ?

1191. Shots were fired only once in the 1970 movie *M*A*S*H*. What were they for?

1192. What was used to power the engines of the starship Enterprise in the *Star Trek* television series?

1193. In the Arab world, what popular TV show is known as "Iftah Ya Simsim" ?

1194. What television show featured fictional Russian spies Boris Badenov and Natasha Fatale?

1195. How many freckles did early TV puppet Howdy Doody have?

1196. What male TV heartthrob appeared nude in *The Harrad Experiment*, a 1973 film about a college experiment in premarital sex?

1183. Amahl and the Night Visitors, *by Gian-Carlo Menotti. It was first presented in 1951.*

1184. From it's star, Redd Foxx, who was born John Elroy Sanford.

1185. The airwaves were used for entertainment for the first time, with Fessenden performing "O Holy Night" on his violin, playing some records and reading from the Bible—all from his transmitter in Brant Rock, Massachusetts.

1186. The Beverly Hillbillies.

1187. What's the Question?

1188. Clark Gable—the movie was the 1934 comedy classic It Happened One Night. *Bugs made his film debut in 1940 in* A Wild Hare.

1189. Betty White. The youngest was Rue McClanahan.

1190. Victoria Principal's. The two had feuded earlier, when Rivers was guest-hosting on The Tonight Show.

1191. Timekeeping at a football game.

1192. Antimatter.

1193. Sesame Street.

1194. The Bullwinkle Show. *In the satirical cartoon series, Natasha's last name sometimes was given as Nogoodnik.*

1195. 48—one for each state in the Union at the time.

1196. Don Johnson, who portrayed the campus stud.

1197. What TV sitcom couple was the first to share a double bed?

1198. What actor—best known for his straight-man TV sitcom role as a befuddled husband—appeared on Broadway with Deborah Kerr in *Tea and Sympathy* and with Kim Stanley in *Bus Stop* ?

1199. Who was the first entertainer shown diapering a baby in full view on television?

1200. On what popular TV sitcom were the two female stars pregnant at the same time—although the story line only acknowledged one of the pregnancies?

1201. What was the name of the *U.S.S. Enterprise* in the original draft for the *Star Trek* TV series?

1202. What popular TV and movie actor once appeared in a television commercial as a package of lemon chiffon pie mix, all decked out in a yellow box and matching yellow tights and flanked by actors playing chocolate, vanilla and butterscotch pie mix?

1203. Who played Oscar Madison's secretary, Myrna Turner, on the TV sitcom *The Odd Couple* ?

1204. What title role did Norman Lloyd—best known as the cranky but good-hearted Dr. Daniel Auschlander on TV's *St. Elsewhere*—play in an Alfred Hitchcock thriller more than 50 years ago?

1205. Whose photo did Michael J. Fox, in his role as Alex P. Keaton, keep on his nightstand in the popular TV sitcom *Family Ties* ?

1206. What popular 1960s TV sitcom was based on the novel *The Fifteenth Pelican* by Tere Ross?

1207. How often is it necessary for Mr. Spock of *Star Trek* to have sex?

1208. On TV's *Petticoat Junction,* what were the names of the three Bradley girls and their uncle?

1197. *The Munsters, Lily and Herman, played by Yvonne De Carlo and Fred Gwynne, during the 1964-65 season of the mock-horror show.*

1198. *Dick York, who played Darrin Stephens in* Bewitched.

1199. *Carroll O'Connor, as Archie Bunker, in the sitcom* All in the Family. *The baby was his TV grandson, Joey Stivic.*

1200. Cheers. *In its third season (1984-85), both Shelley Long (Diane Chambers) and Rhea Perlman (Carla Tortelli) were expecting. Long's pregnancy was concealed on camera while Perlman's was worked into the script.*

1201. *The* U.S.S. Yorktown.

1202. *Ted Danson, who's much better known for his portrayal of Sam Malone in the TV sitcom* Cheers.

1203. *Penny Marshall—who went on to make a name for herself as Laverne in the sitcom* Laverne & Shirley, *and as the director of such movies as* Big *and* Awakenings.

1204. *The saboteur who falls from the Statue of Liberty at the climax of Hitchcock's 1942 film* Saboteur, *starring Robert Cummings and Priscilla Lane.*

1205. *Richard Nixon's. A poster of William F. Buckley, Jr., was over Alex's bed.*

1206. The Flying Nun, *which starred Sally Field in the title role.*

1207. *Once every seven years.*

1208. *Billie Jo, Betty Jo, Bobbie Jo, and Uncle Joe.*

1209. Whose TV contract stipulated that she stay overweight and wear dumpy dresses so she'd look frumpier than the show's star?

1210. What role did mystery writer Erle Stanley Gardner, creator of the character of Perry Mason, play in the last TV episode of *The Perry Mason Show*?

1211. What was the "line" of the very first contestant on *What's My Line*, which premiered on February 16, 1950?

1212. What was the name of Col. Sherman Potter's horse in the *M*A*S*H* TV series?

1213. How did the last episode of TV's *Mary Tyler Moore Show* end?

1214. Where did Rocket J. Squirrel and Bullwinkle Moose live in the animated TV mock adventure series *Rocky and His Friends* ?

1215. What was Archie Bunker's address in the TV sitcom *All in the Family* ?

1216. Gore Vidal wrote a satirical TV comedy called *State of Confusion* for what comedian?

1217. On *The Andy Griffith Show*, what did deputy sheriff Barney Fife keep in his shirt pocket?

1218. What was Groucho Marx's real first name?

1219. What TV sitcom did Carl Reiner write and hope to star in?

1220. Who danced a pas de deux from "Swine Lake" with Miss Piggy on TV's The Muppet Show ?

1221. Who played Ronnie Burns, son of George Burns and Gracie Allen, on their TV show?

1222. On what TV show did Nancy Walker get her training for the maid's job on *McMillan and Wife*?

1209. *Vivian Vance's contract—to play Ethel Mertz on the* I Love Lucy *show.*

1210. *He played the judge.*

1211. *Hat check girl at the Stork Club.*

1212. *Sophie.*

1213. *Everyone but incompetent newscaster Ted Baxter was fired.*

1214. *Frostbite Falls, Minnesota.*

1215. *Archie resided at 704 Houser St., in the Corona section of Queens, New York City.*

1216. *Milton Berle, in 1955.*

1217. *His one bullet.*

1218. *Julius.*

1219. The Dick Van Dyke Show, *in which he ended up playing boss Alan Brady.*

1220. *Rudolf Nureyev.*

1221. *Ronnie Burns, their son.*

1222. *She portrayed a part-time maid on* Family Affair.

1223. What was the name of the lawyer who never lost a case on TV's cartoon sitcom *The Flintstones?*

1224. What was the name of TV detective Baretta's pet cockatoo?

1225. What TV character did *Time* magazine describe as a "human oil slick"?

1226. On the TV sitcom *My Mother, the Car,*who was the voice of the car?

1227. As a struggling young actor, James Dean helped support himself by testing stunts for what TV game show?

1228. What was the name of Phyllis Diller's short-lived 1968 TV variety show?

1229. The producer of what TV series once said that sometimes his actors' "faces get so green you can't shoot them"?

1230. Why did the fourteenth screen Tarzan, former LA Rams linebacker Mike Henry, sue for physical and mental injury following his third and final film?

1231. What was the name of the lurid novel written by Det. Ron Harris on the *Barney Miller TV* show?

1232. How much were Dean Martin and Jerry Lewis paid for their appearance on the first *Ed Sullivan Show* in June 1948?

1233. What was Maxwell Smart's cover on the TV spy comedy *Get Smart?*

1234. What was the Skipper's full name on TV's *Gilligan's Island* ?

1235. For what film role did Telly Savalas first shave his head?

1236. What popular actor once noted, "I am a slob, but nobody will believe it"?

1237. Comedienne Joan Rivers has a registered trademark. What is it?

1223. *Perry Masonry.*

1224. *Fred.*

1225. Dallas *villain J. R. Ewing.*

1226. *Ann Southern.*

1227. Beat the Clock.

1228. The Beautiful Phyllis Diller Show.

1229. Sea Hunt—*he was referring to his regularly seasick cast.*

1230. *Dinky the Chimp bit him.*

1231. Blood on the Badge.

1232. *They shared $200.*

1233. *Salesman for the Pontiac Greeting Card Co.*

1234. *Jonas Grumby, played by Alan Hale Jr.*

1235. *Pontius Pilate, in* The Greatest Story Ever Told, *in 1965.*

1236. *Tony Randall, who portrayed Felix Unger, the fussy roommate in the* Odd Couple *television series.*

1237. *Her famous line: "Can we talk?"*

1238. What were the names of cartoon superstars Tom and Jerry when they made their debut in 1940 in *Puss Gets the Boot* ?

1239. What television soap opera was the very first to use plastic surgery to explain a cast change?

1240. What was the working title of the TV series "Dynasty" before it went on TV in 1981?

1241. What television personality won America's Junior Miss crown in 1963?

1242. What TV sex symbol appeared as a contestant on "The Dating Game"—and wasn't chosen?

1243. Debbie Allen, who portrayed dance teacher Lydia Grant on TV's "Fame," has a sister who also became well-known through a popular television series. Who is she?

1244. Who appeared on the TV soap "All My Children" as Verla Grubbs, daughter of a carnival snake charmer, who was searching for her long-lost father?

1245. What is the apartment number of "The Jeffersons" on the popular television series?

1246. What was the name of the first female member of TV's "Mission Impossible" team?

1247. What famous cowboy's horse had its own TV series?

1248. In May 1977 Bill Cosby was awarded a doctor of education degree by the University of Massachusetts. What was the subject of his 242-page dissertation?

1249. At what age did Lucille Ball become a redhead?

1250. Who played Mr. Spock's mother in both film and television episodes of "Star Trek"?

1251. Why was Simon Templar—portrayed on television by Roger Moore—called "The Saint"?

1238. *Tom, the cat, was called Jasper; Jerry, the mouse, was unnamed.*

1239. One Life to Live, *in 1969 when Michael Storm replaced his brother Jim as Dr. Larry Wolek.*

1240. *"Oil."*

1241. *News show host Diane Sawyer.*

1242. *Tom "Magnum, P.I." Selleck.*

1243. *Phylicia Raschad, better known as Clair Huxtable on* The Cosby Show.

1244. *Comedienne and former TV regular Carol Burnett, in 1983.*

1245. *Apartment 12-D.*

1246. *Cinnamon Carter. She was portrayed by Barbara Bain.*

1247. *Gene Autry's Champion, the* Wonder Horse. *Autry produced but never appeared in the series,* The Adventures of Champion, *which ran from September 1955 to February 1956.*

1248. *Fat Albert and the Cosby Kids. It was called "An Integration of the Visual Media via Fat Albert and the Cosby Kids into the Elementary School Curriculum as a Teaching Aid and Vehicle to Achieve Increased Learning."*

1249. *At age 30, after 12 years as a platinum blonde and 18 as a natural brunette.*

1250. *Jane Wyatt, who prepared for Trekkie motherhood by playing Margaret Anderson on TV's* Father Knows Best.

1251. *Because of his initials, S.T.*

1252. On what TV sitcom did the schnauzer-cocker-poodle mix we know as Benji appear before he made it big in the movies?

1253. What popular TV personality claims he was once fired as a weekend TV weatherman for describing a storm as having "hailstones the size of canned hams"?

1254. What famous actress had a plumbing fixture named after her?

1255. On what TV program did Johnny Carson first team up with Ed McMahon?

1256. What was the first Hollywood film shown on TV after the U.S. movie industry ended its ban and started selling television rights to its films in late 1955?

1257. What was the radio classic *Amos 'n' Andy* originally called when it went on the air in Chicago in 1926?

1258. What actor-comedian, before attaining stardom, performed with a popular folksinging group called The Tarriers?

1259. What female entertainer, as a five-year-old kindergarten student in 1953, appeared regularly on television on the *Horn & Hardart Children's Hour*?

1260. What famous actor, offered the role of the Penguin in the *Batman* TV series, said he would only take the part if he could kill Batman?

1261. Remember all the promotional hoopla in 1980 about "Who shot J.R." on TV's *Dallas*? Well, who did?

1262. How did Batman disguise the lever that opened the secret panel hiding the bat slides he and Robin used to get to the bat cave?

1263. What is the diameter of TV's famous *Wheel of Fortune*?

1264. Bob Hope had a reputation for delivering six punch lines a minute. How many a minute has Phyllis Diller been known to reel off?

1252. *On* Petticoat Junction, *as Uncle Joe's dog. At the time Benji was known as Higgins.*

1253. *David Letterman.*

1254. *Farrah Fawcett. The fixture was the gold-plated "Farrah faucet."*

1255. *On the daytime quiz show* Who Do You Trust, *in 1958.*

1256. King Kong, *starring Fay Wray.*

1257. Sam 'n' Henry.

1258. *Alan Arkin.*

1259. *Bernadette Peters, who was Bernadette Lazzara at the time.*

1260. *Spencer Tracy.*

1261. *Ewing's pregnant mistress, his sister-in-law Kristin Shepard, played by Mary Frances Crosby.*

1262. *As a bust of Shakespeare.*

1263. *Eight and a half feet.*

1264. *Twelve.*

1265. Which of Jim Henson's Muppets was the first to become a regular on national television?

1266. What well-known actor has been known to carry a small battery-powered fan to blow cigarette and cigar smoke back at the offending source?

1267. What famous couple appeared in the 1958 television play *A Turkey for the President* ?

1268. In what film did actor Leonard Nimoy—best known as Mr. Spock on *Star Trek*—first appear as an alien from outer space?

1269. What TV series did David Hartman star in before he became the host of *Good Morning America* in 1975?

1270. What fellow performer's Congressional candidacy did Beverly Hillbilly Buddy Ebsen oppose in a 1984 radio commercial?

1271. Name the third baseman in the Bud Abbott-Lou Costello *Who's on First* comedy routine.

1272. On what television show did Julie Newmar portray a robot?

1273. Actor Robert Blake worked with a cockatoo named Fred on the *Baretta* TV series. With what famous animal did he share credits much earlier in his career?

1274. Before he legally changed his name, what was strongman-actor Mr. T's name?

1275. Where did actor Jim Backus' radio character Hubert Updyke III (a fabulously wealthy forerunner of his Thurston Howell III on TV's *Gilligan's Island*) claim his ancestors landed when they arrived in America?

1276. How did Lauren Bacall entertain the audience when she made her television debut on in 1954?

1277. Which of TV's card-carrying private eyes was an indirect namesake of Dashiell Hammett's Sam Spade?

1265. *Rowlf the Dog. The Muppet hound, created for a dog food commercial, appeared for three seasons on* The Jimmy Dean Show.

1266. *Larry (J. R. Ewing) Hagman.*

1267. *President-to-be Ronald Reagan and his wife Nancy. The dramatization was the Thanksgiving feature on* General Electric Theater, *which Reagan hosted.*

1268. *In* The Zombie Vanguard, *the first of 12 episodes in the serial* Zombies of the Stratosphere. *Nimoy, 20 at the time, played a Martian in the zombie army.*

1269. Lucas Tanner, *in which he played the title role.*

1270. *That of Nancy Kulp, who played homely Jane Hathaway on* The Beverly Hillbillies. *She lost her bid for the Pennsylvania seat.*

1271. *"I Don't Know."*

1272. *On* My Living Doll, *starring Robert Cummings. The show ran from September 1964 to September 1965.*

1273. *Rin Tin Tin III—in the 1947 film* The Return of Rin Tin Tin.

1274. *Lawrence Tero.*

1275. *On Cadillac Rock.*

1276. *She recited the poem* Casey at the Bat.

1277. *Richard Diamond, played by David Janssen. His name was taken from another suit of cards.*

1278. What was the first American television series acquired for screening in the Soviet Union?

1279. What was the name of the 1973 TV movie that co-starred twice-wed, twice-divorced entertainers Elizabeth Taylor and Richard Burton?

1280. Why did gunslinger Matt Paladin on TV's *Have Gun, Will Travel* have a knight chesspiece inscribed on his calling card?

1281. How did Kukla, the bubble-nosed puppet featured on the TV kiddie show *Kukla, Fran and Ollie*, get his name?

1282. What was wacky *Today Show* weatherman Willard Scott's first television job?

1283. How many miles per gallon did the 19 ½-foot long, 8-foot-wide crime-fighting Batmobile get on the campy *Batman* TV show starring Adam West?

1284. How many 25-foot mobile vans did TV's traveling newscaster Charles Kuralt wear out in logging a million miles for his *On the Road* show?

1285. What were the names of Johnny Carson's first three wives?

1286. Where did Captain Benjamin Franklin Pierce, the irreverent doctor portrayed by Alan Alda on the popular *M*A*S*H* TV series, get his nickname, Hawkeye?

1287. What was the name of Buffalo Bob Smith's replacement on the *Howdy Doody Show* during the 1954-55 TV season when the puppet's best pal was incapacitated by a heart attack?

1288. What percentage of the episodes of TV's Gilligan's Island dealt with getting off the island?

1289. Who showed up disguised as a man at a stag Friars Club roast for Sid Caesar in 1983—and got through the entire evening undetected by any of the 2,200 male guests?

1290. What popular television series was originally going to be called *The Alley Cats* ?

1278. Fraggle Rock, *the children's educational show developed by Muppet creator Jim Henson. The Soviets bought 24 half-hour episodes.*

1279. Divorce His/Divorce Hers.

1280. *Because paladin is another word for knight.*

1281. *Kukla means "puppet" in Russian.*

1282. *He appeared as Bozo the clown on TV in Washington, D.C., in 1959.*

1283. *Four miles per gallon.*

1284. *Seven.*

1285. *From first to third: Joan, Joanne and Joanna.*

1286. *From James Fenimore Cooper's 1826 novel, "The Last of the Mohicans," in which the principal character, frontier scout Natty Bumppo, is known as Hawkeye.*

1287. *Bison Bill—Buffalo Bob's brother. He was played by Ted Brown, who went on to become a leading New York City disc jockey.*

1288. *32 percent.*

1289. *Phyllis Diller, who attended the roast under the alias Phillip Downey.*

1290. *"Charlie's Angels."*

1291. Who got his big break on TV when he filled in at the last minute for Red Skelton after the slapstick comic was injured during rehearsal?

1292. Why was madcap comedienne Lucille Ball kicked out of drama school in New York City when she was 15?

1293. What did Bugs Bunny drink to become invisible?

1294. What heavyweight actor portrayed Marshall Matt Dillon in the long-running 1950's radio version of *Gunsmoke*?

1295. Who was the left fielder in the Bud Abbott and Lou Costello comedy skit *Who's on First*?

1296. What was the original theme song of the *Happy Days* TV series, starring Ron Howard and Henry Winkler?

1297. What was Oprah Winfrey's first name supposed to be—before it was misspelled on her birth certificate?

1298. In the TV sitcom *Cheers*, what was the legal capacity of the popular Boston bar?

1299. On the TV kiddie show *Howdy Doody*, to what tribe did Chief Thunderthud belong? Hint: It's the name of an animal spelled backward.

1300. What is the name of the production company Tom Arnold formed after he and Roseanne Barr split?

1301. On the hit TV sitcom *Seinfeld*, what role did Kramer land on the "Murphy Brown" show when he moved to Hollywood to pursue an acting career?

1302. What is the significance of the name actor Michael J. Fox gave his production company, Snowback Productions?

1303. Who played Don Johnson's partner in the pilot for the hip TV police drama *Miami Vice*?

1304. What popular movie star appeared as Michael J. Fox's alcoholic uncle on the TV sitcom *Family Ties*?

1291. *Johnny Carson, in 1954. He was a staff writer for Skelton's network variety show at the time.*

1292. *Her teacher thought she was too quiet and shy.*

1293. *Hare remover.*

1294. *William Conrad, best known to TV viewers for his title roles in the* Cannon *and* Jake and the Fatman *series.*

1295. *Why.*

1296. *"Rock Around The Clock," by Bill Haley and the Comets.*

1297. *Orpah, after Ruth's sister-in-law in the Bible. (Ruth 1:4) The midwife transposed the second and third letters when she filled out Winfrey's birth certificate.*

1298. *75. The number was in a notice posted over the front door.*

1299. *Ooragnak—that's kangaroo spelled backward.*

1300. *Clean Break Productions.*

1301. *He played one of Murphy's many short-term secretaries. Kramer is played by Michael Richards.*

1302. *Snowback is Canadian slang for a native who crosses the border into the United States. Fox was born in Canada.*

1303. *Jimmy Smits, before he achieved fame as lawyer Victor Sifuentes in* L.A. Law. *Philip Michael Thomas ended up playing Johnson's partner, Det. Ricardo Tubbs, on* Miami Vice.

1304. *Tom Hanks.*

1305. What was the name of the newspaper started by cross-dressing corporal Max Klinger on the hit TV sitcom *M*A*S*H* ?

1306. What famous catchphrase delivered by Peter Falk indicated that Columbo, TV's rumpled detective, was closing in on the criminal?

1307. What one-time TV Western star got his acting start in college when someone strong was needed to carry bodies in a student production of Arsenic and Old Lace?

1308. What new career did actor Jay Silverheels, best known for his portrayal of the Lone Ranger's faithful companion, Tonto, launch after retiring from show business in 1984?

1309. What TV show featured radio station KBHR? How about radio station KJCM?

1310. On the TV sitcom *The Munsters,* what was Lily Munster's maiden name?

1311. What did the American Lung Association call the "awards" it issued in 1996 to TV dramas it felt wrongly glamorized smoking?

1312. In what role did Helen Hunt, star of the TV sitcom *Mad About You,* appear on *The Mary Tyler Moore Show* when she was seven years old?

1313. What Hollywood sexpot played the wicked Siren on the *Batman* television series?

1314. Who plays Captain Kangaroo, and what other well-known television character did he play?

1315. The only time Ralph Edwards did not host *This Is Your Life,* was on January 30, 1957. Who was the substitute host that night?

1316. What actress, appearing in the TV series *Dynasty,* made her television debut in 1957 in *Bachelor Father* with her *Dynasty* co-star John Forsythe?

1305. *M*A*S*H Notes.*

1306. *"Oh, one more thing."*

1307. *Dan Blocker, who played Hoss Cartwright on* Bonanza.

1308. *He became a harness-racing driver.*

1309. *KBHR was on* Northern Exposure; *KJCM, on* Midnight Caller.

1310. *Dracula.*

1311. *Phlemmys. The big winners were* Chicago Hope *and* NYPD Blue.

1312. *The daughter of head newswriter Murray Slaughter.*

1313. *Joan Collins.*

1314. *Bob Keeshan, who was also the first Clarabell the Clown on* The Howdy Doody Show.

1315. *Ronald Reagan.*

1316. *Linda Evans.*

1317. CBS-TV's *60 Minutes* ran a feature called "Point Counterpoint" from 1971 to 1979, in which conservative James L. Kilpatrick debated two liberal adversaries. Can you name them?

1318. To what fraternal organization did Ralph Kramden and Ed Norton belong in the TV series, *The Honeymooners*?

1319. Who was the four-foot-tall, hairy character in the TV series, *The Addams Family*?

1320. What was the first film released in CinemaScope?

1321. "Man-woman-birth-death-infinity" were the opening words of what television series and who said them?

1322. Who commanded the *U.S.S. Enterprise* in TV's *Star Trek* before Capt. James T. Kirk came on board?

1323. What well-known movie actor once played the role of Ben Harper on the TV soap opera, *Love of Life*?

1324. *Laverne and Shirley, Mork and Mindy* and Joanie *Loves Chachi* were spin-offs of the more successful TV series, *Happy Days*. From what series was *Happy Days* itself a spin-off?

1325. In the Walt Disney cartoons, what was the name of Goofy's brilliant nephew?

1326. In the old *Mickey Mouse Club* TV series, each day of the week had a theme. What were the themes for Monday through Friday?

1327. What school did Beaver Cleaver attend in the television series, *Leave It To Beaver*?

1328. What TV cartoon characters belonged to the Royal Order of Water Buffaloes?

1329. Who was the first black person to host a network television game show?

1317. *Nicholas Von Hoffman (in the 1971—74 seasons), and Shana Alexander (from 1975 to 1979).*

1318. *The Royal Order of Raccoons, also known as the International Order of Friendly Raccoons.*

1319. *Cousin Itt, played by Felix Silla.*

1320. The Robe, *in 1953.*

1321. *"Ben Casey," spoken by Sam Jaffe.*

1322. *Capt. Christopher Pike, played by Jeffrey Hunter.*

1323. *Christopher Reeve.*

1324. Love, American Style.

1325. *Gilbert.*

1326. *Fun With Music Day, Guest Star Day, Anything Can Happen Day, Circus Day, and Talent Roundup Day.*

1327. *Grant Avenue Grammar School.*

1328. *Fred Flintstone and Barney Rubble of* The Flintstones.

1329. *Singer Adam Wade, who hosted* Musical Chairs *(1975).*

1330. What brand of stopwatch is seen in the TV program, *60 Minutes*?

1331. Humphrey Bogart acted for television only once—in a 1955 live production of what play?

1332. Ferdy and Morty are the two mischievous nephews of what well-known cartoon figure?

1333. In the TV series, *Wild Bill Hickok*, what was the name of Wild Bill's horse?

1334. In the TV series, *Three's Company*, what was the full name of Chrissy, played by Suzanne Somers?

1335. What is the name of the television series which began: "There is nothing wrong with your television set; do not attempt to adjust the picture. We are controlling transmission"?

1336. What was the working title of the TV series, *Dallas*?

1337. Who was the only Dumont television network star ever to win an Emmy Award?

1338. On the television series *Batman*, who played Batman and Robin's nemesis, Chandell?

1339. *Primrose Lane* was the theme song of what TV series starring Henry Fonda?

1340. What company always supplied the numerous devices used by Wile E. Coyote in his efforts to capture the Road Runner?

1341. In the TV series, *Mork and Mindy*, what was the capital city of Mork's home planet, Ork?

1342. Two actors who played high school students on the TV series, *The Many Loves of Dobie Gillis*, went on to become big stars, both renowned for "many loves" of their own. Who are they?

1330. *Heuer.*

1331. *The Petrified Forest, in which he played Duke Mantee.*

1332. *Mickey Mouse.*

1333. *Buckshot.*

1334. *Christmas Snow.*

1335. *The Outer Limits. The introduction and closing words were spoken by Vic Perrin.*

1336. *Houston.*

1337. *Bishop Fulton J. Sheen, who was voted the Most Outstanding Personality for the 1952 season.*

1338. *Liberace.*

1339. *The Smith Family.*

1340. *Acme.*

1341. *Kork.*

1342. *Warren Beatty and Ryan O'Neal.*

1343. When Elizabeth Montgomery played the dual roles of Samantha Stevens and her cousin, Serena, in the TV series, *Bewitched*, she was credited by what name for the role of Serena?

1344. Which well-known newsman narrated the TV series, *The Untouchables?*

1345. On the TV series, *M*A*S*H*, B. J. Hunnicutt was often pining for his wife and daughter back home. What were their names?

1346. Mayor La Trivia, Wallace Wimple and Myrt, the telephone operator, were characters on what classic radio program?

1347. Who was the first guest host of NBC-TV's *Saturday Night Live* ?

1348. What was the longtime sponsor of the radio series, *Jack Armstrong, the All-American Boy*, and where did Jack go to school?

1349. The NBC-TV game show, *Hollywood Squares*, first aired on October 17, 1966. Who occupied the center square on that telecast?

1350. Identify the father, mother and brother of Olive Oyl, Popeye's girlfriend.

1351. What was the name of the dirty old man, played by Arte Johnson, who always offered a Walnetto to Gladys Ormphby (played by Ruth Buzzi) in TV's *Laugh-In* ?

1352. Husband and wife Martin Landau and Barbara Bain starred together in which two television series?

1353. Vinko Bogataj has been seen once a week on ABC-TV for several years. What does he do?

1354. Which actress won the top prize on the TV quiz show, *The $64,000 Question*, by answering questions on Shakespeare?

1343. *Pandora Sparks.*

1344. *Walter Winchell.*

1345. *Peg and Erin, respectively.*

1346. Fibber McGee and Molly.

1347. *Comedian George Carlin, on October 10, 1975.*

1348. *Wheaties, and Hudson High, respectively.*

1349. *Ernest Borgnine. (For the record, the other squares housed Nick Adams, Abby Dalton, Charlie Weaver, Wally Cox, Sally Field, Morey Amsterdam, Agnes Moorehead and Rose Marie.)*

1350. *Cole Oyl, Nana Oyl and Castor Oyl, respectively.*

1351. *Tyrone F. Horneigh.*

1352. Mission: Impossible *and* Space: 1999.

1353. *He is the skier shown going off the side of the ski jump in the introduction to* Wide World of Sports.

1354. *Barbara Feldon.*

1355. What was Laverne De Fazio's favorite drink in the TV series, *Laverne & Shirley*?

1356. What was the first ABC-TV series to be rated number one for an entire season?

1357. "All aboard for Anaheim, Azusa and Cucamonga." Who uttered that phrase and on what program?

1358. Who was Johnny Carson's first guest when he took over the *Tonight Show* on October 1, 1962?

1359. *The Mary Tyler Moore Show* spawned three successful spin-off series. What were they?

1360. Who sings the theme song of the TV series, *The Love Boat*?

1361. In the late 1950's, Steve McQueen played the bounty hunter, Josh Randall, in what western TV series?

1362. The British television program, *Till Death Us Do Part*, inspired what extremely popular American TV series?

1363. What was the name of Tonto's horse in the TV series of *The Lone Ranger*?

1364. Jessica Tandy and Hume Cronyn were the stars of a 1954 NBC-TV situation comedy called, *The Marriage*—an otherwise unremarkable series, were it not for what pioneering distinction?

1365. On December 31, 1970, something disappeared from television. What was it?

1366. Whom did actress Joan Crawford replace in four episodes of the TV soap opera The Secret Storm in 1968?

1367. What word did censors ban from I Love Lucy scripts during the 1952-53 TV season?

1355. *Pepsi and milk.*

1356. Marcus Welby, M.D., *in 1970-71.*

1357. *Mel Blanc, on both the radio and television versions of* The Jack Benny Program.

1358. *Groucho Marx.*

1359. Rhoda, Phyllis *and* Lou Grant.

1360. *Jack Jones.*

1361. Wanted: Dead Or Alive.

1362. All In The Family.

1363. *Scout.*

1364. *It was the first network show to telecast regularly in color.*

1365. *The cigarette commercial.*

1366. *Her adopted daughter, Christina—who later poison-penned the bestseller* Mommie Dearest. *Christina appeared as Joann Kane on the show. Her mother filled in for her while she was hospitalized.*

1367. *The word* pregnant*—even though Lucy was obviously expecting and the birth of her son was the highlight of the season.*

1368. By what more popular name do TV viewers know fictional Old West hero Don Diego de la Vega?

1369. What is the name of the more famous actor-brother of TV's Steve Forrest, who appeared as Hondo in *S.W.A.T.* and as Ben Stivers on *Dallas*?

1370. What popular actor's father appeared as Clem, the deputy sheriff, on TV's long-running Western series *Bonanza*?

1371. How did TV's Emmy Awards get their name?

1372. What popular actor fell in love with a woman he saw in a Maxwell House commercial—and married her?

1373. What was the name of the baby born to Ted Baxter and his wife Georgette on the popular TV sitcom *The Mary Tyler Moore Show*?

1374. What burly character actor provided the voices of Charlie the Tuna and the Jolly Green Giant in television commercials?

1375. What famous entertainer appeared on educational TV in the 1970s as the milkman on *The Electric Company*?

1376. Whom did actor John Forsythe replace as multimillionaire Blake Carrington on TV's *Dynasty* 16 days after filming had begun?

1377. In the Abbott and Costello *Who's on First* routine, what was the pitcher's name?

1378. Why was the *Muppet Show* banned from TV in Saudi Arabia?

1379. Meredith Baxter-Birney played the mother, Elyse Keaton, on the hit TV sitcom *Family Ties*. On what sitcom did her mother play a mother?

1380. What popular actress was once a regular in the Peanut Gallery of TV's *The Howdy Doody Show*?

1368. *Zorro.*

1369. *Dana Andrews.*

1370. *Kurt Russell's father, Bing Russell.*

1371. *From the feminized form of "immy", a nickname for the image orthicon—the TV camera tube in wide use when the awards were first given in 1949.*

1372. *Michael Caine. His wife is Shakira Baksh.*

1373. *Mary Lou—for Mary Richards and Lou Grant, the show's two leading characters.*

1374. *Herschel Bernardi.*

1375. *Bill Cosby.*

1376. *George Peppard, who disagreed with the producers on how the part should be played. He ended up on* The A-Team.

1377. *Tomorrow.*

1378. *Because one of its stars was a pig.*

1379. *On* Hazel—*her mother, Whitney Blake, appeared as Dorothy Baxter.*

1380. *Sigourney Weaver—whose father, Pat Weaver, was president of NBC.*

1381. What actress-comedienne was a dancer until she was spotted in the chorus line of an Andy Griffith TV special in 1966 and became a regular on a popular TV show?

1382. How large a crew did *Star Trek's* Captain Kirk command?

1383. What size pumps did cross-dressing Corporal Max Klinger wear on the TV sitcom *M*A*S*H* ?

1384. What question did TV quiz show contestant Herb Stempel answer incorrectly to set the stage for Charles Van Doren's reign as champion on *Twenty-One* ?

1385. Why did CBS-TV display a blank screen for seven minutes following its coverage of the women's tennis semi-finals at the 1987 U.S. Open?

1386. What is the Canadian equivalent of the Emmy?

1387. What popular entertainer portrayed the first openly homosexual character on a nationally broadcast TV series?

1388. What long-running TV series was based on the 1963 movie *Spencer's Mountain*, starring Henry Fonda and Maureen O'Hara?

1389. What was the name of Walt Disney's family dog?

1390. Actors Jack Klugman and Tony Randall played roommates in the TV sitcom *The Odd Couple*. What actor was Klugman's real-life roommate in New York City before both became stars?

1391. What entertainer, upset at the high decibel level of the commercials shown during the TV premiere of one of her movies, called NBC and ordered an engineer to lower the volume?

1392. What famous entertainer first appeared onstage under the name Earl Knight?

1381. *Goldie Hawn. Her first acting role wa*s as a gossipy neighbor in the one-season comedy series *Good Morning, World in 1967. From there she went to "Rowan and Martin's Laugh-In" and stardom.*

1382. *Kird's crew numbered 430. His successor, Captain Picard, had 1,012—in crew and civilians—under his command.*

1383. *Size 10.*

1384. *As shown in the 1994 film* Quiz Show, *Stempel was asked to name the 1955 Oscar winner for Best Picture. Following instructions to muff the question, he answered* On the Waterfront *instead of* Marty.

1385. *The* CBS Evening News *was scheduled to go on, but anchorman Dan Rather walked out of the studio, disturbed that the long match between Steffi Graf and Lori McNeil had pushed back the start of the show.*

1386. *The Nelly.*

1387. *Billy Crystal, who played Jodie Dallas in the prime-time sitcom* Soap *from 1977 to 1981.*

1388. The Waltons, *which was on TV from 1970 to 1981, featuring Richard Thomas as John-Boy. James MacArthur played the role in the movie—where the character was known as Clay-Boy.*

1389. *Lady. She was a poodle, not a cocker spaniel like Lady in Disney's 1955 film* Lady and the Tramp.

1390. *Charles Bronson.*

1391. *Barbra Striesand, in February 1995. The film was* The Prince of Tides.

1392. *Alan King, who was born Irwin Kniberg. As a teen he formed a combo called Earl Knight and His Musical Knights, which performed at weddings and bar mitzvahs—with Kniberg/Knight/King on the drums.*

1393. What was Kramer's first name on the TV sitcom *Seinfeld?*

1394. To what lodge do Fred and Barney of TV's *The Flintstones* belong?

1395. On *The Mary Tyler Moore Show*, how did Chuckles the Clown die?

1396. How many times were Madonna's remarks bleeped during her first appearance on *Late Night with David Letterman*? How about her second appearance?

1397. Why was Merv Griffin dumped as a featured vocalist on Kate Smith's TV show in the early 1950s?

1398. How many fingers and toes do Fred Flintstone, Barney Rubble and their relatives have on the animated TV sitcom *The Flintstones*?

1399. What was the name of the adult son born to Mork on the TV sitcom *Mork and Mindy*, starring Robin Williams and Pam Dawber?

1400. In TV's Bonanza series, how did each of Ben Cartwright's three wives die?

1401. What message is written on the tombstone of Mel Blanc, the Man of 1,000 Voices—including those of Bugs Bunny, Porky Pig, Sylvester the Cat, Tweetee pie and Jack Benny's Maxwell?

1402. On what TV show did Jim Dial, the uptight senior anchor on TV's *Murphy Brown*, begin this television career?

1403. What moneymaking scheme did bus driver Ralph Kramden, of TV's *The Honeymooners,* claim would cut down on electricity bills?

1404. Mailman Cliff Claven on the TV sitcom *Cheers* hated two things about his job. One was a dog on his route, what was the other?

1393. *Cosmo. Kramer, Seinfeld's eccentric next-door neighbor, was played by Michael Richards.*

1394. *The Loyal Order of Water Buffaloes.*

1395. *He was dressed as a peanut for a parade—and was killed when an elephant tried to shell him.*

1396. *12 the first time; once the second time.*

1397. *His last name was the same as one of the chief competing brands of the show's sponsor—Esquire Shoe Polish.*

1398. *Four fingers on each hand; three toes on each foot.*

1399. *Mearth.*

1400. *Adam's mother, Elizabeth, died after childbirth; Inger, Hoss's mother, was killed by Indians; and Marie, Little Joe's mother, was thrown from a horse and died. (Elizabeth was played by Geraldine Brooks, Inger by Inga Stevens, and Marie by Felicia Farr.)*

1401. *"That's all folks," the sign-off line of all Porky Pig cartoons. Blanc is buried in the Hollywood Memorial Park Cemetery.*

1402. *A local kiddie show called "Poop Deck Pete and Cartoons Ahoy," on which he served as host.*

1403. *Glow-in-the-dark üwallpaper. Jackie Gleason, of course, played Kramden.*

1404. *The day the Sears catalog came out.*

1405. How did a salt shaker serve as a prop in early episodes of TV's original *Star Trek* series?

1406. What was The Fonz's full name on the TV sitcom *Happy Days*?

1407. In what city is the building whose exterior was used for Jerry Seinfeld's apartment house on the TV sitcom *Seinfeld*?

1408. Who demonstrated a chin lock that left comedian Richard Belzer bloodied and unconscious on his cable TV show *Hot Properties*?

1409. How many hours of television a day does the average person watch, according to Nielsen Media Research?

1410. What TV news anchor was once described in *Life* magazine as looking "eerily like a police composite made up of the best features of the more famous anchors"?

1411. What popular TV show is called *Rehov Sumsum* in Hebew and *Shaara Simsim* in Arabic?

1412. On TV game shows, what's a *Bambi*?

1413. What was the name of Porky Pig's father?

1414. In what TV sitcom town would you find Foley's Market, Floyd's Barbershop and the Bluebird Diner?

1415. Under federal law, how many minutes of advertising per hour are permitted during children's TV shows on weekdays? How about on weekends?

1416. What kind of feathers are used in making Big Bird's costume?

1417. What stands a in 1983 in the 20th Century-Fox parking lot in Hollywood?

1405. *It was used as Dr. McCoy's medical scanner.*

1406. *Arthur Herbert Fonzarelli. The part was played by Henry Winkler.*

1407. *Los Angeles—not New York City, which is the setting of the sitcom.*

1408. *Hulk Hogan.*

1409. *About 4 hours—or more precisely, 27 hours and 53 minutes a week.*

1410. *Peter Jennings, in 1983, when he replaced Frank Reynolds on ABC-TV.*

1411. Sesame Street.

1412. *A contestant who freezes in front of the camera—as deer do in the glare of headlights.*

1413. *Phineas Pig.*

1414. *Mayberry, North Carolina, the setting of The* Andy Griffith Show.

1415. *Weekdays, 10 minutes per hour; weekends, 10½. The time limits were set by the Children's Television Act of 1990.*

1416. *Turkey—dyed, of course.*

1417. *A Marriott Hotel. No marker was put on the site when the capsule—containing mementos from the show—was buried.*

1418. As a youngster, what popular TV show host won seven spelling-bee and four science-fair championships?

1419. What TV personality authored a cookbook entitled *Sweetie Pie*?

1420. What were the names of the seven castaways on TV's *Gilligan's Island*?

Bonus Trivia

1421. For many years, the globe on the *NBC Nightly News* spun in the wrong direction. On January 2, 1984, NBC finally set the world back in the proper direction.

1422. Before his comedian days, Bob Hope boxed, under the name of Packy East.

1423. On the night of October 31, 1938, Orson Welles and his Mercury Theatre troupe provided "the panic broadcast that shook the world," when they performed *The War of the Worlds* by H. G. Wells as a terrifying real-life episode.

1424. The doomed TV series, *Turn On*, hosted by Tim Conway, established a record on February 5, 1969: it was aired and canceled on the same day.

1425. Novelist Jacqueline Susann once hosted the TV game shows, *Your Surprise Store* and *Ring the Bell*.

1426. Actress Mary Tyler Moore made her television debut as Happy Hotpoint in a commercial. In an early acting role, she was Sam in *Richard Diamond, Private Detective*. Playing a woman at an answering service, you could only see her legs and hear her voice.

1418. *Alex Trebek, of* Jeopardy.

1419. *Diet guru Richard Simmons, in 1997.*

1420. *Gilligan; the Skipper (Jonas Grumby); the Professor (Roy Hinkley); Mary Ann (Summers); Ginger (Grant); Thurston Howell III and Lovey Howell.*

Business, Advertising & Inventions

Questions

1427. According to Raymond Loewy, the industrial designer who introduced streamlining to packaging, what are the two most perfectly designed containers ever made?

1428. What essential piece of office equipment did Johann Vaaler invent in 1900?

1429. What Scottish innkeeper's son invented the thermos bottle in 1892?

1430. Who started the first airship passenger service in 1910?

1431. Who invented the aerosol valve in 1949?

1432. Who invented the Johnny Mop, the disposable toilet bowl cleaner on a stick?

1433. What did Englishman Edwin Budding invent in 1830?

1434. On what wardrobe item did zipper inventor Whitcomb Judson use his first "clasp locker" in the late nineteenth century?

1435. Who invented charcoal briquettes?

1436. With what product did the term "brand name" originate?

Answers

1427. *The old Coca-Cola bottle and the egg.*

1428. *The paper clip.*

1429. *Sir James Dewar, who later invented cordite, the first smokeless explosive.*

1430. *Ferdinand, Graf von Zeppelin, who flew passengers 300 miles between Düsseldorf and Friedrichshafen.*

1431. *Richard Nixon's buddy, Robert Abplanalp.*

1432. *Dorothy Rodgers, wife of composer Richard Rodgers.*

1433. *The lawn mower, or as he described it: "machinery for the purpose of cropping or shearing the vegetable surface of lawns."*

1434. *A pair of boots.*

1435. *Henry Ford, to make use of scrap wood left over in the manufacture of the Model T.*

1436. *Whiskey. Producers branded their names on the barrels they shipped out.*

1437. What do the initials S.O.S. stand for in the brand of steel-wool soap pads marketed under that name?

1438. A certain Capt. Hanson Gregory is credited with a curious invention: It has neither weight nor density; it can be seen but not felt. What is it?

1439. What is the economic status of someone referred to by the acronym DINK?

1440. To a Wall Streeter, what is a shark repellent?

1441. For what is the NOW in NOW bank accounts an acronym?

1442. What is the derivation of the trademark name Velcro?

1443. In the world of economics, what does the acronym GATT represent?

1444. What do the letters represent in the over-the-counter stock market acronym NASDAQ?

1445. What did John Matthews do with all the scrap marble he bought from the St. Patrick's Cathedral construction site in New York City in 1879?

1446. What famous statesman sold 18 canvases to Hallmark cards for reproduction on greeting cards?

1447. How many years after the total assets of America's mutual funds hit $1 billion did it take for them to reach $1 trillion?

1448. What was megacorporation IBM known as before its name was changed in 1924?

1449. What did the George N. Pierce Co. manufacture before it began producing the Pierce-Arrow and other automobiles?

1450. What piece of modern office equipment was first developed in 1842 by Scottish clockmaker Alexander Bain?

1437. *Save Our Saucepans.*

1438. *The doughnut hole.*

1439. *Double income, no kids. The acronym is used to describe either half of a career couple.*

1440. *Any device or strategy used to ward off a hostile takeover.*

1441. *Negotiable order of withdrawal.*

1442. *It's from the words velvet and crochet, which means "hook" in French.*

1443. *General Agreement on Tariffs and Trade. GATT is an international organization, headquartered in Geneva and associated with the U. N. that was established in 1948 to reduce tariffs and other barriers to international trade.*

1444. *National Association of Securities Dealers Automated Quotations.*

1445. *Matthews, a manufacturer of soda fountain equipment, made 25 million gallons of soda water by dissolving the marble (calcium carbonate) with dilute acid.*

1446. *Winston Churchill, in 1950. He was paid an undisclosed sum, which he donated to Churchill College at Cambridge.*

1447. *45 years. They hit $1 billion in 1945, $1 trillion in 1990.*

1448. *C-T-R, for Computing-Tabulating-Recording Company.*

1449. *Bird cages.*

1450. *The facsimile machine—better known as the fax. Bain was granted a patent in 1843 for his electro-chemical duplicating telegraph system, which was capable of transmitting crude images short distances.*

1451. What unusual use did non-drinker Andy Warhol make of Absolut Vodka, the Swedish liquor for which he and other artists created a series of innovative print ads?

1452. What was the last 12-cylinder car produced in the United States?

1453. For whom was the Mercedes automobile named?

1454. What mother's aid did Marion Donovan patent in 1951?

1455. Why are the annual awards given for the best billboards called Obies by the Outdoor Advertising Association of American Marketing?

1456. What phrase is said to be the most oft-printed warning in the history of the printed word?

1457. What famous children's book author created an imaginative ad campaign for an insect spray called Flit?

1458. Where did Robert Fulton launch his first steamboat?

1459. Prior to 1953, what product was advertised with the slogan, "Just what the doctor ordered"?

1460. An illustration of what TV and movie "celebrity" appeared on the teal-blue bottle of a unisex fragrance called Amphibia in 1995?

1461. What American industry introduced the 5-day, 40-hour work week?

1462. What famous circus performer introduced the flying trapeze?

1463. What was the name of the car that followed Ford's 1932 Model B, the last in the automaker's series of cars known by letter designations?

1464. Who is second only to Thomas Edison in the number of U.S. patents granted for inventions?

1451. He claimed he used it as perfume.

1452. The 1948 Lincoln Continental.

1453. Mercedes Daimler, the daughter of German automaker Gottlieb Daimler.

1454. The disposable diaper.

1455. They're named after the ancient obelisks of Egypt, which are considered by the association to be the precursors of today's outdoor advertising.

1456. "Close Cover Before Striking"—the words of caution that appear on most matchbooks.

1457. Dr. Seuss, whose real name was Theodor Seuss Geisel. He worked on the ad campaign—which featured his trademark bugs—for 17 years.

1458. In Paris, on the Seine, in 1803. It sank. But Fulton made history four years later when his steamboat Clermont traveled the Hudson River from New York City to Albany.

1459. L & M cigarettes.

1460. Kermit the Frog. The scent "pour homme, femme, et frog" was marketed by Jim Henson Productions, creator of the Muppets.

1461. The steel industry, in 1923. Henry Ford adopted it in 1926.

1462. French aerialist Jules Leotard, who also invented the tights we call leotards.

1463. The Model 18—the 8 indicated it had an eight-cylinder engine; the 1 that it was Ford's first V-8.

1464. Edwin Land, inventor of the Polaroid camera.

1465. What state was the home of the U.S. auto industry before World War I and the rise of Michigan?

1466. How much did the first three minutes of a call cost when commercial telephone service was introduced between New York and London in 1927?

1467. What did a horse named Nita beat in a famous race in 1830?

1468. What is the blue crayon in Crayola's box Magic Scents crayons designed to smell like?

1469. What was Henry Ford's first mass-produced car?

1470. Who invented the coffee filter?

1471. What were the first products marketed in aerosol containers?

1472. What fast-food chain founded in 1964 was named for brothers Forrest and LeRoy Raffel?

1473. On the New York Stock Exchange, what is the ticker-tape symbol for the Anheuser-Busch company?

1474. Frank W. Woolworth started selling 5-cent goods in 1878 and added 10-cent items in 1880. When did he begin offering 20-cent items?

1475. What toy did American author John Dos Passos invent and have patented in 1959?

1476. What was produced when sewing machines were first set up in a French factory in 1841?

1477. What was Lifebuoy soap called when it was first introduced in 1897?

1478. In the 1925 edition of the Encyclopaedia Britannica, who was credited with writing the article on mass production?

1465. *Indiana, where there were once hundreds of automakers. The last, Studebaker, shut down its operations in 1963. The Indianapolis 500 auto race, held annually on Memorial Day weekend, dates back to 1911, when Indianapolis was an auto-manufacturing center.*

1466. *$75.*

1467. *Tom Thumb, the first locomotive built in America. Nita, a part-Mustang gray mare, outran the iron horse after its engine broke down.*

1468. *A new car. It was initially given a blueberry aroma, but Crayola changed all its scents after parents suggested that kids would be less likely to eat crayons that were not food-scented. The sepia crayon, formerly chocolate-scented, now smells like dirt; white went from coconut to baby powder; black, from licorice to leather; pink, from bubblegum to shampoo.*

1469. *The Model N—which sold for $500 in 1906.*

1470. *Melitta Bentz, in Germany in 1908. To improve the quality of coffee for her family, she pierced holes in a tin container, put a circular piece of absorbent paper in the bottom of it and put her creation over a coffee pot.*

1471. *Insecticides. The aerosol dispenser was developed and patented by American chemist Lyle D. Goodhue in 1941.*

1472. *Arby's. The name stands for RB—Raffel Brothers.*

1473. *BUD. The company manufactures Budweiser beer.*

1474. *In 1932.*

1475. *A "toy pistol that blows soap bubbles," which he coinvented with three friends. They designed it in Dos Passos's kitchen for his daughter, Lucy, when she was six years old.*

1476. *Uniforms for the French army. Rioting tailors—fearing they'd be put out of work—broke into the factory and destroyed the machines.*

1477. *Lifebuoy soap.*

1478. *Henry Ford, although the entry was actually written by the Ford Motor Company's official spokesman, William Cameron.*

1479. How often did the spark plugs in the Model T Ford have to be cleaned—in miles driven?

1480. In the world of business, what is the meaning of the acronym IPO?

1481. What household appliance designed for Sears, Roebuck and Company by visionary engineer Raymond Loewy won first prize at the Paris International Exposition in 1937?

1482. For what product was the term twofers first used?

1483. Who invented the first hideaway bed ever patented in the United States?

1484. What common plastic product do we owe to Nathaniel C. Wyeth—son of artist N.C. Wyeth, brother of artists Andrew, Carolyn and Henriette Wyeth, and uncle of artist Jamie Wyeth?

1485. What role did Mrs. P.F.E. Albee of Winchester, New Hampshire—widow of a U.S. senator—play in American sales history?

1486. What was the only product ever promoted by Elvis Presley in a television commercial?

1487. How did secure, relatively high-yielding stocks get to be called blue chips?

1488. What century-old product was originally promoted with the advertising slogan "You press the button—we do the rest"?

1489. What company is both the oldest corporate enterprise still in existence and the largest corporate landowner in history?

1490. What product was first introduced in 1906 as Blibber-Blubber?

1491. What popular baby device was inspired by something former Peace Corps member Anne Moore saw while serving in West Africa?

1479. *Every 200 miles.*

1480. *Initial public offering—it's a company's first sale of stock to the public.*

1481. *The refrigerator.*

1482. *Cigars. The term was used as early as 1892 for two-for-a-nickel cigars. It's been used for selling two-for-the-price-of-one theater tickets since 1948.*

1483. *Thomas Jefferson. The bed was hoisted and secured to the ceiling when it wasn't in use.*

1484. *The now-ubiquitous plastic soda bottle. He developed it as an engineer for the DuPont Company.*

1485. *She was the first Avon lady—although the company she worked for before the turn of the century was not yet called Avon. Mrs. Albee sold Little Dot Perfume Sets door-to-door for Avon founder David McConnell and set up a door-to-door sales network for him by recruiting and training other women.*

1486. *Donuts—the commercial, for Southern Made Donuts, was aired in 1954.*

1487. *The term was taken from the game of poker, where blue chips are more valuable than white or red chips.*

1488. *The Kodak camera. The slogan was first used in 1888.*

1489. *The Hudson Bay Company. Founded in 1670, its realm once covered nearly 3 million square miles. The company now operates Canada's largest department store chain.*

1490. *Bubblegum. Developed and marketed by the Frank H. Fleer Corporation, it was soon abandoned because it was too sticky and brittle. In the 1920s the company came up with a winning formula, which it marketed under the name Dubble Bubble.*

1491. *The strap-on baby pouch known as the Snugli. Moore made the first one for herself when she had a baby shortly after returning to the United States from Africa in 1964.*

1492. Joan Collins, Elizabeth Taylor and Cher all have marketed perfumes. Can you name their scents?

1493. What is the maximum number of individual memberships—or seats—permitted on the New York Stock Exchange?

1494. In 1985 officials of a New York supermarket chain advertised for "part-time career associate scanning professionals." What job position were they trying to fill?

1495. In 1985 a Denver hotel published an ad offering guests a "Free Hotel Room" in large type. What was the catch in the fine print below?

1496. What hand-rolled device did Marvin Chester Stone of Washington, D.C., patent in 1888? Hint: although no longer hand rolled, it's still very much on the scene today.

1497. How many miles per gallon did the 22-horsepower, 4-cylinder Model T Ford get when it was introduced in 1908?

1498. What food industry innovator invented a recoilless harpoon for whaling and a fast process for converting sugar cane waste into paper pulp?

1499. Who invented the whistle for the railroad train?

1500. How many exposures were there on the roll of film sold with Kodak's first box camera in 1888?

1501. What was the source of billionaire recluse Howard Hughes' original fortune?

1502. The makers of Ivory soap claim their product is 99 and $^{44}/_{100}$ percent pure. What are the "impurities" in the remaining $^{56}/_{100}$ percent?

1503. In 1851, how much money did newspaper publisher Horace Greeley recommend that the average workingman set aside weekly for rent if he were supporting a family of five?

1504. What was the price of a gross of metal suspender buttons in the 1908 Sears, Roebuck and Co. catalog?

1492. Collins, *"Spectacular"*; Taylor, *"Passion"*; and Cher, *"Uninhibited."*

1493. 1,366. The number is set in the exchange's constitution.

1494. Checkout clerk.

1495. *"Parking $55.00 / night (Parking is mandatory)."*

1496. The wax paper drinking straw.

1497. It got between 25 and 30 miles per gallon.

1498. Frozen food king Clarence Birdseye.

1499. George Washington Whistler—father of artist James Abbott McNeill Whistler.

1500. One hundred. The price of camera and film together was $25.

1501. His father's invention of an oil drill bit capable of boring through subterranean rock.

1502. Uncombined alkali, carbonates and mineral matter. Fatty acids and alkali make up the *"pure"* part of the soap.

1503. $3.

1504. Nine cents.

1505. What was the dowry of Consuelo Vanderbilt, daughter of multimillionaire William Henry Vanderbilt, when she married the Duke of Marlborough in 1895?

1506. To celebrate its one-hundredth anniversary in 1860, what did the Lorillard Company put at random in packages of its Century brand of tobacco?

1507. Who invented flexible greasepaint—the first natural-looking cosmetic used in the movies?

1508. In what year was the first American car sold for export—and where was it shipped?

1509. What famous Christmas legend did a Montgomery Ward advertising man create as part of his job?

1510. In 1933, how much did a night's stay in a double room cost at the famous Waldorf-Astoria Hotel in New York City?

1511. What was the first consumer product purchased on the installment plan?

1512. What enduring advertising symbol was created by a Virginia schoolboy as part of a drawing competition held in 1916?

1513. What was plastic first used for in America?

1514. In 1937, an American company built the very first auto-airplane combination. What was it called?

1515. When Gillette first marketed its safety razor at the turn of the century, it sold 20 blades for $1. How much did the razor handle cost?

1516. What was the name of the first major deodorant company in the Untied States?

1517. Why was Sam Colt—inventor of the six-shooter—expelled from school at the age of 16?

1518. Who wrote the Ford Motor Co., "While I still have got breath in my lungs, I will tell you what a dandy car you make"?

1505. *The duke received $2.5 million in railroad stock.*

1506. *$100 bills.*

1507. *Russian-born makeup expert Max Factor.*

1508. *In 1893. An Olds gasoline steam carriage was shipped to Bombay, India, for use by the branch office of a British patent medicine company. It's price: $400.*

1509. *Rudolph, the Red-Nosed Reindeer. Adman Robert May first wrote of the now famous reindeer in a pamphlet distributed to children by store Santas in 1939.*

1510. *In 1933, a double cost $9; a single, $6; a suite, $20.*

1511. *A Singer sewing machine, in 1856. It was purchased by Margaret Hellmuth of New York for $50 down, with the remaining $100 paid in six monthly installments. Later customers were able to buy machines for $5 down and payments of $3 a month.*

1512. *Mr. Peanut—the trademark of Planters Peanuts. Schoolboy Antonio Gentile of Suffolk, Virginia, received $5 for his winning entry.*

1513. *Billiard balls. Brothers Isaiah and John Wesley Hyatt developed celluloid in 1869 while competing for a $10,000 prize offered by a company looking for a substitute for ivory in billiard balls.*

1514. *The Arrowbile.*

1515. *$5.*

1516. *Odorono—its magazine ad mentioning underarm odor in 1919 led hundreds of offended women to cancel their subscriptions to the "Ladies' Home Journal."*

1517. *For experimenting with explosives.*

1518. *Killer Clyde Barrow, who added, "I have drove Fords exclusively when I could get away with one." Lawmen killed him during an ambush—in the last Ford he stole.*

1519. What actress was billed as "Miss Deepfreeze" when she toured the country demonstrating refrigerators?

1520. On a February afternoon in 1959, the TV game show "Haggis Baggis" was interrupted with the announcement, "Ladies and gentlemen, Mrs. Franklin D. Roosevelt." What followed?

1521. How many shades of blue are there in the 64-crayon box sold by Crayola?

1522. "She kissed the hairbrush by mistake. She thought it was her husband Jake." What is the origin of this rhyme?

1523. All automaker Henry Ford's cars were black until 1925, when he introduced two new colors. What were they?

1524. One hundred years ago today Griswold "Grizzy" Lorillard wore the first tailless dinner coat for men in the U.S. Where did he wear it and what did it come to be called?

1525. How did the term "the 400" come to mean the wealthiest and most fashionable members of society in 1892?

1526. What are the street lights in Hershey, Pennsylvania designed to look like?

1527. What U.S. department store was the first to install electric lighting?

1528. What was sold in the Burpee mail-order catalog when it was introduced by 17-year-old Washington Atlee Burpee in 1876?

1529. What product used Bobby Darin's 1958 hit song "Splish Splash" in its commercials?

1530. What American innovation did Walter Scott of Providence, Rhode Island, introduce in a converted horse-drawn freight wagon in 1872?

1531. What famous American, in a bid to show the commercial potential of the soybean, appeared at a convention in 1939 outfitted in clothes made entirely from that very versatile vegetable?

1519. *Kim Novak.*

1520. *A commercial for Good Luck Margarine delivered by the former First Lady.*

1521. *Eleven: aquamarine, blue, cadet blue, cornflower, green blue, midnight blue, navy blue, periwinkle, sky blue, turquoise blue, and violet blue. (Not counted: blue gray, blue green, and blue violet.)*

1522. *Burma Shave roadside jingle, 1940.*

1523. *Green and maroon.*

1524. *He wore it to New York City's exclusive Tuxedo Park Club, from which it took its name—tuxedo.*

1525. *It was the number of people Mrs. William Astor's ballroom could accommodate.*

1526. *Foil-wrapped Hershey's chocolate kisses.*

1527. *Wanamaker's of Philadelphia, in 1878.*

1528. *Chickens. Burpee soon added chicken feed and then the vegetable and flower seeds the catalog has long been famous for.*

1529. *Drano.*

1530. *The diner.*

1531. *Henry Ford. His shoes were the only part of his wardrobe not made from soybeans.*

1532. The first paid radio commercial ever aired promoted a cooperative apartment house in New York City in 1922. The ad cost $100. How long did it last?

1533. What legendary American folk hero was popularized in pamphlets written and illustrated by adman W. B. Laughead in the early twentieth century?

1534. Where did Uniroyal get the steel frame for the 80-foot-tall tire that stands near Detroit's Edsel Ford Freeway?

1535. What was unusual about the Sexto-Auto manufactured by the Reeves Manufacturing Company of Columbus, Indiana, in 1912?

1536. The Ford Motor Company manufactured one million cars for the first time in 1922. In what year did it hit the two-million mark?

1537. What were Kleenex tissues marketed as when they were first introduced in 1924?

1538. What did the Jacuzzi brothers manufacture when they first opened up shop in 1915—long before their grandchildren gave the bathtub business a whirl?

1539. What product was the first to use animated characters in its television commercials?

1540. Woolworth's 5-and-10-cent store chain was founded in 1879. For how long did 10 cents remain its top price?

1541. How many buildings are there in the landmark Rockefeller Center complex in New York City?

1542. What American city bills itself as the home of the first push-button car radio, the first canned tomato juice, the first mechanical corn picker and the first commercially built car?

1543. Who was the only American to have two cars named after him?

1544. What is the full name of Barbie, the doll?

1532. *10 minutes.*

1533. Giant lumberjack Paul Bunyan. The pamphlets were for the Red River Lumber Company of Minnesota.

1534. It was the Ferris wheel at the 1964 New York World's Fair.

1535. It had six wheels—two in front and four in the rear. The same company previously had manufactured the eight-wheel Octo-Auto.

1536. In 1923.

1537. A cold-cream remover.

1538. Farm pumps.

1539. Ajax cleanser. The Ajax pixies used to tell us, "You'll stop paying the elbow tax when you start cleaning with Ajax."

1540. For 53 years, until 1932—but only in its U.S. stores east of the Missouri River. Prices west of the Missouri and in Canada were higher because of greater freight costs.

1541. 19.

1542. Kokomo, Indiana, which calls itself the "city of firsts."

1543. Ransom E. Olds—who gave us the Oldsmobile and the long-discontinued Reo, which was produced from 1904 to 1936 and got its name from its manufacturer's initials.

1544. Barbara Millicent Roberts.

1545. What famous American showman had his obituary published before his death?

1546. What is the largest American corporation named for an owner's daughter?

1547. Which were the only four of the contiguous 48 states that never had rhyming Burma-Shave signs on their highways?

1548. What was the longest flight ever made by aviation pioneer Wilbur Wright?

1549. What American bank adopted its cable address as its official name?

1550. What did the first vending machines in the United States dispense?

1551. How tall is the Barbie doll?

1552. Largelamb, an anagram pseudonym of a famous inventor, was one of the founders of "National Geographic" magazine. Who was he?

1553. How was Coca-Cola originally billed when it appeared on the market in 1886?

1554. Where does the Barbie Doll get its name?

1555. Where did Levi Strauss come from, and what did his blue jeans first sell for in 1850?

1556. In 1937, the grocery business was revolutionized by Sylvan Goldman's simple invention. What was it?

1557. What is the name of the camel on the Camel cigarettes pack?

1558. What was the original name of the Bank of America?

1559. What children's product does Binney and Smith manufacture?

1545. *P.T. Barnum.*

1546. *The Sara Lee Corp. It's named for the daughter of Chicago bakery owner Charles Lubin, who first named a cheesecake after his daughter and then, in 1951, his company, which was originally known as the Kitchens of Sara Lee.*

1547. *Arizona, Massachusetts, Nevada and New Mexico.*

1548. *77 miles. He made the flight in 1908 (five years after Kitty Hawk) from Camp d'Auvours, France, setting a world record and winning the Michelin Prize of 20,000 francs.*

1549. *Citibank, which originally was the City Bank of New York.*

1550. *Chewing gum. The machines were installed on New York City train platforms in 1888.*

1551. *11½ inches.*

1552. *Alexander Graham Bell.*

1553. *As an "Esteemed Brain Tonic and Intellectual Beverage."*

1554. *It was named after Barbara Handler, the daughter of its designer, Ruth Handler.*

1555. *He came from Bavaria, and the original price was $13.50.*

1556. *The shopping cart.*

1557. *Old Joe.*

1558. *The Bank of Italy.*

1559. *Crayola Crayons.*

1560. What cigarette company first used a woman in its advertisements, and what was the headline?

1561. What do J.C. Penney's initials stand for?

1562. Where did the soft drink Dr. Pepper get its name?

1563. What western hero was featured in comic book advertisements for Daisy air rifles?

1564. What was the name of multimillionaire fur trader John Jacob Astor's hometown in Germany?

1565. What was the original source of the Hearst publishing family's fortune?

1566. How much did supermarket "coupon queen" Susan Samtur pay for $130 in groceries when she went shopping with a TV consumer reporter in 1978?

1567. What did eccentric Texas businessman Stanley Marsh have planted in an Amarillo cornfield?

1568. Who sent the next message after the historic words "What hath God wrought" were transmitted over Samuel F. B. Morse's telegraph in 1844?

1569. What husband did two of the richest women in the world—five-and-dime heiress Barbara Hutton and tobacco heiress Doris Duke—have in common?

1570. How long did it take Robert Fulton's steamboat, the Clermont, to make its historic 150-mile maiden voyage up the Hudson River from New York City to Albany in 1807?

1571. What famous American inventor ran twice for mayor of New York City—in 1836 and 1841—and lost both times?

1572. Who uttered the famous words, "Mr. Watson, come here. I want you"?

1573. In how many articles did the word "recession" appear in *The Wall Street Journal* in 1990?

1560. Chesterfield, with the caption, "Blow some my way."

1561. James Cash.

1562. Chemist Charles Alderton named his drink after the father of a girl he was dating, Dr. Charles Kenneth Pepper.

1563. Red Ryder.

1564. Waldorf—which explains both halves of the name of the Waldorf-Astoria Hotel.

1565. Gold mining. George Hearst struck it rich in Nevada in 1859, nine years after crossing the plains from Missouri to join the California gold rush.

1566. Only $7 in cash—coupons covered the rest.

1567. Ten Cadillacs—half-buried, nose-down, each slanted toward California at the same angle as one side of the Great Pyramid in Egypt. Marsh dubbed the sculpture "The Great American Dream."

1568. Dolly Madison. The words: "Message from Mrs. Madison. She sends her love to Mrs. Wethered." Mrs. Wethered was a friend of the 76-year-old former First Lady.

1569. Dominican playboy-diplomat Porfirio Rubirosa. He was the fifth of Hutton's seven husbands; the second of Duke's two.

1570. 32 hours.

1571. Samuel F. B. Morse.

1572. Alexander Graham Bell—not Sherlock Holmes. This was the first complete sentence heard over the newly invented telephone. Blurted out by Bell on March 10, 1876, when he spilled acid on his trousers, the words were picked up by his assistant, Thomas A. Watson, at the other end of the line.

1573. 1,583, by the paper's own count.

1574. What fuel did Stuart Perry of New York City use in the engine he invented in 1844—the very first gasoline engine patented in the United States?

1575. The title of what film classic was used in the *Variety* headline reporting the stock market crash of October 29, 1987—a day now known as Black Monday?

1576. What famous American actress was the first woman to run a U.S. airline?

1577. The Dow Jones average closed at over 3,000 for the first time in 1991. When did it first top 2,000? How about 1,000?

1578. What was the horsepower of the four-cylinder engine in the Flyer, the plane piloted by Orville Wright in his historic flight on December 17, 1903?

1579. In 1884, what enterprising American helped squelch doubts about the stability of the Brooklyn Bridge—and how?

1580. Who invented rubber dental plates in 1855?

1581. Who kept Thomas Edison's dying breath in a bottle?

1582. What automobile made the first U.S. cross-country journey in 1903?

1583. In March 1981 students at an Allentown, Pennsylvania high school got into trouble for a money-making extracurricular venture. What was it?

1584. What colonial American devised the first wet suit for divers as well as a primitive version of today's flippers?

1585. In what city was the world's first electric traffic light installed 75 years ago?

1586. By how much did "steel-driving man" John Henry best a steam drill in the legendary face-off?

1587. When was power steering first offered in an automobile?

1574. *Turpentine.*

1575. Gone With the Wind. *The headline was* Bull Market Gone With the Wind.

1576. *Maureen O'Hara. From 1978 to 1981, she was president of 27-plane Antilles Air Boats, an airline based in the Virgin Islands that had been operated by her pilot husband until his death.*

1577. *It passed 2,000 in 1987; 1,000 in 1972.*

1578. *12 horsepower.*

1579. *P. T Barnum—he led a herd of twenty-one elephants over it.*

1580. *Charles Goodyear, who accidentally discovered how to vulcanize rubber in 1839 when he dropped a mixture of rubber and sulfur on a hot stove.*

1581. *Henry Ford. It's now on display at the Ford Museum in Greenfield Village, Michigan.*

1582. *A chauffeur-driven 1903 Winton touring car. It left San Francisco on May 23, 1903 and arrived in New York City on July 26.*

1583. *They were manufacturing counterfeit $1 and $5 bills on the school's offset printing press.*

1584. *Benjamin Franklin.*

1585. *In Cleveland, Ohio—at the intersection of Euclid Avenue and East 105th Street.*

1586. *By 5 feet—John Henry drove his 20-pound hammer 14 feet while the steam drill went only 9.*

1587. *In 1895, in the Sweany Steam Carriage manufactured by the C. S. Caffre Company. The first mass-produced gas-powered automobiles with power steering were marketed by Chrysler and Buick in 1951.*

1588. Where did pioneering American newspaperwoman Elizabeth Cochrane get her pseudonym Nellie Bly, the name she made famous when she circled the globe faster than Phileas Fogg, hero of *Around the World in 80 Days* ?

1589. Who issued the first mail-order catalog in the United States?

1590. During his most creative years, how often did Thomas Edison believe he should come up with a new invention?

1591. Who was aviatrix Amelia Earhart's wealthy husband?

1592. What nicknames did inventor Thomas A. Edison give to his first two children, Marion and Thomas Jr.?

1593. What stock exchange was the first in the United States to be completely computerized, with all transactions handled without benefit of a physical trading floor?

1594. When Charles Lindbergh made his pioneering transatlantic flight on May 20-21, 1927, he covered 3,610 miles in 33½ hours. How long did it take Amelia Earhart to make her solo crossing exactly five years later?

1595. In 1989, who became the first foreign monarch to patent an invention in the United States?

1596. What was the average yearly salary of an American public school teacher at the turn of the century?

1597. What would have been Charles Lindbergh's name if his paternal grandfather hadn't changed it when he fled to the United States to escape being jailed in Sweden for his political beliefs?

1598. In what year was the first mutual fund introduced in the United States?

1599. Why was there a big uproar about the 12-foot-high statue honoring steelworkers that was unveiled at a Pittsburgh arts festival in 1990?

1600. How much did Levi Strauss get for his first pair of jeans in 1850?

1588. From a Stephen Foster song called "Nellie Bly."

1589. Benjamin Franklin, in 1744. He was selling books.

1590. In his own words: "A minor invention every 10 days and a big thing every 6 months or so."

1591. Publisher G. P. Putnam.

1592. Dot and Dash—in honor of telegraphy. Edison married twice and had six children.

1593. The Cincinnati Stock Exchange (CSE), in 1978.

1594. Just under 15 hours—14 hours and 56 minutes, to be exact. But Earhart's crossing covered fewer miles (2,026).

1595. King Hassan II of Morocco, who was issued patent No. 4,805,631 for an invention that combines videotape and an electrocardiogram to study heart performance.

1596. $325.

1597. Charles Mannson.

1598. In 1924—it was the Massachusetts Investors Trust and had no set minimum investment.

1599. It wasn't made of steel. Sculptor Luis Jimenez used fiberglass, claiming that "it holds up better than steel."

1600. Six dollars—in gold dust.

1601. What was financier J. P. Morgan's reply when a journalist asked, "Mr. Morgan, will the market go up or down"?

1602. Who was the first person to officially walk across the Brooklyn Bridge when it opened on May 24, 1883?

1603. What famous American roasted a turkey on a rotating electric spit—in 1749?

1604. How did Robert S. Brookings amass the fortune that enabled him to found and underwrite the work of the Brookings Institution, the highly respected Washington, D.C., think tank?

1605. In what year did the New York Stock Exchange have its first million-share trading day?

1606. What was the nickname of the Lockheed Electra in which Amelia Earhart was flying when she disappeared over the Pacific in 1937?

1607. Which record-setting aviation mechanic was the godfather of Robert Cummings, the actor?

1608. How fast—in miles per hour—did the Wright brothers' Model A biplane fly in test flights conducted for the U.S. Army in 1909?

1609. What was Charles Lindbergh's average speed on his historic, 3,610-mile, nonstop flight across the Atlantic in 1927?

1610. When the first home TV set was demonstrated in 1928, what was the size of the screen?

1611. What life-saving device did Philip Drinker and Louis Agassiz Shaw build with two vacuum cleaners at Harvard University in 1927?

1612. What product did Armenian-born Sarkis Colombosian introduce to the United States in 1929?

1613. Where did American drivers buy gasoline for their automobiles before 1912, when the first gasoline stations were opened?

1601. "*Yes.*"

1602. President Chester A. Arthur.

1603. Benjamin Franklin, in a cooking experiment he conducted on the banks of the Schuylkill River in Philadelphia.

1604. He manufactured clothespins.

1605. 1886.

1606. The Flying Laboratory.

1607. Orville Wright.

1608. 42 mph. The price the army paid for the plane was based on its speed in the test flight. The base price was $25,000 plus a 10 percent bonus for every mile per hour over 40—so the Wright brothers were paid $30,000.

1609. About 108 mph.

1610. 3 inches by 4 inches.

1611. The first iron lung. Iron lungs are known as Drinker respirators.

1612. Yogurt. Colombosian produced it at his Colombo dairy in Methuen, Massachusetts.

1613. From coal merchants, lumberyards and hardware stores.

1614. What company's stock has been included in the Dow Jones Transportation Average ever since the index was created more than a century ago?

1615. What was the first Japanese car imported to the United States?

1616. What significant event occurred at 5 Exeter Place in Boston, in 1876?

1617. There were 15,700,003 of them manufactured, all in black. What were they?

1618. Who established what is believed to be America's first department store?

1619. Who designed the original 1936 Volkswagen?

1620. Asa Griggs Candler purchased the formula for Coca-Cola from fellow pharmacist John Pemberton for $2,300 in 1887. How much did Candler's sons get when they sold out in 1916?

1621. What singing commercial became a Top 10 hit in 1972?

1622. How much did Eastman Kodak's Brownie camera cost when it was introduced in 1900?

1623. How did denim, the fabric used for blue jeans, get its name?

1624. What department-store chain marketed its own car in 1952 and 1953?

1625. What modern convenience owes its discovery to a melted Hershey bar in scientist Percy LeBaron Spencer's pocket?

1626. Why did Proctor and Gamble decide to drop its century-old moon and stars trademark from its packaging in 1985?

1627. Which was the first well-known auto company to install steering wheels in its cars?

1628. The U.S. record for the greatest number of patented inventions is 1,093. Who holds it?

1614. *Union Pacific's.*

1615. *The Datsun, in 1958. A total of 83 were sold in the U.S. that year.*

1616. *The first telephone conversation. On March 10, Alexander Graham Bell spoke the first sentence transmitted directly over wire when he yelled to his assistant in another room, "Mr. Watson, come here; I want you."*

1617. *Model T Ford's.*

1618. *Mormon leader Brigham Young, in 1868. His Zion's Co-operative Mercantile Institution still exists in Salt Lake City, Utah, where it is known as ZCMI.*

1619. *Ferdinand Porsche, who later went on to build sports cars bearing his name.*

1620. *They were paid $25 million.*

1621. *The New Seekers' "I'd Love to Teach the World to Sing," which originated as a Coca-Cola ad.*

1622. *Just $1.*

1623. *From the city in which it originated—Nimes, France. It's a shortened version of serge de Nimes, or serge of Nimes.*

1624. *Sears, Roebuck & Company. The car, the Allstate, was built by the Kaiser-Frazer Corporation.*

1625. *The microwave oven. The Raytheon Company, where he worked, developed the oven after Spencer saw what a microwave signal had done to the chocolate.*

1626. *There was a rumor circulating nationwide that the logo—showing a man in the moon and 13 stars—was the mark of the devil.*

1627. *Packard. In 1900 it replaced the tiller with a steering wheel, mounting it on the right side.*

1628. *Thomas Alva Edison.*

1629. What was the inspiration for Campbell's red-and-white soup can?

1630. What is believed to be the first coin-operated machine ever designed?

1631. What famous American appeared in a 1947 soft-drink advertisement boasting, "My wife is a pretty smart Jane"?

1632. How long did Thomas Alva Edison's first incandescent lightbulb burn when he tested it in 1879?

1633. Why were featherless chickens—developed by avian scientists in 1975—a commercial failure?

1634. What did David Dunbar Buick build before he began manufacturing automobiles in 1901?

1635. What popular TV star appeared in Salem cigarette commercials for four years—with his green eyes colored blue?

1636. What was the original name of the Xerox Corporation?

1637. What did Christopher Cockerell invent with his wife's vacuum cleaner in 1950?

1638. What special payment arrangement was made in 1973 when Pepsi-Cola became the first American company to market a consumer product in Russia?

1639. *Garbo Talks* was the famous ad that promoted the reclusive screen star's first talkie, *Anna Christie*. What film did the later *Garbo Laughs* ad boost?

1640. What letter designations did Henry Ford use for his cars before he introduced the Model T in 1909?

1641. What was the name of the plane in which Orville Wright made his historic 12-second flight 85 years ago today?

1642. What was the Pennsylvania Fireplace?

1629. *The Cornell University football team uniform. Campbell's company treasurer was inspired by the brilliant Cornell colors when he attended a Penn-Cornell football game on Thanksgiving Day in 1898.*

1630. *A holy-water dispenser that required a five-drachma piece to operate. It was the brainchild of the Greek scientist Hero in the first century A.D.*

1631. *Ronald Reagan. The magazine ad, for Royal Crown Cola, also featured his former wife, actress Jane Wyman.*

1632. *Forty hours.*

1633. *It cost more to heat their houses than to defeather them.*

1634. *Bathtubs and other plumbing fixtures.*

1635. *Tom ("Magnum PI") Selleck.*

1636. *The Haloid Company.*

1637. *The Hovercraft. He created his air-cushion boat by reversing the vacuum's blower so it blew air out instead of sucking it in.*

1638. *Pepsi accepted payment in Stolichnaya vodka.*

1639. *"Ninotchka."*

1640. *Models A, B, C, F, K, N, R and S. He built nearly 29,000 of them between 1903 and 1909.*

1641. *Flyer I—now popularly known as Kitty Hawk I, after its North Carolina takeoff site.*

1642. *The original name of the Franklin stove, invented by Benjamin Franklin.*

1643. On October 21, 1929, inventor Thomas Edison returned to his laboratory to reenact the moment he created the incandescent lightbulb. Where was he?

1644. What did London blacksmith Charles Moncke invent?

1645. From what crop did agricultural genius George Washington Carver produce tapioca, ink, synthetic rubber and postage stamp mucilage?

1646. What American engineer supervised construction of a rail link between Moscow and St. Petersburg for Russia's Czar Nicholas I in 1842?

1647. What startling creation did French engineer-designer Louis Reard unveil in June 1946?

1648. Who invented the power lawn mower?

1649. Who invented waxed paper, an electric pen and a process that turned goldenrod plants into synthetic rubber?

1650. When was the rocket first invented?

1651. When searching for a manufacturing hub, what city had the Ford Company originally favored as center of its operations?

1652. What America merchandising pioneer used to shoplift from his own stores to check the alertness of his employees?

1653. What did Joseph C. Gayetty invent in 1857?

1654. How much did the first ballpoint pens cost when they were offered for sale in 1945?

1655. What was the Schwimmwagen?

1656. How much did the first Rolls-Royce sell for when the opulent auto was first marketed in 1906?

1643. *In Dearborn, Michigan's Greenfield Park—where his Menlo Park, New Jersey, lab had been reassembled, stick by stick, by Henry Ford.*

1644. *The monkey wrench, which was originally called Moncke's wrench.*

1645. *The sweet potato.*

1646. *Artist James Abbot McNeill Whistler's father, George Washington Whistler. The famous portrait of his wife hangs in the Musée d'Dorsay in Paris.*

1647. *The bikini—which he named after Bikini atoll, where the U.S. had just conducted a nuclear test.*

1648. *Car maker Ransom E. Olds (of Oldsmobile fame), in 1915.*

1649. *Thomas Edison.*

1650. *In the thirteenth century, by the Chinese. Bamboo tubes stuffed with gunpowder were used against the Mongols in 1232 at the Battle of K'ai-fung-fu.*

1651. *Oswego, New York. Due to complications Ford encountered with the local government, the site was switched to Detroit—which would later become known as "The Motor City."*

1652. *Woolworth.*

1653. *Toilet paper.*

1654. *$12.*

1655. *An amphibious Volkswagen with a retractable propeller that the Germans used during World War II.*

1656. *$600. The cheapest model now goes for close to $200,000.*

1657. Which oil company opened the first drive-in service station in the United States?

1658. On Wall Street, what's a "quack"?

1659. Which American passenger car was the first to pass the one-million production mark in a single year?

1660. What did manufacturers add to wood cement to discourage glue-sniffing by people seeking highs in the 1970s?

1661. What was the first automobile to have air-conditioning?

1662. How many copies per minute did the first Xerox machine produce when it was marketed 40 years ago?

1663. What is traded on NYMEX, the New York Mercantile Exchange?

1664. What is the oldest registered food trademark still in use in the United States?

1665. What was unique about the wristwatch for which Zeppo Marx obtained a patent?

1666. What are Hoot the Owl, Tabasco the Bull, Peanut the Elephant, Rex the Tyrannosaurus and Peking the Panda?

1667. How many burgers were there to a pound at the original McDonald's drive-in opened by brothers Maurice and Richard McDonald in San Bernardino, California in 1948?

1668. How did Swedish immigrant John W. Nordstrom make the fortune with which he founded the shoe store that grew into today's Nordstrom fashion-retail empire?

1669. What color is Martha Stewart's "Himalayan Eyes" paint?

1670. What does "cutting a melon" mean to a Wall Streeter?

1657. *Gulf—on December 1, 1913, in Pittsburgh, Pennsylvania.*

1658. *A quarter-point change in a stock's price.*

1659. *Chevrolet, 1949, when a record 1,109,958 were manufactured.*

1660. *Pungent oil of mustard.*

1661. *The Packard, in 1939.*

1662. *Seven. At the time, the company that developed and manufactured the copying machine was known as Haloid. It later took on the name of its breakthrough process.*

1663. *Metal and energy futures. The exchange is also known as the Merc.*

1664. *The red devil on cans of Underwood's deviled ham. It dates back to 1866.*

1665. *It included a heartbeat monitor.*

1666. *Beanie Babies—among the many seven-inch-long, plush-covered polyvinyl-chloride-pellet-stuffed animals first introduced in 1993 by Ty Inc.*

1667. *10. Ray Kroc established the nationwide chain in 1955 and introduced the quarter-pounder in 1972.*

1668. *He struck gold during the Klondike Gold Rush in 1897.*

1669. *Blue—dusty blue. It's one of the hundreds of colors produced by Sherwin-Williams bearing the imprimatur of the queen of the domestic scene.*

1670. *The declaration of an extra-large dividend by a company.*

1671. What roadside signs did the Burma-Shave admen erect a short time after they made the tempting offer: "Free, free, a trip to Mars for 900 empty jars"?

1672. What automobile company produced a car called the Dictator from 1927 to 1936?

1673. What was William Wrigley selling when he started handing out free packages of chewing gum to his customers as a premium?

Bonus Trivia

1674. On July 28, 1933, the first singing telegram was delivered to Rudy Vallee on the occasion of his birthday.

1671. Signs cautioning, *"If a trip to Mars you'd earn, remember friend there's no return."*

1672. Studebaker.

1673. Baking powder—*a product he soon abandoned when he realized his customers were more interested in his sticks of gum.*

Religion, the Bible & Mythology

Questions

1675. Can you name the nine daughters of Zeus and Mnemosyne —the nine Muses of Greek mythology?

1676. How much time did Jonah spend in the belly of the whale?

1677. Why did a Bible published in London in 1632 become known as the Wicked Bible?

1678. The name of God is not mentioned in only one book of the Bible. Which one?

1679. What kind of wood was used to make Noah's Ark?

1680. Who was the only Englishman to become Pope?

1681. If you lived as long as Methuselah, what age would you live to?

1682. What sculpted bird sits atop the Mormon temple in Salt Lake City—and why?

1683. What mythological beast has the head of a man, the body of a lion, and the tail and feet of a dragon?

Answers

1675. *Calliope, Clio, Erato, Euterpe, Melpomene, Polyhymnia, Terpischore, Thalia, and Urania.*

1676. *Three days and three nights.*

1677. *Because "not" was missing from the seventh commandment, making it "Thou shalt commit adultery."*

1678. *The Book of Esther.*

1679. *Gopher wood, according to Genesis 6:14.*

1680. *Nicholas Breakspear, who was Adrian IV from 1154 to 1159.*

1681. *According to Genesis 5:27, you'd be 969 years old.*

1682. *A seagull—honored for devouring an 1848 plague of crickets in that city.*

1683. *A manticore.*

1684. For what event in February 1964 did evangelist Billy Graham break his strict rule against watching TV on Sunday?

1685. What celebrated evangelist baptized a little girl named Norma Jeane Mortensen, and by what name was that girl later known?

1686. According to the Bible, what substance was used to caulk Noah's ark and to seal the basket in which the infant Moses was set adrift on the Nile?

1687. The diet of what mythical monster periodically included seven youths and seven maidens?

1688. How old was Moses when he died?

1689. In Greek mythology, who was the goddess of the rainbow?

1690. How tall was Goliath, the Philistine giant slain by David with a stone hurled from a sling?

1691. In ancient Athens, what tree was considered sacred—with all its fruit belonging to the state, and death the penalty for anyone caught cutting one down?

1692. What Biblical Babylonian king cast Daniel into the lion's den for praying to God in defiance of a royal decree?

1693. What is the longest name in the Bible?

1694. What day of the week is the sabbath for Muslims?

1695. What legendary fire-breathing female monster had a lion's head, a goat's body and a dragon's tail?

1696. What famous structure in Greek mythology was built by a man named Epeius?

1697. According to legend, who fired the arrow that hit Achilles in the heel, his only vulnerable spot?

1684. *The Beatles' first appearance on "The Ed Sullivan Show."*

1685. *Aimee Semple McPherson christened the child who would be Marilyn Monroe, in December 1926.*

1686. *Pitch, or natural asphalt.*

1687. *The Minotaur's.*

1688. *He was 120 years old, according to the Bible (Deuteronomy 34:7).*

1689. *Iris.*

1690. *"Six cubits and a span," according to the Bible (I Samuel 17:4). That would put Goliath's height somewhere between 9 feet 3 inches and 11 feet 9 inches. The cubit measure (the distance from the elbow to the end of the middle finger) varied from about 17 to 22 inches, and the span (the distance from the thumb to the little finger when extended) was approximately 9 inches.*

1691. *The olive tree.*

1692. *Darius the Mede (Book of Daniel, Chapter 6).*

1693. *Mahershalalhashbaz, which is also written Maher-shalal-hash-baz (Isaiah 8:1).*

1694. *Friday.*

1695. *The chimera.*

1696. *The Trojan Horse. According to the legend, Epeius was a skilled woodworker commissioned by Odysseus to build the huge gift horse.*

1697. *Paris.*

1698. What mythological god was portrayed as the Colossus of Rhodes, the more than 100-foot-high sculpture that was one of the Seven Wonders of the World?

1699. In Greek mythology, who was the queen of the underworld and wife of Hades?

1700. In the Bible, which of the four horsemen of the Apocalypse rides a red horse?

1701. In Greek mythology, who were Arges, Brontes and Steropes?

1702. How many books of the Bible are named for women?

1703. Who was the ancient Greek god of dreams?

1704. What bird was credited with saving Rome from attack by the Gauls in 390 B.C.?

1705. What is the latest day in the year on which Easter Sunday can fall in Western Christian churches?

1706. What language is Jesus believed to have spoken?

1707. In the Bible, for what "price" did Esau sell his birthright to his younger twin brother, Jacob?

1708. According to classical mythology, who was the first mortal woman?

1709. Janus—the ancient Roman god of good beginnings for whom January is named—is pictured on early coins with two faces looking in opposite directions. What did the faces represent?

1710. What did the lords of the Philistines offer Delilah for revealing the secret of Samson's strength?

1711. In the Old Testament, who was Jezebel's husband?

1712. How were Noah and Methuselah related?

1713. What bird is named for the apostle Peter?

1698. *Helios, the sun god. The statue was destroyed by an earthquake in 224 B.C.*

1699. *Persephone.*

1700. *War (Book of Revelation).*

1701. *Cyclopes.*

1702. *Two—Ruth and Esther.*

1703. *Morpheus. (Hypnus was the god of sleep.)*

1704. *The goose. According to legend, the honking of geese alerted the Romans to a night raid by the Gauls.*

1705. *April 25th. The earliest is March 22nd. Under guidelines established by the Council of Nicaea in 325 A.D., Easter Sunday is the first Sunday after the first full moon that occurs on the day of the vernal equinox or on one of the next 28 days.*

1706. *Aramaic—an ancient language in use on the north Arabian Peninsula at the time of Christ. A modern version of the language is spoken today in Syria and among Assyrians in Azerbaijan.*

1707. *Pottage of lentils (Genesis 25:29-34).*

1708. *Pandora.*

1709. *The future and the past.*

1710. *They promised the sum of 1,100 pieces of silver each, according to the Bible (Judges 16:5).*

1711. *Ahab, King of Israel (I Kings 16:28-31).*

1712. *Methuselah was Noah's paternal grandfather (Genesis 5:25-29).*

1713. *The petrel, from a diminutive form of Petrus, or "Peter," in Latin. The reason—it appears to walk on water when it hunts for food, reminiscent of St. Peter's walking on water (Matthew 14:29).*

1714. What political-religious movement is named after former Ethiopian emperor Haile Selassie?

1715. What is the name of the imaginary city built in the air in *The Birds*, the comedy written by the Greek playwright Aristophanes in 414 B.C.?

1716. In Greek mythology, what were the names of Oedipus's parents?

1717. According to legend, what is the color of the horn in the middle of the unicorn's forehead?

1718. What was comic W. C. Fields's explanation when actor Thomas Mitchell caught him thumbing through a Bible?

1719. According to early Christian theologians, how many grades of angels are there?

1720. How many locks of hair did Delilah have cut from the mighty Samson's head to render him powerless?

1721. What was the first town in the United States to be given a biblical name? Hint: Its name is the most common biblical place name in the country.

1722. In the Bible, who did the sun and moon stand still before?

1723. According to Norse legend, what animals pulled Thor's chariot across the sky?

1724. What Biblical name did writer Dorothy Parker give to her pet canary?

1725. What country was the world's first constitutionally atheistic state?

1726. Who is the only woman whose age is mentioned in the Bible?

1727. Why is the egg a symbol of Easter?

1714. The Rastafarians. The movement gets its name from Selassie's title before his coronation—Ras Tafari, or Prince Tafari.

1715. Cloud-Cuckoo-Land—or Nephelococcygia in Greek.

1716. Laius, King of Thebes, and his queen, Jocasta.

1717. White at the base, black in the middle and red at the tip.

1718. "Looking for loopholes."

1719. Nine. The hierarchy of angels, from highest rank to lowest, is seraphim, cherubim, thrones, dominions, virtues, powers, principalities, archangels and angels.

1720. Seven, according to the Bible (Judges 16:19).

1721. Salem, Massachusetts. Salem is the shortened form of Jerusalem, which means "the city of peace" in Hebrew.

1722. Joshua. The passage is in Joshua 10:12-13.

1723. Two goats. Thor was the god of thunder.

1724. Onan. He was so named, she said, because he spilled his seed.

1725. Albania, between 1967 and 1990, when all churches and mosques were closed and religious observances were banned.

1726. Sarah. Her age is mentioned twice: In Genesis 17:17, when she is 90 and Abraham is told that she will bear him a child (Isaac); and in Genesis 23:1, when she dies at age 127.

1727. As an ancient symbol of new life, it's considered a fitting symbol for the Resurrection.

1728. What is the most common name in the Bible—shared by 32 people in the Old Testament and one in the New Testament?

1729. According to legend, what Hindu god died as Achilles did—from an arrow shot into his heel?

1730. The name of what brave Trojan warrior once was a synonym for hero, but now means bully?

1731. Along what body of water is there a low salt mountain some believe is the pillar of salt that Lot's wife was turned into after the destruction of the cities of Sodom and Gomorrah?

1732. In Greek mythology, who were the parents of the love child Harmonia?

1733. What was the Bedouin Muhammad adh-Dhib looking for when he discovered the Dead Sea Scrolls in 1947?

1734. According to the Bible, what weapons was the Philistine giant Goliath carrying when he was slain by David?

1735. In Greek mythology, what sea did Jason sail across in search of the legendary Golden Fleece?

1736. What is the meaning of orbium phonographicorum theca, one of the words the Vatican has added to the Latin language in a bid to keep it up to date?

1737. In the heavens above, at what constellation is the archer Sagittarius aiming his arrow?

1738. According to Roman mythology, in what volcano's crater did Vulcan, the god of fire, work at his forge?

1739. How did the Vatican's Sistine Chapel get its name?

1740. What does the word "amen" mean?

1741. What two constellations are named for mythical centaurs?

1742. Who was the founder of the International Church of the Foursquare Gospel?

1728. Zechariah.

1729. Krishna. He was shot by a hunter who mistook him for a deer. His heel was his only vulnerable spot.

1730. Hector, the eldest son of Priam. The present meaning of the name can be traced back to a seventeenth-century London street gang whose members called themselves hectors—or heroes.

1731. The Dead Sea—which is known for its high salt content. The Arabs call it the Sea of Lot; the Israelis, the Salt Sea.

1732. Aphrodite and Ares.

1733. A lost goat.

1734. A sword and a spear, according to I Samuel 17:45.

1735. The Black Sea.

1736. "Discotheque."

1737. Scorpius—to avenge the death of fellow hunter Orion, who, according to legend, died of a scorpion sting.

1738. Mount Etna's, in Sicily.

1739. From the fifteenth-century pope who had it built as a private papal chapel—Pope Sixtus IV.

1740. "So be it," or "Let it be."

1741. Centaurus and Sagittarius.

1742. Evangelist Aimee Semple McPherson, in 1927.

1743. How wide and deep was the moat dug around the famous 21-foot-high wall that protected the biblical city of Jericho in 7000 B.C.?

1744. In what language was the New Testament originally written?

1745. How many of the 150 psalms in the Bible's Book of Psalms are attributed to Moses?

1746. According to the Bible, on what day did God divide land and water?

1747. In Norse mythology, who was Ull?

1748. What was the playing time of the Bible when the American Foundation for the Blind recorded the entire 774,000-word King James version in 1944?

1749. In classical Greek mythology, who was the third and better-known sister of the trio of siblings that included Stheno and Euryale?

1750. According to the Bible, how many pearly gates are there?

1751. What was the total population of the world at the time of Christ?

1752. According to the Bible, in what city were the disciples of Jesus first called Christians?

1753. In the Bible, who saw the handwriting on the wall?

1754. Who was the only ugly male god among the immortals in Roman mythology?

1755. According to legend, what tragedian died when an eagle, looking for a stone on which to smash a tortoise shell, mistakenly dropped the shell on his bald head?

1756. What were the names of the three wise men?

1757. How high were the walls of Jericho before they came tumbling down?

1743. *It was 15 feet wide and 9 feet deep.*

1744. *In Greek.*

1745. *One—Psalm 90, "A Prayer of Moses, the man of God."*

1746. *On the third day (Genesis 1:9).*

1747. *The god of snowshoes.*

1748. *84½ hours.*

1749. *Medusa. The three were Gorgons—monstrously ugly women with serpents for hair and tusks for teeth.*

1750. *12 (Revelation 21:12-21).*

1751. *About 200 million.*

1752. *In Antioch, one of the earliest centers of Christianity (Acts 11:26).*

1753. *The Babylonian king Belshazzar (Daniel 5:1-5).*

1754. *Vulcan, the god of fire (known as Hephaestus in Greek mythology).*

1755. *The Greek tragic dramatist Aeschylus, who lived from 525 to 456 B.C.*

1756. *Balthazar, Caspar and Melchior.*

1757. *Twenty-one feet. They enclosed a 10-acre area.*

1758. How many people were on Noah's Ark?

1759. How did the ancient Greeks spread word about the winners of Olympic Games held between 776 B.C. and A.D. 393?

1760. What are the seven cardinal virtues?

1761. What are the seven deadly sins?

1762. How many decks were there on Noah's Ark?

1763. "Salt of the earth."
"Feet of clay."
"Apple of my eye."
All are clichés. What is their common source?

1764. Who were the parents of King Solomon?

1765. What was the first imprisonment recorded in the Bible?

1766. How many times a day do observant Muslims pray?

1767. According to Indian legend, how did the sacred thunderbird produce thunder and lightning?

Bonus Trivia

1768. Pope John Paul II's talents extend beyond the realm of his calling: He is also a gifted writer and musician. His 1979 record album, "At the Festival of the Sacro Song," sold over a million copies.

1758. *Eight—Noah, his wife; and his sons, Shem, Ham and Japheth, and their wives.*

1759. *By carrier pigeon.*

1760. *Prudence, temperance, fortitude, justice, faith, love, and hope.*

1761. *Pride, covetousness, lust, gluttony, anger, envy and sloth.*

1762. *Three, according to Genesis 6:16.*

1763. *The King James Version of the Bible.*

1764. *David and Bathsheba.*

1765. *The jailing of Joseph by Potiphar, the captain of the Egyptian pharoah's guards, after Joseph was falsely accused of trying to seduce Potiphar's wife (Genesis 39:6-20).*

1766. *Five—at daybreak, noon, midafternoon, sunset and evening.*

1767. *It produced thunder by beating its wings; lightning by blinking its eyes.*

America—
Past & Present
Questions

1769. What room in the average American home is the scene of the greatest number of arguments?

1770. How much does the 555-foot-5-⅛-inch-high Washington Monument in Washington, D.C., weigh?

1771. What does Separation Creek in Oregon separate?

1772. How many figures were tattooed on the body of Captain George Costentenus, one of the human curiosities put on exhibit by legendary showman P. T. Barnum in 1876?

1773. In what year did motor vehicle registrations in the United States pass the million mark?

1774. How many hours a year are Americans expected to spend waiting in traffic jams by the year 2005?

1775. What is the length and width of the dollar bill?

1776. Under California law, what fish may only be caught using bare hands?

Answers

1769. The kitchen.

1770. 90,854 tons.

1771. Two mountains known as The Husband and The Wife.

1772. From head to toe, 386—including fish, animals, birds, mummies and hieroglyphics.

1773. In 1913, when there were 1,258,070 vehicles registered—1,190,393 of them passenger cars; 67,677 of them trucks and buses.

1774. 8.1 billion, according to the Federal Highway Administration.

1775. Length, 6.14 inches; width, 2.61 inches.

1776. The tiny grunion, which comes ashore to spawn.

1777. In 1960, the citizens of Hot Springs, New Mexico, voted to rename their town in honor of a popular radio show. What is it now called?

1778. What are the names of the two landmark stone lions sitting in front of the New York Public Library at Fifth Avenue and 42nd Street in New York City?

1779. How many windows are there on the 102-story Empire State Building?

1780. How much time—in months—does the average American motorist spend during his lifetime waiting for red lights to turn green?

1781. Borden is the name of a county in Texas. What is the name of its county seat?

1782. Two states bill themselves as the "Sunshine State." Can you name them?

1783. In 1954 the Pennsylvania coalmining communities of Maunch Chunk and East Maunch Chunk merged and adopted a new name in honor of a famous athlete. What was it?

1784. What are school teams nicknamed at Jack Benny Junior High, the school the citizens of Waukegan, Illinois, named after their most famous son?

1785. What was the name of the first series of U.S. postage stamps ever produced outside the country?

1786. What employee-grooming regulation at Disney World would prevent the hiring of Walt Disney—if he were alive and job hunting today?

1787. What was put between the steel framework and the copper skin of the restored Statue of Liberty to prevent corrosion?

1788. On the reverse side of the $100 bill, what time is shown on the Independence Hall clock?

1777. *Truth or Consequences—known as T or C for short. The change was made after radio (and later TV) show host Ralph Edwards promised to hold a program there annually.*

1778. *Patience and Fortitude, names given them by Mayor Fiorello LaGuardia.*

1779. *6,000.*

1780. *Six months.*

1781. *Gail, for Gail Borden, the man who brought us condensed milk—but only after drawing the first topographical map of Texas and surveying and laying out the city of Galveston.*

1782. *Florida and South Dakota.*

1783. *Jim Thorpe, after the great Oklahoma Indian athlete. The renaming was part of a plan to establish the town as a shrine to Thorpe, who was buried there.*

1784. *The 39ers—39 was the age comedian Benny claimed for more than 39 years of his life.*

1785. *Great Americans. The series, introduced in 1991, was printed in Canada.*

1786. *The ban on facial hair. Disney had a mustache.*

1787. *Teflon.*

1788. *4:10.*

1789. In what state can you find the towns of Romance, Sweet Home and Success?

1790. Where are the only remaining free-roaming panthers in North America?

1791. Why was the entire village of Hibbing, Minnesota, relocated?

1792. What physical handicap afflicted Juliette Low, founder of the Girl Scouts of America?

1793. Where did Samuel McPherson Hunt, gangster Al Capone's feared hitman, carry his submachine gun when he went out on a job?

1794. In what unusual manner did Ashrita Furman retrace the 13 ¼-mile route taken by Paul Revere on his historic 1775 ride?

1795. What U.S. city is at almost the same latitude as Mexico City?

1796. In what state can you visit Athens, Carthage, Damascus, Egypt, England, Formosa, Hamburg, Havana, Holland, Jerusalem, London, Manila, Melbourne, Oxford, Palestine, Paris, Scotland and Stuttgart?

1797. What was the first poll ever taken by national pulse-taker George Gallup?

1798. What famous gangster, posing as a reporter for a detective magazine, convinced some cops to take him on a tour of the weapons arsenal in their police station—and later returned to steal everything in it?

1799. What state is most dependent on tourism, with almost 30 percent of its jobs tourist related?

1800. To whom was columnist Grantland Rice referring when he wrote: "Outlined against the blue-gray October sky, the Four Horsemen rode again"?

1801. American naturalist George B. Grinnell founded the Audubon Society. What did his middle initial stand for?

1789. *Arkansas.*

1790. *In Southern Florida—in the Everglades and Big Cypress Swamp.*

1791. *The village was sitting atop huge beds of iron ore. After it was moved south, the original site became one of the largest open-pit iron mines in the world—covering over 1,600 acres and running 535 feet deep.*

1792. *She was deaf.*

1793. *In a golf bag, rather than in the traditional violin case. His nickname was Golf Bag.*

1794. *She somersaulted the entire way.*

1795. *Hilo, on the Big Island of Hawaii. It's at 19°42′ north; Mexico City is at 19°25′ north.*

1796. *Arkansas—which has towns with all of those names.*

1797. *A survey to find the prettiest girl on campus at the University of Iowa, where he was editor of the student newspaper in the early 1920s. Gallup ended up marrying the winner, Ophelia Smith.*

1798. *John Dillinger, in 1934. The police station was in Peru, Indiana.*

1799. *The state of Nevada.*

1800. *Notre Dame's undefeated 1924 backfield, Elmer Layden, Harry Stuhldreher, Don Miller, and Jim Crowley.*

1801. *Bird.*

1802. Who gave his red hand-knitted cardigan sweater, size 38, to the Smithsonian Institution in 1984?

1803. What's on the flip side of the Susan B. Anthony $1 coin?

1804. How many Ringling Brothers were there?

1805. Which is the smallest of New York City's five boroughs—with a total area of 22.6 square miles?

1806. What unique distinction does Maine's 5,268-foot Mt. Katahdin enjoy?

1807. What is the only car that consumer crusader Ralph Nader has ever owned?

1808. What oft-played American song's tune, meter, and verse form were borrowed from an English drinking song?

1809. Mistletoe is the state flower of what state?

1810. The names of 48 states are engraved on the frieze of the Lincoln Memorial, which was completed in 1922. How many are in the etching of the memorial on the back of the $5 bill?

1811. What U.S. canyon is the deepest gorge on the North American continent?

1812. What was the official New York City weather forecast on the day of the Great Blizzard of 1888?

1813. What inland state has the longest shoreline?

1814. What are the only four states to share a common boundary?

1815. How did John Luther Jones, the engineer of the "Cannonball Express" whose death in a collision with a freight train is memorialized in ballad and legend, get his nickname "Casey"?

1816. What three national parks does the Continental Divide pass through?

1802. Fred Rogers of public television's "Mister Rogers' Neighborhood."

1803. An eagle landing on the moon, commemorating the Apollo II moon landing on July 20, 1969.

1804. Seven: John, who headed the circus empire, and brothers Albert, Otto, Alfred, Charles, August, and Henry.

1805. Manhattan. (Queens is the largest borough with 118.6 square miles.)

1806. It is the first spot in the U.S. to be touched by the rays of the rising sun.

1807. A 1949 Studebaker, which he sold thirty years ago when he was a Harvard Law School student.

1808. "The Star Spangled Banner," which was based on the song "Anacreon in Heaven."

1809. Rhode Island.

1810. Twenty-six. Use a magnifying glass to check—they're in two rows on the frieze above the colonnade.

1811. Hell's Canyon, also known as the Grand Canyon of the Snake River, which reaches a depth of 7,900 feet.

1812. "Clearing and colder, preceded by light snow." The city was hit with 20.9 inches of snow and a temperature of -6°F.

1813. Michigan. Its more than 3,100 miles of freshwater shoreline includes four of the five Great Lakes—Michigan, Superior, Huron and Erie.

1814. Arizona, Colorado, New Mexico, and Utah.

1815. From his hometown: Cayce, Kentucky.

1816. Yellowstone, Rocky Mountain and Glacier national parks.

1817. According to the folklore of the early American lumber camp, how was the Grand Canyon created?

1818. How much does the Liberty Bell weigh?

1819. What unearthly attraction can visitors find in Coconino National Forest, outside Flagstaff, Arizona?

1820. How many islands are there in the Hawaiian Islands?

1821. What is the origin of the name Baton Rouge, the capital of Louisiana?

1822. What is the size of automobile license plates issued by the 50 states, Canada, and Mexico?

1823. What is the name of the island on which Newport, Rhode Island, is located?

1824. How long is the Grand Canyon of the Colorado River?

1825. How did the town of Snowflake, Arizona, get its name?

1826. How much does it cost the U.S. government to produce a quarter?

1827. How much does Plymouth Rock weigh?

1828. What U.S. government agencies are known as Freddie Mac and Sallie Mae?

1829. The Algonquin Hotel is a famous New York literary landmark. What is the name of the hotel down the street where the struggling young James Dean once lived?

1830. How did Goon Dip Mountain, in Alaska, get its name?

1831. What does verdigris have to do with the Statue of Liberty?

1832. How many crayons does the average American child wear down in his or her coloring lifetime (ages 2 to 8)?

1833. Where are the oldest church bells in the United States?

1817. *By Paul Bunyan dragging his pick behind him.*

1818. *Just over a ton—2,080 pounds.*

1819. *A 640,000-square-foot re-creation of the lunar landscape blasted in the volcanic ash and cinders of a dry lake bed.*

1820. *There are 132—8 major islands and 124 islets.*

1821. *The name, translated from French, means "red stick"—for the red cypress tree that once marked the boundary between local Indian tribes.*

1822. *They're 12 inches wide by 6 inches high.*

1823. *Rhode Island—formerly Aquidneck. It gave its name to the state.*

1824. *217 miles.*

1825. *From two early settlers—Erastus Snow and William J. Flake.*

1826. *2½ cents—which gives Uncle Sam a profit (or seigniorage) of 22½ cents.*

1827. *Approximately four tons.*

1828. *Freddie is the Federal Home Loan Mortgage Corporation; Sallie, the Student Loan Marketing Association.*

1829. *The Iroquois.*

1830. *It was named in 1939 for Goon Dip, who had been the Chinese consul in Seattle.*

1831. *It's the green patina on her copper body.*

1832. *730, according to the folks at Crayola.*

1833. *In Boston's Old North Church. They were made in England in 1744 and shipped to Boston.*

1834. Where in the U.S. will you find both Neon and Krypton?

1835. How did the town of Disco, Michigan, get its name?

1836. What are the numbers of the three interstate highways that run from coast-to-coast?

1837. How many elevators are there in the Empire State Building in New York City?

1838. How many windows are there in the Pentagon, the world's largest office building?

1839. What was the given name of Doc Holliday, the frontier dentist, gambler and gunman who befriended Wyatt Earp and was at his side during the shootout at the O.K. Corral?

1840. Which American city was the first to establish a police department?

1841. What comic strip character did the grateful farmers of Crystal City, Texas, honor with a six-foot-high stone mountain in 1937?

1842. Who came in second to Eleanor Roosevelt in a 1945 *Fortune* magazine poll taken to determine the most famous woman in America?

1843. Who once said: "The hardest thing in the world to understand is the income tax?"

1844. Whose appearance in a nearly transparent white fishnet bathing suit in the 1978 *Sports Illustrated* swimsuit issue led an editor to promise, "We never have, and never will, run anything so revealing again"?

1845. What was the average amount of money left per visit by the tooth fairy in 1950?

1846. Why did Trinity College in Durham, North Carolina, change its name to Duke University in 1924?

1834. *In Kentucky. They're small towns named after the two elements.*

1835. *From a school once located there that was called Disco—which in Latin means "I learn."*

1836. *I-10, I-80 and I-90.*

1837. *73.*

1838. *7,754.*

1839. *John Henry.*

1840. *Boston. Regular-duty officers were appointed on May 5, 1838.*

1841. *Popeye—for his role in popularizing spinach, their main crop.*

1842. *The fictitious Betty Crocker, the symbol created in 1921 for General Mills' baking products.*

1843. *Albert Einstein.*

1844. *Cheryl Tiegs.*

1845. *A quarter.*

1846. *To honor its leading benefactor, tobacco tycoon James Buchanan Duke, and his family.*

1847. How many official time zones are there in the United States—including Puerto Rico, the Virgin Islands and American Samoa?

1848. Who owns the 45.52-carat Hope diamond?

1849. What is the most frequently stolen street sign in New York City?

1850. What was the total weight of the identical Dionne quintuplets—Annette, Cecile, Emilie, Marie and Yvonne—when they were born on May 28, 1934?

1851. Prior to their complete 1998 redesign, how did $20 bills differ from those printed before 1948?

1852. What name was originally spelled out in the huge mountainside sign that welcomes visitors in Hollywood?

1853. Why is Arizona sometimes referred to as the Valentine State?

1854. When you translate "revenue enhancement" from government doublespeak, what have you got?

1855. What is the name of the tiny pond in New York's Adirondack Mountains where the 315-mile-long Hudson River originates?

1856. What four state capitals are named after cities in England?

1857. What was the name of pioneer Daniel Boone's family cat?

1858. What words appear on the front of the penny, nickel, dime and quarter—alongside the likenesses of Presidents Lincoln, Jefferson, Franklin D. Roosevelt and Washington, respectively?

1859. What is the name of the periodical published by the Procrastinators Club of America?

1860. How deep is Oregon's Crater Lake, the deepest lake in the United States?

1847. *Eight. From Puerto Rico to Samoa, they are Atlantic, Eastern, Central, Mountain, Pacific, Alaska Standard, Hawaii-Aleutian and Samoa Standard.*

1848. *The United States. It was given to the Smithsonian Institution by jeweler Harry Winston in 1958.*

1849. *Hooker Place.*

1850. *13½ pounds.*

1851. *The engraving of the White House on the back of the bill was changed in 1948 to include structural alterations made during Harry S. Truman's presidency. Additions include a balcony on the front portico and two more chimneys. Also different on the revised bill are the words below the engraving, which were changed from "White House" to "The White House."*

1852. *Hollywoodland, the name of a real-estate subdivision on the site of what is now the nation's film capital.*

1853. *It joined the Union as the 48th state on February 14, 1912.*

1854. *A tax increase.*

1855. *Lake Tear of the Clouds.*

1856. *Hartford, Connecticut; Dover, Delaware; Boston, Massachusetts; and Richmond, Virginia.*

1857. *Bluegrass—which is also the nickname of Kentucky, the state he helped found.*

1858. *"LIBERTY" and "IN GOD WE TRUST."*

1859. *"Last Month's Newsletter"*

1860. *1,932 feet deep. The lake is in the crater of Mount Mazama, an extinct volcano.*

1861. What car is shown in front of the U.S. Treasury Building on the back of the $10 bill?

1862. How much garbage—in tons—is generated daily in the twin towers of the World Trade Center in New York City?

1863. Which is the only state on the eastern seaboard to fall partially in the central time zone?

1864. What city—more than 2½ times the size of Rhode Island—is America's largest in area?

1865. Through how many states does U.S. 80—the main northern route from New York to California—pass?

1866. Which two states have neighboring towns named for explorers Meriwether Lewis and William Clark?

1867. Which of the 50 states takes in the least amount of tourist dollars?

1868. What animals—besides horses—accompanied Buffalo Bill Cody when he sailed his Wild West Show to London in 1887 to appear before Queen Victoria?

1869. What are roller coasters classified as by the U.S. Patent Office?

1870. What is the name of the boulevard on which Fort Knox is located?

1871. Which of the states uses the Napoleonic code rather than English common law as the basis of its civil law?

1872. How many U.S. states and their capital cities have names that begin with the same letter?

1873. What major vegetable crop was grown in Beverly Hills, California, before it became home to the rich and famous?

1874. What is the only place below sea level in the United States that is not in the California desert? Hint: It's a major city.

1861. *A 1926 Hupmobile.*

1862. *65—of which about 37½ tons are waste paper.*

1863. *Florida.*

1864. *Juneau, Alaska. It covers an area of 3,108 square miles. Rhode Island covers 1,214 square miles.*

1865. *12—from east to west: New York, New Jersey, Pennsylvania, Ohio, Indiana, Illinois, Iowa, Nebraska, Wyoming, Utah, Nevada, California.*

1866. *Idaho and Washington. The towns—Lewiston, Idaho, and Clarkston, Washington—are separated by the Snake River. Lewiston was a Lewis and Clark campsite.*

1867. *Rhode Island. California takes in the greatest amount.*

1868. *Buffalo (18), elk (10), mules (10), steers (5), donkeys (4) and deer (2). His cowboy-and-Indian entourage also included 180 horses.*

1869. *Scenic railways. The classification was first used for roller coasters in 1886.*

1870. *Bullion Boulevard.*

1871. *Louisiana.*

1872. *Four. Dover, Delaware; Indianapolis, Indiana; Oklahoma City, Oklahoma; and Honolulu, Hawaii.*

1873. *Lima beans.*

1874. *New Orleans.*

1875. What aptly named village has the highest post office in the United States?

1876. What newspaper, launched in 1982, was dubbed the *McPaper* because it provided its readers with "McNuggets" of news?

1877. How fast—in words per minute—does the average American adult read?

1878. How many steps are there to the top of the Empire State Building?

1879. What is the best-selling magazine in the United States, and who founded it?

1880. In 1949, Mrs. Ralph E. Smafield of Rockford, Ill., won first prize in what event with her Water-Rising Twists?

1881. Who appeared on the cover of the maiden issue of *People* magazine on March 4, 1974?

1882. What was Walt Disney's original title for his dream world, Disneyland?

1883. Between 1835 and 1837 a now perennial feature of American life was blissfully absent. What was it?

1884. Where is it illegal for a portrait of a living person to appear in the United States.

1885. Who was *Time* magazine's Man of the Year for 1952?

1886. In what connection is Anne Reese Jarvis remembered today?

1887. Where is the longest street in the United States?

1888. How was the three-mile territorial limit from the U.S. coastline determined?

1889. What was the working title of Hugh Hefner's *Playboy* magazine, before it made its debut in December 1953?

1875. *Climax, Colorado. It's located in the Rockies at 11,320 feet above sea level.*

1876. *USA Today.*

1877. *275 words per minute.*

1878. *1,575.*

1879. *"TV Guide," first published in 1953 by Walter Annenberg.*

1880. *The first annual Pillsbury Bake-Off.*

1881. *Mia Farrow.*

1882. *Mickey Mouse Park.*

1883. *The national debt.*

1884. *On our postage stamps.*

1885. *Queen Elizabeth II of Great Britain. It was her coronation year.*

1886. *She was the inspiration for Mother's Day, which was dreamed up by her daughter, Anna M. Jarvis.*

1887. *Los Angeles, where Figueroa Street runs for 30 miles.*

1888. *It was the distance that coastal cannons could fire a shell.*

1889. *"Stag Party."*

1890. What was the full name of the 8-year-old girl, Virginia, who wrote to the *New York Sun*, asking if there really is a Santa Claus?

1891. In what city did Will Rogers serve as honorary mayor?

1892. Eighty-seven-year-old Democrat Rebecca Latimer Selton held what distinction in the political arena?

1893. In 1992, the governor of Hawaii received a 30,000-signature petition to change the name of the island of Maui—to what?

1894. Which territory in North America did Detroit's founder, Antoine Laumet de la Mothe Cadillac, the man for whom the car is named, serve as governor from 1713 to 1716?

1895. Whose body was the first to lie in state in the rotunda of the Capitol Building in Washington, D.C.?

1896. What country benefited from the first foreign aid bill approved by the United States Congress?

1897. What was the first building erected by the federal government in Washington, D.C.?

1898. In a 1989 newspaper survey, only 9 percent of those polled knew William Rehnquist was chief justice of the U.S. Supreme Court. What judge was identified by 54 percent of those polled?

1899. Of the 32 civil rights cases Thurgood Marshall argued before the U.S. Supreme Court as the lawyer for the National Association for the Advancement of Colored People, how many did he win?

1900. Who was the first black American to win the Nobel Prize for Peace?

1901. Which American colony was the first to enact anti-slavery legislation?

1902. To what amount did Congress vote to raise the minimum wage on October 26, 1949?

1890. *Virginia O'Hanlon.*

1891. *Beverly Hills.*

1892. *She was the first woman to become a U.S. Senator, when she was appointed by the governor of Georgia to serve the remaining day of a vacated Senate seat, November 21-22, 1922.*

1893. *Gilligan's Island, in honor of the TV sitcom. Needless to say, the island is still called Maui.*

1894. *Louisiana.*

1895. *Senator Henry Clay's. He died in 1852.*

1896. *Venezuela. In May 1812, Congress appropriated $50,000 for relief following an earthquake in Venezuela.*

1897. *The executive mansion—later known as the White House. It was first occupied in 1800 by John Adams.*

1898. *Retired California judge Joseph Wapner, of television's "The People's Court."*

1899. *29.*

1900. *American statesman and United Nations official Ralph Bunche, in 1950, for his mediation of the 1948-49 Arab-Israeli War. Dr. Martin Luther King, Jr., whose birth we celebrate today, won the coveted award in 1964.*

1901. *Massachusetts, in 1641, in its "Body of Liberties."*

1902. *They raised it to 75 cents an hour; it had been 40 cents.*

1903. What did the U.S. government buy for Alaska's Eskimos in 1891?

1904. What state was the last to adopt the secret ballot?

1905. Uncle Sam made his first appearance—beardless—in 1852. When did he acquire whiskers?

1906. What state abolished its personal income tax in 1980 and refunded $185 million already collected to its taxpayers?

1907. What senator gave the longest filibuster on record—24 hours, 18 minutes?

1908. How many years of schooling did Benjamin Franklin have?

1909. John Jay, John Marshall, Roger B. Taney, and Salmon P. Chase were all chief justices of the U.S. Supreme Court. What other distinction did they share?

1910. What was the name of the father of Sioux Indian leader Sitting Bull?

1911. In 1812 New York City's Federal Hall—the site of America's first presidential inauguration—was torn down and sold for scrap at auction. How much did the city get for it?

1912. What was Martin Luther King, Jrs.'s name at birth?

1913. Did Captain Miles Standish ever marry? You remember Standish, the Pilgrim leader who, according to legend, sought Priscilla Mullins' hand in marriage by having John Alden do the asking for him.

1914. Who was the first civilian astronaut launched into space by the U.S.?

1915. French daredevil aerialist Philippe Petit walked a tightrope linking the twin towers of New York's World Trade Center in 1974. How did he attach his 270-pound steel cable tightrope between the towers?

1903. *Sixteen Siberian reindeer—the start of the state's herd.*

1904. *South Carolina, in 1950.*

1905. *In his seventeenth year, in 1869, in "Harper's Weekly" magazine.*

1906. *Alaska, which has the highest per capita income in the country.*

1907. *South Carolina Republican Strom Thurmond. He was opposing the 1957 voting rights bill.*

1908. *Two—one year in grammar school and one with a private teacher.*

1909. *They never went to law school.*

1910. *Jumping Bull.*

1911. *$425.*

1912. *Michael Luther King Jr.*

1913. *Standish married twice. Rose, his first wife, died during the Pilgrims' first winter in the New World. Barbara, whom he married in 1624, bore him six children. Standish was between wives when John supposedly spoke for himself and married Priscilla.*

1914. *Neil Armstrong. The former Navy pilot went into space twice: in 1966 as commander of Gemini 8; in 1969 as commander of Apollo 11.*

1915. *Friends used a bow and arrow to shoot a fishing line across the 131-foot gap—and then used the fishing line to pull the cable across.*

1916. What is the significance of latitude 39°43' N in American history?

1917. How long did America's first space flight, made by astronaut Alan ShepardJr., last?

1918. Who wrote "Fish and visitors smell in three days"?

1919. What was the name of the huge Newfoundland dog that accompanied explorers Meriwether Lewis and William Clark on their famous expedition to the Pacific northwest in the early nineteenth century?

1920. What did Thomas Jefferson smuggle out of Italy in 1784 to help boost America's post-Revolution economy?

1921. How many states were created—in part or in their entirety—from the Louisiana Territory, purchased from France in 1803?

1922. How many cherry trees had to be cut down to prepare the site for the Jefferson Memorial in Washington, D.C., in 1938?

1923. Who gained fame as Richard Saunders during America's colonial days?

1924. Who was the last man on the moon?

1925. How many chests of tea were dumped overboard at the Boston Tea Party on December 16, 1773.

1926. How long did the black boycott against the Montgomery, Alabama, bus system last?

1927. What crime led to Billy the Kid's first run-in with the law?

1928. When and where was the first recorded report of a UFO sighting made in the United States?

1929. Which were the only four states to vote against the Sixteenth Amendment, the amendment ratified 80 years ago that gave Congress the power to "lay and collect taxes on incomes, from whatever sources derived"?

1916. *It's the location of the Mason-Dixon Line, surveyed in the mid-eighteenth century to settle a boundary dispute between Pennsylvania and Maryland and considered the dividing line between North and South.*

1917. *Shepard's suborbital flight in a 6-by-9-foot capsule lasted 15 minutes and 22 seconds.*

1918. *Benjamin Franklin, in his wisdom-packed "Poor Richard's Almanack."*

1919. *Scammon.*

1920. *Jefferson snuck out two sacks of an improved strain of rice—despite a ban on its export from Italy—to help revitalize the Georgia and Carolina rice crops destroyed by the British during the Revolution.*

1921. *Thirteen: the entire states of Arkansas, Missouri, Iowa and Nebraska; and parts of Louisiana, Oklahoma, Kansas, Colorado, Wyoming, Montana, North Dakota, South Dakota and Minnesota.*

1922. *171.*

1923. *Benjamin Franklin. Richard Saunders was the pen name he used in his "Poor Richard's Almanack" between 1732 and 1757.*

1924. *Astronaut Eugene Cernan, commander of Apollo 17—in December 1972.*

1925. *342.*

1926. *The boycott, led by the Rev. Martin Luther King, Jr., lasted 382 days. It ended when the city of Montgomery began integrated bus service on December 21, 1956.*

1927. *The theft of some butter. His second known offense was receiving stolen property—clothes taken from a Chinese laundry.*

1928. *In June 1947, near Mount Rainier, Washington. Idaho businessman Kenneth Arnold reported seeing nine silvery, saucer-shaped disks flying in formation at very high speed.*

1929. *Connecticut, Florida, Rhode Island and Utah.*

1930. What article of clothing were women required to wear on the beach at New Jersey's Atlantic City until 1907—along with their standard attire of long bathing dresses, bathing shoes and straw hats?

1931. How did Massachusetts sea captain Joshua Slocum—the first man to sail solo around the world—fight off pirates attacking his sloop?

1932. What famous American's father headed the investigation into the Lindbergh kidnapping in 1932?

1933. What triggered the legendary feud between the hillbilly Hatfields and McCoys in 1873?

1934. What was the powder used by America's Founding Fathers to keep their wigs white?

1935. Judge Roy Bean gained fame as the Law West of the Pecos. What was his brother, Josh, known for?

1936. What was astronaut Neil Armstrong's total annual salary when he walked on the moon on July 20, 1969?

1937. What was the name of the prospector who discovered gold in the Alaska panhandle in 1880?

1938. In what year did the average American salary pass $100 a week?

1939. Which state was the first in the nation to recognize Labor Day as a legal holiday?

1940. What famous Cherokee Indian was known to the Americans of his time as George Guess?

1941. What famous words did Francis Bellamy write to commemorate the 400th anniversary of Columbus's discovery of America?

1942. What was the name of the very first ocean-going vessel built by Englishmen in the New World?

1930. Stockings.

1931. He turned away the barefoot pirates by spreading carpet tacks on the deck of his boat. Slocum completed his historic 46,000-mile, 38-month voyage in 1898.

1932. General H. Norman Schwarzkopf's. The senior Schwarzkopf was a retired brigadier general who was New Jersey's state chief of police at the time of the kidnapping.

1933. The alleged theft of a pig.

1934. Ground rice.

1935. He was the first mayor of the city of San Diego, California.

1936. Just over $30,000.

1937. Joseph Juneau—the man for whom the capital of Alaska is named.

1938. In 1963.

1939. Oregon, in February 1887—followed later the same year by Colorado, Massachusetts, New Jersey and New York.

1940. Sequoya.

1941. "The Pledge of Allegiance"—which was published in "The Youth's Companion" magazine. Bellamy was on the magazine's staff.

1942. Virginia. The 30-ton ship was built by settlers who landed in Maine in 1607, established a colony, but found life and the winter weather so harsh that they built a ship to escape a second winter.

1943. What was the name of the first permanent settlement in Kentucky, established in 1775 by frontiersman Daniel Boone?

1944. What role did the ships "Discovery," "Sarah Constant" and "Goodspeed" play in American history?

1945. What house is the second-most-visited American home in the United States—outdrawn only by the White House?

1946. In 1784 American settlers established an independent state named Franklin, in honor of Benjamin Franklin. Where was it?

1947. How much expense money did Congress allot Meriwether Lewis and William Clark for their expedition across America that lasted from May 1804 to September 1806?

1948. What famous frontierswoman was buried in Deadwood, South Dakota, wearing a white dress and holding a gun in each hand?

1949. Who designed the Statue of Liberty's iron skeleton for French sculptor Frédéric Auguste Bartholdi?

1950. What fashion was introduced by and named after Civil War Gen. Ambrose Burnside?

1951. Why couldn't surgeon Charles Richard Drew, who organized the first blood bank in the U.S., donate his own blood?

1952. What foreign government contributed the greatest amount of money for the relief of victims of the 1906 San Francisco earthquake?

1953. What famous Northern publisher signed the bail bond for Confederate leader Jefferson Davis in 1867?

1954. In 1867, how much per acre did the U.S. pay Russia for what is now the state of Alaska?

1955. What movie had John Dillinger just seen when federal agents gunned him down outside the Biograph Theater in Chicago?

1943. Boonesborough.

1944. They landed in what is now Jamestown, Virginia, in 1607, carrying the colonists who established the first permanent English settlement in the United States.

1945. Graceland, the home of Elvis Presley in Memphis, Tennessee.

1946. In what is now eastern Tennessee. The territory had been ceded to the federal government by North Carolina.

1947. The sum of $2,500.

1948. Calamity Jane, aka Martha Jane Burke.

1949. Alexandre Gustave Eiffel, who is best known for the tower that bears his name.

1950. Sideburns—an anagram of his name.

1951. Segregation laws in 1941 prohibited it—he was black.

1952. Japan.

1953. Horace Greeley, editor of the "New York Tribune."

1954. Just under 2 cents, compared to 4 cents an acre paid for the Louisiana Territory in 1803.

1955. "Manhattan Melodrama," in which "gangster" Clark Gable dies in the electric chair.

1956. Who gave the "in" party for the Black Panthers that inspired the phrase "Radical Chic"?

1957. What American institution did Napoleon's grandnephew Charles Bonaparte found in 1908?

1958. Who was the first U.S. citizen to be canonized as a saint?

1959. Which state was the first to pass a right-to-die law?

1960. The U.S. bought the Virgin Islands for $25 million in 1917—from what country?

1961. What concession earned $862,000 in just five months at the Chicago World's Fair in 1933?

1962. What was the Mayflower's cargo before it was chartered to carry the pilgrims to America in 1620?

1963. What speed limit was set by Connecticut in 1901 in the first statewide automobile legislation passed in the U.S.?

1964. What state was the first to proclaim Christmas a holiday?

1965. What sentence did Patty Hearst receive in 1976 for the bank robbery she participated in while she was with the Symbionese Liberation Army?

1966. What event was precipitated by a book entitled "Civic Biology"?

1967. What historical trial gave birth to the phrase "sharp as a Philadelphia lawyer"?

1968. With what story did the tiny German-language newspaper "Philadelphische Staatshote" scoop the world?

1969. What famous early American once boasted: "I can't say I was ever lost, but I was bewildered once for three days"?

1970. How did the town of Showlow, Arizona, get its name?

1956. *Conductor-composer Leonard Bernstein.*

1957. *The F.B. I. He was attorney general of the U.S. at the time.*

1958. *Mother Frances Xavier Cabrini, in 1946.*

1959. *California, in 1976.*

1960. *Denmark, which had established its first settlement there in 1672.*

1961. *The rest room, at 5 cents a visit.*

1962. *Wine. Just prior to its Atlantic crossing, the Mayflower transported 153 tuns and 16 hogsheads (39,564 gallons) of wine from Bordeaux to London.*

1963. *On country highways, 15 mph; on highways within city limits, 12 mph.*

1964. *Alabama, 150 years ago.*

1965. *Seven years, but she served only 22 months—President Carter commuted her sentence.*

1966. *The 1925 "Monkey Trial." "Civic Biology" was the text science teacher John Scopes read to his students in defiance of a Tennessee law banning the teaching of evolution.*

1967. *The landmark 1735 libel trial of New York newspaperman John Peter Zenger, who was defended by Philadelphia lawyer Andrew Hamilton. Zenger was acquitted when the jury found his charges against the colonial governor were based on fact.*

1968. *The adoption of the Declaration of Independence. The Staatshote (which, translated, means "Messenger of the State") was the only Philadelphia newspaper published on Fridays—and July 5th fell on a Friday in 1776.*

1969. *Frontiersman Daniel Boone.*

1970. *From the card draw held to pick the mayor of the mining town. The player who drew and showed the low card became mayor—giving the town its name. Its main street is called Deuce of Clubs in honor of the winning low card.*

1971. From what European country did the ancestors of the people we call Pennsylvania Dutch originally come?

1972. What were Robert E. Lee's dying words?

1973. How many bullet holes did lawmen put in Clyde Barrow's car when they ambushed and killed him and his gangster girlfriend Bonnie Parker in 1934?

1974. Which of the contiguous 48 states was the last to be explored?

1975. What are the six flags that have flown over Texas?

1976. Columbus had three ships on his first exploration of America. How many were under his command on his second expedition?

1977. How did the American Indian brave shave?

1978. How did the Pilgrims celebrate New Year's Day?

1979. How many days did the historic civil rights march from Selma to Montgomery, Alabama, take?

1980. According to poetic legend, Lizzie Borden used her ax to give her mother 40 whacks and her father 41. How many whacks did the police actually accuse her of delivering?

1981. What does Apache chief Geronimo's Indian name—Goyathlay—mean in English?

1982. How long did the April 18, 1906, earthquake in San Francisco last?

1983. What were the dimensions of the "Star Spangled Banner" Francis Scott Key saw flying over Baltimore's Fort McHenry "by the dawn's early light" almost 185 years ago?

1984. What size was the first footprint on the moon—the one made by astronaut Neil Armstrong when he took his historic "one small step for man" on July 20, 1969?

1971. *From Germany—the Dutch designation comes from the word Deutsch, meaning "German."*

1972. *"Strike the tent."*

1973. *They counted 106.*

1974. *Idaho, which was first visited by Meriwether Lewis and William Clark in 1805 during their famous expedition across America.*

1975. *The flags of Spain, France, Mexico, the Republic of Texas, the Confederacy, and the U.S.*

1976. *Seventeen.*

1977. *With clam shells, which he used as tweezers.*

1978. *They didn't. They considered it a blasphemous reverence for the Roman god Janus, for whom the month of January is named. The pilgrims referred to January as First Month.*

1979. *Five days.*

1980. *Dad, 10; stepmom, 19. But Lizzie was acquitted at her trial for the 1892 double slaying.*

1981. *One who yawns. He was given the name Geronimo—Spanish for Jerome—by Mexicans.*

1982. *48 seconds. The San Francisco earthquake of 1989 lasted 15 seconds.*

1983. *30 feet by 42 feet. The fort's commander had it made that large so "the British will have no difficulty in seeing it from a distance."*

1984. *It was 13 inches by 6 inches—the dimensions of Armstrong's boot. The exterior shell is the same size for all the astronauts' boots.*

1985. What were the police in Atlantic City, New Jersey, cracking down on when they arrested 42 men on the beach in 1935?

1986. What is Mary E. Surratt's significance in U.S. history?

1987. What did famed bank robber Charles Arthur "Pretty Boy" Floyd do whenever he pulled off a job, which made him a hero to many people?

1988. How many children did Mormon leader Brigham Young have?

1989. How many crates did it take to transport the Statue of Liberty from France to New York in 1885?

1990. What did gangster Al Capone's oldest brother, Jim—who went by the name Richard "Two Gun" Hart—do for a living?

1991. In an effort to avoid recapture, how did convicted bank robber Robert Alan Litchfield change his features after his 1989 escape from Fort Leavenworth, where he was serving a 140-year term?

1992. Why didn't the anti-porn law passed by the town council of Winchester, Indiana, ever take effect?

1993. What plant's leaves did American colonists use to brew a tea substitute following their Boston Tea Party tax protest?

1994. When police and federal agents finally decoded the notation "K1,P2,CO8,K5" found in a Seattle woman's little black book in 1942, what did it turn out to be?

1995. What was the name of the ship that was supposed to accompany the Mayflower on its historic journey across the Atlantic in 1620?

1996. What well-known millionaire died when the Titanic sank?

1997. What song was the band playing while the Titanic was sinking?

1998. Who gave our country the name, the United States of America?

1985. Topless swimsuits on men.

1986. She was the first woman executed by hanging. A military panel convicted her of conspiracy in the assassination of President Abraham Lincoln. Her guilt, however, is still in question.

1987. He destroyed all first mortgages he could find on the chance they had not been recorded, and tossed money out the window of his getaway car.

1988. 57, with 16 of his 27 wives.

1989. 214.

1990. He was a lawman in Nebraska—serving as a town marshal and a state sheriff.

1991. He underwent plastic surgery so he would look like actor Robert DeNiro.

1992. The editors of the only newspaper in town refused to publish it, claiming the law itself was pornographic. Under local statutes, no law could take effect until published in a newspaper.

1993. The goldenrod's—the drink it yielded was known as "liberty tea."

1994. Knitting instructions: "Knit one, purl two, cast on eight, knit five."

1995. The Speedwell. It was left behind in Plymouth, England, when it started taking on water.

1996. John Jacob Astor.

1997. Not "Nearer My God To Thee," as is popularly believed, but the hymn "Autumn," by Francois Barthelemon.

1998. Thomas Paine.

1999. Who was the only U.S. astronaut to fly in the Mercury, Gemini and Apollo programs?

2000. What exactly did the Apollo II crew declare on a U.S. Customs form upon their return from the moon on July 24, 1969?

2001. Who is infamous for staging the first train robbery?

2002. What was the name of the ship on which Francis Scott Key composed "The Star Spangled Banner" in Baltimore Harbor, in 1814?

2003. French architect Pierre L'Enfant is best remembered in American history for what?

2004. What was the name of the first child born of English parents in the New World?

2005. John Glenn was the first American to orbit the earth. Who was the second?

2006. How many women were among the first 105 colonists to settle in Jamestown, Virginia, in 1607?

2007. When the first census of the United States was taken in 1790, what percentage of the population was African-American?

2008. What was the name of the man who shot frontier legend Wild Bill Hickok in the back while he was playing poker in a Deadwood, South Dakota, saloon in 1876.

2009. On what day of the week in 1492 did Christopher Columbus set sail for the New World?

2010. What was originally on the site of America's first mint, the Philadelphia mint, which opened in 1792?

2011. What bird was imported to the United States from England in 1850 to protect shade trees from voracious, foliage-eating caterpillars?

2012. What were the five tribes in the Iroquois League when it was formed around 1600?

1999. *Walter Shirra.*

2000. *"Moon walk and moon dust samples."*

2001. *Jesse James, at Adair, Iowa, on July 21, 1873.*

2002. *The Minden.*

2003. *He planned the city of Washington, D.C. in 1791. It was known at the time as Federal City.*

2004. *Virginia Dare, who was born in 1587 on Roanoke Island.*

2005. *Scott Carpenter, on May 24, 1962.*

2006. *None. The first two women settlers arrived in 1609.*

2007. *19.3 percent—of which 59,557 were free blacks and 697,624 were slaves.*

2008. *Jack McCall. He was acquitted at a trial the day after the shooting, then retried and hanged.*

2009. *Friday.*

2010. *A distillery.*

2011. *The English (or house) sparrow. Eight pairs were imported by the Brooklyn Institute in New York. They multiplied so prolifically that in 1890, New York City imported starlings to prey on the sparrows in Central Park.*

2012. *The Mohawk, Seneca, Onondaga, Oneida and Cayuga. The league later expanded to six tribes when it admitted the Tuscarora.*

2013. How many stripes were on the official American flag in 1818 before Congress passed a law forever setting the number at 13?

2014. How many signatures are on the Declaration of Independence?

2015. How was Martha's Vineyard spelled on official U.S. government maps before 1933?

2016. Who was the first European explorer to see and cross the Mississippi River?

2017. What famous Old West town was known as Goose Flats before a prospector named Ed Schieffelin discovered silver there?

2018. How much did the multi-layered space suits worn by astronauts on the Apollo moon landings weigh—life-support system included?

2019. What city was the center of gold mining in the United States before the discovery of gold at Sutter's Mill in 1848 triggered the California gold rush?

2020. How many children did Pocahontas and her husband John Rolfe have?

2021. A likeness of what famous legendary figure was on the prow of the first ship to bring Dutch settlers to America?

2022. How many states were there in the United States at the turn of the century?

2023. What is the diameter of each of the two main cables on San Francisco's Golden Gate Bridge?

2024. For what famous historic figure was Marietta, Ohio, named?

2025. What role did the ships Dartmouth, Beaver and Eleanor play in American history?

2026. Which American state capital was originally incorporated as the town of Marthasville?

2013. *15. The number had been increased to 15 in 1795 to include Kentucky and Vermont. But with more and more states joining the Union, the number was reduced to 13 as of July 4, 1818, to represent the original 13 states.*

2014. *56.*

2015. *Marthas Vineyard. The apostrophe making the name possessive was the first apostrophe sanctioned by the U.S. Board on Geographic Names.*

2016. *Hernando de Soto of Spain, in 1541. He died the following year.*

2017. *Tombstone, Arizona. Schieffelin picked the name because soldiers laughingly told him all he'd find there would be his tombstone when he set out to prospect in the area in the 1870s.*

2018. *On earth, 180 pounds; on the moon, with the reduced lunar gravity, 30 pounds.*

2019. *Charlotte, North Carolina. From 1800 to 1848, gold mines in the Charlotte area were the main source of U.S. gold.*

2020. *One, a son named Thomas, who was born and educated in England but settled in Virginia.*

2021. *Sinterklass—a predecessor of Saint Nicholas, better known to us as Santa Claus.*

2022. *45. Oklahoma became the 46th state in 1907; followed by New Mexico and Arizona in 1912; and Alaska and Hawaii in 1959.*

2023. *3 feet—or 36.5 inches, to be exact. There are 25,572 wires contained in each of the cables.*

2024. *Marie Antoinette.*

2025. *They were the three ships targeted by American colonists at the Boston Tea Party on December 16, 1773. Together the three ships had 342 casks of the tea dumped into Boston Harbor by colonists who disguised themselves as Mohawks to carry out their historic protest of the British tax on tea.*

2026. *Atlanta, Georgia, in 1843—in honor of Martha Lumpkin, daughter of the governor of the state. A railroad official changed the name two years later to Atlanta, the feminine of Atlantic, after the Western and Atlantic Railroad, which had selected the town as the last stop on its line.*

2027. What famous Englishman gave us the expression, "Keep your powder dry"?

2028. How long—in days—did the Pilgrims' first Thanksgiving in 1621 last?

2029. How much was suffragette Susan B. Anthony fined for voting in 1872?

2030. What was the source of E pluribus unum—Latin for "one from many"—the motto the Second Continental Congress adopted for the Great Seal of the newly named United States?

2031. How many times does each newly produced U.S. dollar bill have to go through the printing press?

2032. According to the Census Bureau, what are the five most common surnames in the United States?

2033. Where were the Library of Congress's original copies of the U.S. Constitution and the Declaration of Independence kept during World War II?

2034. Which state is America's flattest, with a difference of only 345 feet between its highest and lowest points?

2035. Which state is the most thickly forested, with 89.8 percent of its land area classified as wooded by the U.S. Forest Service?

2036. How many jurors were dismissed during the course of O. J. Simpson's double-murder trial?

2037. How many ballots in the House of Representatives did it take to break the deadlocked presidential election between Thomas Jefferson and Aaron Burr in February 1801?

2038. How fast—in miles per hour—do the fastest roller coasters in the U.S. go?

2039. How many signers of the Declaration of Independence went on to serve as president of the United States?

2040. What was the country of origin of the greatest number of immigrants to pass through Ellis Island between 1892 and 1924?

2027. *Oliver Cromwell. In 1642 at the Battle of Edgehill, he told his troops, "Put your trust in God, but keep your powder dry."*

2028. *Three. It featured bountiful meals, demonstrations by the Plymouth militia, traditional Indian dancing by the native guests, and foot races and other athletic contests.*

2029. *$100.*

2030. *It was from a recipe for salad in a poem entitled "Moretum," attributed to Virgil. The words, chosen by Benjamin Franklin, John Adams and Thomas Jefferson, were known at the time because they appeared as a motto on the cover of Gentlemen's Magazine.*

2031. *Three. First the front is printed in black, then the back is printed in green, and finally, the front is overprinted with the serial number and Treasury Department seal in green.*

2032. *Smith, Johnson, Williams, Jones and Brown, in that order.*

2033. *At Fort Knox, Kentucky*

2034. *Florida. Delaware is the second flattest state, with an elevation range of 442 feet.*

2035. *Maine. It's followed by New Hampshire, at 88.1 percent, and West Virginia, with 77.5 percent.*

2036. *10.*

2037. *36.*

2038. *The two fastest—the Steel Phantom in West Mifflin, Pennsylvania, and the Desperado in Jean, Nevada—reach a speed of 82 miles an hour.*

2039. *Two—John Adams and Thomas Jefferson.*

2040. *Italy, with 2.5 million. It was followed by Austria-Hungary, 2.2 million; Russia, 1.9 million; and Germany, 633,000.*

2041. How many states border an ocean?

2042. Where is the Superman Museum located?

2043. What words did Thomas Jefferson use in his final draft of the Declaration of Independence to describe the truths we now hold to be "self-evident"?

2044. What interest rate was charged when the U.S. government took out its first loan in September 1789 to help pay the salaries of the president and Congress?

2045. How much—in pounds and shillings—did Paul Revere charge in expenses for his ride to New York and Philadelphia to deliver news of the Boston Tea Party in December 1773?

2046. What motto was inscribed on the 1787 Fugio cent, the first coin issued by authority of the United States?

2047. After what famous eatery did railroad innovator George Pullman name his first luxury dining car in 1832?

2048. How many male justices had been appointed to the U.S. Supreme Court before Sandra Day O'Connor became the first woman named to the nation's highest court?

2049. What are the eight Rocky Mountain states?

2050. How long did it take aerialist Philippe Petit to make his 1,350-foot-long tightrope walk between the twin towers of the World Trade Center in New York City in 1974?

2051. What state capital was originally called Pig's Eye?

2052. What famous Indian chief's name was Goyakla or Goyathlay, which means One Who Yawns in his native tongue?

2053. In the early years of America's celebration of Mother's Day, what flower was customarily worn by those honoring their moms?

2054. What did "Little Miss Sure Shot" Annie Oakley do with all her gold shooting medals?

2055. What percent of a newly minted dime is silver?

2041. *23. They are: Maine, New Hampshire, Massachusetts, Rhode Island, Connecticut, New York, New Jersey, Delaware, Maryland, Virginia, North Carolina, South Carolina, Georgia, Florida, Alabama, Mississippi, Louisiana, Texas, California, Oregon, Washington, Alaska and Hawaii.*

2042. *In Metropolis, Illinois. The comic book superhero lived and worked as Clark Kent in a fictional city named Metropolis.*

2043. *Jefferson wrote "sacred and undeniable," but Benjamin Franklin, acting as his editor, changed the wording to "self-evident." In all, 86 changes were made to the draft submitted by Jefferson.*

2044. *Six percent. The loan, for $200,000, was from the Bank of New York. A similar loan was obtained from the Bank of North America.*

2045. *14 pounds, 2 shillings. The trip took him 11 days. His bill, endorsed by John Hancock, was sold at auction in 1978 for $70,000.*

2046. *"Mind your business." The motto was suggested by Benjamin Franklin. Fugio is Latin for "I am fleeing"—meaning time flies.*

2047. *Delmonico's, the fashionable New York restaurant.*

2048. *104. She was nominated to the Supreme Court in 1981 by Ronald Reagan.*

2049. *Idaho, Montana, Wyoming, Nevada, Utah, Colorado, Arizona and New Mexico.*

2050. *50 minutes.*

2051. *St. Paul, Minnesota. Pig's Eye was the nickname of one of the town's first settlers, a French-Canadian trader named Pierre Parrant.*

2052. *The Apache we know as Geronimo, Spanish for Jerome.* **2053.** *The carnation. Pink carnations were worn by those whose mothers were alive; white by those whose mothers had died.*

2054. *She had them melted down, then sold the gold and gave the money to charity.*

2055. *None. As of 1965, the U.S. Mint stopped putting silver in dimes. They contain 75 percent copper and 25 percent nickel, bonded to an inner core of pure copper. Previously, dimes were 90 percent silver and 10 percent copper.*

2056. For what is the telephone number 800-555-0199 reserved?

2057. What three names were given to more than half the females christened in the Massachusetts Bay Colony in the 1600s?

2058. What group of Americans speak a dialect they call Mudderschprooch?

2059. What shipboard position did John Washington, George Washington's grandfather, hold when he sailed from England to Virginia aboard the ketch Sea Horse of London in 1657?

2060. What Ivy League college was the last to go coed?

2061. What Old West city was named after a biblical city that drew its name from the Hebrew word for "grassy plain."

2062. How many U.S. states are there with only four letters in their names? Watch out, this is a trick question.

2063. What American city claims to have the only authentic Dutch windmill in the country?

2064. How long must a person be dead before he or she can be honored with a U.S. commemorative stamp?

2065. In airport code, LAX stands for Los Angeles International Airport and JFK for Kennedy International Airport. What airport is represented by the initials IAD?

2066. What weekly periodical was the first magazine in history to sell a billion copies in a year?

2056. *The movies. It's the 800 number set aside for use in films.*

2057. *Sarah, Elizabeth and Mary.*

2058. *The Amish. The language is Pennsylvania Dutch.*

2059. *He was a ship's mate. Although Washington intended to return to England with the ketch and a cargo of tobacco, the ship sank and he stayed in the colonies.*

2060. *Dartmouth, in 1972.*

2061. *Abilene, Kansas, which was entirely grassland when it was named in the mid-nineteenth century and served as the end of the famous Chisholm Trail. The biblical Abilene (from the Hebrew word abel) is mentioned in Luke 3:1 and was in ancient Syria.*

2062. *Nine. The easy ones are Iowa and Utah. The tough ones are Alabama, Alaska, Hawaii, Indiana, Kansas, Mississippi and Tennessee.*

2063. *Aptly named Holland, Michigan, founded in 1847 by Dutch immigrants and site of an annual tulip festival. The city's centuries-old windmill was dismantled in Vinkel, Holland, and reassembled there in 1965.*

2064. *At least 10 years—except for U.S. presidents. Commemorative stamps can be issued for a deceased president on the first birthday anniversary following his death, or anytime thereafter.*

2065. *Dulles International Airport in Washington, D.C.*

2066. *TV Guide, in 1974.*

2067. What was the dark blue Crayola crayon called before its name was changed to midnight blue in 1958?

2068. What did Wild Bill Hickok toss around his bed so he wouldn't be surprised by anyone sneaking up on him while he slept?

2069. What state has an average of 124 tornadoes a year—more than any other?

2070. What name was given to the largest diamond ever found in the U.S.?

2071. What did the middle initial O stand for in the late Supreme Court Justice William O. Douglas's name?

2072. What number iron did astronaut Alan Shepard use when he took his famous swing at a golf ball on the moon?

2073. What is the flickertail, from which North Dakota gets its official state nickname, the Flickertail State?

2074. What did Robert LeRoy Ripley, creator of the Believe It or Not newspaper cartoons, call his oddity-filled 27-room home?

2075. How many of the ships involved in Columbus's historic 1492 expedition made return voyages to the New World?

2076. American dollar bills are not printed on paper as many believe—what are they printed on?

2077. What famous American statesman made three appearances on national TV as a weather forecaster?

2078. According to Senate tradition, who is assigned the desk once occupied by Daniel Webster?

2079. What famous Old West lawman was appointed deputy U.S. marshal for New York by Theodore Roosevelt?

2080. What state's official bird is the roadrunner?

2081. How many terms did American frontiersman Davy Crockett serve in Congress?

2067. *Prussian blue. It was the first crayon renamed by Binney & Smith, which started producing crayons in 1903.*

2068. *Crumpled newspapers.*

2069. *Texas. In second place is Oklahoma, which averages 56 tornadoes a year.*

2070. *The Uncle Sam diamond. It was 40.23 carats in the rough when it was found in Murfreesboro, Arkansas, in 1924, and it yielded a 12.42-carat gem.*

2071. *Orville.*

2072. *A six. The club actually was a 6-iron head attached to a jointed astronaut tool used to scoop soil.*

2073. *A squirrel—the Richardson ground squirrel—widely found in North Dakota.*

2074. *Bion—for Believe It or Not.*

2075. *Only one—the Niña. The Santa Maria, Columbus's flagship, ran aground off Hispaniola and was abandoned on the first expedition; the Pinta sailed home from the New World and disappeared from history.*

2076. *Fabric—a cotton linen blend.*

2077. *Former secretary of state and national security advisor Henry Kissinger, in 1991.*

2078. *The senior senator from New Hampshire. The tradition was established by New Hampshire Senator Styles Bridges, who discovered the desk in the basement of the Capitol. (Webster, who represented Massachusetts in the Senate, was born in New Hampshire.)*

2079. *Bat Masterson.*

2080. *New Mexico's.*

2081. *Three.*

2082. What figure in American history is believed to have inspired the exclamation "Great Scott"?

2083. How fast was New York City cabbie Jacob German driving when he became the first motorist arrested in the U.S. for speeding?

2084. What was the first word spoken on the moon?

2085. What was Benjamin Franklin explaining when he said, "An ounce of prevention is worth a pound of cure"?

2086. How many banks and trains did the notorious Jesse James rob?

2087. What was the name of De Tour Village, Michigan, before it was changed?

2088. What was the first country to which the United States sent a woman as ambassador?

2089. Of the 14 states bordering on the Atlantic, which has the least oceanfront—only 13 miles?

2090. What did the town of Ismay, Montana, change its name to in 1993?

2091. How did Embarrass, Wisconsin, get its name?

2092. What was the weekly salary paid to Chief Sitting Bull when he was part of Buffalo Bill Cody's traveling Wild West Show?

2093. What is the only crime defined in the U.S. Constitution?

2094. When the first U.S. Congress set the president's pay at $25,000 a year, what salary did it establish for the vice president?

2082. *Gen. Winfield Scott—the hero of the Mexican War and the losing candidate for president in 1852.*

2083. *12 miles an hour. The year was 1899, and the arresting officer was on a bicycle.*

2084. *"Houston." Astronaut Neil Armstrong's first message on July 20, 1969, was: "Houston, Tranquillity Base here. The Eagle has landed."*

2085. *Why he had just attached a lightning rod to his house.*

2086. *Banks, 12; trains, 7.*

2087. *Detour. It was changed to avoid confusion with road signs. The village is located on Lake Huron at the eastern tip of Michigan's Upper Peninsula.*

2088. *Denmark, in 1933. Ruth Bryan Owen, a two-term congresswoman and the daughter of William Jennings Bryan, served until 1936 when she married Danish citizen Borge Rohde.*

2089. *New Hampshire. Florida has the most, 580 miles.*

2090. *Joe, Montana, in honor of the star quarterback.*

2091. *The village's founding fathers weren't commemorating an event that left them red-faced. They took the name from a local river that lumberjacks often found impassable—and embarras is French for "hindrance" or "obstacle."*

2092. *$50.*

2093. *Treason—in Article III, Section 3.*

2094. *$5,000.*

2095. What state owes its name to its having been discovered during Eastertime?

2096. In what state was the Battle of Tippecanoe fought in November 1811?

2097. El Paso is known as the Four C City. What attractions do the four C's represent?

2098. Under the rules of the Senate Ethics Committee, what is the maximum number of times a senator's name can appear in a newsletter to his or her constituents?

2099. Who represented Aaron Burr's wife, Eliza Jumel, when she sued her 80-year-old husband for divorce on grounds of adultery in 1836?

2100. What was the name of Paul Bunyan's pet moosehound?

2101. What state has official neckwear?

2102. In what year did the F. B. I, established in 1908 as the Bureau of Investigation, start hiring women as special agents?

2103. The flag of what American state was designed by a 13-year-old- boy?

2104. At what constant speed does the cable that pulls San Francisco's famous cable cars move—in miles per hour?

2105. Who was the first African-American to have his portrait engraved on a U.S. coin?

2106. What was the late Supreme Court Justice Thurgood Marshall's first name at birth?

2107. What was the featured attraction between the Indian elephant act and the ape-man act at the Barnum & Bailey Circus in 1896?

2108. Where was Billy the Kid, the notorious Wild West outlaw, born?

2109. In what city did the high-kicking Rockettes of New York's Radio City Music Hall get their start?

2095. *Florida. Spanish explorer Juan Ponce de Leon named the land Pascua Florida— "flowery Easter"—when he discovered it in 1513.*

2096. *Indiana.*

2097. *Cattle, climate, copper and cotton.*

2098. *An average of eight times per page. The rule applies to franked (postage-exempt) mail.*

2099. *Alexander Hamilton, Jr., son of the man Burr killed in his famous duel. Jumel was granted a legal divorce on the day of Burr's death.*

2100. *Elmer.*

2101. *Arizona—the bolo tie.*

2102. *In 1972—after the death of longtime director J. Edgar Hoover, who had banned women agents.*

2103. *Alaska. Seventh-grader Benny Benson entered the design—of the Big Dipper and the North Star on a field of blue—in an American Legion contest in 1927. It was adopted as the territorial flag, and later as the state flag.*

2104. *9 mph.*

2105. *Booker T. Washington, on a commemorative silver half-dollar issued from 1946 to 1951.*

2106. *Thoroughgood—he shortened it when he was in the second grade.*

2107. *An automobile. American auto pioneer Charles Duryea drove around in one of the 13 autos his Duryea Motor Wagon Company produced that year.*

2108. *In New York City, as Henry McCarty, in 1859. He later changed his name to Henry Antrim, then to William (Billy the Kid) Bonney.*

2109. *In St. Louis. The dancing group was organized there in 1925 as the Missouri Rockets. After changing the name to the Roxyettes, the group moved to Radio City, becoming the Rockettes in 1932.*

2110. How has American veterinarian and U.S. Agriculture Department inspector Daniel E. Salmon (1850-1914) been immortalized?

2111. What was the last institution of higher learning in the United States established by royal decree?

2112. What mountain has the most extensive glacial system of any single peak in the contiguous 48 states?

2113. What was the Declaration of Sentiments, drafted in Seneca Falls, New York, in 1848?

2114. What was the name of strongman-bodybuilder Charles Atlas's son?

2115. What was Benjamin Franklin's last official act?

2116. What body of water did the early American settlers describe as "too thick to drink, too thin to plow"?

2117. What is the name of the 600-mile-long California trail that the Spanish blazed from mission to mission from San Diego to Sonoma?

2118. What role did Garret A. Hobart play in American history?

2119. In what city was the first stock exchange in the United States established?

2120. Who wrote the unofficial anthem of Hawaii, "Aloha Oe"?

2121. What famous early Americans named North America's whistling swan?

2122. How many single-serving jars of baby food does the average American baby eat in one year?

2123. In 1910 there were 32 million Americans living on farms. How many were living on farms in 1990?

2124. How was a man named Fred Ott immortalized by Thomas Edison?

2110. Salmonella—*the sometimes deadly bacteria*—*is named for him.*

2111. Dartmouth College, which received its royal charter from England's King George III in 1769.

2112. Mount Rainier, in Washington State. It has a total of 26 named glaciers.

2113. A treatise, patterned after the Declaration of Independence, that declared "All men and women are created equal." It was signed by 100 people— 68 women and 32 men—at the nation's first women's rights convention.

2114. Hercules. He grew up to become a math teacher.

2115. Two months before his death in 1790, he signed a petition to Congress calling for the abolition of slavery. He did so as president of the Pennsylvania Society for Promoting the Abolition of Slavery.

2116. The Mississippi River, which is nicknamed the Big Muddy.

2117. El Camino Real. It linked 21 missions and 4 forts.

2118. Vice president (1897-99) to William McKinley—Hobart died while in office.

2119. In Philadelphia, in 1790—two years before a New York exchange was set up.

2120. Queen Liliuokalani—the last royal ruler of the Hawaiian Islands.

2121. Explorers Meriwether Lewis and William Clark, who discovered the swan and named it for its song during their expedition to the West Coast.

2122. 630, according to the folks at Gerber Products.

2123. 4.6 million.

2124. Edison filmed him sneezing in the first copyrighted film in history.

2125. What late Nobel Peace Prize-winning world leader was once a wanted terrorist with a $50,000 bounty on his head?

2126. How did Charles Lindbergh's Spirit of St. Louis get back to the U.S. after its historic 1927 transatlantic flight to Paris?

2127. Where was the flower known as the Yellow Rose of Texas first found in the United States?

2128. How wide are the stars from point to point on the flag that inspired Francis Scott Key to write "The Star-Spangled Banner"?

2129. What two changes have been made in the wording of the U.S. Pledge of Allegiance since it was first published in 1892?

2130. How many birthday cards does the average person receive annually?

2131. What magazine regularly publishes a column called "Streetwalker"?

2132. The name of what American state capital means "sheltered harbor."

2133. Why were many private clubs able to serve alcoholic beverages legally during Prohibition?

2134. What is the waist size of the Statue of Liberty?

2135. Who opened the first public aquarium in the United States?

2136. What group of Americans were the first to use the term rub out as a synonym for killing?

2125. *Israeli Prime Minister Menachem Begin. The bounty was offered by British authorities in 1946 when Begin led the Irgun underground guerrillas in their fight for Zionist homeland. He shared the Nobel Prize with Egyptian President Anwar Sadat in 1978.*

2126. *In a pine packing crate, measuring 27 by 12 by 9 feet, that was put aboard the cruiser USS Memphis.*

2127. *In New York City. A lawyer named George Harrison found it as a seedling in the 1830s on his farm near what is now Penn Station. The rose was brought out west by settlers and—according to legend—adopted by Texans after Mexican General Santa Anna was distracted by a beautiful woman wearing it in her hair.*

2128. *Two feet across. The flag is now on display at the Smithsonian Institute in Washington, D.C.*

2129. *The words "the flag of the United States of America" replaced the original words "my flag" in 1923; and the phrase "under God" was added in 1954.*

2130. *Eight, according to the folks at Hallmark.*

2131. *Forbes. The street referred to, of course, is Wall Street.*

2132. *Honolulu.*

2133. *Their alcohol had been purchased before Prohibition went into effect. The Eighteenth Amendment didn't ban the purchase, possession or consumption of alcohol—it banned its manufacture, sale, transportation, importation or exportation.*

2134. *The statue measures 35 feet in diameter at the waist. But there is no real "waistline"—the robe forms the outer shell of the statue and there is no "torso" underneath.*

2135. *Showman P.T. Barnum, in New York City in 1856.*

2136. *Trappers—not gangsters—during the early nineteenth century. The term was derived from Plains Indian sign language, which used a rubbing motion to indicate killing.*

2137. What magazine did the Library of Congress cease publishing in braille in 1985 after Congress voted to withhold funding?

2138. Who was the first chairman of the Securities and Exchange Commission?

2139. For whom were Mount Wayne, Mount Powell and Mount Hughes named in Utah's Escalante Desert?

2140. What six Americans states were named after English kings or queens?

2141. Which is the only one of the original 48 states to have a fjord—a narrow sea inlet bordered by steep cliffs?

2142. What state's official motto has the capital of another state in it?

2143. What famous American was listed in the 1920 Chicago telephone directory as "second hand furniture dealer, 2220 S. Wabash Ave."?

2144. By law, how long must information collected in a U.S. census remain confidential?

2145. What is the unusual state gem of Washington?

2146. Who coined the word hello and introduced it as the proper way to answer a telephone call?

2147. How soon after gold was discovered at Sutter's mill in 1848 did the United States acquire California?

2148. What post office—zip code 33843—is the smallest in the country?

2149. What cities served as the seat of government for the fledgling U.S.A. before Washington, D.C., became the nation's capital in December 1800?

2137. *Playboy, which it had been publishing in braille—without ads or pictures—for 15 years. Publication resumed in 1986 after the courts ruled Congress's action illegal. At the time Playboy was the sixth most popular of the 36 publications the Library was printing in braille.*

2138. *Joseph P. Kennedy—father of President John F. Kennedy.*

2139. *John Wayne, Dick Powell and Howard Hughes. The three mountains were named in their honor after they filmed The Conqueror—about Mongol leader Genghis Khan—on location in the desert in 1954.*

2140. *Georgia, named for King George II; North Carolina and South Carolina, named for King Charles I (from Carolana, "land of Charles," in Latin); Maryland, for Queen Henrietta Maria, wife of Charles I; and Virginia and West Virginia, named for Elizabeth I (who was known as the Virgin Queen).*

2141. *Maine—its six-mile-long fjord, Somes Sound, is located at Mount Desert Island, the largest island in the state.*

2142. *Colorado's—Nothing without providence (Nil sine numine). Providence, of course, is the capital of Rhode Island.*

2143. *Alphonse Capone, better known to us as gangster Al Capone.*

2144. *For 72 years—which is considered a normal lifetime.*

2145. *Petrified wood.*

2146. *Thomas Edison. Alexander Graham Bell favored ahoy but lost out to Edison, whose hello was derived from halloo, the traditional call to rouse hounds to the chase.*

2147. *Nine days. California was part of the territory Mexico ceded to the U.S. in the Treaty of Guadalupe Hidalgo.*

2148. *The converted 8- by-7-foot fertilizer shed that serves the 200 families living in and around Ochopee, in the Florida Everglades.*

2149. *Philadelphia, York and Lancaster, Pennsylvania; Baltimore and Annapolis, Maryland; Princeton and Trenton, New Jersey; and New York City.*

2150. How did a postage stamp convince the U.S. Congress to build a canal across Panama rather than the original choice, Nicaragua?

2151. In June 1939 a New York City magistrate ruled nose-thumbing legal with one reservation. What was it?

2152. What two state flags include a Confederate flag in their design?

2153. Where did the prefabricated Quonset hut get its name?

2154. How did Manhattan get its name—and what does it mean?

2155. Who were Robert Leroy Parker and Henry Longbaugh?

2156. Why did Benjamin Franklin call himself "perhaps the loneliest man" attending the First Continental Congress in 1774?

2157. How did San Francisco policemen save important city records from the devastating fires sparked by the 1906 earthquake?

2158. What city has the country's highest zip code number—99950?

2159. How many crisp new dollar bills to the pound?

2160. In 1925 what did con man Arthur Ferguson "lease" to a wealthy cattle rancher for 99 years at $100,000 a year?

2161. In 1814 when Francis Scott Key wrote what is now our National Anthem, how many stars and stripes were on the flag flying over Fort McHenry in Baltimore Harbor?

2162. Who was Florence Nightingale Graham?

2163. How much did Texas millionaire H. Ross Perot pay for a copy of the Magna Carta in 1984?

2150. *The Nicaraguan postage stamp showed a belching volcano, triggering fears that an eruption might destroy the canal.*

2151. *That the "thumber" be at a safe distance— "about 10 feet"—from the "thumbee."*

2152. *Those of Georgia and Mississippi.*

2153. *From Quonset, Rhode Island, where it was first manufactured during World War II.*

2154. *It's a derivative of the Indian word Manahachtaniek, which means "the island where we all got drunk," apparently referring to a spirited encounter between the Native Americans and some newly arrived Dutchmen.*

2155. *The inspiration for "Butch Cassidy and the Sundance Kid," portrayed on film by Paul Newman and Robert Redford in 1969 and William Katt and Tom Berenger in 1979.*

2156. *He had chosen his country over his only son, William, who had pledged loyalty to the British crown.*

2157. *They hauled them to a downtown square and soaked them with beer from nearby saloons.*

2158. *Ketchikan, Alaska. The lowest 00401, belongs to the Reader's Digest company in Pleasantville, New York.*

2159. *Exactly 490, according to the Bureau of Engraving and Printing.*

2160. *The White House. He fled after collecting the first year's rent but got caught a short time later trying to sell the Statue of Liberty to an Australian.*

2161. *Fifteen each. They represented the original 13 states plus Vermont and Kentucky.*

2162. *Beauty entrepreneur Elizabeth Arden. (Consistent with her given name, she briefly pursued a nursing career.)*

2163. *He paid $1.5 million for a version issued in 1297 and believed to be the most complete of the 17 copies known to exist. The original was issued in 1215, and 4 copies of that still exist: 2 in the British Museum, 1 at Lincoln Cathedral and 1 at Salisbury Cathedral.*

2164. Which six states have more senators than representatives in Congress?

2165. Where did the family of Thomas Mellon, founder of the prosperous banking dynasty, settle after immigrating to the U.S. from northern Ireland?

2166. What state has designated "Home on the Range" its official song?

2167. When Charles Lindbergh soloed across the Atlantic in 1927, what did he bring along to keep him company?

2168. Podunk has come to mean Smalltown, U.S.A. Where is Podunk?

2169. What organization in 1972 began encouraging its members to learn how to treat rat bites and read subway maps?

2170. What two cities were linked by the Chisholm Trail, the cattle drivers' route first used in 1867?

2171. Which American state legislature is the only one to have a single chamber?

2172. What city promotes itself as the "air capital of the world" because it produces more aircraft than any other city?

2173. What special training was required of the first airline stewardesses, hired by United Airlines in 1930?

2174. What is the foggiest place in the United States?

2175. At 11:03 p.m. on February 28, 1983, why did water usage in New York City rise by an unprecedented 300 million gallons?

2176. In what year were FBI agents first allowed to carry guns?

2177. What American statesman, in his later years, regularly received mail deliveries at a park bench in Lafayette Square, opposite the White House?

2164. *Alaska, Delaware, North Dakota, South Dakota, Vermont and Wyoming have only one representative each.*

2165. *Poverty Point, Pennsylvania.*

2166. *Kansas.*

2167. *The "Lone Eagle" took a Feliz the Cat doll on his 33½-hour flight.*

2168. *In Massachusetts, near Worcester.*

2169. *The Boy Scouts, by offering merit badges in those two areas of achievement.*

2170. *San Antonio, Texas, and Abilene, Kansas.*

2171. *The Nebraska legislature.*

2172. *Wichita, Kansas.*

2173. *They had to be registered nurses. The requirement was dropped 12 years later.*

2174. *Cape Disappointment, Washington. It's foggy there an average of 2,552 hours a year—or 106 complete days.*

2175. *The final episode of M*A*S*H had just ended, and an estimated one million New Yorkers flushed their toilets in unison.*

2176. *In 1934—26 years after the agency was established, and the year in which the careers of John Dillinger, Pretty Boy Floyd and Baby Face Nelson came to abrupt and bloody ends.*

2177. *Financier Bernard Baruch, who became known as the "Park Bench Statesman" during World War II when he used the unpainted oak bench as his office.*

2178. How many children were born to the Mayflower's Priscilla Mullins and "Speak for yourself John" Alden, whose romance was immortalized in "The Courtship of Miles Standish" by Henry Wadsworth Longfellow?

2179. What unwanted distinction did the Red Lantern in Chicago gain on February 1, 1920?

2180. The motto "In God We Trust" first appeared on U.S. currency in 1864. What was the denomination of the coin?

2181. What was on the site of the Empire State Building before the 102-story skyscraper was erected in 1931?

2182. To whom was Santa Claus delivering Christmas gifts in the Thomas Nast cartoon that first depicted him with a sleigh and reindeer?

2183. What did the town of Lovelady, New Jersey, change its name to in 1962?

2184. When was "In God We Trust"—which first appeared on an American coin in 1864—adopted as the national motto?

2185. What are the vital statistics of the 72-foot-high Betty Boop balloon in the Macy's Thanksgiving Day Parade?

2186. What famous Old West duo threw an elegant five-course Thanksgiving dinner for their neighbors as a thank-you for not being turned in to the law?

2187. When television cameras moved into the Senate in 1986, who advised its members, "You learn your lines, don't bump into the furniture, and, in the kissing scenes, keep your mouth closed?"

2188. When was the site of the Washington Memorial—completed in 1885—first proposed?

2189. What was the real name of criminal George "Baby Face" Nelson, who was Public Enemy Number One when he was gunned down by F.B.I. agents in 1934?

2190. How many American astronauts have walked on the moon?

2178. Ten. *According to "Families of the Pilgrims," by the Massachusetts Society of Mayflower Descendants, there were six girls and four boys.*

2179. *It was the first speakeasy raided by federal agents during Prohibition.*

2180. Two cents.

2181. The original Waldorf-Astoria Hotel.

2182. Soldiers fighting in the Civil War. *The cartoon, entitled "Santa Claus in Camp," appeared on the cover of "Harper's Weekly" on January 3, 1863.*

2183. Loveladies.

2184. In 1956.

2185. A shapely 34-24-36 (feet, that is).

2186. Butch Cassidy and the Sundance Kid. *The dinner, from oysters to plum pudding with brandy sauce, took place in Brown's Park, a valley at the junction of Utah, Colorado and Wyoming.*

2187. President Reagan, who said the advice came from his Hollywood days.

2188. In 1791, in Pierre L'Enfant's original master plan for the District of Columbia.

2189. Lester Gillis, who adopted his famous alias when he was arrested in his teens.

2190. Twelve, between July 1969 and December 1972. *In order of their lunar visits: Neil Armstrong, Edwin Aldrin, Charles Conrad, Alan Bean, Alan Shepard, Edgar Mitchell, David Scott, James Irwin, John Young, Charles Duke, Eugene Cernan and Harrison Schmitt.*

2191. What was Montana's capital, Helena, called when it was a mining camp in the 1860s?

2192. What unique monetary service has the St. Francis Hotel in San Francisco provided for the past 60 years?

2193. Colonial New York paved its first street—using stones—in 1657. What was its name?

2194. How much was Tennessee schoolteacher John T. Scopes fined after he was found guilty of teaching evolution at his famous "monkey trial" in 1925?

2195. How did John Paul Scott, the only prisoner known to have survived an escape from Alcatraz, make it across the perilous waters of San Francisco Bay?

2196. What state, of the contiguous 48, touches only one other state?

2197. Where did Yale students find the name "Whiffenpoof" for their singing society and song?

2198. Congress established the nation's first minimum wage in 1938. What was it?

2199. Who is the source of the U.S. Post Office's unofficial motto: "Neither snow, nor rain, nor heat, nor gloom of night stays these couriers from the swift completion of their appointed rounds"?

2200. What American city was founded in 1733 as a haven for British debtors?

2201. The highest and lowest points in the contiguous 48 states are within 75 miles of one another. What are they?

2202. The sign in front of a building on George Washington Parkway in Langley, Virginia, used to say Fairbank Highway Research. What does it say now?

2203. What was the source of the green copper used to repair the Statue of Liberty for her 100th birthday in 1986?

2191. *Last Chance Gulch.*

2192. *Its guests are given only freshly washed coins. The hotel employs a full-time coin washer.*

2193. *Stone Street.*

2194. *He had to pay $100.*

2195. *With water wings he fashioned from surgical gloves. Although he survived, he was recaptured after a 2½-mile swim.*

2196. *Maine—it touches only New Hampshire.*

2197. *From an imaginary character in the 1908 Victor Herbert operetta "Little Nemo."*

2198. *Twenty-five cents an hour.*

2199. *Greek historian Herodotus, who was referring to the couriers of Persia's King Xerxes I in the fifth century B.C.*

2200. *Savannah, Georgia.*

2201. *Mount Whitney, which is 14,494 feet above sea level, and Death Valley, which drops to 282 feet below sea level at a spot known as Bad Water. Both are in California.*

2202. *CIA—it was changed in 1974 in a Nixon administration move toward more open government.*

2203. *A Bell Laboratory roof in Murray Hill, New Jersey. New copper would have been penny-bright.*

2204. How much did NASA charge for America's first paying space passenger, scientist Charles Walker, on his trip aboard the shuttle Challenger in August 1984?

2205. How much did industrialist-philanthropist John D. Rockefeller—America's first billionaire—give to charity during his 97-year lifetime?

2206. What was civil libertarian Henry David Thoreau's response when his friend Ralph Waldo Emerson visited him in jail and asked: "Why are you in there, Henry?"

2207. How many sisters and brothers did Benjamin Franklin have?

2208. According to legend, why did Betsy Ross suggest making the stars on the American flag five-pointed instead of six-pointed, as originally planned?

2209. By what names do we know twin sisters Pauline and Esther Friedman, born on the Fourth of July, 1918?

2210. Why was astronaut John Young reprimanded after returning from the first multi-manned space flight with Gus Grissom in March 1965?

2211. What American city boasts a Moon Walk?

2212. What American diversion did the London *Times* label a "menace" in 1924 for "making devastating inroads on the working hours of every rank of society"?

2213. How long was Prohibition in effect in the U.S.?

2214. What name did Pocahontas, the Indian princess who saved Captain John Smith, adopt after she married settler John Rolfe and converted to Christianity?

2215. Who is the only king to be included in the National Statuary Hall in the U.S. Capitol building?

2216. What is the English translation of Sputnik—the name Russia gave to the first artificial satellite to orbit the earth?

2204. *NASA was paid $80,000 by McDonnell Douglas, for whom Walker manufactured a batch of rare hormones at zero gravity.*

2205. *He gave away more than a half billion dollars—$531,326,842.*

2206. *"Why are you out there?" Thoreau, as a protest against slavery, had refused to pay his poll tax.*

2207. *Sixteen—seven sisters and nine brothers. He was the fifteenth child and youngest son.*

2208. *Because she could easily cut them with a single snip of the scissors after folding the fabric in a special way.*

2209. *We know Pauline as* Dear Abby, *advice columnist Abigail Van Buren; Esther as advice columnist Ann Landers.*

2210. *For eating a smuggled corned beef sandwich during the flight, creating crumbs that threatened the craft's sensitive machinery.*

2211. *New Orleans. The crescent-shaped promenade along the Mississippi River is named for a former city mayor, Moon Landrieu.*

2212. *The crossword puzzle, which the introduced as a Christmas treat in its Sunday supplement in 1913.*

2213. *Almost 14 years, from January 1920 to December 1933.*

2214. *Rebecca.*

2215. *Hawaii's King Kamehameha.*

2216. *"Traveler."*

2217. What were the first words spoken by aviation great Charles Lindbergh when he landed in Paris following his historic nonstop solo flight across the Atlantic?

2218. How long did it take news of the "shot heard 'round the world" at the Battle of Lexington on April 19, 1775, to reach New York City?

2219. How many Finger Lakes are there in central New York?

2220. To whom did "New York" magazine present its 1985 "More Clothes Than Nancy Reagan Award"?

2221. For what 1961 story did the Associated Press issue its first public apology since it prematurely announced the end of World War II?

2222. How did the town of Ink, Arkansas, get its name?

2223. In what special way did Chicago mayor Richard J. Daley commemorate St. Patrick's Day in 1965?

2224. Where were the first parking meters in the U.S. installed?

2225. How much was the tax on tea when the colonists held the Boston Tea Party in 1773?

2226. What four states have active volcanoes?

2227. According to Indian legend, Lake Itasca in northwest Minnesota is named for I-tesk-ka, daughter of Hiawatha. What is its other claim to fame?

2228. Who was Marie Joseph Paul Yves Roch Gilbert du Motier?

2229. Which state was the first to outlaw slavery?

2230. How much was black seamstress Rosa Parks fined for refusing to give up her bus seat to a white man in the incident that launched the Reverend Martin Luther King Jr.'s civil rights career?

2231. What did the high-living gastronomical giant Diamond Jim Brady buy when his doctor ordered him to get some exercise?

2217. *"Are there any mechanics here?" When he was unable to understand the flurry of replies in French, he shouted, "Does anyone here speak English?"*

2218. *Four days.*

2219. *Eleven. According to Indian legend, they are the water-filled fingerprints of the Great Spirit.*

2220. *Barbie, the doll—because of the 20 million designer fashions sold for her.*

2221. *A story that First Lady Jackie Kennedy had been spotted doing the twist in a Palm Beach nightclub.*

2222. *When the Post Office application for the community was being filled out, someone wrote "ink" where the form requested "Name of town (write in ink)."*

2223. *He had 100 pounds of emerald green dye poured into the Chicago River.*

2224. *In Oklahoma City, Oklahoma, in 1935. Motorists paid a nickel for a 20-foot space.*

2225. *Three pence per pound.*

2226. *Alaska, California, Hawaii and Washington.*

2227. *The 1.8-square-mile lake is the main source of the 2,348-mile-long "father of waters," the Mississippi River.*

2228. *America's Revolutionary War ally, the Marquis de Lafayette.*

2229. *Rhode Island, in 1774.*

2230. *She was fined $14.*

2231. *A gold-plated bicycle with diamonds and rubies embedded in the handlebars.*

2232. On what college campus was Phi Beta Kappa—the oldest Greek letter society in the U.S.—first established in 1776?

2233. What was the name of the 1,550-pound bison at the New York Zoo that served as a model for the buffalo nickel, introduced in 1913?

2234. What wood is most widely used in making pencils in the United States?

2235. What two states produce the greatest number of Christmas trees?

2236. What creature serves as the mascot of the University of California at Santa Cruz?

2237. What was the name of Yale University's original bulldog mascot—and all namesakes that have followed?

2238. What did philanthropist Andrew Carnegie contribute to Princeton University in 1906?

2239. With what word did most people answer the telephone when it was first introduced at the end of the nineteenth century?

2240. What is May Day known as in Hawaii?

2241. The name of what Florida city means "rodent mouth" in Spanish?

2242. Before it got its present name in 1847, what American city was known as Yerba Buena— "good herb" in Spanish—for an aromatic herb that grew in the area?

2243. What monument is the tallest in the United States—at 630 feet?

2244. Where was the first library in North America established in 1638?

2245. What percentage of the United States is officially designated wilderness?

2232. The College of William and Mary in Williamsburg, Virginia.

2233. Black Diamond. It was sold for $700 in 1915 and turned into 750 pounds of usable meat.

2234. Cedar—more specifically, the incense cedar of the high Sierra Nevada in northern California. It has a straight grain and is soft enough to be sharpened without splintering. It replaced the red cedar of the southern U.S. after those forests were depleted.

2235. Oregon and Michigan.

2236. The banana slug.

2237. Handsome Dan.

2238. A 3½-mile-long lake to "take the young men's minds off football," a game he detested.

2239. "Ahoy." Thomas Edison later suggested replacing it with a simple "Hello."

2240. Lei Day. Ever since 1928, Hawaiians have dedicated the day to the garland of flowers that is their symbol of friendship—celebrating with Polynesian songs and pageantry.

2241. Boca Raton. The name is believed to come from the shape of the city's Atlantic Ocean shoreline.

2242. San Francisco.

2243. The Gateway Arch, in St. Louis, Missouri.

2244. At Harvard College. The initial collection consisted of 329 religious and philosophical texts.

2245. 3.8 percent.

2246. What was unusual about the hand-carved Great Seal of the U.S. that Soviet diplomats gave Averell Harriman in 1945 when he was U.S. ambassador to Moscow?

2247. How often can the design of an American coin be changed without Congressional approval?

2248. How many islands, reefs and shoals make up the Hawaiian archipelago?

2249. What city on the Virginia-North Carolina border is named for the two states?

2250. Who was the first U.S. citizen to cross the Continental Divide?

2251. How many shots were fired in the famous gunfight at the O.K. Corral?

2252. What building in Hayward, Wisconsin, is shaped like a muskie?

2253. The life expectancy of the average American born in 1990 is 72.7 years for males and 76.1 for females. What was it for the average American born in 1900?

2254. What animal served as Yale's mascot before the bulldog?

2255. How did Washington Post reporter Bob Woodward signal his anonymous Watergate source, Deep Throat, when he wanted to make contact?

2256. What major American city passed an ordinance in 1838 making it necessary to get a license before serenading a woman?

2257. What was the size of the standard lot in Levittown, New York, when it was developed as the first mass-housing suburb in the country following World War II?

2258. How many burglars were arrested inside the Democratic Party's national headquarters at the Watergate complex in Washington, D.C., on June 17, 1972?

2259. Who was the first American to get oil drilling concessions in Saudi Arabia and Kuwait?

2246. *It contained a listening device that enabled the Soviets to monitor all conversations in Harriman's private study, where the seal was displayed on the wall. The bug wasn't discovered until 1952.*

2247. *Once in 25 years.*

2248. *132.*

2249. *Virgilina.*

2250. *Meriwether Lewis, on August 12, 1805, during his historic expedition with William Clark.*

2251. *34—evenly split between the Earps and the Clantons. But the Earps were better marksmen, scoring 13 hits and killing three (Billy Clanton, and Frank and Tom McLowery). The Clantons had three hits, wounding two (Morgan and Virgil Earp) and ripping a hole in Wyatt Earp's coat.*

2252. *The National Fresh Water Fishing Hall of Fame.*

2253. *Males, 46.6; females, 48.7.*

2254. *A cat. The bulldog replaced the cat in the late 1800s.*

2255. *He put a red flag in a flowerpot on his apartment balcony.*

2256. *Los Angeles.*

2257. *60 by 100 feet. More than 17,000 one-story, two-bedroom, one-bath, wood-frame ranch houses were built—and sold for about $6,000 each.*

2258. *Five. They were adjusting wiretapping equipment that had been installed in May.*

2259. *John Paul Getty.*

2260. Whose statue stands in front of the headquarters of the Organization of American States in Washington, D.C.?

2261. Which state averages the greatest number of shark attacks annually?

2262. How much of the currency in circulation in the United States was believed to be counterfeit in 1865, when the Secret Service was established to combat counterfeiting?

2263. How many British bullets tore through the flag flying over Fort McHenry during the War of 1812 bombardment that inspired Francis Scott Key to write The Star-Spangled Banner?

2264. What state is nicknamed the Pelican State?

2265. The average shower Americans take lasts 10.4 minutes. How many gallons of water does it use up? Bonus: What's the most popular water temperature?

2266. What is the very appropriate state flower of Massachusetts?

2267. How old was Billy the Kid when he was shot to death by Sheriff Pat Garrett?

2268. How long did the jury deliberate at the sensational 1925 "Monkey Trial" of Tennessee science teacher John Scopes?

2269. What was the total weight—to the closest pound—of the septuplets born to Iowa parents Bobbi and Kenny McCaughey in 1997?

2270. What was the highest price ever paid by the United States for a territorial acquisition?

2271. What was the native tribe of Sacagawea, the Indian woman who helped guide Lewis and Clark on their historic 1804 journey of discovery?

2272. What was the name of the ship that carried the second group of colonists to Plymouth, Massachusetts?

2260. *Queen Isabella I, who financed Christopher Columbus's expedition to America. The statue was a gift from Spain.*

2261. *Florida, with an average of 13 a year.*

2262. *One-third.*

2263. *11.*

2264. *Louisiana. Its state bird is the pelican.*

2265. *Gallons, 12.4; temperature, 105 °F.*

2266. *The mayflower.*

2267. *21.*

2268. *Nine minutes. Scopes—whose trial was the setting for the play and film Inherit The Wind—was found guilty of violating a state law banning the teaching of evolution in public schools.*

2269. *20 pounds—or to be precise, 19 pounds 14 ounces.*

2270. *$25 million—to Denmark in 1917 for what is now the U.S. Virgin Islands.*

2271. *Shoshone. She was captured by the Hidatsas and sold into marriage to French Canadian trader/trapper Toussaint Charbonneau, who subsequently joined the Lewis and Clark expedition as a paid interpreter.*

2272. *The Fortune. It landed at Plymouth with 30 settlers on December 13, 1621—just under a year after the colonists aboard the Mayflower disembarked there.*

2273. How much did Baltimore seamstress Mary Young Pickersgill charge for materials and labor for the 30- by 42-foot woolen flag immortalized in Francis Scott Key's "The Star-Spangled Banner"?

2274. How high was the 1,340-foot-long wall that gave New York's Wall Street its name?

2275. Which U.S. Supreme Court justice wrote the greatest number of majority opinions?

2276. What historic name did Buffalo Bill Cody give to his buffalo gun?

2277. How many rest rooms are there along the 17½ miles of corridors in the Pentagon?

2278. Which is the only state ever to have two decorated Vietnam War combat veterans serving as U.S. senators at the same time?

2279. What was the municipal "cremator" built in New York City in 1885?

2280. When Benjamin Franklin was living in England, what stroke did he use in his regular swims across the Thames River?

2281. What is taught at the California Academy of Tauromaquia in San Diego?

2282. How many sides does a Navajo hogan have?

2283. What name was given to the baby born aboard the Mayflower during its historic voyage to the New World?

2284. Who was the first person honored as Man of the Year by Time magazine?

2285. In whose honor did the city of Modesto, California, erect a bronze sculpture of a teenage boy and girl sitting on the fender of a 1957 Chevrolet?

2286. Which state capital is situated on the Delaware River?

2287. What famous frontier outlaw once handed a press release to a robbery victim and told him to fill in the amount taken?

2273. *$405.90.*

2274. *12 feet. It was erected in 1653 by the Dutch colonists as protection against their enemies.*

2275. *Oliver Wendell Holmes. He wrote 873 majority opinions while serving on the Court from 1902 to 1932. Morrison H. Waite, chief justice from 1874 to 1888, wrote just one less-872.*

2276. *Lucrezia Borgia.*

2277. *284.*

2278. *Nebraska. The two are Democrat Bob Kerrey and Republican Chuck Hagel.*

2279. *An incinerator—the first city-run incinerator in the U.S. The first one built in England, in 1894, was called a "destructor."*

2280. *The breast stroke—the same stroke used by Matthew Webb in 1875 when he became the first person to swim across the English Channel.*

2281. *Bullfighting.*

2282. *Six; the entry always faces east, toward the morning sun.*

2283. *Oceanus. A second baby, who was named Peregrine, was born aboard ship after the Mayflower set anchor. The full names of the two boys were Oceanus Hopkins and Peregrine White.*

2284. *Charles Lindbergh, in 1927.*

2285. *Director-producer George Lucas. The sculpture, erected in 1997 on a plot renamed Lucas Square, pays tribute to the Modesto-born filmmaker's 1973 movie classic American Graffiti.*

2286. *Trenton, New Jersey.*

2287. *Jesse James. The victim was a train conductor.*

2288. How did Wisconsin come to be called the Badger State?

2289. On which holiday are the greatest number of collect calls generally made in the United States?

2290. What famous American inventor and diplomat compiled a list of more than 200 synonyms for "drunk," including cherry-merry, nimptopsical, and soaked?

2291. What did Paul Revere shout on his famous midnight ride from Boston to Lexington on April 18, 1775? Hint: Longfellow had it wrong in his poem.

2292. English ships once carried limes to protect sailors from scurvy; what did American vessels carry?

2293. What is the official state dessert of Massachusetts?

2294. How much was the tax per pound of tea that triggered the Boston Tea Party in 1773?

2295. How did Zilwaukee, Michigan, get its name?

2296. What American coin was the first to have nickel in it?

2297. Why do old firehouses have circular staircases?

Bonus Trivia

2298. General Henry "Lighthorse Harry" Lee, who said, "to the memory of the man, first in war, first in peace, and first in the hearts of his countrymen," in reference to George Washington, was the father of Confederate General Robert E. Lee.

2299. Ohio, known as the 17th state, technically did not become a state until August 7, 1953. Due to an oversight, Congress never voted on the resolution to admit Ohio to the Union until that date.

2300. Contrary to popular opinion, the "Saturday Evening Post" was not founded by Benjamin Franklin. It was founded by Charles Alexander and Samuel C. Atkinson in 1821. The "Saturday Evening Post" was, however, begun in the same building in which Franklin had published his "Pennsylvania Gazette."

2288. *"Badger" was the nickname given to Wisconsin's early miners—mostly Cornish immigrants—who worked underground in lead mines and, like badgers, dug caves in hillsides to survive the coldest winter months.*

2289. *Father's Day.*

2290. *Benjamin Franklin.*

2291. *"The Regulars are out!" The Regulars were the British troops.*

2292. *Cranberries.*

2293. *Boston cream pie.*

2294. *3 cents per pound.*

2295. *The owners of a local sawmill devised it, hoping German immigrants would confuse it with Milwaukee and settle in their town.*

2296. *The one-cent piece issued in1857. It contained 12 percent nickel and 88 percent copper. It was not until 1866 that five-cent pieces containing nickel were put into circulation.*

2297. *Because in days of yore the horses that pulled fire engines were stabled on the ground floor of fire houses and figured out how to walk up straight staircases.*

The World

Questions

2301. Where is Rock English spoken?

2302. In 1519 Portuguese navigator Ferdinand Magellan set out to circumnavigate the globe with five ships and 250 men. How many ships and men were left when the expedition ended in 1522?

2303. Where in the world is there a place called Disko Island?

2304. What recreational activity did Joseph Merlin of Belgium demonstrate for the first time in 1760 at a London masquerade party?

2305. What great thinker proved a lunar eclipse is the circular shadow of the earth on the moon?

2306. What is the longest strait in the world?

2307. In what country is the most remote weather station in the world located?

2308. How many members did the United Nations have when it celebrated its 50th anniversary in 1995?

Answers

2301. *On Gibraltar, which is commonly known as the Rock. It is a mixed patois of Spanish and English spoken by the natives of the strategic Mediterranean island.*

2302. *One ship, the Victoria, and 18 men—Magellan not among them. He was killed during the expedition.*

2303. *In Greenland. Although it's been renamed Qeqertarsuup, it is still widely known by its old name.*

2304. *Roller skating. Unfortunately, Merlin crashed into a mirror and was seriously injured, discouraging others from giving skating a whirl. Another 103 years passed before the first modern four-wheeled skates were introduced.*

2305. *Aristotle.*

2306. *The Strait of Malacca, between the Malay Peninsula and the island of Sumatra. It's about 500 miles long and connects the Andaman and South China seas.*

2307. *Canada. Its Eureka weather station is 600 miles from the North Pole.*

2308. *185. The last to join was the Pacific island chain of Palau, in December 1994.*

2309. How many loincloths did archaeologists find in King Tut's tomb after it was discovered in 1922?

2310. What percentage of the earth's land has a temperate climate?

2311. Which European country has two elements on the Periodic Table named after it?

2312. The capitals of what two South American countries are located on the mouth of the same river—the Rio de la Plata?

2313. What famous geological feature was named for the man who headed the Great Trigonometrical Survey of India in the first half of the nineteenth century?

2314. What country produces the world's largest crop of soybeans?

2315. Why did the English call their gold coins guineas?

2316. In what country did the automat originate?

2317. What floral symbol do the state of Kansas and the country of Peru have in common?

2318. What famous statesman was known as Dizzy to his supporters?

2319. Why did the rulers of ancient Sparta mint large, unwieldy iron coins?

2320. On international automobile license plates, what country is represented by the letter E?

2321. What was the first colony in the New World put to agricultural use—with sugar cane plantations?

2322. Which continent is the highest—with more than half of it 6,562 feet above sea level?

2323. What was the name of the first public theater built in England?

2309. 145. *The loincloths have been in storage in the Cairo Museum since 1939, along with Tut's jewel-encrusted sandals, beaded tunics, leopard skins and other items of apparel.*

2310. *Seven percent. But nearly half the earth's population lives in temperate zones.*

2311. *France. The elements are No. 31, gallium (Ga), and No. 87, francium (Fr). The name gallium is derived from Gallia, the Latin name for almost all the region we now know as France.*

2312. *Argentina's capital, Buenos Aires; and Uruguay's capital, Montevideo.*

2313. *Mount Everest, which was named for Sir George Everest.*

2314. *The United States. China is the second-largest producer.*

2315. *The gold used for the coins was originally mined in Guinea, in West Africa. Although the coins haven't been minted since 1813, the term guinea is still used to denote a value of 21 shillings.*

2316. *In Sweden. There had been automats there for half a century before Horn & Hardart opened the first U.S. automat in Philadelphia in 1902.*

2317. *The sunflower.*

2318. *Benjamin Disraeli, Queen Victoria's favorite prime minister.*

2319. *To make it difficult for citizens to take the coins with them when they left the country.*

2320. *Spain—the E is for Espana.*

2321. *Brazil, in the mid-1500s, under the Portuguese. By 1600, it was producing half the world's sugar supply.*

2322. *Antarctica.*

2323. *The Theatre. It was built in 1576, a half-mile outside London because the city fathers barred the performance of plays inside city limits.*

2324. Who was the first American to have a monument erected in his honor in India?

2325. What did Chinese businessmen in the third century B.C. use to put their personal seals on documents?

2326. What percentage of all English surnames are derived from animal names such as Lamb, Fox, Wolf, Hawk and Bird?

2327. How did the Red Sea get its name?

2328. What country is represented by the letters SF on international license plates?

2329. What California city is directly across the border from the Mexican city of Mexicali—and has a name to match it?

2330. How many writing systems appear on the Rosetta Stone, found near Rosetta, Egypt, in 1799 by a Napoleonic expedition?

2331. What article of clothing worn by Roman emperor Caligula as a child gave him his name?

2332. What famous seafarer called his ship the Adventure Galley?

2333. At what speed was the Titanic traveling when it hit an iceberg and sank on its maiden voyage in 1912?

2334. What are the three largest islands in the Mediterranean?

2335. The name of what part of the world is derived from a Latin verb that means "to rise"?

2336. What is the distance—in yards—between the corral and the bull ring at the famous bull runs held annually in Pamplona, Spain?

2337. How did Lake Itasca, the source of the Mississippi River, get its name?

2338. What is the largest desert in Europe?

2324. *George Washington Carver. The monument, erected in Bombay in 1947 by the peanut growers of India, honored Carver for his contributions in making the peanut a popular crop. India is the world's largest peanut-producing country.*

2325. *Their fingerprints. Chinese tablets dating back to 200 B.C. bear fingerprint impressions to prove their authenticity.*

2326. *Three percent.*

2327. *From the occasionally extensive blooms of algae that, upon dying, turn the Red Sea's normally intense blue-green waters red.*

2328. *Finland. SF stands for Suomi Finland.*

2329. *Calexico.*

2330. *Three. The inscription is written in the Greek alphabet, Egyptian hieroglyphics, and demotic script (a cursive form of Egyptian hieroglyphics). The stone is now housed in the British Museum.*

2331. *His sandals. He grew up among his father's soldiers and wore small shoes similar to their iron-nailed military sandals, called caligae in Latin. As a result, he became known by the diminutive Caligula, or Little Shoes. His real name was Gaius Caesar.*

2332. *Captain Kidd.*

2333. *22 knots—to landlubbers, a little over 25 miles per hour.*

2334. *Sicily, Sardinia and Cyprus.*

2335. *The Orient, so named because the sun rises in the east.*

2336. *825 yards.*

2337. *Not from an Indian tribe or word, but from Latin. An early explorer called it Lake Veritas Caput, meaning "true source" or "true head." His companion decided that was too long and chopped off letters at both ends.*

2338. *Europe has no deserts—it's the only continent without one.*

2339. Where is Hillary's Chimney?

2340. What city is the southernmost state capital in the United States?

2341. The region known as Lapland comprises parts of what four countries?

2342. What is the unit of currency of both North and South Korea?

2343. What is the average temperature at the South Pole?

2344. What country has a massive mountain chain known as the Southern Alps?

2345. What city was the first to mint its own gold coins?

2346. What was the name of the daughter Lady Emma Hamilton bore Admiral Horatio Nelson?

2347. How was the great lover and adventurer Casanova earning his livelihood when he died?

2348. What Asian countries are known in economic circles as the Four Tigers?

2349. After Faisal I was deposed as king of Syria in 1920, what country did he serve as king until his death in 1933?

2350. Geographically speaking, what is the area north of latitude 66(30'N called?

2351. How long is the standard single oar used by gondoliers in Venice?

2352. How many stone monoliths are there on Easter Island?

2353. What British statesman was born in a ladies' cloakroom?

2354. How many yards of silk and lace were used to make actress Grace Kelly's wedding gown for her 1956 marriage to Prince Rainier of Monaco?

2339. *On Mount Everest—it's a 40-foot vertical path near the summit of the world's highest mountain (29,028 feet), and the toughest obstacle for those attempting to scale it. It is named for Sir Edmund Hillary, who conquered the mountain in 1953 with Sherpa guide Tenzing Norgay.*

2340. *Austin, Texas—it's about 11 miles farther south than runner-up Tallahassee, Florida.*

2341. *Norway, Sweden, Finland and Russia.*

2342. *The won.*

2343. *-56° Fahrenheit. At the North Pole, the average temperature is -21° F.*

2344. *New Zealand. Located on South Island, the chain has 16 snow-covered peaks over 10,000 feet. The highest, Mount Cook, is named for the explorer who named the chain for its "prodigious height" in 1770.*

2345. *Florence, Italy, in 1252. The coin, the fiorino ("little flower"), became known as the florence, then florin—a name that has been used for coins in a number of countries.*

2346. *Horatia.*

2347. *As a librarian for a count in Bohemia.*

2348. *Hong Kong, Singapore, South Korea and Taiwan. All are major Asian exporting nations that, along with Japan, are responsible for a big part of the U.S. trade deficit.*

2349. *Iraq—the British installed him on the Iraqi throne in 1921.*

2350. *The Arctic Circle.*

2351. *14 feet.*

2352. *838.*

2353. *Winston Churchill, whose mother went into labor while attending a fancy-dress ball.*

2354. *450 yards.*

2355. What country has the world's oldest surviving parliament?

2356. What is the only country in Southeast Asia never ruled by a European nation?

2357. What did Agamemnon and the French revolutionary Jean Marat have in common?

2358. Where is the Louisiana Museum of Modern Art?

2359. What words are missing from this old Irish maxim: "Only two things in this world are too serious to be jested on: ___and___"?

2360. In what four European countries are motorists required to drive on the left-hand side of the road?

2361. What toll was American adventure writer Richard Halliburton charged when he swam the length of the Panama Canal in 1928?

2362. What Italian city receives about 1,000 letters addressed to Juliet every Valentine's Day?

2363. The Germans call it Donou; the Russians call it Dunay. What do people in English-speaking countries call it?

2364. What was the first European city to pave all its streets?

2365. Where was the first Neanderthal fossil excavated in 1856?

2366. How did the ancient Romans keep dry when it rained at the Colosseum?

2367. How did Venice's centuries-old Bridge of Sighs get its name?

2368. What European capital is located in the crater of an extinct volcano?

2369. How many baths did France's King Louis XIV take during his lifetime of almost 77 years?

2370. What is London's equivalent of Wall Street?

2355. *Iceland. Its parliament, the Althing, first met in 930 when Viking chieftains gathered at an open-air assembly to iron out their differences.*

2356. *Thailand.*

2357. *Each was slain in his bath—Agamemnon by his wife, Clytemnestra; Maaraat by Charlotte Corday.*

2358. *In Denmark, in the city of Humlebaek. The museum, established in 1958, features art from the mid-twentieth century to the present.*

2359. *Potatoes and matrimony.*

2360. *Great Britain, Ireland, Malta and Cyprus.*

2361. *36 cents. Halliburton, who weighted 140 pounds, was charged as though he were a vessel—in terms of cargo tonnage.*

2362. *Verona—the city in which Shakespeare's most famous lovers, Romeo and Juliet, lived.*

2363. *The Danube.*

2364. *Florence, Italy. All its streets were paved by 1339.*

2365. *In the Feldhofer Grotto of Germany's Neander Valley—from which the name Neanderthal is derived.*

2366. *An awning known as a velarium shielded them from both rain and sun. It was pulled across the great amphitheater by sailors operating an elaborate network of guy ropes.*

2367. *From the sighs of prisoners taken across the bridge from the judgment hall in the Doge's Palace to the dungeons and place of execution in the state prisons on the other side.*

2368. *Edinburgh.*

2369. *Only three—when he was baptized, when a mistress insisted, and when a doctor lanced a sore on his rear end and ordered him to soak in a tub of water.*

2370. *Throgmorton Street. It's where the London Stock Exchange is located.*

2371. In what country does Domino's Pizza have a reindeer sausage pie on its menu?

2372. Where is the White Sea?

2373. What cape is at the southernmost point of Africa?

2374. Which foreign airline has the longest record of continuous scheduled service?

2375. Why did Flemish artists once belong to the same guild as physicians and pharmacists?

2376. In the Bahamas, what's a banana wind?

2377. What city is the southernmost national capital in the world?

2378. How many judges are on the International Court of Justice, headquartered in The Hague, in the Netherlands?

2379. In what village was Leonardo da Vinci born?

2380. What company produced the world's first front-wheel-drive motor vehicle?

2381. What is the national bird of India?

2382. What is the official language of Andorra, the tiny Pyrenees principality on the French-Spanish border?

2383. What country boasts the highest per capita ownership of Rolls Royces in the world?

2384. What country includes the islands of New Britain and New Ireland?

2385. What group of people won the right to vote in India in 1994?

2386. Which is the only Central American nation that does not border the Caribbean Sea?

2387. What city is home to the International War Crimes Tribunal?

2371. *Iceland.*

2372. *In northern Russia. It's an almost-landlocked extension of the Arctic Ocean.*

2373. *Cape Agulhas. It is about 100 miles southeast of the Cape of Good Hope, which many people mistakenly believe is the answer. The cape was named agulhas, Portuguese for "needles" for its many saw-edged reefs and sunken rocks.*

2374. *Avianca (Aerovias Nacionales de Colombia SA). It was established in 1919.*

2375. *Because they used the same grinding and mixing techniques in preparing their pigments and varnishes as doctors and pharmacists sued in preparing their salves and potions.*

2376. *A strong wind—strong enough to blow fruit off the trees, but not as dangerous as a hurricane.*

2377. *Wellington, New Zealand.*

2378. *15. No country can have more than one citizen on the court. Judges are elected by the United Nations General Assembly and Security Council to nine-year terms and are eligible for reelection.*

2379. *Vinci, in what is now Italy.*

2380. *Citroen, in 1934.*

2381. *The peacock.*

2382. *Catalan.*

2383. *Monaco. A survey in the early 1990s put the figure at one for every 65.1 people.*

2384. *Papua New Guinea.*

2385. *Eunuchs.*

2386. *El Salvador.*

2387. *The Hague, in the Netherlands.*

2388. Who was the first non-head of state—living or dead—to be depicted on a postage stamp?

2389. How did Russian leader Boris Yeltsin lose the thumb and forefinger of his left hand?

2390. Who is the only woman in history to have married the kings of both France and England?

2391. What river did Alexander the Great believe was the boundary of the universe?

2392. Where is the world's biggest airport—covering 91 square miles?

2393. What country, after the United States, has the world's greatest number of tornadoes?

2394. Who was the last czar of Russia?

2395. Where was the world's first boardwalk built?

2396. In England, how did a quarter of a penny come to be called a farthing?

2397. What country is the world's largest tobacco producer?

2398. What European country was founded by a German-born nobleman known as William the Silent?

2399. What country is the source of most of the blackthorn used to make shillelaghs?

2400. Who was the first living ruler to have his own face on a coin?

2401. What country is the largest importer of American cars?

2402. Which country established the world's first national theater in 1680? Hint: The theater is still in existence.

2388. *Benjamin Franklin, America's first postmaster general. He was on a U.S. 10-cent stamp issued in July 1847.*

2389. *In a hand-grenade explosion. As an 11-year-old, Yeltsin and some friends stole two grenades from a weapons warehouse. One of the grenades detonated when they tried to disassemble it.*

2390. *Eleanor of Aquitaine. Her husbands were Louis VII of France and Henry II of England.*

2391. *The Ganges, in India.*

2392. *In Saudi Arabia, near Riyadh. The King Khalid International Airport is more than four times the size of Bermuda.*

2393. *Australia. It has a few hundred a year—a distant second to the U.S., which has about 1,000 a year.*

2394. *Nicholas II, the last of the Romanov dynasty. He was executed by the Bolsheviks in 1918.*

2395. *In Atlantic City, New Jersey. Opened in June 1870, the mile-long boardwalk rested on the sand. It was built in 8-foot sections that were removed every September and stored for the winter.*

2396. *It was originally called a fourthing—when coins were cut into pieces to make change. Farthing is a corruption of fourthing.*

2397. *China. Brazil is the largest exporter.*

2398. *The Netherlands—which was established as the United Provinces of the Netherlands in 1579 by William, the prince of Orange.*

2399. *Germany. The wood is imported from the Black Forest.*

2400. *Ptolemy I of Egypt.*

2401. *Canada.*

2402. *France. Its national theater, the Comédie-Française, was created by Louis XIV.*

2403. What body of water was originally called the Strait of the Eleven Thousand Virgins?

2404. What is the lowest body of water on the earth?

2405. Where in the world was the bridge of San Luis Rey—immortalized by Thornton Wilder in his Pulitzer Prize-winning novel?

2406. Who was the first person other than royalty to be portrayed on a British stamp?

2407. What are the only two countries in the world whose names begin with the letter Z?

2408. What is the most common domestic animal on the African continent?

2409. What river is the muddiest in the world?

2410. What country was liberated by Bernardo O'Higgins in 1818?

2411. How tall is the Eiffel Tower?

2412. Halloween is a remnant of an ancient Druid celebration—of what?

2413. How many of the Great Lakes are in both the United States and Canada?

2414. What are the natives of Monaco called?

2415. What percentage of the Sahara Desert is covered by sand?

2416. Who was Roderigo de Triana?

2417. What English king died from a lethal dose of morphine and cocaine administered by his personal physician—with the royal family's approval?

2418. Of what land was Helen of Troy queen?

2419. What great ruler died of a nosebleed on his wedding night?

2403. *The Strait of Magellan, the winding, 350-mile-long channel linking the Atlantic and Pacific oceans at the southern tip of South America. It was navigated by explorer Ferdinand Magellan in 1520 and given its original name by his crew. It also has been called Victoria Strait, Strait of All Saints, and Strait of the Patagonians.*

2404. *The Dead Sea. At its lowest point, it's 1,315 feet below sea level.*

2405. *In the Peruvian Andes, spanning the Apurimac River.*

2406. *William Shakespeare, in 1964.*

2407. *Zambia and Zimbabwe. Both countries are in Africa.*

2408. *The goat.*

2409. *The Yellow River, known as the Hwang Ho in China. It gets its name from the yellowish silt it carries to an arm of the Yellow Sea.*

2410. *Chile. O'Higgins, the son of a Spanish officer of Irish origin, served as Chile's head of state until 1823.*

2411. *984 feet.*

2412. *New Year's Eve. The Druids' new year started on November 1.*

2413. *Four. Only one—Lake Michigan—is entirely within the United States.*

2414. *Monegasques.*

2415. *About 20 percent—the rest is comprised of barren rocks, rocky plateaus and gravel-covered plains.*

2416. *The sailor aboard Columbus's ship the Pinta, who made the first definite sighting of land in the New World on October 12, 1492.*

2417. *King George V—grandfather of Queen Elizabeth II—who was comatose and on his deathbed at the time.*

2418. *Sparta.*

2419. *Attila the Hun, in A.D. 453.*

2420. What is the only country in the Middle East that does not have a desert?

2421. In what country was geothermal energy first harnessed to produce electricity?

2422. What animal was the symbol of liberty in ancient Rome?

2423. What are Rum, Eigg, Coll, Mull, Muck, and Canna?

2424. What do workers in the mangrove forests of West Bengal, India, wear to protect themselves from tiger attacks?

2425. Following the bridal tradition of wearing something old, new, borrowed and blue, what new item did divorcée Wallis Warfield Simpson have in her left shoe at her wedding to Edward VIII, who had abdicated the British throne to marry her?

2426. What was the first name of the Queen of Sheba, who visited King Solomon bearing great riches?

2427. In England, a citizen of Birmingham is called a Brummagem, and a student at Cambridge is called a Cantabrigian. What is a resident of Manchester called?

2428. In what country did India ink originate?

2429. When did the world's first daily newspaper begin publishing?

2430. Where was St. Patrick, the patronß saint of Ireland, born?

2431. In classical mythology, what god dressed as a woman, spun wool and performed other womanly tasks for three years to appease his fellow gods?

2432. The fictitious name John Doe was first used in British courts to represent the unknown plaintiff in a real—property suit. What fictitious name was used for the defendant?

2433. Split is an important seaport—in what European country?

2434. What is the Temple of the Tooth?

2420. *Lebanon.*

2421. *In Italy—at the Larderello hot springs in Tuscany, where steam has been producing electricity since 1904.*

2422. *The cat.*

2423. *Some of Scotland's Inner Hebrides islands.*

2424. *Rubber masks tied to the back of their heads—because tigers are known to attack humans only from behind.*

2425. *A gold coin minted just 18 months earlier for Edward's coronation.*

2426. *Balkis.*

2427. *A Mancunian.*

2428. *In China.*

2429. *In 59 B.C.—it was a government-controlled daily bulletin called Acta Diurna (Action Journal) that Julius Caesar had posted throughout Rome.*

2430. *In Scotland, in the town of Kilpatrick, near Dumbarton. He was captured at age 16 by Gaels and taken to Ireland, where he was sold as a slave.*

2431. *Hercules.*

2432. *Richard Roe.*

2433. *Yugoslavia. It's on the Adriatic Sea.*

2434. *A Buddhist temple in Kandy, in central Sri Lanka (formerly Ceylon), where a sacred relic reputed to be a tooth of the Buddha has been enshrined since the fourth century A.D.*

2435. What nation do we have to thank for Florida's orange crop?

2436. What rousing song was originally known as the "Battle Song of the Rhine Army"?

2437. How many time zones are there in China?

2438. What is the basic monetary unit of Zimbabwe called?

2439. On what island are one-third of the world's languages spoken?

2440. What two boundaries lie between Big Diomede Island and Little Diomede Island?

2441. What did 5-and-10-cent-store magnate F. W. Woolworth call the chain of stores he opened in England in 1909?

2442. What famous French landmark is named after a German city?

2443. Archaeologists believe they have located the burial site of Boudicca, the British queen who led a bloody revolt against Roman rule in the first century A.D. Where is it?

2444. When was the first kissaten—coffee shop—established in Tokyo?

2445. What piece of construction equipment is named after an early seventeenth-century British hangman?

2446. What island nation was named after a Dutch province?

2447. What river is the longest in Europe?

2435. *Spain. During the seventeenth century, every Spanish explorer was required to bring 100 orange seeds with him when he set sail for the New World.*

2436. *"La Marseillaise," the French national anthem.*

2437. *Only one. Although the country covers 3,691,521 square miles and geographically could be in five different zones, the government requires clocks throughout the nation to conform to those in the capital (Beijing).*

2438. *The dollar.*

2439. *On New Guinea, where more than 700 distinct native languages can be heard.*

2440. *The U.S.-U.S.S.R. border and the International Date Line. The islands, in the Bering Strait, are 2 miles apart and 25 miles from both mainland U.S. and mainland U.S.S.R. They were named by Danish explorer Vitus Bering, who discovered them on St. Diomede's Day (August 16) in 1728.*

2441. *"Three-and-Sixpence" stores.*

2442. *The Eiffel Tower. It was built by Gustave Eiffel, whose upholsterer grandfather moved to Paris from Eifel, Germany, and became known as Eifel because his friends couldn't pronounce his name, Boenickhausen. Eventually granddad added another "f" and legally changed his name to Eiffel.*

2443. *Under Platform 8 of the King's Cross Railway Station in London.*

2444. *In 1889.*

2445. *The derrick, which is named for Thomas Derrick—who carried out more than 3,000 executions during his career at Tyburn, near what is now the Marble Arch in London.*

2446. *New Zealand, which was discovered by Dutch explorer Abel Tasman in 1642 and named Nieuw Zeeland after Zeeland, a Dutch province bordering the North Sea.*

2447. *The Volga, the principal waterway in Russia, which is approximately 2,293 miles long.*

2448. What is the northernmost city in Europe?

2449. How are 99 percent of the buildings heated in Reykjavik, the capital of Iceland?

2450. In what country did the windmill originate?

2451. Parts of which existing European countries once were included in the nation known as Flanders?

2452. What famous philosopher said, "Children today are tyrants. They contradict their parents, gobble their food, and tyrannize their teachers"?

2453. What Middle Eastern country's name includes the name of its first ruler?

2454. What famous philosopher is known by the name given to him by his wrestling teacher?

2455. Where was Nero when Rome burned in 64 A.D.?

2456. What European country was once known as the Batavian Republic?

2457. How many children did Cleopatra have?

2458. According to Greek legend, who cut the Gordian Knot?

2459. How is the Balinese national holiday known as Njebi (pronounced nn-YEH-pee) celebrated?

2460. What was blamed for the deaths of Emperor Claudius and Tiberius, Czar Alexander I, Pope Clement VII and Charles V of France?

2461. What was Mahatma Gandhi's reply when he was asked what he thought of Western civilization?

2462. Lutetia, which means "mid-water dwelling" in Latin, is the original name of what European city?

2448. *Hammerfest, Norway—which is at 70° 38' north.*

2449. *With geothermal power—from natural hot (140°F) water from an underground reservoir. The water (from Ice Age glaciers trapped by hardened lava from volcanic eruptions) is piped to radiators and hot-water tanks throughout the city.*

2450. *In Iran, in A.D. 644. It was used to grind grain.*

2451. *France, Belgium and the Netherlands.*

2452. *Socrates, who lived in Greece from 470 to 399 B.C.*

2453. *Saudi Arabia. Ruler Abd al-Aziz ibn Saud unified his dual kingdoms of Hejaz and Nejd and their dependencies under the name Saudi Arabia in 1932.*

2454. *Plato, who was originally named Aristocles. According to historians the nickname Plato, which means "broad" in Greek, referred to either his broad shoulders or broad forehead.*

2455. *At his villa at Antium (now Anxio), 35 miles from Rome. And he wasn't fiddling—the violin had not yet been invented.*

2456. *The Netherlands, between 1795 and 1806, during the French Revolutionary Wars. The name came from the Batavi, a Germanic tribe that originally inhabited the region.*

2457. *Four: with Julius Caesar a son, Caesarion; with Mark Antony twins, Alexander Helios and Cleopatra Selene, and a son, Ptolemy Philadelphus.*

2458. *Alexander the Great (356-323 B.C.).*

2459. *In silence. It is the national day of silence.*

2460. *Mushroom poisoning.*

2461. *"I think it would be a good idea."*

2462. *Paris. It was named Lutetia by the Romans in the first century B.C. after Julius Caesar's forces defeated the original settlers, a Gallic people known as the Parisii. The city became known as Paris in the early fourth century after the Romans were defeated by Barbarian invaders.*

2463. According to Roman mythology, what was the name of the daughter born to Cupid and Psyche?

2464. American children get their Easter eggs from the Easter Bunny. Who delivers Easter eggs to Swiss youngsters?

2465. Where is Pushtu spoken?

2466. What nation has the city of Godthaab as its capital?

2467. What happened to the Latin inscription on the Blarney Stone?

2468. Russia's space station program is called Salyut, which means salute. To whom is it a salute?

2469. What are the Near Islands near?

2470. How many languages are spoken in the Republic of Sudan, the largest country on the African continent?

2471. The latitude of the North Pole is 90° north; what is its longitude?

2472. Haiti and the Dominican Republic are the only two independent nations in the world to be located on the same island. What is the island called?

2473. What is the most popular first name in the world?

2474. The Russian Czarevitch, Alexis, inherited Queen Victoria's hemophilia from his mother's side of the family. Did he eventually die from the disease?

2475. What is the name of Moscow's largest department store?

2476. What is London's Big Ben?

2477. How many diamonds are there on Britain's Imperial State Crown, which is worn by the reigning monarch on state occasions?

2478. How long did the Trojan War last?

2463.   *Pleasure—or Volupta in Latin.*

2464.   *The Easter Cuckoo.*

2465.   *In Afghanistan. It's one of the country's two official languages. The other is Dari Persian.*

2466.   *Greenland.*

2467.   *The words were rubbed off the stone after years of removing the lipstick left by women who kissed it.*

2468.   *The first man in space, cosmonaut Yuri Gargarin, who died in a MiG-15 test in 1968.*

2469.   *The Alaska mainland, although they were named for their relatively close proximity to Russia. They are part of the Aleutian chain off the southern tip of the Alaska peninsula and became part of the U.S. with the purchase of Alaska in 1867.*

2470.   *115—most of them tribal dialects.*

2471.   *No longitude is given since all degrees of longitude pass through the North Pole.*

2472.   *Hispaniola.*

2473.   *Muhammad.*

2474.   *No. He was executed with other members of the royal family in 1918.*

2475.   *GUM.*

2476.   *The bell in the clock tower of the Houses of Parliament; not the clock tower itself, as is usually supposed.*

2477.   *There are 1,783—including the 309-carat Star of Africa. The crown also has 277 pearls, 17 sapphires, 11 emeralds, and 5 rubies.*

2478.   *Ten years.*

2479. Who was the first member of the English royal family to wear a pair of silk stockings?

2480. In Middle Eastern legend, what is widely considered to be the forbidden fruit?

2481. Which continent is the only one to have no glaciers?

2482. What world leader was originally known as Karl Herbert Frahm?

2483. What was the given name of the long-time Yugoslavian communist leader we knew as Marshal Tito?

2484. What was the source of the earliest eye glitter ever used—that devised by the ancient Egyptians?

2485. What country was once known as New Holland?

2486. What is the native language of the Fiji Islands?

2487. How was Queen Victoria trained to keep her chin up as a child?

2488. What Dutch colony was ceded to the British in 1667 in exchange for Dutch Guiana—the South American country now known as Suriname?

2489. What is the claim to fame of the Turkish site known as Hissarlik?

2490. Where do the Blue Nile and White Nile meet?

2491. Where were Panama hats—woven from jipijapa leaves—first made?

2492. Which ocean is the smallest and shallowest?

2493. How long is the Suez Canal, the water link between the Gulf of Suez and the Mediterranean Sea?

2494. Who was Somdetch Phra Paramendr Maha Mongkut?

2479. *Oft-married Henry VIII, in 1509. The stockings were a gift from Spain.*

2480. *The banana.*

2481. *Australia.*

2482. *Former German chancellor Willy Brandt. He changed his name to escape the Gestapo.*

2483. *Josip Broz.*

2484. *Iridescent beetle shells.*

2485. *Australia, in the mid-seventeenth century.*

2486. *Fijian.*

2487. *A sprig of holly was placed beneath her collar.*

2488. *New York—then known as Nieuw Amsterdam. The exchange was part of the Treaty of Breda.*

2489. *It is the site of ancient Troy.*

2490. *At Khartoum, the capital of Sudan.*

2491. *In Peru. They're also made in Colombia and Eucador—but not in Panama. They were misnamed after being discovered by North Americans in Panama.*

2492. *The Arctic Ocean.*

2493. *It's 105 miles long.*

2494. *The monarch immortalized by writer Margaret D. Langdon in her book "Anna and the King of Siam" and portrayed by Yul Brynner in stage and screen productions of "The King and I."*

2495. How long was the reign of Louis XIV, the French king who proclaimed, "L'état, c'est moi"—"I am the state"?

2496. What great discovery were Ooqueah, Ootah, Egingwah and Seegloo part of on April 6, 1909?

2497. Where do you have to go to find Le Restaurant de la Tour Eiffel, which was located on the first level of Paris' landmark Eiffel Tower from 1937 to 1981?

2498. In England, what are the five grades of peerage—or nobility—entitled to seats in the House of Lords?

2499. What major European country does not belong to the United Nations?

2500. Serendip was the early name for Ceylon. What is it now called?

2501. What are the Soo Locks and where are they located?

2502. Where was the world's first successful oil well drilled?

2503. Where is Interpol, the international police organization, headquartered?

2504. "Confound their politics. Frustrate their knavish tricks" is part of what country's national anthem?

2505. It took Fred Newton 742 hours over a six-month period to take the world's longest swim. He went 1,826 miles in what body of water?

2506. How did the world's highest waterfall—the Angel Falls in Venezuela—get its name?

2507. What lake, once part of a sea, has the only freshwater sharks in the world?

2508. What well-known scientist was offered the presidency of Israel, but turned it down, after the death of Chaim Weizmann in 1952?

2495. *Seventy-two years—he acceded to the throne at age 5, in the year 1643*

2496. *The discovery of the North Pole. The four Eskimos, with Robert Peary and his assistant Matthew Henson, were the first men to reach latitude 90 degrees north.*

2497. *To New Orleans, Louisiana, where the dismantled restaurant was reassembled and put back in business in 1986.*

2498. *In descending order: duke, marquess, earl, viscount and baron.*

2499. *Switzerland, on grounds that membership would jeopardize its neutrality.*

2500. *Sri Lanka.*

2501. *They are the busiest locks in the world, linking Lake Superior and 22-foot-lower Lake Huron in Sault Ste. Marie, Michigan.*

2502. *Titusville, Pennsylvania, in 1859.*

2503. *In Saint Cloud, a suburb of Paris. Its popular nickname comes from its cable designation.*

2504. *Great Britain's "God Save the Queen."*

2505. *The Mississippi River, from Minneapolis to New Orleans, in 1930.*

2506. *From American bush pilot Jimmy Angel, who crash-landed nearby in 1937.*

2507. *Lake Nicaragua, in Nicaragua.*

2508. *Albert Einstein.*

2509. In 1872 what three cities, located near the Danube, merged into one?

2510. What mountain is the largest on earth?

2511. In what year during this century did England have three kings?

2512. If you flew due east from Cape Horn where would you next pass over land?

2513. What kind of car did Communist leader Nikolai Lenin equip with skis and half-tracks in order to overcome Russia's heavy snows?

2514. What breed was Sir Winston Churchill's favorite pet dog, Rufus?

2515. During what war was the Battle of the Herrings fought?

2516. What kings were named by Egypt's King Farouk when he predicted, after being overthrown by Gamal Abdel Nasser, that "one day there will be only five kings left"?

2517. How was Kublai Khan related to Genghis Khan?

2518. What career was Casanova preparing for before he distinguished himself as a rogue and libertine?

2519. What great ruler's name at birth was Sophie Friederike Auguste?

2520. What unusual museum is located in Pontedassio, Italy?

2521. Who was the last British monarch to ascend to the throne as a teenager?

2522. How large—in acres—is the area in France where grapes for Champagne are grown?

2523. Chinese writings dating back to the fourth century B.C. mention fishing with a bamboo rod, silk line and a hook made from a needle. What was used for bait?

2509. Buda, Obuda, and Pest joined to become Budapest.

2510. Mauna Loa (Long Mountain), Hawaii. A 13,680-foot-high volcano, its dome measures 75 miles by 64 miles.

2511. In 1936—when George V died, Edward VIII abdicated to marry divorcée Wally Simpson, and George VI began his sixteen-year reign.

2512. Cape Horn—there's no other land at the same latitude, 56° 00'S.

2513. A Rolls-Royce.

2514. Poodle.

2515. The Hundred Years' War. It took place on February 12, 1429, while the British were laying siege to Orléans and their Lenten rations of herring were intercepted by the French.

2516. "Hearts, spades, diamonds, clubs and England."

2517. He was the grandson of Genghis, the great Mongol conqueror.

2518. The priesthood.

2519. Catherine the Great's.

2520. The Museo Storico degli Spaghetti—or the Historical Museum of Spaghetti.

2521. Queen Victoria, who was 18 when she became queen in 1837. She went on to reign a record 63½ years.

2522. 85,000 acres—in the Pernay-Reims region, 90 miles east of Paris.

2523. Cooked rice.

2524. Where are the volcanoes Shira, Kibo and Mawenzi located?

2525. What famous explorer included a photograph of his nude mistress in a book about his travels?

2526. What does Chinese leader Deng Xiaoping's name mean in English?

2527. What is the meaning of the nickname Rasputin, bestowed upon Grigory Yefimovich Novykh, the notorious Siberian monk and mystic who wielded great influence over the Russian imperial family?

2528. The French knew the first ruler of the Holy Roman Empire as Charlemagne. What did the Germans call him?

2529. What was the name of the pug that shared Napoleon and Josephine's bed?

2530. What was the profession of Edmund Hillary, the New Zealander who conquered Mount Everest with Sherpa guide Tenzing Norkay in 1953?

2531. How many beds were listed in the palace inventories of France's King Louis XIV?

2532. The British prime minister's official residence is at Number 10 Downing Street. Whose official residence is at Number 11?

2533. What Middle Eastern capital was once known as Philadelphia?

2534. There was a major mistake in the 1968 film "Krakatoa, East of Java." What was it?

2535. In 1305, what did England's King Edward I decree should be used to determine the length of an inch in shoemaking and other trades?

2536. In what country was World War I German spy Mata Hari born?

2524. *In Tanzania—they are the three principal volcanoes that make up Mount Kilimanjaro.*

2525. *Robert Peary, discoverer of the North Pole. His Eskimo mistress, Aleqasina, was shown bathing.*

2526. *Little Peace. Born Kan Tse-kao, he began using the name Deng Xiaoping as an underground alias when he joined the Chinese Communist Party in 1924.*

2527. *Rasputin—derived from the Russian word rasputny—means "debauchee" or "libertine."*

2528. *Karl der Grosse—which, like Charlemagne, means Charles the Great.*

2529. *Fortunè.*

2530. *Beekeeper, or apiarist.*

2531. *413.*

2532. *The Chancellor of the Exchequer's.*

2533. *Amman, Jordan.*

2534. *The location given in the title. The famous volcano is west of Java. The mistake was remedied when the movie was released on videocassette under a new title, "Volcano."*

2535. *Barleycorns. According to his decree, three contiguous dried barleycorns were an inch.*

2536. *In Holland, as Margaretha Geertruida Zelle.*

2537. Four years after King Edward VIII abdicated the British throne, he became governor—of what?

2538. In what country is the austral the basic monetary unit?

2539. What country was the second in the world to adopt communism?

2540. What did the late King Prajadhipok, the last absolute ruler of Siam (now Thailand), do to prepare himself financially for life after his anticipated overthrow in the early 1930s?

2541. The name of what South American capital city means "I see a hill"?

2542. What is the highest large navigable lake in the world—at 12,500 feet above sea level?

2543. Where is the city of Batman?

2544. When the swallows return to California's Mission San Juan Capistrano every year, where are they coming from?

2545. What is the significance of the shamrock, the emblem of Ireland?

2546. How many icebergs are there in the world?

2547. If you weigh 154 pounds in America, how many stone do you weigh in England; how many kilograms in France?

2548. What did the Queen Mother say to Queen Elizabeth II when her elder daughter considered having a second glass of wine with lunch shortly after her coronation?

2549. In what country was the first English-language newspaper published?

2550. What country was the world's largest producer of potatoes in 1990?

2537. *The Bahamas. He retired after serving from 1940 to 1945.*

2538. *Argentina.*

2539. *Mongolia, in 1921—four years after the Bolshevik revolution in Russia. In 1990, Mongolia became the first Asian country to desert communism.*

2540. *Prajadhipok took out unemployment insurance with French and British insurance companies. He collected on the policies after his ouster, and lived comfortably in England for the remaining six years of his life.*

2541. *Montevideo, Uruguay.*

2542. *Lake Titicaca, which lies between Bolivia and Peru.*

2543. *In southeastern Turkey.*

2544. *Their winter home in Goya, Argentina.*

2545. *According to legend, St. Patrick chose the three-leaflet plant as the symbol of the Trinity. He is said to have used it to drive the snakes of Ireland into the sea. The word shamrock is derived from the Irish seamrog, meaning "trefoil."*

2546. *Approximately 320,000.*

2547. *You weigh 11 stone in England; and 70 kilograms in France. A stone is equal to 14 pounds; a kilogram to 2.2 pounds.*

2548. *"Don't forget, my dear, you have to reign all afternoon."*

2549. *In Holland, in 1620. The newspaper was published by Puritan refugees from England—the same community of Puritans that provided the Pilgrims who crossed the Atlantic on the Mayflower in 1620.*

2550. *The Soviet Union. The United States was fifth, after China, Poland and India.*

2551. What was the most common first name given to children born in China during the years of the Cultural Revolution (1966-1977)?

2552. What is the last remaining British colony in the South Pacific?

2553. What country was the first to produce lace?

2554. How many islands are there in the Indonesian archipelago?

2555. Why did the Coca-Cola Company change the name of its popular soft drink in China in 1986?

2556. Sir Laurence Olivier once held a press conference in London to complain about railroad service. What was his beef?

2557. Where was the first tunnel in recorded history?

2558. What political party emblem was the first to be used on a national flag?

2559. What is the origin of the Russian title czar for ruler?

2560. What common sight on the English street scene is named for Sir Robert Peel?

2561. What capital is the oldest continuously inhabited city in the world?

2562. What country was the first to produce the leather we know as suede?

2563. What is the traditional salute to a royal birth in Great Britain?

2564. What silver hood ornament does Queen Elizabeth II have installed on any car in which she is traveling?

2565. Who are the Hottentots?

2551. *Hong—which means "red" in Chinese.*

2552. *Pitcairn Island—made up of tiny, remote Pitcairn, where the nine mutineers from the HMS Bounty landed in 1790, and the uninhabited islands of Oeno, Henderson and Ducie.*

2553. *Italy, in the early sixteenth century.*

2554. *There are 13,677—most of which are uninhabited.*

2555. *Company officials learned that the phonetic equivalent, ke kou ke la, means "bite the wax tadpole" in Chinese.*

2556. *Kippers had been dropped from the dining car menu.*

2557. *In Babylon. Built by the Assyrians in about 2100 B.C., the secret 3,000-foot-long passageway linked the royal palace on one side of the Euphrates River with the Temple of Jupiter on the other side.*

2558. *The Nazi's swastika. The black swastika in a circle of white on a red background was introduced as the banner of Germany's National Socialist Party in 1919; it became the flag of the Third Reich in 1935.*

2559. *It was derived from Caesar, after Julius Caesar—as was kaiser, in Germany, and qaysar, in the Islamic world.*

2560. *English bobbies, or policemen—originally known as Bobby's boys. Peel is the man who organized the London police force in 1829.*

2561. *Damascus, Syria.*

2562. *Sweden, which is what Suède means in French. The name was first used in the phrase gants de Suède, or "gloves from Sweden."*

2563. *A 41-gun salute.*

2564. *A sculpture of St. George—the patron saint of England—slaying a dragon.*

2565. *Members of a semi-nomadic pastoral tribe, the Khoikhoin, living in southwestern South Africa. The name is a pejorative label the Dutch bestowed on them because of their clipped way of speaking.*

2566. How many children of England's oft-married King Henry VIII sat on the British throne?

2567. How many trunks and suitcases did the Duchess of Windsor take with her on her honeymoon with England's ex-king Edward XIII, who had abdicated to marry her?

2568. What is the basic monetary unit of Venezuela?

2569. What day followed September 2nd in Great Britain and its American colonies in 1752?

2570. How old was England's youngest monarch, Henry VI, when he ascended to the throne?

2571. The tallest wave ever observed was spotted in the North Pacific in 1933. How tall was it?

2572. Whose bowlegs inspired a furniture style?

2573. What country has the most phones per capita?

2574. What rare metal was used to make coins in Russia between 1818 and 1845?

2575. What financially ailing country's bid to be annexed by the United States failed to win passage in the Senate in 1870?

2576. The Isle of Man is in the Irish Sea, off the British coast. Where is the isle called Male?

2577. What French city was home to Anthelme Brillat-Savarin, the famous gastronome?

2578. In Persia, what is the color associated with mourning?

2579. What is the diameter of the earth at the equator?

2580. What did Ludwig I, King of Bavaria from 1825 to 1848, have stuffed inside his velvet-covered mattress?

2581. There are 12 locks on the Panama Canal. How many are there on the Suez Canal, which is twice as long?

2566. *Three—Edward VI (son of wife #3, Jane Seymour); Queen Mary I (daughter of wife #1, Catherine of Aragon); and Queen Elizabeth I (daughter of wife #2, Anne Boleyn).*

2567. *186 trunks and 83 suitcases.*

2568. *The bolivar—named for the nation's liberator, Simon Bolivar.*

2569. *September 14th. Parliament omitted 11 days from September that year when it adopted the new Gregorian calendar. Cutting the 11 days put the calendar and the seasons back in line with one another.*

2570. *He was just under nine months—269 days old to be exact.*

2571. *It was 112 feet high—a towering ten stories.*

2572. *England's Queen Anne.*

2573. *Sweden.*

2574. *Platinum—which wasn't highly valued at the time.*

2575. *The Dominican Republic's. The Senate vote was 28 to 28.*

2576. *In the Indian Ocean, off the coast of India. It's the capital of the Maldives.*

2577. *Belley.*

2578. *Pale brown, the color of withered leaves.*

2579. *7,926 miles. (The circumference is 24,902 miles.)*

2580. *The beards and mustaches of soldiers from his father's old Alsatian regiment.*

2581. *None.*

2582. Where did the umbrella originate?

2583. Who made it fashionable to leave undone the bottom button on the vest of a man's three-piece suit?

2584. What country has more volcanoes than any other?

2585. What is the destination of an airline passenger whose luggage tags are marked AZO? or YYZ?

2586. What historic leader was the first to be called the "Father of His Country"?

2587. What size were the 2,400 pairs of shoes Imelda Marcos left behind when she and her husband, deposed Philippine president Ferdinand Marcos, went into exile in 1986?

2588. On the Chinese lunar calendar, the year of the horse began January 27, 1990. Can you name the other eleven animals on the calendar?

2589. How much did Aga Khan III weigh in 1946 when his followers gave him his weight in diamonds in celebration of his sixtieth year as leader of the Ismaili sect of the Shiite Muslims?

2590. What sport did King Jigme Singye Wangchuck, then 34-year-old ruler of the isolated Himalayan nation of Bhutan, engage in daily in 1990?

2591. What unique wedding gift did Indian leader Mahatma Gandi send to England's Princess Elizabeth and Prince Philip when they wed in 1947?

2592. What country was the first to impose a general income tax?

2593. How many of Canada's 10 provinces do not border on the United States?

2594. Which is the only one of the Seven Wonders of the Ancient World still in existence today?

2595. What country has a glacier located on the Equator?

2582. *In Mesopotamia, in 1400 B.C. It was used for shade, which is why its name is derived from the Latin word for a shade, umbra.*

2583. *The Prince of Wales (later King Edward VII), at the turn of the century—because he was too portly to button his bottom button.*

2584. *Indonesia—it has 167 of the 850 active volcanoes known in the world.*

2585. *AZO is Kalamazoo, Michigan; YYZ is Toronto, Canada.*

2586. *Augustus Caesar, earlier known as Octavian, grandnephew of Julius Caesar and the first Roman emperor. He was granted the title Pater Patriae in 2 B.C. by the Roman senate and people.*

2587. *There were size 8½.*

2588. *The sheep (or goat), monkey, hen (or rooster), dog, pig, rat, ox (or bull), tiger, rabbit (or hare or cat), snake and horse.*

2589. *He tipped the scale at 243¼ pounds, which translated into $2.5 million in diamonds. His followers contributed that amount in cash to charities he sponsored.*

2590. *Basketball.*

2591. *A hand-spun loincloth.*

2592. *Great Britain—in 1799. It was done to finance the Napoleonic Wars.*

2593. *Three—Newfoundland, Nova Scotia and Prince Edward Island.*

2594. *The Pyramids of Egypt at Giza. The other six wonders were the Hanging Gardens of Babylon, the Tomb of Mausolus at Helicarnassus, the Temple of Artemis (Diana) at Ephesus, the Colossus of Rhodes, the Statue of Zeus (Jupiter) by Phidias at Olympia, and the Pharos of Alexandria.*

2595. *Ecuador. The glacier is on a volcano known as Cayambe.*

2596. Who was the only English king to be honored with the epithet "the great" after his name?

2597. What is the largest island in the South Pacific archipelago known as the Society Islands?

2598. Where in the world are there geological features known as ergs, regs and hamadas?

2599. How many countries joined the United Nations when it was formed in 1945?

2600. The United States is the oldest independent country in the Americas. What country is the second oldest?

2601. The name of what East African country means "land of sunburned faces" in Greek?

2602. What river divides the Dutch capital of Amsterdam in two?

2603. Where is the 1,300-mile-long Orange River?

2604. In what country are the natives known as Malagasy?

2605. What is the sacred animal of Thailand?

2606. What is Canada's highest city?

2607. What was Casablanca called when it was first built by the Portuguese in 1515?

2608. How much does the jewel-studded Crown of England— worn only at coronations—weigh?

2609. What is the largest river delta in the world?

2610. In the African version of the Hansel and Gretel story, what is the house of the wicked witch made of instead of gingerbread?

2611. Where is the iron key to the Bastille—the notorious French prison—kept today?

2612. What country's flag consists of a single solid color?

2596. *Alfred the Great, who ruled from 871 to 899.*

2597. *Tahiti. The French-controlled islands are named for the group of scientists from the Royal Society brought to visit some of the islands in 1769 by Lt. (later Capt.) James Cook.*

2598. *In the Sahara—where ergs are sandy expanses, regs are gravelly plains and hamadas are stony upland plateaus.*

2599. *51.*

2600. *Haiti, which gained its independence from France in 1804.*

2601. *Ethiopia.*

2602. *The Amstel. The city's name is derived from a dam built between dikes bordering the river.*

2603. *In South Africa.*

2604. *Madagascar. They're also called Madagascans.*

2605. *The white elephant.*

2606. *Kimberley, British Columbia.*

2607. *Casa Branca. Both names mean "white house"—for the city's many white houses.*

2608. *The crown, also known as St. Edward's Crown, weighs just under seven pounds.*

2609. *The Ganges Delta, or Ganges-Brahmaputra Delta, in India and Bangladesh. It extends for about 250 miles north to south, and ranges from 80 to 200 miles west to east.*

2610. *Salt, which is highly prized south of the Sahara.*

2611. *At George Washington's home, Mount Vernon, where it is on display in the central hallway. The key was sent to Washington by the Marquis de Lafayette, "as a missionary of liberty to its patriarch."*

2612. *Libya's. Its flag is green.*

2613. What is the state language of Luxembourg?

2614. What Canadian province is named for the Great Spirit of the Algonquin Indians?

2615. What country or countries would you be visiting if you traveled the length of the Mosquito Coast?

2616. What European country uses the initials CH on its automobile license plates and in its postal codes?

2617. The name of what former world leader, translated into English, means "Mr. Clean"?

2618. What is the heroine's name in the version of "Snow White" told to children in Africa, where snow is virtually unknown?

2619. Hot springs are known as geysers after the Great Geysir. In what country is it located?

2620. What famous woman, using a diamond, scratched the following message on her prison window: Much suspected of me, Nothing proved can be.

2621. What mammal do fishermen in China train to help them increase their catch?

2622. Where in the world is Spa, the resort town that gave its name to mineral springs everywhere?

2623. In 1512 why did France's King Louis XII order the removal of all the garbage that for years had been routinely tossed over the walls surrounding the city of Paris?

2624. What daily exercise routine did seventeenth-century French statesman Cardinal Richelieu perform to stay in shape?

2625. How did the Caribbean island of Curaçao get is name?

2626. What was the name of the space vehicle in which Yuri Gagarin, the Soviet Union's first cosmonaut, orbited Earth on April 12, 1961?

2613. *Luxembourgish, which is also known as Letzeburgesch. The language is used by most Luxembourgers in their daily lives. French, however, is Luxembourg's administrative language, and students are taught German in primary school. Many also study English.*

2614. *Manitoba. The Algonquin god is Manitou.*

2615. *Nicaragua and Honduras. The approximately 225-mile-long stretch of lowland skirting the Caribbean is named for the Miskito—or Mosquito—Indians.*

2616. *Switzerland.*

2617. *U Thant, the Burmese diplomat who served as secretary general of the United Nations from 1961 to 1971.*

2618. *Flower White.*

2619. *Iceland. Geysir is Icelandic for "gusher."*

2620. *England's Queen Elizabeth I, while she was confined at Woodstock in the mid-sixteenth century before she attained the throne.*

2621. *The otter. The Chinese train otters to chase fish under large nets, which are then dropped and pulled in.*

2622. *In Belgium.*

2623. *He feared invaders would climb the mounds of garbage and scale the walls.*

2624. *He jumped over furniture.*

2625. *From the word cure—for the cure for scurvy it unexpectedly provided to Portuguese sailors set ashore with the disease. When they were later picked up, all were in good health—having partaken of the island's abundant crop of citrus fruit.*

2626. *Vostok I.*

2627. The French were so taken with a particularly beautiful double pink rose back in 1797 that they named it Blushing Thigh of the Aroused Nymph. What was it renamed by the prim and proper English?

2628. What percentage of the world's land area is occupied by Asia, the largest continent?

2629. What was the name of Sir Walter Raleigh's black greyhound?

2630. What was the first continental European city to build a subway?

2631. How many vessels were in the Spanish Armada, the great fleet sent by Spain's King Philip II to conquer England in 1588?

2632. What nation's symbol is an eagle perched on a cactus with a writhing snake in its beak?

2633. How many republics were there in the Union of Soviet Socialist Republics before its dissolution in 1991?

2634. Where is the world's largest sculpted strawberry?

2635. What percentage of the world's ice is contained in the continental ice sheet that covers Antarctica?

2636. What famous royal rulers were the first in-laws of England's oft-married King Henry VIII?

2637. What three Italian cities have lent their names to reddish hues?

2638. How many women named Cleopatra served as rulers of ancient Egypt before the most famous one—the one linked romantically to Julius Caesar and Marc Antony?

2639. What colors do the flags of North Korea and South Korea have in common?

2640. Where was the world's first paper money used?

2627. *Great Maiden's Blush.*

2628. *About 30 percent.*

2629. *Hamlet.*

2630. *Budapest, Hungary—in the 1890s.*

2631. *130.*

2632. *Mexico's.*

2633. *15.*

2634. *In Strawberry Point, Iowa.*

2635. *90 percent.*

2636. *Spain's King Ferdinand and Queen Isabella. Their daughter Catherine of Aragon was the first of Henry's six wives.*

2637. *Magenta, Siena and Venice (for Venetian red).*

2638. *Six.*

2639. *Red, white and blue. The South Korean flag also has a fourth color— black.*

2640. *In China in the ninth century. It was introduced due to a scarcity of the copper used for coins.*

2641. What two cities were linked by the Orient Express?

2642. What two American entertainers believe that in a previous life they were Queen Hatshepsut, ruler of Egypt from 1503 to 1482 B.C.?

2643. What city was the first in the world to have a population over one million?

2644. Into how many standard time zones is the world divided?

2645. What country's language is composed of the dialects of Gheg and Tosk?

2646. What nation owns Easter Island, the Polynesian outpost in the eastern Pacific known for its mysterious 50-ton monolithic sculptures?

2647. What was the cargo of the Cutty Sark when the famous three-masted clipper ship returned to England on its maiden voyage in 1869?

2648. What is the only place in the world where alligators and crocodiles coexist?

2649. What was 21-year-old Captain Nathaniel Brown Palmer, of Stonington, Connecticut, credited with discovering while hunting for seals in 1820?

2650. What were Mexican revolutionary Pancho Villa's dying words?

2651. What is the oldest European settlement in the Americas?

2652. Where did the pawnbroker's symbol—three gold balls—originate?

2653. How many years did the Hundred Years War between England and France last?

2654. What wildlife gave the Canary Islands their name?

2641. *Paris and Istanbul.*

2642. *Hoofer Ann Miller and singer Tina Turner.*

2643. *London. It passed the million mark in 1811.*

2644. *Twenty-four.*

2645. *Albania. Its official language has been based on Tosk since 1945.*

2646. *Chile, which is 2,300 miles away.*

2647. *Tea from China. The ship, now restored, is on view in Greenwich, England.*

2648. *Southern Florida.*

2649. *The continent of Antarctica.*

2650. *"Don't let it end like this. Tell them I said something."*

2651. *Santo Domingo, in the Dominican Republic. It was founded in 1496 by Bartholomew Columbus, brother of Christopher.*

2652. *On the coat of arms of the Medici banking family.*

2653. *It went on for 116 years, from 1337 to 1453.*

2654. *Wild dogs—canis in Latin. The songbirds we call canaries were named after the islands.*

2655. Simon Bolivar was the liberator of five South American countries, one of them his native land. Can you name them?

2656. What noted Englishman did singer Texas Guinan rush into her nightclub kitchen and arm with a chef's hat and skillet, so he would escape arrest during a Prohibition raid?

2657. What did a man named George Harrison sell for $50 in 1886?

2658. What great act of courage brought scorn upon British philanthropist Jonas Hanaway in 1750?

2659. In what geological era are we living?

2660. How did the War of the Roses (1455-1485) get its name?

2661. What 10 European countries still have crowned heads of state?

2662. How old was Joan of Arc when she was burned at the stake?

2663. What popular children's rhyme was an outgrowth of the bubonic plague?

2664. What unique distinction is shared by Spain's Paseo del Prado, Germany's Schlossalle and France's Rue de la Paix?

2665. Whose Day-Glo orange-and-yellow striped mini-dress, with matching headband and tights, is on view at the Victoria and Albert Museum in London?

2666. Who was K'ung Fu-tzu?

2667. Lusitania was the Roman name for what country?

2668. When Ugandan officials rummaged through the home of deposed president Idi Amin in April 1979, they found a case of old film reels. What were they?

2669. What area of the world is the only place where the insect-eating Venus's-flytrap grows naturally?

2655. *Bolivia, Colombia, Ecuador, Peru and Venezuela, the last being his homeland.*

2656. *The Prince of Wales, who later became Edward VIII, the king who abdicated to marry divorcée Wallis Warfield Simpson.*

2657. *The Rand in South Africa—the world's major source of gold.*

2658. *He was the first man to carry an umbrella in public. Previously, only women carried them.*

2659. *The Cenozoic Era, which started 65 million years ago.*

2660. *It was fought between England's House of York, whose symbol was the white rose, and the House of Lancaster, whose symbol was the red rose. The Tudor rose, a combination of the two, is now England's floral emblem.*

2661. *Belgium, Denmark, England, Liechtenstein, Luxembourg, Monaco, the Netherlands, Norway, Spain and Sweden.*

2662. *The Maid of Orleans was 19 years old.*

2663. *"Ring-a-ring o'roses," which refers to the rosy red rash that was a symptom of the Black Death.*

2664. *Each, like Boardwalk in the U.S., is the most expensive property on its country's version of the Monopoly game board.*

2665. *Platinum-haired Deborah Harry's. She wore the outfit during Blondie's 1979 European tour.*

2666. *Chinese philosopher Confucius.*

2667. *Portugal.*

2668. *Segments of the "I Love Lucy" show and Tom and Jerry cartoons.*

2669. *A narrow, 100-mile-long strip of swampy coastland in the Carolinas.*

2670. What special device did Saudi Arabia's King Fahd have installed in the ceiling of each room in his $150-million "Flying Palace"?

2671. What three civilizations are believed to have been the only ones in history to invent the zero?

2672. What were the last words of Queen Elizabeth I when she died in 1603?

2673. Where are the highest tides in the world?

2674. What country is the only one to have been represented in all modern Olympic games—both summer and winter?

2675. What nation's flag has remained unchanged the longest?

2676. In the Indonesian village of Wirakan in 1985, what unusual payment were couples required to make in order to get married?

2677. What role did France's King Louis XIV play in a ballet written especially for him?

2678. At what age did Cleopatra take her first lover?

2679. What was the toll charged when the 66,851-ton, 963-foot Queen Elizabeth II traveled through the Panama Canal in January 1980?

2680. What was the name of the ill-fated Titanic's sister ship?

2681. What country has diverted roads to avoid disrupting "elf mounds"—communities of elves?

2682. What nation was in one continent in 1902 and another in 1903?

2683. Swat, once a principality, is now part of what country?

2684. Who was the first woman head of state in the Western Hemisphere?

2670. *A dial with a needle that automatically points to the holy city of Mecca.*

2671. *The Babylonian, Hindu and Mayan civilizations.*

2672. *"All my possessions for one moment of time."*

2673. *In the Bay of Fundy in southeastern Canada. Tides have reached 70 feet at the head of the bay.*

2674. *Great Britain.*

2675. *Denmark's.*

2676. *Ten rats—in a bid to combat a plague of rats threatening the rice harvest. Divorces cost 20 rats.*

2677. *The Sun King appeared as the sun.*

2678. *At the age of 12.*

2679. *Exactly $89,154.62.*

2680. *The Olympic. Launched on the same day as the Titanic, it collided with a Royal Navy warship on its maiden voyage two weeks later.*

2681. *Iceland.*

2682. *Panama. After winning its independence from Colombia in 1903, the new government decided to switch continents—from South America to North America.*

2683. *Pakistan.*

2684. *Isabel Peron, who succeeded her husband, Argentine dictator Juan Peron, after his death. She was ousted by a military junta in March 1976 after 20 months as president.*

2685. A hundredweight is 100 pounds in the U.S. How much is it in England?

2686. What happened to Captain William Bligh when he was governor of New South Wales in 1808—almost 20 years after he was set adrift in the famous mutiny on the Bounty?

2687. Who were the two women who joined Napoleon during his 10-month exile on the Italian island of Elba?

2688. Who coined the phrase "Third World"?

2689. What was Israeli prime minister Golda Meir's response when someone asked her how it felt to be a woman minister?

2690. What was the name of the cardinal in office in the Philippines in 1986 when strongman Ferdinand Marcos was ousted?

2691. How many member nations were there in NATO—the North Atlantic Treaty Organization—when it was founded in 1949?

2692. Who was the famous wife of Leofric, earl of Mercia and lord of Coventry?

2693. Where is the world's highest railway?

2694. What did 16-year-old Louis-Auguste, France's future King Louis XVI, write in his diary for the day of his wedding to Marie Antoinette in 1770?

2695. Where is the Valley of Ten Thousand Smokes?

2696. Why did Western Australia build a three-foot-high, 1000-mile-long fence between its northern and southern coasts in 1907?

2697. Whom did Catherine II of Russia keep in an iron cage in her bedroom for more than three years?

2698. What did Czar Nicholas II of Russia buy from Hammacher Schlemmer in 1914?

2685. *It's 112 pounds.*

2686. *Another mutiny. British Army officers rebelled, captured him and forced him to resign—for stifling the colony's rum trade.*

2687. *Maria Walenska, the Polish countess who bore him a son, and his mother, Letizia Ramolino Bonaparte.*

2688. *Indian leader Jawaharlal Nehru.*

2689. *"I don't know—I've never been a man minister."*

2690. *Cardinal Sin.*

2691. *Twelve: Belgium, Canada, Denmark, France, Iceland, Italy, Luxembourg, the Netherlands, Norway, Portugal, the United Kingdom and the U.S. Four others—Greece, Spain, Turkey and West Germany—joined later.*

2692. *Lady Godiva, who accepted her husband's challenge to ride naked through the marketplace in return for his vow to lower Coventry's taxes.*

2693. *In Peru. The Central Railway climbs to 15,694 feet in the Galera Tunnel, 108 miles from Lima. Tourists take it to get from Cuzco to the Inca ruins of Machu Picchu.*

2694. *He wrote just one word: "Nothing."*

2695. *In southwest Alaska—its name comes from the steam that rises from volcanic fissures.*

2696. *To keep its booming and destructive rabbit population from migrating from the east. The rabbits, however, were not stopped by the "No. 1 Rabbit-proof Fence."*

2697. *Her wig maker. She didn't want anyone to know her hair wasn't her own.*

2698. *One of everything the store offered.*

2699. What nation was the first to be represented on both U.S. and Russian space missions?

2700. What was the cost of a first-class ticket on the first and only around-the-world flight by an airship, made by the Graf Zeppelin in 1929?

2701. What South American country is named for an Italian city?

2702. How long did King Edward VIII sit on the English throne before he abdicated for the woman he loved?

2703. What are the citizens of Rio de Janeiro, Brazil, called?

2704. For what country did Florentine explorer Giovanni da Verrazano sail to the New World?

2705. What world-famous family changed its name from Wettin early in this century?

2706. What country's highest mountain is named for Thaddeus Kosciusko, the Polish general who fought in the American Revolution?

2707. What was Pago Pago, the administrative capital of American Samoa, formerly known as?

2708. What was 18-year-old Queen Victoria's first act after her coronation in 1838?

2709. In what country can you find Europe's last remaining herd of bison?

2710. What natural phenomenon did the ancient Egyptians use to mark the start of their New Year?

2711. Shang-tu in China was the summer palace of a great ruler. What name do we know it by?

2712. What two unique physical characteristics did Anne Boleyn—second wife of King Henry VIII—have?

2699. *France. It had representatives aboard a Soviet space flight in June 1982 and on an American flight in June 1985.*

2700. *The ticket for the 20,000 miles, 21-day trip was $9,000.*

2701. *Venezuela—which, translated, means "Little Venice."*

2702. *Eleven months, from January 20 to December 10, 1936.*

2703. *Cariocas.*

2704. *France.*

2705. *England's royal family. Wettin—the family name of Queen Victoria's German husband—was changed to Windsor when Great Britain was fighting Germany during World War I.*

2706. *Australia.*

2707. *Pango Pango, which is how Pago Pago is pronounced in the Samoan language, with "g" pronounced "ng."*

2708. *She had her bed moved from her mother's room to the very first room of her own.*

2709. *In Poland, in the Bialowieza Forest.*

2710. *The annual flooding of the Nile River.*

2711. *Xanadu, the "stately pleasure-dome" of Kubla Khan in the poem by Samuel Taylor Coleridge.*

2712. *Three breasts and an extra finger on one hand.*

2713. What distinctive emblem, descriptive of his family name, was on Dutchman Peter Minuit's coat of arms?

2714. What colors did Cleopatra paint her eyelids?

2715. Whom did Queen Elizabeth II name baron of Brighton, a peer of the realm, in 1970?

2716. In what city did Polish-born Helena Rubinstein launch her cosmetics and beauty-care business?

2717. What did the ancient Japanese use to get bricks to the top of the tall buildings they constructed?

2718. The fiber of what plant was used to make the fine linen sheets upon which Mary, Queen of Scots, slept?

2719. In 1653, what city became the first in the world to install an organized system of roadside mailboxes?

2720. According to legend, what did Cleopatra have her mattresses stuffed with every night?

2721. In England, what's a bap?

2722. What do the French refer to when they speak of "La Manche"?

2723. In the U.S. a pig says "oink." How do the French describe the sound?

2724. What's the British slang for white-collar worker?

2725. In the United States, a redcap is a baggage porter at an airport or a train or bus station. What's a redcap in Great Britain?

2726. What were the GPU, the NKVD and the MVD?

2727. Russian emperors were known as czars—but what was a czarevich?

2728. In medieval days, what were the narrow windows in thick castle walls called?

2713. A bat—symbolizing midnight, which in French is minuit.

2714. Lower lids, green; upper lids, blue-black.

2715. Laurence Olivier—or, more appropriately, Lord Olivier of Brighton. He was the first actor in English history to reach the House of Lords.

2716. Melbourne, Australia, in 1902. She opened a salon in London in 1908, in Paris in 1912 and in New York in 1915.

2717. Kites.

2718. The stinging nettle.

2719. Paris. The boxes, used for mail bound for other parts of the city, were emptied three times a day. They were in use only briefly and then abandoned because of vandalism.

2720. Fresh roses.

2721. A hamburger bun.

2722. The English Channel. La manche means "the sleeve" in French.

2723. "Grwahng."

2724. Black-coat worker.

2725. A military policeman.

2726. Earlier names of the KGB, the secret political police of the now-dissolved Soviet Union.

2727. The eldest son of a czar. The czar's wife was a czarina.

2728. Loopholes. Modern-day loopholes are usually sought in contracts and laws.

2729. In an ancient Roman amphitheater or stadium, what was a vomitory?

2730. The Romans had three words for kissing—basium, osculum and suavium. What were the distinctions among them?

2731. What topographical feature is known as elv in Danish, gang in Korean, and reka in Russian?

2732. In the German version of Monopoly, it's Goethestrasse; in the British, it's Piccadilly; and in the French, Rue Lafayette. What is this property in the American version?

2733. In Cockney rhyming slang, what is the meaning of the phrase "Would you Adam and Eve it"?

2734. How many islands are there in Hong Kong?

2735. During Napoleon's rule in France (1799-1815), what was the only year-long period he was not at war?

2736. Where in ancient Rome would you find a frigidarium?

2737. Which Caribbean island nation is closest to Mexico?

2738. What does Sinter Klaas, the Santa Claus of The Netherlands, ride when he delivers gifts to children on December 5th, St. Nicholas's Eve?

2739. What is the largest city north of the Arctic Circle?

2740. Future kings Louis XVII of France and George IV of England are both shown playing with what toy in boyhood portraits?

2741. The name Mesopotamia means "between two rivers" in Greek. What are the two rivers?

2742. What world leader-to-be lived in exile in England using the pseudonym Jacob Richter?

2743. What are the only two towns in England allowed to use the word "Royal" in their names?

2729. *A large opening that served as an entrance to or exißt from a tier of seats.*

2730. *Basium was the kiss exchanged by acquaintances; osculum, the kiss between close friends; and suavium, the kiss between lovers.*

2731. *A river.*

2732. *Marvin Gardens.*

2733. *Would you believe it?*

2734. *235 islands.*

2735. *1802-1803.*

2736. *In a Roman bath. The third of the three chambers in a Roman bath, it consisted of a cold bath and sometimes a swimming pool. The two other chambers were the caldarium (hot water bath) and the tepidarium (warm room).*

2737. *Cuba.*

2738. *A white horse. And instead of the white-trimmed red suit that Santa wears, Sinter is decked out in a red cape.*

2739. *Murmansk, in Russia.*

2740. *A yo-yo.*

2741. *The Tigris and Euphrates. Much of what was Mesopotamia is in present-day Iraq.*

2742. *Lenin, founder of the Russian Communist Party and premier of the first Soviet government.*

2743. *Royal Tunbridge Wells and Royal Leamington Spa. The right to use "Royal" as a prefix was granted to commemorate visits by Queen Victoria.*

2744. Who was Egypt's only woman pharaoh?

2745. What dog is named for an area along the coast of Croatia?

2746. The House of Windsor rules England. What house rules the Netherlands?

2747. By what means did Swedish explorer Salomon Andrée try to reach the North Pole with two companions in 1897?

2748. By what nickname is the infamous Ilich Ramirez Sanchez more commonly known?

2749. In what country is the historic city of Timbuktu located?

2750. What destination is indicated as MME in airport code?

2751. What country's thriving film industry has been nicknamed "Bollywood"?

2752. What famous teenager lived at 263 Prinsengracht?

2753. What common fate was shared by millionaires John Jacob Astor, Isidor Straus and Benjamin Guggenheim?

2754. If you saw a daibutsu in Japan, what would you be looking at?

2755. What country includes several groups of islands, including the Laccadives, the Andamans and the Nicobars?

2756. The flagship known as Queen Anne's Revenge belonged to what famous pirate?

2757. On what continent have more meteorites been discovered than have been found in all the rest of the world?

2758. How many rooms are there in Buckingham Palace?

2759. Where is the only recorded flying saucer pad on earth located?

2744. *Hatshepsut, who ruled from 1492 to 1458 B.C. The daughter and heiress of Thutmose I, who proclaimed her his successor, she ruled jointly with her half-brother, Thutmose III, whom she married.*

2745. *The dalmatian. The popular spotted dog is believed to have been originally bred along the Dalmatian coast.*

2746. *The House of Orange.*

2747. *By balloon. They failed and perished when their balloon became weighed down by ice and they were forced to land.*

2748. *Carlos the Jackal. He's the Cold War terrorist who claimed responsibility for 83 murders. His nom de guerre was Carlos, but he was dubbed "The Jackal" after a copy of the Frederick Forsyth best-seller The Day of the Jackal reportedly was found in one of his safe houses.*

2749. *Mali.*

2750. *Marseilles, France.*

2751. *India's. The bulk of the Indian film industry is based in Bombay.*

2752. *Anne Frank. The address is in Amsterdam, Holland.*

2753. *They all died when the Titantic hit an iceberg and sank on the night of April 14-15, 1912.*

2754. *A gigantic statue of Buddha.*

2755. *India. The Laccadives are in the Arabian Sea; the Andamans and Nicobars in the Bay of Bengal.*

2756. *Blackbeard, whose real name was Edward Teach. The ship sank in 1718 after it was attacked and hit a sandbar off the North Carolina coast.*

2757. *Antarctica. More than 6,000 have been found there.*

2758. *600.*

2759. *In Canada—in St. Paul, Alberta. It was built in 1967.*

2760. What formal wearing apparel—never before worn in public—led to the arrest of James Hetherington in England in 1797?

2761. What nation has an AK-47 assault rifle on its flag?

2762. Which European country was the first to establish a trading post and colony in India?

2763. What is the warmest month of the year in the Arctic?

2764. What is England's Queen Elizabeth II referring to when she mentions "Granny's chips"?

2765. Where is Mount Harvard?

2766. Where in the world are the Glasshouse Mountains?

2767. What did the Inuit use to waterproof the sea lion skins that covered their kayaks?

2768. Whose legs were banned from posters in the Paris Metro because they were considered too distracting for riders?

2769. What wood did Thor Heyerdahl use in building Kon-Tiki, the raft he sailed across the Pacific in 1947 to prove that Polynesian islanders originally came from South America?

2770. What does the dragonfly signify in Japan?

2771. Who was the first European to visit Cuba?

2772. Which national flag has the largest animal emblem?

2773. What gem served as Cleopatra's signet?

2774. In airport code, TYO stands for Tokyo. What does YTO stand for?

2775. What are the six official languages of the United Nations?

2776. To what Caribbean island territory do Bonaire, Curaçao, Saba, St. Eustatius and St. Maarten belong?

2760. The top hat. The charge was that he "appeared on the public highway wearing upon his head a tall structure of shining luster and calculated to disturb timid people."

2761. Mozambique.

2762. Portugal, in 1502.

2763. July, when the average temperature is no more than 50°F 10°C.

2764. Her 94 and 63-carat diamonds. "Granny" was Queen Mary, wife of King George V.

2765. In Colorado, near Buena Vista, in the Sawatch Range of the Rocky Mountains. Its peak, at 14,399 feet, is the third highest in the state. Peaks to its south include 14,196-foot Mount Yale and 14,197-foot Mount Princeton.

2766. In Queensland, Australia. They were named in 1770 by explorer James Cook, who apparently observed that the volcanic mountains' smooth rock surface reflected the sun like glass.

2767. Whale fat.

2768. Marlene Dietrich's.

2769. Balsa. He lashed 12 giant balsa logs together.

2770. Good luck, courage, manliness. Japanese warriors wore the dragonfly emblem in battle.

2771. Christopher Columbus. He stepped ashore there on October 28, 1492, during his historic exploration of the New World.

2772. The flag of Sri Lanka. The animal is a lion.

2773. The amethyst. She believed it had magical powers.

2774. Toronto.

2775. English, French, Arabic, Chinese, Russian and Spanish.

2776. The Netherlands Antilles. A sixth island, Aruba, broke from the group in 1986.

2777. Why do the natives of the Duke of York Islands in the South Pacific send a canoe adrift, once a year, loaded with money and decorated with green leaves?

2778. In what country will you find a city called Zagazig? How about a city called Wagga Wagga?

2779. What would happen if the Grimaldis, the ruling family of Monaco, should ever be without a male heir?

2780. What country once was plagued by a murderous religious sect whose members were called thugs?

2781. What is the largest city, in population, south of the Equator?

2782. What is the name of the highest mountain peak in the the former Soviet Union?

2783. In what year did Hong Kong lose its status as a Crown Colony of the United Kingdom to become a part of China again?

2784. What river is the only one that flows both north and south of the equator?

2785. What street is London's equivalent of New York's Wall Street?

2786. What was the name of polar explorer Admiral Richard Byrd's dog?

Bonus Trivia

2787. The Roman Emperor, Caligula, once wanted to appoint his favorite horse, Incitatus, a consul of Rome

2777. *To pay the fish for their relatives who were caught.*

2778. *Zagazig is in Egypt. It's a cotton and grain center in the Nile delta about 40 miles from Cairo. Wagga Wagga is in Australia, in New South Wales, 320 miles southwest of Sydney. It's an agricultural area and important livestock-selling center.*

2779. *Under a treaty that dates back to 1918, Monaco would cease to exist as a sovereign state and would become a self-governing French protectorate.*

2780. *India. The group was wiped out by the British in the nineteenth century, but its name is still used to describe criminals.*

2781. *Sao Paolo, Brazil.*

2782. *Communism Peak, or "Pik Kommunizma." The 24,590-foot-high mountain is in modern-day Tajikistan, in the Pamir Range.*

2783. *In 1997.*

2784. *The Congo River, which crosses the Equator twice.*

2785. *Lombard Street. It's named for the Lombard family, the first modern bankers of Europe, whose residence was once located there.*

2786. *Igloo.*

Language

Questions

2788. What is the last letter of the Greek alphabet?

2789. What is the measurement, "one foot," based on?

2790. What is the word "laser" an acronym for?

2791. Who invented the word, "carport"?

2792. What do the letters "Z", "I", and "P" stand for in zip codes?

2793. What ails you if you have a bilateral perorbital hematoma?

2794. In ballet, what's a promenade?

2795. A milligram is a thousandth of a gram. What's a picogram?

2796. What is the meaning of the Greek word kosmetikos, from which we get the word cosmetics?

2797. The first two letters of what three words were combined to form wohelo, the watchword of the Campfire Girls?

2798. What do noologists study?

Answers

2788. Omega.

2789. One third the length of the arm of King Henry I (1068-1135) of England.

2790. Light amplification by stimulated emission of radiation.

2791. Frank Lloyd Wright.

2792. Zone Improvement Plan.

2793. You have a black eye.

2794. A slow turn of the body, pivoting on the heel.

2795. A trillionth of a gram.

2796. Skilled in decorating.

2797. Work, health, and love.

2798. The mind.

2799. How fast is hypersonic?

2800. What are you afraid of if you have ergophobia?

2801. What is a dentiloquist?

2802. What does an ammeter measure?

2803. In the world of computers, what is spam?

2804. What kind of voice does someone have if he or she is oxyphonic?

2805. In the world of gardening, what is a clairvoyee?

2806. What are zoonoses?

2807. In weaving, what's the weft, or woof?

2808. What is a neuroblast?

2809. Synonyms are words with the same or nearly the same meaning. What are heteronyms?

2810. What words were combined to form the word contrail—the visible cloudlike streak left behind by jet airplanes?

2811. In Japan, what automobile accessory is known as a bakkumira?

2812. What is the meaning of the legal term involuntary conversion?

2813. What is a triolet?

2814. When it comes to waves in the ocean, what is a wavelength?

2815. SPAM is an acronym formed from what two words?

2816. What do the letters DC stand for in the airplane known as the DC-10?

2799. *More than five times the speed of sound—or above Mach 5. The speed of sound is about 740 miles an hour at sea level.*

2800. *Work.*

2801. *Someone who speaks through clenched teeth.*

2802. *Electric current—it measures the strength of an electric current in amperes.*

2803. *Junk e-mail.*

2804. *Unusually shrill.*

2805. *A windowlike hole cut in a hedge.*

2806. *Animal diseases communicable to man.*

2807. *The yarn that's threaded over and under the strands of yarn that run parallel along the length of the cloth. The parallel strands are known as the warp.*

2808. *A newly formed nerve cell.*

2809. *Words that are spelled the same but have different meanings and often different pronunciations—such as minute, meaning "60 seconds," and minute, meaning "tiny."*

2810. *Condensation and trail.*

2811. *The rear-view mirror. The Japanese word was drawn from two English words—back and mirror.*

2812. *Loss or destruction of property through theft, accident or condemnation.*

2813. *A poem. It's an eight-line poem having a rhyming scheme of ab aa ab ab, with its first line repeated as the fourth and seventh lines, and the second line repeated as the eighth line.*

2814. *The linear distance between the crests of two successive waves.*

2815. *Spiced ham.*

2816. *Douglas Commercial.*

2817. What is poliosis?

2818. What words were combined and shortened to form the radio code response "wilco"?

2819. What's the difference between a nook and a cranny?

2820. In business jargon, what does the term glocal mean?

2821. What part of an airplane is the empennage?

2822. What is a bicorn?

2823. In what profession is the scruple used as a measure?

2824. "En la komenco, Dio kreis le cielon kaj la teron." Can you translate this famous line from Esperanto into English?

2825. What is the chief symptom of someone suffering from oniomania?

2826. How did the duffel bag get its name?

2827. What does the word climax mean in Greek?

2828. In the field of accounting, what does the abbreviation "dr." signify?

2829. What is your problem if you have trichottilomania?

2830. Dublin theater manager James Daly was credited with inventing and introducing what word into the English language during the late eighteenth century by scrawling it in bathrooms and other public places?

2831. What sort of words does a sesquipedalian speaker use?

2832. What is the more common name we use for the physical affliction known as furfur?

2833. What is your problem if you have sitomania?

2817. *The graying of the hair. It comes from polios, the Greek word for "gray." The disease poliomyelitis was so named because it involves the inflammation of the gray matter of the spinal cord.*

2818. *Will comply.*

2819. *A nook is a corner; a cranny is a crack.*

2820. *A combination of the words global and local, it means taking a global view of the market and adjusting it to local needs, or making global products fit the local market.*

2821. *The complete tail assembly. Empennage is a French word meaning "the feathers at the end of an arrow," which the tail unit resembles.*

2822. *The crescent-shaped hat worn by Napoleon. The three-cornered hat worn by early American colonists is known as a tricorn.*

2823. *Pharmacy—the scruple is an apothecary weight equal to 20 grains, or ¹/₂₄ ounce.*

2824. *"In the beginning, God created the heaven and the earth," the first sentence of the Bible.*

2825. *An uncontrollable desire to buy things.*

2826. *From the Belgian town of Duffel, where the coarse, thicknapped woolen fabric used for the bags was manufactured.*

2827. *"Ladder." In Greece it is spelled klimax.*

2828. *Debtor.*

2829. *You have an overwhelming urge to tear your hair out.*

2830. *Quiz. Daly reportedly bet a friend he could introduce a new word into the language within 24 hours—and won.*

2831. *Long ones—like sesquipedalian.*

2832. *Dandruff.*

2833. *An abnormal craving for food.*

2834. What are you afraid of if you have pogonophobia?

2835. What is the meaning of the oft-quoted Latin phrase "O tempora! O mores!"?

2836. Where does the expression "out of the mouths of babes" come from?

2837. What word originated as the nickname for an English insane asylum?

2838. In Gaelic, what is the literal meaning of the name Campbell?

2839. What is the origin of the word hoax?

2840. What is the meaning of the Latin word veto?

2841. What do we call a phrase that combines two contradictory words—such as pretty ugly, jumbo shrimp or unbiased opinion?

2842. When truck drivers talk about green stamps, what are they discussing?

2843. What game is known as ajedrez in Spain and Schachspiel in Germany?

2844. What are you suffering from if you have ozostomia?

2845. What do the letters in the computer-world acronym BASIC represent?

2846. What are you studying if you're into oology?

2847. What do the letters in the acronym LED stand for?

2848. In computerese, what are pixels?

2849. What was the original meaning of the Latin word musculus, meaning muscle?

2850. What language gave us the word honcho, for big shot or boss?

2834. *Beards, or men wearing beards.*

2835. *"What times! What manners!"—suggesting that both have changed for the worse. The line is from Cicero's "In Catilinam."*

2836. *The Bible, Psalms 8.2, which begins: "Out of the mouth of babes..."*

2837. *Bedlam. It was the nickname for the Hospital of St. Mary of Bethlehem in London.*

2838. *"Crooked Mouth."*

2839. *It's believed to be a contraction of "hocus," from the expression hocus pocus.*

2840. *"I forbid."*

2841. *An oxymoron.*

2842. *Speeding tickets.*

2843. *Chess.*

2844. *Halitosis—or bad breath.*

2845. *Beginner's all-purpose symbolic instruction code.*

2846. *Birds' eggs.*

2847. *Light-emitting diode. It's the light on a computer product that indicates the power is on.*

2848. *More formally known as picture, or pix, elements (pix-els), they are the individual dots on a computer monitor. In combination, they form characters as well as graphics. The more dots, the clearer the image.*

2849. *Little mouse.*

2850. *Japanese. Hancho means "squad commander" in Japanese. American flyers picked up the term during the American occupation of Japan following World War II and started using it to mean top boss.*

2851. What does the name Jonah mean when translated from Hebrew?

2852. How did April get its name?

2853. How did the ampersand become a symbol for the word "and"?

2854. What flower's name means nose-twitching in Latin—a name bestowed on it because of its pungent aroma?

2855. What is the meaning of katzenjammer, the German word used in the name of the early comic strip "The Katzenjammer Kids"?

2856. What is the name of the international association of women helicopter pilots?

2857. A bibliophile is a collector of rare books. What is a bibliopole?

2858. How did the paisley fabric design get its name?

2859. How did the airgun known as the BB gun get is name?

2860. What was the original meaning of the word clue?

2861. What do the letters in the abbreviation e.g. stand for?

2862. What is the origin of the expression "on the Q.T."?

2863. What is the origin of the word Thursday?

2864. How did Mrs. come to be the abbreviation for a married woman?

2865. What does Iwo Jima mean in Japanese?

2866. In the world of dolls, who is Midge Hadley?

2867. What are hackles—the things that get raised with anger or agitation?

2868. What do Eskimos mean when they refer to the "Big Nail"?

2851. *Dove.*

2852. *From the Latin name of the month, Aprilis—derived from the verb aperire, "to open," signifying the time of the year buds begin to open.*

2853. *The symbol is a representation of the Latin word et, which means "and." It combines a capital "E" with a lowercase "t".*

2854. *The nasturtium.*

2855. *Hangover.*

2856. *Whirly-Girls.*

2857. *A seller of rare books.*

2858. *From the Scottish manufacturing town of Paisley, where copies were made of shawls sent home by soldiers serving in India.*

2859. *From the ball bearing pellets it fires.*

2860. *A ball of thread or yarn—which makes the concept of unraveling a clue all the more meaningful.*

2861. *Exempli gratia—which in Latin means "for example."*

2862. *The word quiet—from which it takes the first and last letters.*

2863. *It is the day of Thor, the god of thunder in Norse mythology. In the past it was sometimes called Thunderday.*

2864. *It's the abbreviation of Mistress, which originally was a title and form of address for a married woman and was always capitalized. It later became missus, and mistress lost both its capitalization and its respectability.*

2865. *Sulfur Island.*

2866. *The Barbie doll's best friend.*

2867. *They are the feathers on the neck of a rooster or hen.*

2868. *The North Pole.*

2869. What is the origin of the expression "knock on wood"?

2870. What does the German word "bad" mean?

2871. In the international civil aviation alphabet used by airport control towers, the letters A, B, and C are represented by Alfa, Bravo, and Charlie. What about X,Y, Z?

2872. What is the literal translation of the pasta "vermicelli"?

2873. What are yurts?

2874. What is the origin of the word "flak"?

2875. What is the name of the layer of atmosphere between the stratosphere and the ionosphere?

2876. What letter was the last to be included in our alphabet?

2877. What is a funambulist?

2878. In computerese, what is the difference between a bit and a byte?

2879. How did the nautical measure of speed known as the knot get its name?

2880. What is the origin of "buck" in the phrase "passing the buck"?

2881. What is a gigaton?

2882. What is the origin of the word "radar"?

2883. What were the very first items referred to as gadgets?

2884. How many feet of fabric are there in a bolt of cloth?

2885. What does "Erin go bragh" mean?

2869. *It dates back to ancient European cultures whose members believed guardian spirits lived in trees and could be summoned to help with a little knocking.*

2870. *Bath.*

2871. *They're X-ray, Yankee, Zulu.*

2872. *"Little worms"—describing its shape.*

2873. *The domed, circular portable tents used by the nomads of Mongolia and Siberia.*

2874. *It's an acronym for the German Fliegerabwehrkanonen, an anti-aircraft gun.*

2875. *The mesosphere.*

2876. *The "j", which became the 26th letter during the fifteenth century. Before then, the "i" represented both the "i" and "j" sounds.*

2877. *A tightrope walker.*

2878. *A bit is a single, basic unit of information; a byte is generally eight bits.*

2879. *From sixteenth-century mariners who let out a line with knots tied at regular intervals and then counted the number of knots played out in a given time to determine their ship's approximate speed.*

2880. *A buckhorn-handled knife that was placed in front of the next card dealer. A card player who didn't want to deal would pass the knife—or buckhorn.*

2881. *The explosive force of a billion tons of TNT—or 1,000 megatons.*

2882. *It comes from radio detecting and ranging.*

2883. *Miniatures of the Statue of Liberty sold in Europe in 1886 to mark the statue's dedication. The word "gadget" came from the name of the man— Gaget—who came up with the replica idea.*

2884. *One hundred and twenty feet.*

2885. *"Ireland forever."*

2886. What are the alevin, parr, smolt and grilse?

2887. In soda fountain slang, what's a bucket of mud?

2888. Why was the Chevrolet Nova renamed the Caribe in Spanish-speaking countries?

2889. Where does the term "maverick" come from?

2890. What character in Richard Sheridan's comedy *The Rivals* has become part of the English language?

2891. How did bloomers—ladies pantaloons—get their name?

2892. Where did the term "strike" originate?

2893. When an Englishman refers to an "affiliation order," what is he talking about?

2894. A pony is a horse that measures 14.2 hands or less in height. How big is a hand?

2895. A "hairbreadth" away—just how close is that?

2896. Where did the term "the real McCoy" originate?

2897. What is a gluteusmaximusplasty?

2898. English poet John Philips wrote: "Lewd did I live & evil I did dwel." What is this an example of?

2899. What is arachibutyrophobia?

2900. What does the Japanese word "judo" mean?

2901. What is the meaning of the Latin phrase "annus mirabilis?"

2902. What word did critics of brilliant thirteenth-century Scottish philosopher-theologian John Duns Scotus contribute to the English language?

2903. What does the name Noah mean?

2886. *Names for a salmon at various stages in its life cycle.*

2887. *A dish of chocolate ice cream.*

2888. *In Spanish, no va means "does not go."*

2889. *Texas cattleman Sam Maverick's practice of not branding his calves.*

2890. *Mrs. Malaprop, whose misuse of words led to the word "malapropism."*

2891. *From suffragette Amelia Bloomer.*

2892. *With British sailors in 1768, who backed their refusal to work by striking (lowering) their sails.*

2893. *A paternity suit.*

2894. *Four inches.*

2895. *Exactly ¹⁄₄₈ inch.*

2896. *In a nineteenth century advertisement for a McCoy sewing machine.*

2897. *A tush tuck.*

2898. *The palindrome—it reads the same backward and forward.*

2899. *Fear of peanut butter sticking to the roof of the mouth.*

2900. *The gentle way.*

2901. *"Wonderful year."*

2902. *Dunce. Two centuries after Scotus's death, during the Renaissance, his followers were labeled Dunsmen or Dunses—and, ultimately, Dunces—for resisting change.*

2903. *Rest.*

2904. What is the meaning of the Latin term ad hoc?

2905. What is the unfriendly meaning of the acronym NIMBY?

2906. In mining, what is a manway?

2907. How do the British pronounce the name Beauchamp?

2908. What is an undecennial?

2909. The Pennsylvania Dutch call it schmierkäse. What do most of us know it as?

2910. What is a parsec?

2911. In space lingo, what does the acronym EVA stand for?

2912. What is trokenbeerenauslese?

2913. What is a valetudinarian?

2914. How did the loosely woven fabric we know as gauze get its name?

2915. In agriculture, what is a windfall?

2916. What does a deltiologist collect?

2917. When a knight of yore sported a panache, what was he wearing?

2918. What is Guido's scale?

2919. What is the definition of "zax"—the highest-scoring three-letter word possible in the game Scrabble?

2920. In the radio communications alphabet that begins "Alpha, Bravo, Charlie," what names of Shakespearean characters are used to denote letters?

2921. What is "wagger pagger bagger" slang for in England?

2904. *"For this"—in the sense of "for this task only."*

2905. *Not in my backyard.*

2906. *A passage wide enough for just one person.*

2907. *BEE-cham.*

2908. *An eleventh anniversary.*

2909. *Cottage cheese.*

2910. *It's a unit equal to 3.26 light years, or 19.2 trillion miles, used in astronomy to measure interstellar space.*

2911. *Extra-vehicular activity, which refers to all movement outside the spacecraft.*

2912. *A German wine made from vine-dried grapes so rare that it can take a skilled picker a day to gather enough for a single bottle.*

2913. *A professional invalid—a sickly person who thinks constantly and anxiously about his or her health.*

2914. *From the city of Gaza, in Palestine, where it was first made.*

2915. *Ripening fruit knocked down from a tree by the wind.*

2916. *Postcards.*

2917. *Plumes of feathers atop his helmet.*

2918. *The musical exercise we know as do, re, mi, fa, sol, la—devised by eleventh-century Benedictine monk Guido d'Arezzo. The last two syllables-ti and do-were added later.*

2919. *A zax is a tool for cutting and trimming roof slates. In Scrabble, it earns a minimum score of 19 points—and much more if one or more of the consonants is placed on a bonus square.*

2920. *Romeo and Juliet.*

2921. *Wastepaper basket.*

2922. What are the only two words in the English language that contain all the vowels, including "y," in alphabetical order?

2923. What does dingbats mean in Australia?

2924. You've no doubt heard the French children's ditty "Alouette." Just what or who is alouette?

2925. What's a trilemma?

2926. What does dottle have to do with pipe smoking?

2927. What are descriptive word combinations such as brunch, motel and smog called?

2928. What is a chiromancer?

2929. How did lb. come to be the abbreviation for a pound?

2930. What does a vexillologist study?

2931. What is the origin of the popular dog's name Fido?

2932. What does volvo—the name of the Swedish automaker—mean in English?

2933. What is the occupational origin of the name Walker?

2934. What is sneet?

2935. What are you afraid of if you have stenophobia?

2936. In hospital slang, what is a GOMER?

2937. In America's horse-and-carriage days, what was a curricle?

2938. What was the original meaning of ezel, the name seventeenth-century Dutch artists gave to the three-legged stand we know today as an easel?

2939. What is pseudogyny?

2940. What is brontology the study of?

2922. Facetiously and abstemiously.

2923. Delirium tremens.

2924. It's a skylark.

2925. It's similar to a dilemma, but involves three alternatives rather than two.

2926. It's the caked ash left in the bottom of the bowl after a pipe of tobacco has been smoked.

2927. Portmanteau words.

2928. A palm reader.

2929. It's the abbreviation for libra, from the Latin phrase libra pondo—libra meaning "a unit of measurement," and pondo meaning "by weight."

2930. Flags.

2931. It's from the Latin fidus, meaning "faithful."

2932. "I roll"—the name comes not from Swedish, but from Latin.

2933. In the Middle Ages a walker was someone who cleaned cloth.

2934. In California, where smoke and fog combine to become smog, a downpour of snow and sleet is known as sneet.

2935. Narrow places.

2936. A patient seeking emergency treatment for a minor complaint. The term is an acronym for Get Out of My Emergency Room.

2937. A two-wheeled chaise usually drawn by two horses running abreast.

2938. Ezel is Dutch for "donkey." The artist's stand was so named because like a donkey, it too carried a burden.

2939. The use of a woman's pen name by a male writer. When a female writer uses a man's pen name it's pseudandry.

2940. Thunder.

2941. What does the acronym NOEL mean to those who test food additives on animals?

2942. In England, what is the hobby of people known as "twitchers"?

2943. What are you afraid of if you have siderodromophobia?

2944. What is a zeedonk?

2945. What is measured in nits?

2946. What did the term skyscraper originally mean—before it was used to describe a tall building?

2947. What's an ananym?

2948. What was the nautical origin of the expression, "not enough room to swing a cat"?

2949. In the newspaper business, the night staff is known as the lobster shift. What is it known as in mining?

2950. What is a squab?

2951. What is the ylang-ylang?

2952. In the world of computers, what are megaflops?

2953. What does the Australian slang word hooroo mean?

2954. Why is a car's instrument panel called a dashboard?

2955. When the bald eagle was first named, what was the meaning of the word bald?

2956. What does the word koala mean in Australia's Aborigine language?

2941. *No observed effect level. It means that no adverse effects were seen.*

2942. *Bird-watching. In the United States, they'd be called birders.*

2943. *Trains.*

2944. *The offspring of a zebra and a donkey.*

2945. *Luminance. A nit is a unit of brightness equal to one candela per square meter.*

2946. *It was the name of the small triangular sail set above the royals on square-riggers to catch wind in calm weather. It was later used to describe tall men and horses, and eventually buildings.*

2947. *A name spelled backwards that is sometimes used as a pseudonym. Oprah Winfrey uses an ananym of her first name for her production company—Harpo.*

2948. *The cat referred to was a cat-o'-nine-tails, which was used for lashings at sea.*

2949. *The hoot owl.*

2950. *A young pigeon that has not yet flown.*

2951. *A tree with fragrant flowers widely used in perfume making. The tree is found in southeast Asia; the scent from its blossoms is found in such popular perfumes as Chanel No. 5 and Arpège.*

2952. *Processing—or operating—speeds of a million floating-points per second. FLOPS is an acronym for floating-point operations per second.*

2953. *"Good-bye."*

2954. *The name dates back to horse-and-buggy days when dashing horses kicked up mud, splashing the passengers riding behind them. The dashboard was devised to protect them.*

2955. *White.*

2956. *It means "no drink." This Australian marsupial gets all the liquid it needs from the eucalyptus leaves it eats.*

2957. The word peninsula is derived from the Latin words paene and insula. What do they mean?

2958. What information is sought in a Schick test? How about a Dick test?

2959. How could the word mile be derived from the Latin phrase mille passuum, which means 1,000 paces, when it takes at least twice that many steps to walk a mile?

2960. What letter of the alphabet is the oldest?

2961. On sailboats, what are barnacles and binnacles?

2962. What is the only word in the English language that both begins and ends with the letters u-n-d?

2963. What two dances are among the words used in the radio communications alphabet that begins Alpha, Bravo, Charlie?

2964. What is the meaning of the word Siberia?

2965. What physical phenomenon are you experiencing if you have horripilation?

2966. What is the meaning of the legal term pro se?

2967. What is the meaning of the Huron-Iroquois Indian word kanata—from which Canada derives its name?

2968. How much does a bushel of apples weigh?

2969. What punctuation mark is derived from the Latin word for joy?

2970. What is the meaning of the word aprosexia?

2971. What astronomical term comes from the Greek word for milk?

2957. *Paene means "almost"; "insula," island.*

2958. *Both are skin tests—the first to determine an individual's susceptibility to diphtheria, and the second to determine susceptibility to scarlet fever.*

2959. *The 1,000 paces referred to were those of the Roman Legion, whose formal parade step consisted of two steps that covered a distance of 5.2 feet. That would make a mile 5,200 feet—very close to today's statute mile of 5,280 feet.*

2960. *The O.*

2961. *A barnacle is a marine animal that attaches itself to a boat's bottom; a binnacle is a covered, nonmagnetic case that contains a ship's compass and a light.*

2962. *Underground.*

2963. *Foxtrot and Tango.*

2964. *It's from sibir, which means "sleeping giant" in the language of the Tatars who once dwelled in the area.*

2965. *Gooseflesh—the bristling of hair on your head or body caused by fear, cold, or disease.*

2966. *"By oneself"—without a lawyer.*

2967. *The name of the world's second largest country comes from a word that means "small village." Explorer Jacques Cartier first used it for the area around what is now Quebec city.*

2968. *About 42 pounds.*

2969. *The exclamation point (!). Joy in Latin is io, which was abbreviated by putting the i above the o.*

2970. *"Abnormal inability to concentrate."*

2971. *Galaxy. In Greek, gala means "milk." The Greeks thought the Milky Way looked like milk spilled across the sky.*

2972. What is garbo slang for in Australia?

2973. What do the initials o.g. mean to a stamp collector?

2974. What is the meaning of the acronym GRAS when it is used by the U.S. Food and Drug Administration?

2975. What is the literal meaning of the word Eskimo?

2976. What is poliosis?

2977. When people in New Orleans speak about Mardi Grass, what are they talking about?

2978. What is a pulicologist's area of expertise?

2979. How many letters are there in the Hawaiian alphabet?

2980. How many words are given for the color yellow in the revised and updated Roget's International Thesaurus, published in 1992?

2981. What do you fear if you have nephophobia?

2982. What is Koninklijke Luchtvaart Maatschappij?

2983. What on earth is the lithosphere?

2984. What is a kakistocracy?

2985. Who wears an item of clothing known as a sporran?

2986. Feline means "catlike," bovine means "cowlike," but what does aquiline mean?

2987. What is cat ice?

2988. What is the arched handle of a bucket or kettle called?

2989. For whom was the fabric poplin named?

2990. From what phrase is the oath zounds derived?

2972. *"Garbageman".*

2973. *"Original gum"—which indicates that the gum that was on the back of a stamp when it was first issued is still there.*

2974. *Generally recognized as safe.*

2975. *"Eaters of raw flesh." It's an Algonquin word, one the Eskimos themselves don't use. They call themselves Inuit, which means "The People."*

2976. *Premature graying of the hair.*

2977. *The artificial turf used at the Superdome.*

2978. *Fleas.*

2979. *12—A, E, I, O, U, H, K, L, M, N, P and W.*

2980. *58.*

2981. *Clouds.*

2982. *KLM—or Royal Dutch Airlines.*

2983. *The layer of hard rock that makes up the earth's outer shell.*

2984. *A government ruled by the worst people in the state.*

2985. *Scottish Highlanders. The sporran is the pouch, or purse, worn with a kilt.*

2986. *Eaglelike.*

2987. *Very thin ice, from which the water underneath has receded—making it unable to bear virtually any weight, even that of a cat.*

2988. *A bail.*

2989. *The pope. The name dates back to at least the sixteenth century, when Avignon, France—where the finely ribbed fabric originated—served as a papal seat.*

2990. *God's wounds.*

2991. What do the lowercase initials U.S. stand for in England?

2992. What does the word yoga mean in Sanskirt?

2993. In postal circles, ZIP is an acronym for Zone Improvement Plan. What do the same letters mean to psychologists? How about bankers?

2994. What is the English translation of the Olympic motto, Citius—Altius—Fortius?

2995. What is pogonology the study of?

2996. What is a nightjar?

2997. What does the acronym LION stand for at the National Aeronautics and Space Administration (NASA)?

2998. What is a Nilometer?

2999. On what part of the body would a man wear a gibus?

3000. What is a callithump?

3001. In the days when last names were linked to a person's trade, what was the occupation of someone named Travers?

3002. What is philematology?

3003. What is the definition of the word manumission?

3004. What would you do if you found a sign written in Latin that said "Cave Canem"?

3005. How did Christmas become Xmas?

3006. Where did the word vamp—meaning seductress— originate?

3007. In political slang, what does it mean if you call a candidate drab?

3008. How did the phrase "cold shoulder" come to mean a polite snub?

2991. Useless. The initials, originally used in the army, are derived from the word unserviceable.

2992. Union.

2993. To psychologists, ZIP means Zero Intelligence Potential—or a person of low intelligence; to bankers, Zero Interest Payment.

2994. Faster—Higher—Stronger.

2995. Beards.

2996. A nocturnal bird common to Europe and Asia. It's also known as a goatsucker.

2997. Lunar International Observer Network.

2998. A gauge devised by the ancient Egyptians to measure the water level of the Nile during flood time.

2999. On his head—it's a collapsible opera hat named for its inventor, Antoine Gibus, a nineteenth-century Parisian hat-maker.

3000. A noisy, boisterous serenade or parade.

3001. Toll bridge collector.

3002. The science of kissing.

3003. The liberation of a slave from bondage; emancipation.

3004. You would "beware of the dog."

3005. X is the Greek letter chi, the first letter of Christ's name written in Greek. It has been a symbol for Christ since the Middle Ages.

3006. With Theda Bara's arousing performance in the film The Vampire.

3007. Doesn't rock any boats.

3008. In medieval France a guest who had overstayed his welcome was served a cold shoulder of beef or mutton rather than a hot meal.

3009. What is the origin of Mayday, the international radiotelephonic distress signal for ships and aircraft?

3010. What is the longest word in the *Oxford English Dictionary* ?

3011. How did the blimp get named?

3012. What is the literal meaning of "aloha"—the Hawaiian word of greeting and farewell?

3013. What is a tittle?

3014. How did detectives come to be called private eyes?

3015. Which is more, an American billion or a British billion?

3016. In computer slang, a byte is a group of bits. What do you call a group of bytes?

3017. What is the origin of the word "good-bye"?

3018. What is trinitrotoluene?

3019. In the Middle Ages, when last names such as Baker and Taylor reflected a person's occupation, what did "Webster" indicate?

3020. The Sherpa tribesmen of Nepal call the creature we know as the Abominable Snowman "Metohkangmi." What is the literal translation of the name?

3021. If you are taking a class in pistology, what are you studying?

3022. What are pilchards called in their younger schooldays?

3023. What are the plastic or metal tips on shoelaces called?

3024. What does a culicidologist study?

3025. What is a formicary?

3026. In citizens band (CB) slang, what's a bear bite?

3027. What's a long ton?

3009. *The French* m'aidez—*help me.*

3010. *Floccinaucinihilipilifacation, which is defined as "the act or habit of estimating as worthless."*

3011. *During World War II there were two categories of dirigibles: A-rigid and B-limp.*

3012. *Love.*

3013. *The dot over the letters "i" and "j."*

3014. *From the unblinking-eye logo of Pinkerton's detective agency which proclaimed "We Never Sleep."*

3015. *A British billion. It's 1,000,000,000,000—which is a trillion in the U.S. The American billion, 1,000,000,000, is known as a milliard in England.*

3016. *A gulp.*

3017. *It's a contraction of the sixteenth-century phrase "God be with ye."*

3018. *The chemical compound we know as TNT.*

3019. *A female weaver. A male weaver was called Webb.*

3020. *"The indescribably filthy man of the snow."*

3021. *Faith.*

3022. *Sardines.*

3023. *Aglets.*

3024. *The mosquito.*

3025. *An ant hill.*

3026. *A speeding ticket.*

3027. *It's a unit of weight in Great Britain, the equivalent of 2,240 pounds. America's 2,000-pound ton is known as a short ton.*

3028. What is the meaning of the Chinese phrase "gong hay fot choy"?

3029. What is the origin of the word "stentorian," meaning "extremely loud"?

3030. What are you afraid of if you have peccatophobia?

3031. How did the term "red-letter day" originate?

3032. What is the meaning of the Swahili word Kwanzaa—the name adopted for the annual celebration of African-American history and culture?

3033. When the State Department refers to "vertical transportation units," what is it describing?

3034. What is the meaning of deinos and sauros, the two Greek words paleontologists combined to name the long-extinct dinosaur?

3035. What is a dactylogram?

3036. What is vog?

3037. What is the meaning of the Sioux word tonka, which was adopted in 1947 as the name of the toy company known for its sturdy toy trucks?

3038. What is the origin of the expression "upper crust"?

3039. In logging slang, what's a "jackpot"?

3040. Why do we call seedy saloons "dives"?

3041. In trucking circles, what's meant by a "bumper sticker"?

3042. How many letters in our alphabet serve as Roman numerals?

3028. *"Wishing you a prosperous New Year."*

3029. *Stentor, a Greek herald during the Trojan War, whose "voice of bronze," according to Homer's "Iliad," was as "loud as the cry of 50 other men."*

3030. *Sinning.*

3031. *In the fifteenth century it became common practice to print important feast days, saints' days and holidays in red ink on ecclesiastical calendars and in almanacs. Since these were memorable, happy days, "red-letter day" came to mean any lucky day or day recalled with delight.*

3032. *It means "first fruits." The celebration, based on African harvest festivals, runs from December 26 to January 1.*

3033. *Elevators.*

3034. *Deinos means "terrible" or "terrifying"; sauros, "lizard."*

3035. *A fingerprint.*

3036. *A Hawaiian cousin of smog—it's a fog caused when sulfuric volcanic fumes mix with oxygen.*

3037. *Tonka means "great."*

3038. *Etiquette in days of yore required that the choice top crust of a loaf of bread be presented to the king or ranking noble at the table.*

3039. *A messy pile of logs.*

3040. *When the word "dive" first came into use in New York City in the mid-1800s, such an establishment was usually located below street level in a run-down row house, requiring patrons to descend into the building's depths.*

3041. *A tailgater; a driver who is following another vehicle too closely.*

3042. *Seven—I, V, X, L, C, D and M. (I=1; V=5; X=10; L=50; C=100; D=500; M=1,000.)*

3043. What is the British term for the maid of honor at a wedding?

3044. What does the word "bellwether" have to do with sheep?

3045. What are menhirs, cromlechs and dolmens?

3046. How did the term "in the buff" come to mean naked?

3047. What is the meaning of the Dutch word doop, which gave us the word "dope" as a synonym for illegal narcotics?

3048. What is a pilot talking about when he uses the term "cumulo-granite"?

3049. On what part of your body would you wear a shako?

3050. What is the only two-syllable word in the English language with no true vowels?

3051. What is a yoctosecond?

3043. *The chief bridesmaid.*

3044. *The word originated with sheep farmers. A shepherd would hang a bell from the neck of his lead sheep—generally a castrated ram known as a wether—so he would know where the flock was heading.*

3045. *Prehistoric monuments.*

3046. *Buff came to us via the buffalo—and was originally used to refer to the soft yellow leather of buffalo hides. The link between hide and skin eventually led to the term "in the buff," meaning naked, and the color buff.*

3047. *It means sauce or gravy. In English its meaning evolved to refer to any mixture of unknown or suspicious ingredients, and then to drugs.*

3048. *Clouds that obscure tall mountains.*

3049. *On your head. The shako is a tall, cylindrical military hat with a flat top, visor and feather cockade in front. It's often worn by members of marching bands.*

3050. *Rhythm.*

3051. *The smallest designated unit of time—equivalent to .00000000000000000000001 second (that's with 23 zeroes).*

Food

Questions

3052. How did pound cake get its name?

3053. How did the manufacturers of Old Grand-Dad bourbon get away with producing their whisky during Prohibition?

3054. What popular drink did a Dutch medical professor produce in his laboratory while trying to come up with a blood cleanser that could be sold in drugstores?

3055. What breakfast food gets its name from the German word for "stirrup"?

3056. What beverage did Pope Clement VIII officially recognize as a Christian drink in an edict issued in 1592?

3057. In wine making, what is the must?

3058. What animal is the source of the milk used in making Roquefort cheese?

3059. Why was the Animal Crackers box designed with a string handle?

3052. *From the one-pound quantities of the key ingredients (sugar, butter, eggs and flour) in the original recipe.*

3053. *They marked the bottles "for medicinal purposes."*

3054. *Gin. The professor, Franciscus dele Boë Sylvius, was distilling pure laboratory alcohol with the essence of juniper berries when he ended up with the drink—which originally was known as Hollandsch genever (Dutch juniper).*

3055. *The bagel. Originally a horn-shaped roll known as a kipfel, it was reshaped to resemble a riding stirrup and renamed bügel—from the German steigbügel for "stirrup"—to honor Poland's King John III Sobiesky for driving Turkish invaders from Vienna in the late seventeenth century. Riding was the king's favorite hobby.*

3056. *Coffee, which had been introduced to Europe by Arab traders and was considered by many Roman Catholics to be the wine of infidels.*

3057. *The juice drawn from the grapes but not yet fermented into wine.*

3058. *The ewe, or female sheep.*

3059. *The animal-shaped cookie treats were introduced in 1902 as a Christmas novelty—and packaged so they could be hung from Christmas trees.*

3060. What elaborate confection was inspired by St. Bride's Church in London?

3061. On what vegetable did an ancient Egyptian place his right hand when taking an oath?

3062. How was the dish we know as chicken à la king first listed when it was added to the menu at New York's Delmonico's restaurant in the 1880's?

3063. What American city produces most of the egg rolls sold in grocery stores in the United States?

3064. What drink is named for the wormwood plant?

3065. Italy leads the world in pasta consumption with 61.7 pounds eaten per person per year. What country is second?

3066. When Birdseye introduced the first frozen food in 1930, what did the company call it?

3067. What vegetables did the Iroquois plant together and refer to as the "three sisters"?

3068. With what did Queen Victoria mix her claret?

3069. What is the largest food-marketing cooperative in the United States?

3070. What novelty salt shakers did publishing czar William Randolph Hearst have on the refectory table in the dining room of his San Simeon estate?

3071. What two spices are derived from the fruit of the nutmeg tree?

3072. How many different animal shapes are there in the "Animal Crackers" cookie zoo?

3073. How many flowers are in the design stamped on each side of an Oreo cookie?

3060. *The tiered wedding cake—which was based on the tiered spire of the church, designed by Sir Christopher Wren.*

3061. *The onion. Its round shape symbolized eternity.*

3062. *As chicken à la Keene—it was named in honor of Foxhall Keene, a regular at Delmonico's.*

3063. *Houston, Texas.*

3064. *Vermouth, which is flavored with wormwood (vermout in French; wermut in German)—so called because the bitter-tasting plant was once used as a cure for intestinal worms. Only the harmless blossoms of the plant, not its toxic leaves, are used in making vermouth.*

3065. *Venezuela, where the annual pasta consumption is 27.9 pounds. The United States, with 19.8 pounds of pasta consumed per person annually is sixth—after Argentina, Tunisia and Switzerland.*

3066. *Frosted food. Company officials feared the word frozen would suggest flesh burns. The name was changed to frozen soon after.*

3067. *Corn, beans and squash. Planted together on earthen hills, the corn stalks supported the vines of the bean plants and the broad-leafed squash plants blocked the growth of weeds.*

3068. *Whiskey—the mixture was her favorite alcoholic beverage.*

3069. *Land O'Lakes, which markets the products of more than 300,000 farmers and ranchers in 15 midwestern and northwestern states. The co-op, formed in 1921 with $1,375 in seed money from the U.S. Farm Bureau, is now America's top marketer of butter, butter blends and delicatessen cheeses.*

3070. *Mickey and Minnie Mouse shakers.*

3071. *Nutmeg, which is produced from the kernel; and mace, which is produced from the kernel's lacy covering.*

3072. *Eighteen—two bears (one walking, one seated), a bison, camel, cougar, elephant, giraffe, gorilla, hippopotamus, hyena, kangaroo, lion, monkey, rhinoceros, seal, sheep, tiger and zebra.*

3073. *Twelve. Each has four petals.*

3074. What part of the strawberry plant is the true fruit?

3075. Peter Cooper, best known for inventing the locomotive "Tom Thumb," patented a dessert in 1845. What was it?

3076. What percentage of whole milk is water?

3077. In which American city is the greatest amount of ketchup consumed?

3078. How many kernels of durum wheat are used to make a pound of pasta?

3079. What is the official state beverage of Delaware?

3080. What part of the banana is used to make banana oil?

3081. From what part of the cinnamon tree do we get the spice?

3082. According to U.S. Agriculture Department grading regulations, how many ounces must a dozen "jumbo" eggs weigh?

3083. Black-eyed peas are not peas. What are they?

3084. What product was introduced in Japanese supermarkets after a survey showed half the country's young people weren't able to use chopsticks?

3085. The pretzel shape was created by French monks in 610 AD. What was it designed to resemble?

3086. What American brewery was the first to market beer in a bottle?

3087. Two states have official beverages. Florida's is orange juice. What's the other state and its beverage?

3088. In 1867 Emperor Napoleon III had a chemist develop a food product "for the army, navy, and the needy classes of the population." What was it?

3089. The father of what American poet invented peppermint Life Savers?

3090. In cooking, how many drops to a teaspoon?

3074. *The seed. The delicacy that we eat and call the fruit is actually the swollen end of the stem called a drupe.*

3075. *A gelatin treat that eventually became known as Jell-O when it was marketed in 1897.*

3076. *87 percent.*

3077. *New Orleans.*

3078. *Approximately 16,550.*

3079. *Milk.*

3080. *No part. Banana oil, a synthetic compound made with amyl alcohol, is named for its banana-like aroma. It is used primarily as a paint solvent and in artificial fruit flavoring.*

3081. *The inner bark of young wood.*

3082. *Thirty ounces.*

3083. *Beans.*

3084. *Trainer chopsticks, with loops to show users where to put their fingers.*

3085. *A little child's arms in prayer.*

3086. *F & M Schaefer.*

3087. *Ohio; tomato juice.*

3088. *Margarine.*

3089. *Hart Crane; his father's name was Clarence.*

3090. *Sixty.*

3091. Who invented evaporated milk in 1853?

3092. What was the first of H. J. Heinz' "57 varieties"?

3093. What word did Winston Churchill coin to describe Socialist nations where people have to wait in line for everything?

3094. What flavor ice cream did Dolly Madison serve at the inaugural festivities in 1812?

3095. Where was the first automated fortune cookie machine manufactured?

3096. How many pounds of roasted, ground coffee does one coffee tree yield annually?

3097. What does the word "pizza" mean in Italian?

3098. Who said: "Never eat more than you can lift"?

3099. Where does the name "Sanka" come from?

3100. What does VVSOP mean on a cognac bottle?

3101. What was the drink we know as the Bloody Mary originally called?

3102. What capital city is expected to be the most populous in the world—with more than thirty million residents—by the year 2000?

3103. What product did Mother Nature personified endorse in a television commercial, and who played the role?

3104. What is the traditional food served at Wimbledon each year?

3105. Who originally coined the phrase that has been appropriated as the slogan for Maxwell House coffee: "Good to the last drop"?

3106. Who first developed frozen foods?

3107. What was the first commercially-manufactured breakfast cereal?

3108. How tall is gourmet cook Julia Child?

3091. *Gail Borden, who went on to invent a variety of juice concentrates and became known as "the father of the instant food industry."*

3092. *Horseradish, marketed in 1869.*

3093. *Queuetopias.*

3094. *Strawberry.*

3095. *In Japan, for Los Angeles' Hong Kong Noodle Co., which first introduced cookies with messages (written by a Presbyterian minister) in 1918.*

3096. *Just one.*

3097. *Pie, which makes the phrase "pizza pie" redundant.*

3098. *Miss Piggy.*

3099. *Sans caféine, French for without caffeine.*

3100. *Very Very Superior Old Pale.*

3101. *The Red Snapper, which was its name when it crossed the Atlantic from Harry's New York Bar in Paris.*

3102. *Mexico City, Mexico.*

3103. *Chiffon Margarine; Dena Dietrich played Mother Nature.*

3104. *Strawberries and cream.*

3105. *President Theodore Roosevelt.*

3106. *Clarence Birdseye, in 1930.*

3107. *Shredded Wheat, made by Henry Perky in 1882.*

3108. *6 feet 2 inches.*

3109. What is the name of the dog on the Cracker Jack box?

3110. Cleopatra used the juice of what common salad ingredient to preserve her skin?

3111. What did the homesick alien get drunk on in Steven Spielberg's 1982 hit film E.T.—The Extra-Terrestrial?

3112. What words are on the three rings on the Ballantine ale label?

3113. In what country did the beverage we know as punch originate?

3114. What seeds are used to flavor the Scandinavian liquor aquavit?

3115. What color did blue replace in 1995 when it was introduced to the standard package of M&Ms candies?

3116. What two tools were recommended in the instructions for opening a tin of roast veal that was taken on English explorer William Parry's third voyage to the Arctic in 1824?

3117. How many pounds of dried saffron does an acre of crocus plants yield?

3118. On average, how many calories a day are American astronauts given to eat while on missions in outer space?

3119. What do herring, cabbage and carrots represent at New Year's Eve feasts in Germany and Scandinavia?

3120. What is the American name for the British delicacy known as trotters?

3121. For whom was the surf 'n' turf meal originally created?

3122. What country boasts the highest per capita consumption of cereal in the world?

3123. How many lemons does the average lemon tree yield per year?

3109. *Bingo.*

3110. *Cucumber, which is still used in skin care—in facial creams, lotions and cleansers.*

3111. *Coors beer.*

3112. *Purity, body, flavor.*

3113. *India. The British gave the refreshing drink the name punch, most likely from the Hindi word panch, for the number five, because it had five basic ingredients—alcohol, tea, lemon, sugar and water.*

3114. *Caraway.*

3115. *Tan. Blue was the overwhelming choice in a vote taken by Mars, Inc. The runner-up colors were purple and pink.*

3116. *Chisel and hammer. The can opener was not invented until 1858.*

3117. *10 pounds. It takes about 75,000 flowers to produce a pound of saffron—which is why it's the most expensive spice in the world.*

3118. *3,000.*

3119. *Herring represents good luck; cabbage, plenty of silver; and carrots, gold in the year ahead.*

3120. *Pigs' feet.*

3121. *Famous gastronome Diamond Jim Brady. It was served to him at a waterfront restaurant in Brooklyn, New York, in the late 1880s.*

3122. *Ireland, where the annual consumption is over 15 pounds per person.*

3123. *1,500. The trees usually bloom throughout the year, with the fruit picked 6 to 10 times a year.*

3124. What food product, marketed as Elijah's Manna in 1904, was renamed because of objections from the clergy?

3125. What name is shared by a citrus fruit and the citizens of an African capital?

3126. What is Bombay duck?

3127. What popular treat did 11-year-old Frank Epperson accidentally invent in 1905 and patent in 1924?

3128. Where did the pineapple plant originate?

3129. What was margarine called when it was first marketed in England?

3130. What American city lead all others in per capita consumption of pizza in 1990?

3131. How much did Weight Watchers founder Jean Nidetch weigh in 1963 when she came up with the concept that helped her shed pounds and make a fortune?

3132. Under what name did the Domino's Pizza chain get its start?

3133. What are the two top-selling spices in the world?

3134. What European nation consumes more spicy Mexican food than any other?

3135. Under U.S. government regulations, what percentage of peanut butter has to be peanuts?

3136. Drupes are a regular part of the American diet. What are they?

3137. What is the essential ingredient in a dish that's prepared à la DuBarry in honor of King Louis XV's mistress?

3138. What is the literal meaning of the Italian word linguine?

3139. Under federal food-labeling regulations, how much caffeine must be removed from coffee for it to be called decaffeinated?

3124. Post Toasties cereal.

3125. Tangerine (Tangiers is the summer capital of Morocco.)

3126. Dried, salted fish. It's both a snack and a flavoring used in Indian cooking.

3127. The Popsicle, which he originally marketed as the Epsicle. Epperson inadvertently made the first one when he left a glass of lemonade with a spoon in it on a windowsill—and it froze overnight.

3128. In South America. It didn't reach Hawaii until the early nineteenth century.

3129. Butterine.

3130. Milwaukee.

3131. 214 pounds. A year later, she weighed 142.

3132. DomiNick's.

3133. Pepper is the top seller; mustard is second.

3134. Norway.

3135. 90 percent.

3136. Simple, succulent, usually single-pitted fruit—such as plums, apricots, peaches, cherries, almonds and olives.

3137. Cauliflower.

3138. "Little tongues."

3139. 97 percent.

3140. How many quarts of whole milk does it take to make one pound of butter?

3141. What shortbread cookie is named for the heroine of a nineteenth-century English novel?

3142. How much did Americans spend on pizzas in 1988?

3143. Christmas is the biggest candy-selling season in the U.S. What holiday ranks second?

3144. How much money did American Airlines claim it saved in 1987 by eliminating one olive from each of the salads served in first class?

3145. What is the hamburger we know as the Big Mac called in Russia?

3146. What was the name of the breakfast cereal Cheerios when it was first marketed 50 years ago?

3147. What famous dish was named after shipping magnate Ben Wenberg?

3148. Under federal regulation, how much caffeine must be removed from coffee for it to be labeled "decaffeinated"?

3149. What favorite recipe of her and her husband's did First Lady Jacqueline Kennedy have taped to the wall in the White House kitchen?

3150. What beverage was advertised as "good to the last drop" in 1907?

3151. How long would a 130-pound person have to walk at a leisurely pace to burn off the calories in a McDonald's Big Mac? How about a Burger King Double Beef Whopper with cheese?

3152. What popular soft drink contained the drug lithium—now available only by prescription—when it was introduced in 1929?

3153. How did the croissant get its name?

3140. *Almost 10—9.86 to be exact.*

3141. *The Lorna Doone. The novel* Lorna Doone, *by R. D. Blackmore, was published in 1869.*

3142. *$20 billion, according to the National Association of Pizza Operators.*

3143. *Easter—which surpasses Valentine's Day, Mother's Day and Halloween.*

3144. *$40,000.*

3145. *The Bolshoi Mak—bolshoi means "big" in Russian.*

3146. *Cherrioats. The name was changed the following year at the urging of the folks at Quaker Oats.*

3147. *Lobster Newburg. Wenberg, who had sampled the dish in South America, passed the recipe on to the chef at Delmonico's in New York in the late nineteenth century. The dish was named for him until he was involved in a drunken brawl and banned from the restaurant. Then it was altered to Newburg.*

3148. *97 percent.*

3149. *The recipe for the daiquiri.*

3150. *Coca-Cola. The slogan was long forgotten by the time the line was adopted by Maxwell House coffee.*

3151. *Two hours and one minute for the Big Mac; three hours and twenty-six minutes for the Double Whopper.*

3152. *7-Up, which originally was marketed under the name Bib-Label Lithiated Lemon-Lime soda. Lithium, now used to treat manic depression, was eliminated from the formula in the mid-1940s.*

3153. *From the crescent design (creissant in Old French) on the Turkish flag. Viennese bakers created the crescent-shaped rolls to mark their city's successful stand against Turkish invaders in 1683.*

3154. What recipe did Texas ice-cream maker Elmer Doolin buy for $100 from the owner of a San Antonio café in 1933—and use to make a fortune?

3155. What popular drink was marketed as Diastoid when it was first introduced in 1882?

3156. What did the Wrigley Company do to promote its chewing gum nationwide in 1914?

3157. What member of the British nobility received a special award from America's National Pickle Packers Association in 1956 in recognition of an ancestor's invention?

3158. What percentage of the grains used in making bourbon must be corn?

3159. What are the five most frequently consumed fruits in the United States?

3160. In the United States, we call a tall iced drink of gin, lemon or lime, club soda and sugar a Tom Collins. What do they call it in England?

3161. What flavor did Baskin-Robbins introduce to commemorate America's landing on the moon on July 20, 1969?

3162. What general introduced chicle—the main ingredient in chewing gum—to the United States?

3163. What eating utensil was first brought to America in 1630 by Massachusetts Bay Colony governor John Winthrop, who carried it around with him in a specially made, velvet-lined leather case?

3164. Where in a wine shop will you find coiffes?

3165. How long does it take to hard-boil a three-pound ostrich egg?

3166. A pound of ground coffee yields 50 cups. How many cups does a pound of tea yield?

3167. What popular fruit was named after a papal estate outside Rome?

3154. *The recipe for tasty corn chips that he marketed as Fritos. He made them at night in his mother's kitchen and peddled them from his Model-T Ford.*

3155. *The malted milk, which was first sold as a special food supplement for babies and sick people.*

3156. *It mailed Doublemint gum to everyone listed in U.S. phone books.*

3157. *The Earl of Sandwich, whose eighteenth-century ancestor—the fourth earl—is credited with having invented the sandwich. The pickle packers gave the award in appreciation of the sandwich's contribution to the consumption of pickles.*

3158. *51 percent.*

3159. *The banana, apple, watermelon, orange and cantaloupe—in order of their greatest consumption, according to the Food and Drug Administration.*

3160. *A John Collins.*

3161. *Lunar cheesecake.*

3162. *Mexican general Antonio López de Santa Anna, while he was living in exile in New York City more than 30 years after he guaranteed himself a place in American history by storming the Alamo. He enjoyed chewing unflavored chicle and brought it north with him.*

3163. *The fork.*

3164. *On champagne bottles. The coiffe is the metal wire contraption that holds the champagne cork in place.*

3165. *1 hour and 45 minutes.*

3166. *200.*

3167. *The cantaloupe, which was named after the Pope's summer residence of Cantalupo.*

3168. Currants—small seedless grapes—were named for their place of origin. Just where was that?

3169. In what country did the Jerusalem artichoke originate?

3170. What was Charles Elmer Hires originally going to call the drink we now know as root beer?

3171. What is the most widely eaten fish in the world?

3172. How long does it take a ginseng root to reach marketable size?

3173. What snack food commercial was pulled off the air in 1970 because of complaints from an outraged ethnic group?

3174. Vichyssoise—the cold potato and leek soup—was first created in 1917 by chef Louis Diat. Do you know where?

3175. What fruit did the Visigoths demand in ransom when they laid siege to Rome in 408?

3176. What ethnic food did Jeno Paulucci make available in supermarkets nationwide for the very first time in 1947?

3177. What recipe—first published 50 years ago—has been requested most frequently through the years by the readers of "Better Homes and Gardens"?

3178. What were guests at the Buckinghamshire estate of financier Alfred de Rothschild asked when they requested milk with their tea?

3179. Under standards established by the U.S. Food and Drug Administration, what is the minimum a gallon of ice cream must weigh?

3180. What food product is named after Hannibal's brother Mago?

3181. When was coffee first sold in sealed tin cans in the United States?

3168. *Corinth, Greece. They were originally known as raysons de Corauntz, or "raisins of Corinth."*

169. *In the United States. Its name has nothing to do with the biblical city, but is a corruption of the Italian word for sunflower, girasole.*

3170. *Root tea—but a friend convinced him the name would discourage sales.*

3171. *The herring.*

3172. *Seven years.*

3173. *The Frito Bandito commercial for Frito corn chips. The complaints came from Mexican-Americans.*

3174. *In New York City—in the kitchen of the Ritz-Carlton Hotel, where Diat was head chef.*

3175. *Peppercorns—3,000 pounds of them. Pepper was a highly valued spice at the time.*

3176. *Paulucci gave us Chinese food—under the Chun King label. He later brought us Jeno's pizza.*

3177. *The recipe for hamburger pie, which has been updated and republished a number of times over the years.*

3178. *"Jersey, Hereford and Shorthorn?"*

3179. *Four and one-half pounds.*

3180. *Mayonnaise—which is named after the Minorca Island port city of Mahon, which was named for Mago.*

3181. *In 1879—by Chase & Sanborn.*

3182. For over fifty years, Ann Turner Cook's portrait has been the symbol for what well-known food product?

3183. What was the first name of Dom Pérignon, the seventeenth-century French monk who gave us Champagne?

3184. What part of the traditional Thanksgiving dinner is the merrythought?

3185. What is the name of the evergreen shrub from which we get capers?

3186. What is the largest fruit crop on earth?

3187. A California vintner named a Napa Valley wine in honor of Marilyn Monroe. What was it called?

3188. What is the official state beverage of Massachusetts?

3189. What food product overtook ketchup as the top-selling condiment in the United States in 1991?

3190. What fruit was originally named the Chinese gooseberry?

3191. What common salad ingredient belongs to the aster family?

3192. What is Danish pastry known as in Denmark?

3193. What is the only essential vitamin not found in the white potato?

3194. Under federal guidelines, how much alcohol can there be in beer labeled "non-alcoholic"?

3195. What delicacy is named for the city of Cheriton, Virginia?

3196. What is the Asiatic cordial kumiss made from?

3197. Under U.S. Agriculture Department guidelines, what percentage of a meatball has to be meat?

3198. What popular lunch and snack food did an unidentified St. Louis doctor develop in 1890 for patients requiring an easily digested form of protein?

3182. *Gerber's baby food.*

3183. *Pierre.*

3184. *The wishbone of the turkey.*

3185. *The caper, or caper bush.*

3186. *Grapes. Followed by bananas.*

3187. *Marilyn Merlot.*

3188. *Cranberry juice. The state's cranberry crop is the nation's largest.*

3189. *Salsa.*

3190. *The kiwi.*

3191. *Lettuce.*

3192. *Vienna bread—Wienerbrod, in Danish.*

3193. *Vitamin A.*

3194. *Up to .4999 percent.*

3195. *The cherrystone clam (the town was originally known as Cherry Stones).*

3196. *Fermented mare's or cow's milk.*

3197. *At least 65 percent.*

3198. *Peanut butter. Five years later, Dr. John Harvey Kellogg filed for a patent for the "process of preparing nut meal"—a spread of steamed peanuts that was not very popular with patients at his Battle Creek, Michigan, sanitarium.*

3199. How did the ice-cream sundae get its name?

3200. Who introduced standardized level measurements to recipes?

3201. With whom did the shallow champagne glass originate?

3202. Who introduced table knives in the seventeenth century?

3203. What did blind cellarmaster Dom Perignon say when he discovered Champagne in 1668?

3204. What nation produces two thirds of the world's vanilla?

3205. What now famous chef joined the OSS (Office of Strategic Services) during World War II, hoping to become an American spy?

3206. How did the Gatorade fruit drink get its name?

3207. Why did candy maker Milton S. Hershey switch from making caramels to chocolate bars in 1903?

3208. What fruits were crossed to produce the nectarine?

3209. What was used to make the coffee substitute given to American soldiers during World War II?

3210. What food product was discovered because of a long camel ride?

3211. What does cookbook author Julia Child claim is "so beautifully arranged on the plate—you know someone's fingers have been all over it"?

3212. The peanut isn't a nut. What is it?

3213. Where were the first frankfurters sold in the United States?

3214. Wild rice isn't rice. What is it?

3215. Who is credited with having invented the Manhattan cocktail, a combination of sweet vermouth and rye whiskey?

3199. *The sundae was created in Evanston, Illinois, in the late nineteenth century to get around a Sabbath ban on selling ice-cream sodas. It was dubbed Sunday but spelled with an "e" instead of a "y" to avoid religious objections.*

3200. *Fannie Farmer.*

3201. *With Marie Antoinette, from wax molds made of her breasts.*

3202. *Cardinal Richelieu. Daggers were in fashion at the dinner table until he became disgusted with their use as toothpicks and ordered knives with rounded ends.*

3203. *"Oh, come quickly. I am drinking stars!"*

3204. *Madagascar, the world's fourth-largest island (after Greenland, New Guinea and Borneo).*

3205. *Julia Child.*

3206. *From the University of Florida football team—the Gators—after the team tested it.*

3207. *Caramels didn't retain the imprint of his name in summertime; chocolate did.*

3208. *None. The nectarine is a smooth-skinned variety of peach, and not— as many people believe—a cross between a peach and a plum.*

3209. *Peanuts. It was one of hundreds of peanut by-products developed by Tuskegee University scientist George Washington Carver.*

3210. *Cottage cheese. An Arab trader found that milk he was carrying in a goatskin bag had turned into tasty solid white curds.*

3211. *Nouvelle cuisine.*

3212. *A legume—a member of the pea family.*

3213. *At Coney Island, in Brooklyn, New York, in 1871. They were made by Charles Feltmann, a butcher from Frankfurt, Germany.*

3214. *A coarse, annual grass native to shallow, marshy lakes and streams.*

3215. *Winston Churchill's Brooklyn-born mother, Jennie Jerome.*

3216. What do Eskimos use to prevent their food from freezing?

3217. What animal's milk is used to make authentic Italian mozzarella cheese?

3218. What is the world's largest herb?

3219. If you order the 5 Bs for dinner in New England, what will you be served?

3220. In the world of food, what is pluck?

3221. What is a cluster or bunch of bananas called?

3222. What part of the orange is the albedo?

3223. What is the BRAT diet?

3224. Why are canned herring called sardines?

3225. Who introduced the gin and lime juice cocktail we know as the gimlet?

3226. What would you get if you ordered a Mae West in a diner?

3227. Which fruit has a variety known as Winter Banana?

3228. Which is the only U.S. state to produce coffee?

Bonus Trivia

3229. In the early nineteenth century, ketchup was sold in the United States as a medicine—Dr. Miles' Compound Extract of Tomato.

3216. Refrigerators.

3217. The water buffalo's.

3218. The banana.

3219. Boston baked beans and brown bread.

3220. An animal's heart, liver and lungs.

3221. A hand. Individual bananas are known as fingers.

3222. The bitter-tasting white tissue that makes the peel stick to the skin.

3223. A diet of bananas, rice, applesauce and toast that's often prescribed for infants with diarrhea.

3224. The canning process for herring was developed in Sardinia, and the fish were first canned there.

3225. Sir T.O. Gimlette, a British naval surgeon at the turn of the century who believed that drinking straight gin was unhealthy and impaired the efficiency of naval officers—so he began diluting it with lime juice.

3226. A figure-eight cruller.

3227. The apple.

3228. Hawaii.

Music & Theatre

Questions

3230. What is the Internal Revenue Service's "Dinah Shore ruling"?

3231. From what performer did Elvis Presley pick up his pelvic gyrations?

3232. What is Cher's real first name?

3233. What was the brand of pajamas manufactured in the factory in which the 1954 Broadway musical *The Pajama Game* was set?

3234. What American actor—nominated for more Tony Awards than any other—made his New York acting debut in 1947 as the rear end of a cow in a production of *Jack and the Beanstalk* ?

3235. Who was unexpectedly cast in *Hair* after he played the piano at his actor half-brother's unsuccessful audition for the West Coast production of the rock musical in 1969?

3236. What job did Geraldine Page leave to appear off-Broadway in Tennessee Williams' *Summer and Smoke* in 1952?

Answers

3230. *A dress can be deducted as a professional expense if it is too tight to sit down in. The ruling was issued after singer Shore deducted gowns worn in public appearances as business expenses and insisted, when challenged by the IRS, that they were only worn onstage while performing.*

3231. *Bo Diddley.*

3232. *Cherilyn. Her name at birth was Cherilyn Sarkisian.*

3233. *Sleep-Tite.*

3234. *Jason Robards Jr.*

3235. *Keith Carradine. The brother who didn't get the part was David.*

3236. *Clerk and negligee model in a New York City dress shop.*

3237. What actor—long since overshadowed by his celebrity son—won a Tony in 1951 for his portrayal of suave gambler Sky Masterson in the original Broadway production of *Guys and Dolls*?

3238. What famous acting duo's off-stage bickering during a production of Shakespeare's *The Taming of the Shrew* was the inspiration for Cole Porter's musical comedy *Kiss Me Kate*?

3239. Who was Alice Brock?

3240. What famous entertainer helped reimburse dissatisfied customers when an acne medicine he endorsed was found to be ineffective?

3241. What title did famed drama critic George Jean Nathan suggest for a magazine photograph of Mae West posing as the Statue of Liberty?

3242. What was the film inspiration for the Stephen Sondheim musical *A Little Night Music*?

3243. In show biz slang, what's an *Annie Oakley*?

3244. What special imprint did Al Jolson make outside Grauman's Chinese Theatre?

3245. What famous American was code-named Napoleon by the Secret Service?

3246. In 1926, the police raided Mae West's Broadway show *Sex* and jailed her on vice charges. What did the wisecracking blonde sexpot claim when she was freed after serving 8 days of her 10-day sentence?

3247. What Beatles hits were on the first single recorded by the Fab Four on their Apple label?

3248. What business was Latin bombshell Carmen Miranda's father in back home in her native Brazil?

3249. What famous entertainer had two nicknames as a teenager: "Slacksey" because of his extensive wardrobe of trousers, and "Angles" because he was such a smart aleck?

3237. *Robert Alda, father of Alan.*

3238. *Alfred Lunt and Lynn Fontanne.*

3239. *The owner of the Stockbridge, Massachusetts, restaurant of Arlo Guthrie's* Alice's Restaurant, *an album popular in 1967, which in turn was the inspiration for the Arthur Penn movie of the same name.*

3240. *Pat Boone, in 1979.*

3241. *The Statue of Libido.*

3242. *Ingmar Bergman's* Smiles of a Summer Night.

3243. *A free pass to the theater. The legendary sharpshooter would toss a playing card in the air and shoot so many holes in it that it resembled a punched ticket.*

3244. *His knees, commemorating the trademark pose he took whenever he sang "Mammy."*

3245. *Frank Sinatra.*

3246. *That it was the only time she ever got anything for good behavior.*

3247. *"Hey Jude" and "Revolution."*

3248. *He ran a wholesale fruit business—which might explain the fruit-laden headdresses that became her trademark.*

3249. *Frank Sinatra.*

3250. Who was the first person ever awarded a gold record?

3251. For what famous entertainer was the Broadway musical *Hello Dolly!* written?

3252. Bing Crosby's recording of Irving Berlin's "White Christmas" is the best-selling pop record of all time. What rock 'n' roll single is in second place?

3253. What role did Dutch-born Andreas Cornelius van Kuijk play in Elvis Presley's life?

3254. What instrument did "King of Jazz" orchestra leader Paul Whiteman play when he launched his musical career with the Denver Symphony?

3255. Tenor Stefan Zucker held the longest-sustained high note on record during a Carnegie Hall performance in 1972. How long did he hold it?

3256. What distinctive vanity license plates did bandleader Lawrence Welk have in California?

3257. What are the three most frequently sung songs in the English language, according to the *Guinness Book of World Records*?

3258. What was the record number of curtain calls ballet greats Margot Fonteyn and Rudolf Nureyev received following a 1964 performance of *Swan Lake* in Vienna?

3259. What hit song was banned on Canadian radio during a 1960 royal visit by Queen Elizabeth II?

3260. What was the only comedy written by American playwright Eugene O'Neill?

3261. What was Beatle John Lennon's middle name?

3262. Who was Meyer Boston?

3263. Who bought one of rock 'n' roll pioneer Buddy Holly's guitars at auction for $242,000 in 1990?

3250. Glenn Miller, for "Chattanooga Choo-Choo."

3251. Ethel Merman. But she didn't star in the hit show until long after it opened—and only after Carol Channing, Ginger Rogers, Martha Raye, Betty Grable, Bibi Osterwald, Pearl Bailey and Phyllis Diller had appeared in the title role.

3252. "Rock Around the Clock," by Bill Haley and the Comets. The 1954 hit has sold 25 million copies to Crosby's 170 million plus.

3253. He was Elvis's manager, better known to us as "Colonel" Tom Parker. He changed his name in his teens after he fled to the U.S. and joined a traveling carnival as a salesman and publicity agent.

3254. The viola.

3255. 3.8 seconds. It was an A in alt-altissimo.

3256. A1ANA2—his trademark phrase.

3257. "Happy Birthday," "For He's a Jolly Good Fellow" and "Auld Lang Syne."

3258. 89.

3259. Johnny Horton's "The Battle of New Orleans," which celebrates the smashing defeat of the British by American troops led by Andrew Jackson in 1815.

3260. Ah, Wilderness!

3261. Winston, after Winston Churchill.

3262. The gambler after whom Damon Runyon modeled his character Nathan Detroit—best known to us as the operator of "the oldest established permanent floating crap game in New York" in the musical Guys and Dolls.

3263. Gary Busey, who won a best actor Oscar nomination for his portrayal of Holly in the 1978 film The Buddy Holly Story.

3264. What record album was the first ever to be taken directly from a film's musical soundtrack?

3265. What city was the hometown of both Nellie Forbush in the musical *South Pacific* and Lorelei Lee in *Gentlemen Prefer Blondes?*

3266. What sticker message did Capitol Records add to a recording of Delibes' opera *Lakmé* in 1988 in a bid to boost sales among buyers not ordinarily interested in classical music?

3267. Who wrote Yale's "Bulldog" song?

3268. How many of the 107 musicians in the new York Philharmonic Orchestra play second violin?

3269. What singer—called Clara Ann Fowler at birth—adopted the name of the milk company that sponsored her first radio show?

3270. What recipe is recited in the play *Cyrano de Bergerac* ?

3271. Which of U2's songs is a tribute to Martin Luther King Jr.?

3272. What is the only sound heard on the record *The Best of Marcel Marceau* ?

3273. What popular band is named for a hallucinogenic treat made by a member's grandmother?

3274. What led jazz great Dizzy Gillespie to redesign his trumpet so it had an upturned bell?

3275. What stringed instrument was the first to have a keyboard?

3276. What famous entertainer was known as Annie Mae Bullock before she adopted a stage name?

3277. When he was six years old, what did country singer Chet Atkins use to string his first musical instrument—an old, discarded ukulele?

3278. What was American rock star Eddie Money's surname at birth?

3264. *Walt Disney's* Snow White and the Seven Dwarfs, *in 1937.*

3265. *Little Rock, Arkansas.*

3266. *"Includes the Flower Duet from the British Airways TV commercial."*

3267. *Cole Porter, in 1911, when he was a student there.*

3268. *16.*

3269. *Patti Page. The company was the Page Milk Company of Tulsa, Oklahoma.*

3270. *The recipe for tart almondine—it's recited by Ragueneau.*

3271. *Pride (In the Name Love).*

3272. *Clapping, after 40 minutes of silence.*

3273. *Pearl Jam. It's named for lead singer Eddie Vedder's grandmother Pearl and the hallucinogenic preserves she made from peyote.*

3274. *He liked the slightly muted sound of his trumpet after comic James "Stump" Cross fell on it, bending the bell to a 45-degree angle. After the accident, Gillespie had his trumpet custom-made—with an upturned bell.*

3275. *The clavichord, which was developed around 1400.*

3276. *Actress-singer Tina Turner.*

3277. *Wire from a screen door.*

3278. *Mahoney. He changed it in hopes the name Money would bring him fame and fortune.*

3279. What is the significance of the Bon Jovi album title 7800 Fahrenheit?

3280. What famous singer-songwriter met his future wife when he was working as a nightclub bouncer—and threw her out for fighting?

3281. Who was the first performer to win Grammy Awards for jazz and classical recordings in the same year?

3282. What flamboyant pop star auctioned off his costumes for $8.2 million in 1988, explaining "I don't want to go on stage looking like Tina Turner's grandmother anymore"?

3283. What was the color of the streetcar named Desire in Tennessee Williams's Pulitzer Prize-winning play?

3284. The rock group Electric Mayhem made an appearance in what 1979 film?

3285. Who was rumored to be the subject of Carly Simon's 1972 record, "You're So Vain"?

3286. Irving Berlin reworked one of his songs, "Smile and Show Your Dimple." What became the song's more memorable title?

3287. From what other singer did Elvis Presley borrow his characteristic hip-swinging?

3288. Max Born, winner of the 1954 Nobel Prize in Physics, is the grandfather of which well-known pop singer?

3289. The singing duo of Caesar and Cleo only achieved fame under another name. What was it?

3290. What pop singer-songwriter once played the piano at the Executive Lounge in Los Angeles under the name of William Martin?

3291. A song called "I Wish You Peace," recorded by The Eagles, was written by Bernie Leadon and Patti Davis. What is Ms. Davis's more obvious claim to fame?

3279. *It refers to the temperature of an exploding volcano.*

3280. *Garth Brooks. His wife, Sandy Mahl, was in the nightclub's ladies' room when she threw a punch at the jealous ex-girlfriend of a man she had dated—and her hand got stuck in the wall. Brooks, a college student at the time, freed her hand and threw her out. He later began dating her.*

3281. *Trumpet virtuoso Wynton Marsalis, in 1984. He won for the albums* Trumpet Concertos *and* Think of One.

3282. *Elton John.*

3283. *Green*

3284. The Muppet Movie—*it was the muppet rock band.*

3285. *Warren Beatty.*

3286. *"Easter Parade."*

3287. *Bo Diddley.*

3288. *Olivia Newton-John.*

3289. *Sonny and Cher.*

3290. *Billy Joel, who recalled those early days in the 1974 hit record,* Piano Man.

3291. *She is the younger daughter of former President Ronald Reagan.*

3292. What brand of apple was used as the symbol for the Beatles' record label, Apple Records?

3293. In 1948, Peter Goldmark introduced something for which people like Stevie Wonder, Pink Floyd and Fleetwood Mac would be forever grateful. What was it?

3294. "Anywhere the Bluebird Goes" was the original title of which very popular 1939 tune?

3295. In 1970, cult ringleader and convicted killer, Charles Manson recorded an album of his songs. What was its title?

3296. What were the names of the two gangs in *West Side Story* ?

3297. Chip Taylor, the composer of such hit songs as "Wild Thing" and "Angel of the Morning," is the brother of which Oscar-winning actor?

3298. Country music comedienne Minnie Pearl always wears a hat with a price tag on it when she performs. What is the amount on the price tag?

3299. "Palisades Park" was a hit in 1962 for singer Freddy Cannon. Its composer, Chuck Barris, is better remembered for creating and hosting which excruciatingly bad TV show of the 70s?

3300. Radio station WSM in Nashville, Tennessee, has been broadcasting *The Grand Ole Opry* since November 1928. What do the call letters "WSM," stand for?

3301. What three Gershwin songs contain the phrase, "Who could ask for anything more"?

3302. In 1957, a group called The Scholars released the record, "Kan-gu-wa," which failed to hit the charts. Both the composer and the lead singer are probably grateful to be remembered for their other accomplishments—who are they?

3303. Although popularized in *Casablanca*, the song, "As Time Goes By," was introduced in what 1931 musical play?

3292. *Granny Smith.*

3293. *The long-playing, 33⅓ RPM record album.*

3294. *"Don't Sit Under the Apple Tree (With Anyone Else But Me)."*

3295. *"Lie."*

3296. *The Jets and the Sharks.*

3297. *Jon Voight.*

3298. *$1.98.*

3299. The Gong Show.

3300. *"We Shield Millions," the motto of the National Life and Accident Company, which originally owned the station.*

3301. *"I Got Rhythm," "Nice Work if You Can Get it" and "I'm About to Become a Mother."*

3302. *Gossip-columnist, Louella Parsons, who wrote the song; Kenny Rogers, who sang it.*

3303. Everybody's Welcome.

3304. What role did Sarah Bernhardt play in *The Sleeping Beauty* when she was 62 years old?

3305. Which actress is thought to be the first woman to wear trousers?

3306. How did the 1950's instrumental group, The Champs, who had a number one hit with "Tequila" in 1958, get their name?

3307. Who was Pat Boone's famous father-in-law?

3308. What rich and famous singer-songwriter owns the publishing rights to *Stormy Weather* and *Hello Dolly*, as well as the soundtracks of *Grease, Mame, Annie* and *A Chorus Line*, among many others?

3309. In *Peter Pan*, if you traveled "second to the right and then straight on till morning," where would you emerge?

3310. What song, originally recorded in 1958 by Hank Ballard and The Midnighters, became the only recording in *Billboard* history to reach number one in two different years when it was recorded by another artist?

3311. Who was the first performer to sell over half-a-million copies of a quadradisc—a stereo, four-channel record?

3312. In April, 1971, what rock group became the first ever to appear at New York's Carnegie Hall?

3313. What song holds the record for the biggest leap to the number one position on *Billboard's* Hot 100 chart?

3314. An opera written to commemorate the opening of the Suez Canal was first performed on December 24, 1871. What was it?

3315. How much did RCA records pay Sun Records for Elvis Presley's contract in 1955?

3316. Who wrote and recorded the song "Beware of Young Girls" after her husband left her for a young woman?

3304. Prince Charming.

3305. Sarah Bernhardt, in 1876.

3306. The group was named after Champion, Gene Autry's horse. (Autry owned Challenge Records, for which The Champs recorded.)

3307. Country singer Red Foley.

3308. Paul McCartney.

3309. Into Never Never Land.

3310. "The Twist," sung by Chubby Checker, which reached number one in 1960 and again in 1962.

3311. Elvis Presley, with "Elvis: Aloha From Hawaii Via Satellite," in 1973.

3312. Chicago, in April 1971.

3313. The Beatles' "Can't Buy Me Love." On March 28, 1964, it entered the chart at number 37, the next week, it was number 1.

3314. "Aida," by Giuseppe Verdi.

3315. RCA paid $35,000 plus a $5,000 bonus when Elvis signed.

3316. Dory Previn, ex-wife of composer-conductor Andre Previn. The younger woman was actress Mia Farrow.

3317. In addition to singing superstar Michael Jackson, who were the original members of the Jackson Five?

3318. What is the name of the street in Charleston, South Carolina, that served as the prototype for Catfish Row in George Gershwin's opera *Porgy and Bess*?

3319. What was the musical theme of TV's *Captain Video and His Video Rangers* ?

3320. What rock star was christened William Broad?

3321. To whom did super-rocker Elton John pay tribute in his hit "Candle in the Wind"?

3322. How did British actor Charles Laughton, subbing as emcee for Ed Sullivan, introduce Elvis Presley when Elvis made his second appearance on TV's *The Toast of the Town* ?

3323. What was the musical theme played at the beginning of the *Green Hornet* radio series?

3324. Under what name was folksinger Joan Baez satirized in Al Capp's *Li'l Abner* cartoon?

3325. What Nobel Peace Prize-winning American vice-president composed the music for the song "It's All in the Game," which became a hit tune for Tommy Edwards in 1951 and again in 1958?

3326. When the roles in *The Odd Couple* were switched from male to female on Broadway, what names were used instead of Oscar and Felix?

3327. Who invented the saxophone?

3328. What is Fats Domino's real first name?

3329. What famous opera was inspired by a short story written in 1898 by Philadelphia lawyer John Luther Long?

3330. How tall is songwriter Randy Newman, the man who wrote the 1977 hit parody of bigotry *Short People*?

3317. *His brothers Jackie, Jermaine, Marlon and Tito.*

3318. *Cabbage Row.*

3319. *The overture to Richard Wagner's "Der Fliegende Holländer" (The Flying Dutchman).*

3320. *Billy Idol.*

3321. *Marilyn Monroe.*

3322. *As Elvin Presley.*

3323. *"Flight of the Bumble Bee," by Nikolai Rimsky-Korsakov.*

3324. *Joany Phoney.*

3325. *Charles G. Dawes, who served as vice-president to Calvin Coolidge from 1925 to 1929. He wrote the song in 1912.*

3326. *Olive and Florence. They were played by Rita Moreno and Sally Struthers, respectively.*

3327. *Adolphe Sax—he patented it in 1846.*

3328. *Antoine.*

3329. Madame Butterfly, *by Puccini.*

3330. *He's 5 feet 11 inches tall.*

3331. Who sang advertising jingles for McDonald's, Pepsi, Chevrolet, Kentucky Fried Chicken and others before making it big on the music scene?

3332. What popular stage and screen musical was based on *Green Grow the Lilacs*, a 1931 Broadway show starring Franchot Tone and singing cowboy Woodward "Tex" Ritter?

3333. What performer rocketed to stardom from the *Pajama Game* chorus line when star Carol Haney was sidelined by an ankle injury?

3334. How many Beatles songs were at the top of the *Billboard Hot 100* singles list in early April 1964?

3335. What did Buddy Holly originally call "Peggy Sue," the rock 'n' roll classic he recorded with the Crickets in 1957?

3336. What modern musical instrument is based on the medieval sackbut?

3337. Who was the only cast member of the hit rock musical *Hair* to refuse to shed her clothes in the closing number?

3338. What popular singer was heard on the first multi-track vocal—on a recording that was billed as a duet?

3339. Who wrote the title song for the 1973 James Bond film *Live and Let Die* ?

3340. How much did a piano cost in the 1900 Sears, Roebuck and Company catalog?

3341. Carole King's song "The Loco-Motion" was made into a hit record in 1962 by her maid. Who was she?

3342. What Broadway show put performers John Travolta, Richard Gere, Marilu Henner, Treat Williams and Barry Bostwick on the road to stardom?

3343. What are the names of the theme parks established by country singers Dolly Parton and Conway Twitty?

3331. *Singer-composer Barry Manilow.*

3332. Oklahoma*!*

3333. *Shirley MacLaine, in 1954.*

3334. *An unprecedented and never duplicated five. From No. 1 to No. 5 they were: "Can't Buy Me Love," "Twist and Shout," "She Loves You," "I Want to Hold Your Hand," and "Please Please Me."*

3335. *"Cindy Lou." Holly renamed it at the urging of Crickets drummer Jerry Allison, whose girlfriend's name was Peggy Sue.*

3336. *The trombone.*

3337. *Diane Keaton.*

3338. *Patti Page, in 1951. The song was "The Tennessee Waltz."*

3339. *Ex-Beatle Paul McCartney.*

3340. *It cost $98—FOB Chicago.*

3341. *Little Eva—Eva Narcissus Boyd.*

3342. *The 1972 rock musical* Grease.

3343. *Parton's is Dollywood (located in Pigeon Forge, Tennessee); Twitty's is Twitty City (in Hendersonville, Tennessee).*

3344. British songwriter-impresario Gordon Mills gave three rock stars their stage names. Can you name them?

3345. What were the last words of famed ballerina Anna Pavlova?

3346. What classical music inspired the theme music for TV's *Alfred Hitchcock Presents* ?

3347. What famous songwriter supported himself by writing *Topper* TV scripts?

3348. What TV personality asked Dolly Parton, "Is it all you?" and what was her reply?

3349. What song about a rat became a hit single?

3350. What's the name of theatrical rock musician David Bowie's son?

3351. Who wrote *The Coffee Cantata* ?

3352. What former Beatle was convicted of "unconscious plagiarism"?

3353. With what group did Linda Ronstadt launch her musical career as a lead singer in 1964?

3354. What was the site of the Beatles' last performance on August 29, 1966?

3355. What was the musical version of the Broadway show *The Rainmaker* called?

3356. What American songwriter could compose music and play the piano only in the key of F?

3357. What European theater legend resumed her stage career after having a leg amputated?

3358. What pop rock singer-songwriter helped launch Bette Midler's career?

3344. Engelbert Humperdinck (Arnold George Dorsey), Tom Jones (Thomas Jones Woodward) and Gilbert O'Sullivan (Ray O'Sullivan).

3345. "Get my swan costume ready!"

3346. Gounod's "Funeral March of a Marionette."

3347. Stephen Sondheim, before his West Side Story success in 1957.

3348. Barbara Walters asked the question and was told: "If I hadn't had it on my own, I'm just the kind of person who would get it!"

3349. "Ben's Song"—performed by Michael Jackson—the title song from the movie Ben, which is about a rat.

3350. Originally Zowie, now renamed Joey.

3351. Johann Sebastian Bach.

3352. George Harrison, for "My Sweet Lord," which was similar to Phil Spector's "He's So Fine."

3353. The Stone Poneys.

3354. Candlestick Park, San Francisco.

3355. 110 in the Shade.

3356. Irving Berlin.

3357. Sarah Bernhardt.

3358. Barry "I Write the Songs" Manilow, who was the Divine Miss M's accompanist-arranger.

3359. What musician was the first to write down blues music and the first to publish it?

3360. What Broadway musical was staged by a labor union in 1939?

3361. What inspired John, Paul, George, and Ringo to call themselves the Beatles?

3362. What famous actor made his Broadway debut in 1944, as Dagmar's brother Nels in *I Remember Mama* ?

3363. In December 1963, Frank Sinatra Jr. was kidnapped. What ransom did his father pay for his release?

3364. Brothers Jimmy and Tommy Dorsey were famous band leaders. Who is Arnold Dorsey?

3365. What teenaged rock 'n' roller appeared in the film *Hound Dog Man* wearing the same jeans and boots worn by Elvis Presley in "Love Me Tender" three years earlier?

3366. What performer's only Las Vegas booking was a two-week stint with the slapstick Honey Brothers at the Hotel Last Frontier in 1954?

3367. What singer subbed for Brian Wilson during the Beach Boys' 1965 tour?

3368. What rock superstar left $2,500 in her will for a farewell party "so my friends can have a ball after I'm gone"?

3369. What gold-plated 33-rpm record did the Apollo astronauts leave behind on the moon?

3370. What popular performer was named best female singer of the year a record 21 times by *Down Beat* magazine?

3359. *Handy, composer of "The St. Louis Blues," who is known as the "father of the blues."*

3360. Pins and Needles, *produced by and with International Ladies Garment Workers Union personnel.*

3361. *Buddy Holly's group, the Crickets. The "beat" spelling was intended as a musical pun.*

3362. *Marlon Brando.*

3363. *He paid $240,000.*

3364. *Pop singer Engelbert Humperdinck.*

3365. *Fabian, whose name in the film was Clint—the same as Elvis' in* Love Me Tender.

3366. *Ronald Reagan, who later became the 40th President of the United States.*

3367. *Glen Campbell.*

3368. *Janis Joplin.*

3369. Camelot—*a favorite of President John F. Kennedy.*

3370. *Ella Fitzgerald.*

3371. What did opera great Luciano Pavarotti do for a living before he became a professional tenor?

3372. Who is the famous clarinetist who performs with the New Orleans Funeral and Jazz Band?

3373. How long was the train on pianist-showman Liberace's 175-pound Norwegian blue shadow fox coat?

3374. What jazz great was known by the nicknames Dippermouth and Gatemouth?

3375. In disc jockey slang, what is a lunar rotation?

3376. What hat is named after a play written for the great Sarah Bernhardt?

3377. What famous country and western singer recorded under the pseudonym Luke the Drifter, as well as his real name?

3378. In the world of music, adagio is a direction to play slowly. What do the terms adagietto and adagissomo mean?

3379. What did Aretha Franklin wear on her head when she sang "Funny Girl" at the Academy Awards ceremony in 1969?

3380. What popular recording star's real name is Robert Van Winkle?

3381. What musical masterpiece commemorates a battle fought at a place called Borodino?

3382. In ballet, what is a fondu?

3383. What's the name of the Mississippi paddle-wheeler that provides the setting for the stage and movie musical *Show Boat*?

3384. What famous writer co-authored the lyrics to Rosemary Clooney's 1951 hit song "Come On-a My House"?

3385. How many children did Baron von Trapp have in the Broadway show and hit movie musical *The Sound of Music*?

3371. He taught in an elementary school and then sold insurance—because he found teaching too hard on his vocal cords.

3372. Woody Allen.

3373. 16 feet. The coat is on display at the Liberace Museum in Las Vegas.

3374. Louis Armstrong—who is better known as Satchmo, a shortened version of Satchelmouth.

3375. An infrequently played record.

3376. The fedora. The play Fédora, by French dramatist Victorien Sardou, features a Russian princess who wears a brimmed, soft felt hat with a creased crown.

3377. Hank Williams.

3378. Adagietto is a direction to play slightly faster than adagio; adagissomo, to play very slowly.

3379. Antlers.

3380. Vanilla Ice's.

3381. Tchaikovsky's "1812 Overture." Borodino is a village 70 miles west of Moscow. The battle was between Napoleon's troops and the Russian Army.

3382. A lowering of the body by bending the knee of the supporting leg.

3383. "Cotton Blossom."

3384. William Saroyan—with his cousin, songwriter-record producer Ross Bagdasarian (who used the professional name of David Seville to make Alvin and the Chipmunks records).

3385. Seven—Leisel, Friedrich, Louisa, Brigitta, Kurt, Marta and Gretl.

3386. What famous American composer has had two of his songs adopted as official state anthems?

3387. As a child, what famous opera singer was featured as an orphan—a singing orphan, of course—on a radio soap opera?

3388. Who was the first rock or pop performer to appear on the covers of *Time* and *Newsweek* magazines in the same week?

3389. The title of what Broadway show and popular movie was inspired by a painting by Marc Chagall?

3390. What top rock group took its name from a song by blues great Muddy Waters?

3391. What famous American singer-songwriter played the part of slick, name-dropping record-industry promoter Tony Lacey in Woody Allen's 1977 movie hit, *Annie Hall*?

3392. What classical music served as the theme of the 1968 film " *2001: A Space Odyssey* ?

3393. Where is the Tallahatchie Bridge, the site of Billie Joe McAllister's suicide leap in the popular 1967 Bobbie Gentry folk ballad, "Ode to Billie Joe"?

3394. What rock band was the first to perform at New York's Metropolitan Opera House?

3395. Who designed the famous working-zipper album cover for the Rolling Stones' 1971 LP *Sticky Fingers* ?

3396. Who played Captain Hook and Mr. Darling opposite Jean Arthur in the 1950 Broadway production of Sir James M. Barrie's *Peter Pan* ?

3397. What famous performer is heard in the background on Harry Belafonte's 1961 LP *Midnight Special* ?

3398. Why did the members of the rock group Led Zeppelin perform under an alias—The Nobs—when they appeared in Copenhagen, Denmark, in 1970?

3386. *Stephen Foster. His "My Old Kentucky Home" is the state song of Kentucky, and his "Old Folks at Home" is the state song of Florida.*

3387. *Beverly Sills, who was known as the Nightingale of the Mountains on the radio serial* Our Gal Sunday.

3388. *Bruce Springsteen, in 1975—after the release of his third album,* Born to Run.

3389. Fiddler on the Roof. *The title came from the Russian-born artist's painting* The Green Violinist, *which depicts a violinist floating over village rooftops.*

3390. *The Rolling Stones. Waters song, of course, was "Rollin' Stone."*

3391. *Paul Simon.*

3392. *Richard Strauss' "Also sprach Zarathustra (Thus Spake Zarathustra)," written in 1896.*

3393. *In Greenwood, Mississippi.*

3394. *The Who, in 1970—for a performance of the rock opera* Tommy.

3395. *Pop artist Andy Warhol.*

3396. *Boris Karloff.*

3397. *Bob Dylan, playing the harmonica.*

3398. *Airship heiress Eva Von Zeppelin threatened legal action if the group performed under its real name.*

3399. Who was the subject of the 1944 song "Nancy (With the Laughing Face)"?

3400. Where did the British reggae band UB40 get its name?

3401. What famous classical musician was named Harvey Lavan Jr. at birth?

3402. What British rock group took its name from a character in the 1968 science-fiction film spoof *Barbarella*, which starred Jane Fonda?

3403. What is Max Yasgur's claim to fame in the world of music?

3404. What popular entertainer sang "Love Me Tender" on a 1960 TV special co-starring Elvis Presley?

3405. What three rock 'n' roll stars were featured in *The Longest Day*, the 1962 film epic about the Allies' D-Day invasion of Normandy?

3406. How old was country-western singer Loretta Lynn when she became a grandmother for the first time?

3407. What name did Chuck Berry originally use in his 1955 rock 'n' roll hit "Maybelline"?

3408. Why did Dame Edith Evans, the famous British actress, refuse to appear onstage as Lady Macbeth?

3409. Who replaced Chico Marx as the pianist at Manhattan's City Theatre in 1917?

3410. What famous entertainment figure once had a solo hit record called "I've Got a Lovely Bunch of Cocoanuts"?

3411. Under what name did New Wave singer-songwriter Declan McManus gain fame?

3412. What does Yoko Ono's first name mean when translated from Japanese?

3399. *Nancy Sinatra, who was four years old at the time. The song, introduced by her crooner father, Frank, was written by comedian Phil Silvers (lyrics) and Jimmy Van Heusen (music).*

3400. *From the code number on the British unemployment benefit card.*

3401. *Pianist Van Cliburn, who gained international renown in 1958 when he became the first American to win the Tchaikovsky Competition in Moscow.*

3402. *Duran Duran. In the movie, Duran Duran was portrayed by actor Milo O'Shea.*

3403. *He was the owner of the Bethel, New York, farm where the famous Woodstock rock festival was held in 1969.*

3404. *Frank Sinatra. Presley, in turn, sang Sinatra's hit "Witchcraft."*

3405. *Paul Anka, Tommy Sands and Fabian.*

3406. *She was 29 years old.*

3407. *"Ida Red." Maybelline was the name of a cow in a school reading book.*

3408. *She claimed, "I could never impersonate a woman who had such a peculiar notion of hospitality".*

3409. *George Gershwin. His salary was $25 a week, but he quit after one show.*

3410. *Merv Griffin.*

3411. *Elvis Costello.*

3412. *Ocean child.*

3413. What song, with a 21-word title, did Fred Astaire sing and dance to with Jane Powell in the 1951 Hollywood musical *Royal Wedding* ?

3414. What is the source of the lyrics of the Byrds' 1965 hit song "Turn! Turn! Turn!"?

3415. Who co-starred with pop singer Petula Clark in a 1969 musical remake of the 1939 film classic *Goodbye Mr. Chips* ?

3416. Who appeared in a Beatle wig on the cover of the July 1965 issue of *Esquire* magazine?

3417. In 1976 what famous singer snuck onto the grounds of Graceland, Elvis Presley's Memphis home, in an unsuccessful bid to meet his rock idol?

3418. What is the diameter of a compact disc, which holds up to three miles of playing track?

3419. What state was used for the location shots for the 1955 hit musical *Oklahoma!*?

3420. What is the origin of the do-si-do, the square dance call that instructs partners to pass each other right shoulder to right shoulder and circle back to back?

3421. What was playwright George S. Kaufman's reply when *Vanity* Fair magazine asked him to write his own epitaph?

3422. What onstage activity started the fire in 1613 that burned down England's first Globe Theatre, where Shakespeare's greatest plays were first performed?

3423. Who dubbed504

the fiddling in the 1971 film *Fiddler on the Roof?*

3424. What perfume is named after a musical term?

3425. What was the name of the first record label developed by entertainment mogul David Geffen?

3413. How Could You Believe Me When I Said I Love You When You Know I've Been a Liar All My Life *? Lyrics by Alan Jay Lerner; music by Burton Lane.*

3414. *The Bible. Composer Pete Seeger adapted the song from Chapter 3 of the Book of Ecclesiastes, which begins, "To every thing there is a season."*

3415. *Peter O'Toole.*

3416. *TV variety show host Ed Sullivan.*

3417. *Bruce Springsteen, who once said, "Anybody who sees Elvis Presley and doesn't want to be like Elvis Presley has got to have something wrong with him."*

3418. *4 ¾ inches.*

3419. *Arizona. There were too many oil derricks and noisy airplanes in Oklahoma at the time. The filming took place outside Nogales, Arizona, where a field of corn was planted long before shooting so it would get "as high as an elephant's eye."*

3420. *The French phrase dos à dos, which means "back to back."*

3421. *"Over my dead body!"*

3422. *A spark from a stage cannon accidentally set the theater's thatched roof ablaze during a performance of Shakespeare's* Henry VIII.

3423. *Isaac Stern*

3424. *Arpège. In music arpeggio is a chord in which the notes are played individually in quick succession. The perfume was named for it because its various floral essences are intended to strike the senses in a similar way.*

3425. *Asylum.*

3426. What popular crooner won a Grammy in 1992 for an album entitled *Perfectly Frank?*

3427. What famous play begins with the line, "Who's there?"

3428. What husband-and-wife acting duo spent more time in bed together onstage than any other theater couple?

3429. Under what name was Harpo Marx portrayed in the Moss Hart-George S. Kaufman play *The Man Who Came to Dinner?*

3430. What singer has recorded under the alias Apollo C. Vermouth?

3431. What is the meaning of the musical direction estinto?

3432. How old was Stevie Wonder when he signed his first record contract?

3433. What color was Elvis Presley's first Cadillac before he bought it and had it painted pink in 1955?

3434. Who provided the voice of the ghost of Hamlet's father when Richard Burton appeared on Broadway in the title role of *Hamlet* in 1964?

3435. Who is the only playwright to have won four Pulitzer Prizes?

3436. How did Bono, the lead singer and lyricist of the Irish rock band U2, get his name?

3437. What woman's name was originally used in the old barbershop quartet favorite "Sweet Adeline"?

3438. What is the name of the album Madonna released in 1990 to coincide with her appearance in the movie *Dick Tracy* with Warren Beatty?

3439. In the 1968 Beatles cartoon fantasy *Yellow Submarine*, what did Jeremy Boob, Ph.D., use to repair the sub's propeller, enabling the Fab Four to escape His Meaniness and the Blue Meanies?

3426. Tony Bennett. The album contained songs identified with Frank Sinatra.

3427. Shakespeare's Hamlet. *The line is spoken by the soldier Bernardo.*

3428. Jessica Tandy and Hume Cronyn, who appeared together on Broadway and on tour in The Fourposter, *a hilarious history of a 35-year marriage told through a series of bedroom scenes.*

3429. Banjo. The usually mute Marx actually appeared onstage in the role—speaking his first lines as a performer in 25 years.

3430. Ex-Beatle Paul McCartney.

3431. As soft as possible—so soft it can hardly be heard.

3432. 11—it was a five-year contract with Motown.

3433. Blue.

3434. Sir John Gielgud, who directed the highly acclaimed production.

3435. Eugene O'Neill. He won the drama prize for Beyond the Horizon *in 1920, for* Anna Christie *in 1922, for* Strange Interlude *in 1928 and for* Long Day's Journey Into Night *in 1957.*

3436. From a hearing aid store in Dublin called Bono Voz—an adaptation of a Latin phrase meaning "good voice," although Bono, who was named Paul Hewson at birth, says he didn't know what it meant.

3437. Rosalie. Written by Richard Gerard (music) and Henry Armstrong (words) in 1903, it was originally entitled "You're the Flower of My Heart, Sweet Rosalie." When the song didn't sell, they renamed it for popular Italian soprano Adelina Patti and shortened the title.

3438. I'm Breathless. *Madonna played Breathless Mahoney in the film.*

3439. Bubble gum.

3440. What famous singer, after receiving an honorary degree from Georgetown University, enrolled as a freshman and earned a B.A. in theology?

3441. From what poetic source did Noel Coward get the title for his play *Blithe Spirit?*

3442. What musical instrument did bandleader-trumpeter Herb Alpert play during his brief appearance in Cecil B. DeMille's 1956 film spectacular *The Ten Commandments?*

3443. What country singer was given a part as an extra in the 1973 film *American Graffiti* after she was spotted driving her mother's 1957 Chevy in Hollywood?

3444. The premiere of what famous play by a Nobel Prize-winning writer was held in England's Canterbury Cathedral in 1935?

3445. What did Frank Sinatra give forever-39 Jack Benny on his 80th birthday?

3446. Who was the last act at the famous three-day Woodstock festival in 1969?

3447. What popular nursery rhyme provided Neil Simon with the title for his first play?

3448. Kurt Weil wrote the music for "September Song." What famous American playwright wrote the lyrics?

3449. What famous opera is based on the search for the Holy Grail?

3450. What famous American songwriter-entertainer recorded a song about Belgian surrealist painter René Magritte and his wife dancing to doo-wop?

3451. Why did musician Herb Alpert, founder of the Tijuana Brass, name his son Dore?

3452. What Grammy-winning 1959 hit—with music written by Hoagy Carmichael—is an official state song?

3440. *Pearl Bailey. She received her B.A. in 1985 after seven years as a part-time student.*

3441. *From Percy Bysshe Shelley's* To a Skylark, *which begins, "Hail to thee, blithe spirit!*

3442. *A drum, which Alpert beats while Moses, played by Charlton Heston, strides down Mount Sinai with the commandments.*

3443. *Wynonna Judd.*

3444. *Eliot's* Murder in the Cathedral. *Canterbury Cathedral was where the play's central character, Thomas `à Becket, was martyred.*

3445. *Two copies of the book* Life Begins at Forty.

3446. *Jimi Hendrix, who performed "The Star-Spangled Banner."*

3447. *"Little Boy Blue" gave him the title for* Come Blow Your Horn.

3448. *Maxwell Anderson. "September Song" was in their 1938 Broadway musical* Knickerbocker Holiday.

3449. *Parsifal, by Richard Wagner.*

3450. *Paul Simon. The song, "René and Georgette Magritte and Their Dog After the War," is on his 1983 album* Hearts and Bones.

3451. *The name contains the first two notes of the musical scale, do and re.*

3452. *"Georgia on My Mind." The lyrics are by Stuart Gorrell.*

3453. How many marches did John Philip Sousa write?

3454. In what famous person's bed did actress Anne Bancroft sleep (alone) in preparation for a Broadway role?

3455. How much does a 9-foot Steinway concert grand piano weigh? How about a 5-foot 1-inch baby grand?

3456. To whom did the Beatles dedicate the movie *Help!*?

3457. What was singer Ray Charles's name at birth?

3458. Who played Madonna's father in the 1986 music video the popular singer made for her recording of "Papa Don't Preach"?

3459. What former friend did singer Al Jolson knock out in a grudge prizefight in 1933?

3460. What musical instrument did Meredith Willson, author of *The Music Man*, play in his hometown band as well as with the John Philip Sousa band and the New York Philharmonic?

3461. What instrument did Dolly Parton play in her high-school marching band?

3462. What popular recording star owes his name to his resemblance to baseball great Hank Aaron?

3463. In the 1961 James Cagney spy comedy *One, Two, Three*, what American hit song did the East Germans use as a form of torture?

3464. Who composed the pop gospel standard "The Bible Tells Me So"?

3465. In music what is a hemidemisemiquaver?

3466. What was the inspiration for the Paul Simon song "Mother and Child Reunion"?

3467. Who composed the coronation anthem first played for England's King George II in 1727 and used at British coronations ever since?

3453. *136. He also wrote 15 operettas, 15 band suites and 70 songs.*

3454. *Golda Meir's. In 1977, Bancroft visited Meir in Israel and slept in her bed before appearing in the title role of* Golda, *a dramatization of Meir's autobiography,* My Life.

3455. *Grand, 990 pounds; baby, 540.*

3456. *To "Elias Howe who, in 1846, invented the sewing machine."*

3457. *Ray Charles Robinson. He dropped his surname early in his career to avoid confusion with boxer Sugar Ray Robinson.*

3458. *Actor Danny Aiello.*

3459. *Columnist Walter Winchell.*

3460. *The flute.*

3461. *The snare drum.*

3462. *Hammer, who was named Stanley Kirk Burrell at birth. He was nicknamed Little Hammer while a batboy for the Oakland Athletics because of his resemblance to Hammerin' Hank.*

3463. *"Itsy Bitsy Teenie Weenie Yellow Polkadot Bikini."*

3464. *Dale Evans, cowgirl wife of Roy Rogers. She also wrote their theme song, "Happy Trails."*

3465. *A sixty-fourth note.*

3466. *A chicken-and-egg dish of that name on the menu of a restaurant in New York City's Chinatown.*

3467. *George Frederic Handel.*

3468. What middle name did Reginald Kenneth Dwight give himself when he legally changed his name to Elton John in 1971?

3469. What is the name of the broomstick-riding witch in German composer Engelbert Humperdinck's opera Hansel and Gretel?

3470. How many pipes are there in a typical set of Scottish bagpipes?

3471. What did Elvis Presley have lining three walls, the floor and the ceiling of his "Jungle Room" at his Memphis mansion, Graceland?

3472. What is the full name of the theater named for singer Andy Williams in Branson, Missouri, the new country music mecca?

3473. What Irish-born Nobel Prize winner wrote music reviews for a London newspaper under the pseudonym Corno di Bassetto before he established himself as a dramatist?

3474. What famous Broadway show, later made into a movie, was based in part on a short story entitled The Idyll of *Miss Sarah Brown*?

3475. In *Peter and the Wolf*, Sergei Prokofiev's popular symphonic fairy tale for children, what instrument is used to represent the cat?

3476. What top band leader was the first to appear before paying audiences with black and white musicians performing side by side?

3477. What famous American songwriter—discouraged over the failure of his first musical comedy—briefly joined the Foreign Legion?

3478. What song was performed more than any other on TV's *The Hit Parade* during the show's 24-year run?

3479. What great pianist served as premier of his native land?

3480. What folk song was inspired by Laura Foster's death in North Carolina in 1866?

3468. Hercules.

3469. Rosina Daintymouth, or Rosina Sweet Tooth, according to the translation.

3470. Five: the intake pipe, a valved tube connecting the bag to the player's mouth; the chanter, a pipe fitted with a double reed and pierced with eight sounding holes, used to play the melody; and three drones, pipes fitted with single reeds that provide the background.

3471. Green shag carpeting. The fourth wall of the room was covered with a fieldstone waterfall.

3472. The Andy Williams Moon River Theatre. "Moon River," of course, is his signature song.

3473. George Bernard Shaw.

3474. Guys and Dolls. The short story, of course, was written by Damon Runyon.

3475. The oboe.

3476. Benny Goodman, in 1936. Helping him break the color barrier while making music were pianist Teddy Wilson and vibraharpist Lionel Hampton.

3477. Cole Porter, in 1917. His musical flop was called See America First.

3478. "White Christmas." It was presented 32 times.

3479. Ignacy Jan Paderewski, in 1919. The country was Poland.

3480. "Tom Dooley." She was the woman ex-Confederate soldier Tom Dula "met up on the mountain" and stabbed with his knife.

3481. If you dialed the title of the Glenn Miller song "Pennsylvania 6-5000" when he wrote it, who would have answered?

3482. How did singer Riley King get his stage name B.B. King?

3483. Who was the first American invited to conduct at La Scala in Milan?

3484. Who played solo guitar on "While My Guitar Gently Weeps" for the 1968 Beatles "White Album"?

3485. What famous composer wrote ballet music for elephants in the Ringling Brothers, Barnum and Bailey Circus?

3486. What real-life roommates were the inspiration for the Neil Simon play, *The Odd Couple*?

3487. The melody of the song on TV's *The Hit Parade* in 1941, *Tonight We Love*, was drawn from what musical classic?

3488. What patriotic American song first appeared as a poem in the *Atlantic Monthly* in 1862?

3489. What popular singer worked in a pineapple cannery before getting her first taste of show business as an extra in the 1966 film *Hawaii*?

3490. During a Metropolitan Opera tour of *Turandot*, soprano Birgit Nilsson held the high C in a duet longer than Franco Corelli. What did the temperamental tenor do to show his disapproval?

3491. What band leader started in show business at age 15 as a concert violinist with Enrico Caruso?

3492. What opera features characters named Ping, Pang and Pong?

3493. What world-famous ballerina was once jailed for participating in an unsuccessful coup attempt with her husband?

3494. Name the musicians and instruments featured in Benny Goodman's Swing Quartet?

3481. *The switchboard operator at New York's Pennsylvania Hotel—later the Statler Hilton and now the New York Penta.*

3482. *From the nickname Blues Boy, given to him during a stint as a disc jockey on a Memphis radio station.*

3483. *Leonard Bernstein.*

3484. *Eric Clapton.*

3485. *Igor Stravinsky in 1942. His "Circus Polka" was choreographed by George Balanchine.*

3486. *Simon and his director brother, Danny. Neil was the neat freak; his brother, the disorganized slob.*

3487. *Tchaikovsky's "First Piano Concerto (No. 1 in B-Flat Minor)".*

3488. *"The Battle Hymn of the Republic," written by Julia Ward Howe after she saw Union troops marching to "John Brown's Body," the music to which her poem was set.*

3489. *Bette Midler, who was paid $350 for portraying a Christian missionary in the screen adaptation of the James Michener novel.*

3490. *He bit her on the neck when he was supposed to give her a stage kiss.*

3491. *Cuban "Rhumba King" Xavier Cugat.*

3492. Turandot *by Puccini.*

3493. *Margot Fonteyn, in 1959. The country involved was Panama, her diplomat-husband's native land.*

3494. *Goodman on clarinet; Teddy Wilson at the piano; Gene Krupa on drums; and Lionel Hampton on the vibraphone.*

3495. What famous songwriter started his career as an accompanist for singer Vic Damone—and was fired?

3496. What rock group is named after the eighteenth-century English inventor of the seed drill?

3497. Antonio Stradivari made 1,116 violins, cellos and violas. How many are believed to still exist?

3498. What singer, when she was seven years old, won a $200 grand prize on Ted Mack's *Original Amateur Hour* with her renditions of "Too Young," "Because of You," and "Brahms' Lullaby"?

3499. What rock superstar sang backup on the Carly Simon hit "You're So Vain," the song supposedly written about Warren Beatty?

3500. What Elvis Presley hit was based on the Italian folk song, "O Sole Mio"?

3501. What actress portrayed a nude Christine Keeler—the call girl named in Britain's John Profumo sex scandal—in a review sponsored by the Royal Shakespeare Company?

3502. Whose romance inspired the sixteenth-century song, "A Frog Went A-Courting"?

3503. What Beatles song ends with a portion of Shakespeare's "King Lear"?

3504. How did jazz singer Anita O'Day, who was called Anita Colton at birth, pick her stage name?

3505. Composer Cole Porter inherited $250,000 from his wealthy grandfather, J. O. Cole. How did the older man earn his fortune?

3506. What song, written in the 1890s by Sunday school teachers Patty and Mildred Hill, do we still sing today?

3507. The first $1-million rockabilly recording was "Blue Suede Shoes." Who wrote and sang it?

3495. *Burt Bacharach.*

3496. *Jethro Tull.*

3497. *More than half—630 violins, 60 cellos and 15 violas.*

3498. *Gladys Knight, in 1951.*

3499. *Mick Jagger.*

3500. *"It's Now or Never," in 1960.*

3501. *Glenda Jackson, in 1963.*

3502. *The first Queen Elizabeth's romance with the Duc d'Alençon.*

3503. *"I Am the Walrus," recorded in 1967.*

3504. *From what she hoped her career would bring her— a lot of dough, or "ough-day" in Pig Latin.*

3505. *He sold water to thirsty miners in the California gold fields.*

3506. *"Happy Birthday to You," which the sisters rewrote from their earlier song, "Good Morning to All."*

3507. *Carl Perkins, in 1956. His rendition outsold that of Elvis Presley.*

3508. What musical instrument does bearded bandleader Mitch ("Sing Along") Miller play?

3509. Why did Al Jolson first take his trademark pose—singing on one knee with arms outstretched?

3510. What was the original name of the George M. Cohan song, "You're a Grand Old Flag"?

3511. On what show did Elvis Presley make his television debut singing "Heartbreak Hotel"?

3512. At a command performance for King George V of England, what great American musician bowed at the royal box and said, "This one's for you, Rex"?

3513. What was the first song to win the Academy Award when the category was introduced in 1934?

3514. The melody of what famous song is also known as "The Miller's Wedding"?

3515. To whom did Russian-born composer Sergei Rachmaninoff dedicate his "Second Piano Concerto (No. 2 in C Minor)" written in 1908?

3516. What Cole Porter classic was inspired by an Indonesian war dance that the songwriter heard during a world cruise?

3517. The music for what patriotic American song was adapted from an obscure operetta by French composer Jacques Offenbach?

3518. The play with the longest title on record was performed on Broadway in 1965 and called "Marat-Sade" for short. What was its full title?

3519. What singer, performing with the Blue Moon Boys, was turned down after auditioning for *Arthur Godfrey's Talent Scouts* TV show in 1955?

3520. Who wrote the musical score for the 1954 film classic *On the Waterfront* ?

3508. *The oboe.*

3509. *He had a painful ingrown toenail and dropped to one knee to relieve the pressure.*

3510. *"You're a Grand Old Rag."* Cohan *wrote it for his 1906 musical* George Washington Jr., *inspired by a Gettysburg veteran's remark. He changed rag to flag following a public protest.*

3511. *On* Stage Show, *produced by Jackie Gleason and co-hosted by bandleader brothers Jimmy and Tommy Dorsey, on January 28, 1956. Presley didn't make his famous Ed Sullivan Show appearance until the fall of that year.*

3512. *Louis Armstrong, in 1934.*

3513. *"The Continental," from the Fred Astaire-Ginger Rogers film,* The Gay Divorcée.

3514. *"Auld Lang Syne," by Scottish poet Robert Burns.*

3515. *His psychoanalyst, Dr. Nikolai Dahl.*

3516. *"Begin the Beguine."*

3517. *The "Marines' Hymn." Its musical source, Offenbach's "Genevieve de Brambant," was first performed in Paris in 1859.*

3518. The Persecution and Assassination of Marat as Performed by the Inmates of the Asylum of Charenton under the Direction of the Marquis de Sade.

3519. *Elvis Presley.*

3520. *Conductor-composer Leonard Bernstein.*

3521. What award-winning 1979 Broadway offering, later made into an Oscar-winning movie, dealt with the same subject as an eighteenth-century play by Russia's Alexander Pushkin?

3522. What famous actress appeared in the title role in *Hamlet*?

3523. Whose put-down gave the heavy-metal rock group Led Zeppelin its name?

3524. What Broadway composer was first flutist with the New York Philharmonic when it was conducted by Arturo Toscanini?

3525. What 1963 hit song was recorded by Martha and the Vandellas in mid-winter, but not released until July?

3526. What was pop singer Boy George's name at birth?

3527. When Federico Fellini's autobiographical film "8½" was made into a Broadway musical in 1982, what new title was it given?

3528. What two opera stars have had food named after them?

3529. What famous pianist got his start in a Milwaukee piano bar playing under the name Walter Busterkeys?

3530. In what two Broadway hits did opera star Ezio Pinza appear?

3531. What famous baritone broke his contract with the Metropolitan Opera to appear in a movie called "Aaron Slick of Punkin Crick"?

3532. What was the name of the wife of Charles Ives, the avant-garde composer known for his atonal music?

3533. What was the original title of Leonard Bernstein's musical *West Side Story*?

3534. How did Gordon Sumner, the rock star and actor we know as Sting, get his stage name?

3521. Amadeus, *by Peter Schaffer. Pushkin's play was called* Mozart and Salieri.

3522. *Sarah Bernhardt.*

3523. *The Who's late drummer Keith Moon's—he told members of the group they'd go over like a lead balloon.*

3524. *"Music Man" Meredith Willson, who also wrote* The Unsinkable Molly Brown.

3525. *"Heat Wave."*

3526. *George O'Dowd.*

3527. Nine.

3528. *Nellie Melba (peach melba and melba toast) and Luisa Tetrazzini (chicken tetrazzini).*

3529. *Liberace.*

3530. South Pacific *and* Fanny.

3531. *Robert Merrill, in 1951.*

3532. *Harmony.*

3533. East Side Story.

3534. *From the yellow-and-black jerseys he used to wear, which fellow musicians thought made him look like a bumble bee.*

3535. Who did soprano Birgit Nilsson once list as a dependent on her U.S. income tax return, claiming he needed her?

3536. What enduring song was introduced on "Black Tuesday," the day the stock market crashed in 1929?

3537. Whose last words were, "I shall hear in heaven"?

3538. What song did the horn on singer Pat Boone's Ferrari play?

3539. On what label did the British rock trio Police cut its first single, the punk screamer "Fallout," in 1977?

3540. What was crooning bandleader Rudy Vallee's real first name?

3541. What famous actor, as a 14-year-old, played Kate in Shakespeare's *The Taming of the Shrew* at Stratford-upon-Avon, prompting a reviewer to remark, "I cannot remember any actress in the part who looked better?"

3542. What boxer appeared on the cover of the Beatles album "Sgt. Pepper's Lonely Hearts Club Band"?

3543. What was the original title of the song "Let Me Go, Lover," which was a million-record seller for Joan Weber in the mid-1950s?

3544. What is the origin of the musical term honky-tonk?

3545. What is the meaning of the expression "three-dog night"— which most of us know only as the name of a rock group?

3546. Under what name do we know Ferdinand Joseph La Menthe Morton?

3547. What country singer's first two hits were "Dumb Blonde" and "Something Fishy"?

3548. Who was the first entertainer to offer public bonds backed by his future music royalties?

3549. Who was featured on the cover of the very first issue of Rolling Stone magazine?

3535. *Metropolitan Opera boss Rudolph Bing.*

3536. *"Happy Days Are Here Again." (It was played by band leader George Olsen at the Hotel Pennsylvania in New York City.)*

3537. *Ludwig von Beethoven's. The composer was totally deaf during the last eight years of his life.*

3538. *"April Love," the title song of the 1957 movie he made with Shirley Jones.*

3539. *Illegal Records.*

3540. *Hubert. He took the name Rudy in the 1920s from a saxophonist he admired.*

3541. *Laurence Olivier, in 1922.*

3542. *Sonny Liston.*

3543. *"Let Me Go, Devil."*

3544. *It was black slang for "gin mill"—but later was used to describe the spirited music that thrived in such places in the 1930s.*

3545. *The phrase, which originated with the Eskimos, means a very cold night—so cold that you'd have to bed down with three dogs to keep warm.*

3546. *"Jelly Roll" Morton, the jazz great.*

3547. *Dolly Parton. Both were recorded in 1967.*

3548. *David Bowie, in 1997. The 7.9 percent average-life bonds were rated single-A by Moody's.*

3549. *John Lennon.*

3550. What famous country singer is the subject of more than a dozen musical tributes, including "Singing Teacher," "The Long Gone Lonesome Blues," "Midnight in Montgomery" and "The Ride"?

3551. What early rock 'n' roll group performed under the name "Saddle Pals" when it first started out—as singers of country music?

3552. What Polynesian island was the inspiration for Bali H'ai in the Rodgers and Hammerstein musical *South Pacific?*

3553. How many operas did Ludwig van Beethoven write?

3554. What show marked the Broadway debuts of Jerome Robbins, Leonard Bernstein, Betty Comden and Adolph Green?

3555. How much—in tons—does the sound system used on tour by the rock group U2 weigh?

3556. Which two woodwind orchestra instruments are classified as double reeds?

3557. What is the name of Madonna's pet Chihuahua?

3558. What song describes the young woman in its title as "a tomboy in lace"?

3559. Who is the famous sister of gospel singer Susie Luchsinger?

3560. In 1985 what four famous country singers recorded an album together as The Highwaymen?

3561. What song was Michael Jackson performing when he introduced his "moonwalk" to the world on a 1983 TV special?

3562. Who were the famous musicians who made up the original Benny Goodman Swing Quartet?

3563. The name of what musical instrument is derived from a French term meaning "high wood"?

3564. What category of performers do we have to thank for the term "hanky-panky"?

3550. *Hank Williams. The titles of most of the other tributes mention him by name.*

3551. *Bill Haley and the Comets. The group was originally called Bill Haley's Saddle Pals.*

3552. *Bora Bora.*

3553. *Only one, Fidelio. Its libretto was adapted from Jean Nicolas Bouilly's play* Léonore.

3554. On the Town. *It opened on Broadway on December 28, 1944.*

3555. *30 tons.*

3556. *The oboe and the bassoon.*

3557. *Chiquita.*

3558. *"Nancy (With the Laughing Face)." The song was written by comedian Phil Silvers for Frank Sinatra's daughter Nancy.*

3559. *Reba McEntire. Susie, who is four years younger than her country-music superstar sister, is well known in Christian music circles. She has a number of albums to her credit as well as a book,* A Tender Road Home, *which was published in 1997.*

3560. *Johnny Cash, Waylon Jennings, Kris Kristofferson and Willie Nelson. Their album was called* The Highwaymen.

3561. *"Billie Jean". The TV show was* Motown 24: Yesterday, Today and Forever.

3562. *Goodman (clarinet), Teddy Wilson (piano), Gene Krupa (drums) and Lionel Hampton (vibraphone).*

3563. *The oboe. In French, "high wood" is hautbois—which the Italians transcribed into oboe.*

3564. *Magicians. The expression was inspired by their practice of using a handkerchief in one hand to distract the audience from noticing what they were doing with the other hand—with the rhyme influenced by the term hocus-pocus.*

3565. What famous composer always poured ice water over his head before he sat down to work?

3566. What instrument did Arturo Toscanini play before he switched to conducting?

3567. What popular band—led by a single-name star—was originally known as the Strontium 90?

3568. What was the stage name of actor Lincoln Theodore Monroe Andrew Perry?

3569. What names did Dolly Parton give her two dogs—both of them spitzes?

3570. What musical instrument was referred to as the "stomach Steinway" by Mark Twain?

3571. What is the stage name of heavy-metal bandleader Brian Warner?

3572. How much did Warner Communications pay in 1988 for the copyright to the song "Happy Birthday"?

3573. Before playwright Mary Chase created her imaginary 6-foot-1 rabbit named "Harvey," what make-believe animal had she planned on making the centerpiece of a new play?

3574. What singer, as a teenager, ended up in a juvenile detention center for shoplifting a Kiss T-shirt?

Bonus Trivia

3575. Most people know that Abraham Lincoln was shot while watching a performance of *Our American Cousin* at Ford's Theatre in Washington, D.C. The same play was also running at the McVerick Theatre in Chicago on May 18, 1860—the day Lincoln was nominated for president in that city.

3565. *Beethoven. He believed it stimulated his brain.*

3566. *The cello.*

3567. *The Police. The band's lead singer was Sting.*

3568. *Stepin Fetchit.*

3569. *Mark Spitz (after the Olympic swimmer) and Lickety Spitz.*

3570. *The accordion.*

3571. *Marilyn Manson. He created the name by combining screen legend Marilyn Monroe's first name with serial killer Charles Manson's last name.*

3572. *$28 million.*

3573. *A 4-foot-tall canary named Daisy.*

3574. *Courtney Love.*

3576. Lloyd Copeland invented the prototype of what we now call the microwave oven, but he might be enjoying better favor nowadays for another "creation": his granddaughter, Linda Ronstadt.

3577. Only two original TV show theme songs have reached the number one slot on "Billboard's" pop chart: "The Theme From S.W.A.T." by the Rhythm Heritage, in 1975, and "Welcome Back" (from *Welcome Back, Kotter*) by John Sebastian, in 1976.

Presidential Trivia

Questions

3578. What is the only U.S. presidential landmark operated outside the country by the National Park Service?

3579. What four state capitals are named after American presidents?

3580. What was the Secret Service's code name for Barbara Bush?

3581. How many bathrooms are there in the White House?

3582. Who was president when running water was first installed in the White House?

3583. In which White House room did President Monroe play cards, Mrs. Theodore Roosevelt receive visitors, and President John F. Kennedy's casket lie in state?

3584. In 1973 what convicted felon was given a free half-hour of airtime on the three major television networks to declare his innocence?

3585. Which American president turned over 40 years of government paychecks to charity?

3586. Who was the first president to throw out the first ball of the season at a baseball game?

Answers

3578. Campobello, the summer home of Franklin Delano Roosevelt, in New Brunswick Province, Canada.

3579. Jackson, Mississippi; Jefferson City, Missouri; Lincoln, Nebraska; and Madison, Wisconsin

3580. "Tranquillity." President Bush was known as "Timberwolf."

3581. 34.

3582. Andrew Jackson.

3583. The Green Room.

3584. Just-resigned vice president Spiro Agnew, who had pleaded nolo contendere—no contest—to charges of tax evasion on bribes paid to him.

3585. Independently wealthy Herbert Hoover.

3586. William Howard Taft, in 1910. The Washington Senators beat the Philadelphia Athletics in the one-hit shutout pitched by baseball great Walter Johnson.

3587. John Tyler had more children than any other American president. How many did he have?

3588. What precipitated the $5.7-million renovation of the White House during the Truman administration?

3589. What did Woodrow Wilson, America's twenty-eighth president, denounce as a symbol of "the arrogance of wealth"?

3590. At what hour did presidential nominee George McGovern deliver his acceptance speech at the disorganized and discordant 1972 Democratic National Convention in Miami Beach?

3591. President Gerald Ford pardoned Iva D'Aquino in 1977. Who was she?

3592. Who was the only presidential candidate other than George Washington to run unopposed?

3593. What presidential wife was the first to be referred to as the First Lady?

3594. Which American president has the greatest number of cities and towns in the United States named after him?

3595. How many American presidents did not attend college?

3596. What did George Washington suggest building on the land that is now the site of the Washington Monument in Washington, D.C?

3597. What was the name of the horse Teddy Roosevelt rode in the famous Battle of San Juan Hill during the Spanish-American War?

3598. Who was the last of the eight American presidents to be born in Virginia—the state that claims the title Mother of Presidents?

3599. What salary did Benjamin Franklin advocate for the president of the United States during debates at the Constitutional Convention in 1787?

3587. *Fifteen. Married twice, he had a total of eight sons and seven daughters.*

3588. *A leg of Margaret Truman's grand piano broke through her sitting room floor into the family dining room below.*

3589. *The automobile.*

3590. *At 3:00 in the morning.*

3591. *Tokyo Rose—the seductive-voiced Japanese radio propagandist during World War II.*

3592. *James Monroe, for his second term in 1820, during the "Era of Good Feeling."*

3593. *Lucy Hayes, wife of Rutherford B. Hayes, in 1877.*

3594. *Madison, whose name is used in 27 states. He's followed in popularity by Washington (26), Monroe (22), Jackson and Jefferson (20 each), and Lincoln (16).*

3595. *Nine—Washington, Jackson, Van Buren, Taylor, Fillmore, Lincoln, Andrew Johnson, Cleveland and Truman.*

3596. *A monument to an unknown soldier of the American Revolution.*

3597. *Texas.*

3598. *Woodrow Wilson. The Virginians who preceded him were George Washington, Thomas Jefferson, James Madison, James Monroe, William Henry Harrison, John Tyler and Zachary Taylor.*

3599. *None. He felt that only the elite should serve as president and that they could do so without compensation.*

3600. The 1990-91 edition of "Who's Who in America" contained 10 lines about former president Ronald Reagan; how many were devoted to his wife, Nancy?

3601. What famous American explorer was the first presidential candidate of the Republican party?

3602. President Lyndon Johnson called his pet beagles Him and Her; what did President Franklin D. Roosevelt and his wife, Eleanor, name His and Hers?

3603. What position did president-to-be George Bush play on the Yale University baseball team?

3604. What equipment purchased by sixth president John Quincy Adams sparked accusations that he was installing "gaming furniture" in the White House?

3605. What was the presidential retreat in Maryland's Catoctin Mountains—now known as Camp David—originally called by President Franklin Delano Roosevelt?

3606. What presidential candidate coined the phrase, "The New Frontier"?

3607. In April 1793, George Washington attended the nation's first circus in Philadelphia and was paid $150. What was the money for?

3608. What President was ticketed for speeding in Washington, D.C., while he was in office?

3609. What President signed the first federal income tax law—3 percent on incomes over $600?

3610. What was the setting of the 1959 confrontation between Vice-President Richard Nixon and Soviet Premier Nikita Khrushchev?

3600. 28.

3601. *John C. Frémont, in 1856. He lost to James Buchanan. Republican candidate Abraham Lincoln won the presidency four years later.*

3602. *The pistols they kept under their pillows.*

3603. *First base.*

3604. *A chess set and a billiard table.*

3605. *Shangri-La.*

3606. *Alf Landon, in 1936.*

3607. *Allowing Jack, the white charger he had ridden during the Revolutionary War, to be put on exhibit.*

3608. *Ulysses S. Grant, in his horse and buggy. He was fined $5.*

3609. *Abraham Lincoln.*

3610. *The model American kitchen of a U.S. exhibit in Moscow. The setting gave the encounter its name— "The Kitchen Debate."*

3611. In 1868 impeachment proceedings were initiated against President Andrew Johnson for his opposition to black rights and Congress' Reconstruction efforts. By what margin did he escape conviction?

3612. What U.S. President had a special bathtub—big enough to hold four men—installed in the White House to accommodate his great bulk?

3613. What kind of dogs were Nixon's Checkers and FDR's Fala?

3614. Who designed the pillbox hat that Jacqueline Kennedy made famous at her husband's inauguration in 1961?

3615. What did President John F. Kennedy commission Pierre Salinger to do on the eve of signing the Cuban trade embargo?

3616. Who was the smallest U.S. President?

3617. Who invented a metal-locating device to find the bullet lodged in President James Garfield's body after he was shot by assassin Charles Guiteau in 1881?

3618. Whose ghost did Queen Wilhelmina of the Netherlands claim she saw during a 1945 stay at the White House?

3619. What strange pets did John Quincy Adams and his wife, Louisa, bring with them to the White House?

3620. Which of our nation's chief executives could have been known as President King?

3621. How much did President Abraham Lincoln spend on a string of seed pearls and matching earrings purchased from Tiffany's for his wife, Mary?

3622. Who was the only American president to remain a bachelor his entire life?

3623. How short was George Washington's second inaugural address—the shortest in U.S. history?

3611. One vote. The Senate voted 35 to 19 against Johnson, just shy of the two-thirds required to remove him from office.

3612. William Howard Taft, who weighed in at 325 pounds at the time.

3613. Checkers was a black-and-white cocker spaniel; Fala, a Scottish terrier.

3614. Halston, whose full name is Roy Halston Frowick.

3615. Buy and stockpile 1,500 Havana cigars.

3616. James Madison, the fourth President, who was 5 feet 4 inches tall and never weighed more than 100 pounds.

3617. Alexander Graham Bell. The device worked, but not on Garfield—because of interference from his steel-spring mattress.

3618. Abraham Lincoln's.

3619. Several hundred silkworms, which the First Lady fed and cared for while trying to make raw silk.

3620. Gerald R. Ford. He was named Leslie L. King at birth, but later assumed his stepfather's name.

3621. He paid $2,600.

3622. James Buchanan, who preceded Abraham Lincoln as the nation's chief executive, serving from 1857 to 1861.

3623. It contained only 135 words.

3624. What was the message on the one-word telegram Bob Hope sent to President Harry S. Truman after he stunned the odds-makers and beat Thomas E. Dewey in 1948?

3625. How many times during his 12 years as president did Franklin Delano Roosevelt use the veto?

3626. Where did Herbert Hoover's 1932 campaign slogan "A chicken in every pot" originate?

3627. George Washington left America's shores only once. Where did he go?

3628. What did Richard M. Nixon's father raise on his ranch in Yorba Linda, California, before moving his family to Whittier when the future president was nine?

3629. What well-known American woman's maiden name was Elizabeth Anne Bloomer?

3630. Who was the first president paid a salary of $100,000?

3631. Who was president when electricity was installed in the White House?

3632. How much was architect James Horan awarded in 1792 for his winning design for the President's House—now known as the White House?

3633. Who once addressed the Mayflower-minded members of the Daughters of the American Revolution as "my fellow immigrants"?

3634. How many tons of jelly beans did the White House buy during Ronald Reagan's presidency?

3635. What unusual coincidence has been noted about the names of the secretaries who served Presidents Lincoln and Kennedy?

3636. Who said, "Let us begin by committing ourselves to the truth—to see it like it is, and tell it like it is—to find the truth, to speak the truth, and live the truth"?

3624. "Unpack."

3625. He used it 635 times (372 regular vetoes; 263 pocket vetoes).

3626. With France's King Henry IV, who at his coronation said that he hoped "to make France so prosperous that every peasant will have a chicken in his pot on Sunday."

3627. To Barbados, in the West Indies, in 1751 with his ailing half-brother Lawrence. It was during his stay there that he was stricken with smallpox.

3628. Lemons.

3629. Former First Lady Betty Ford.

3630. Harry S. Truman.

3631. Benjamin Harrison. The year was 1889.

3632. Horan was given $500 and a lot in Washington, D.C.

3633. Eleanor Roosevelt.

3634. 12 tons.

3635. Lincoln's secretary was named Kennedy (John); Kennedy's was named Lincoln (Evelyn).

3636. Richard M. Nixon, in accepting the Republican party's presidential nomination in 1968.

3637. Who has been credited with writing George Washington's famous Farewell Address?

3638. Who gave Thomas Jefferson the fur-collared coat he's shown wearing in the famous statue of him at the Jefferson Memorial in Washington, D.C.?

3639. How many children did former President Jimmy Carter have besides his high-profile daughter, Amy?

3640. What famous American political figure worked during his teen years as a summer barker at the Slippery Gulch Carnival in Prescott, Arizona?

3641. What coincidence was there in the timing of the decisions of our two President Johnsons—Andrew and Lyndon—not to seek re-election?

3642. Who changed the presidential seal so that the American eagle faces the talon in which it's holding an olive branch of peace rather than the one in which it clasps arrows of war?

3643. What four American presidents ran unsuccessfully for re-election on third-party tickets?

3644. What national political experience did Abraham Lincoln have before he became president?

3645. What did President Franklin Delano Roosevelt have imprinted on White House matchbooks?

3646. What was George Washington's nickname for his wife, Martha?

3647. How many U.S. presidents had full beards?

3648. What prompted President Harry S. Truman to write a newspaper columnist, "Some day I hope to meet you. When that happens you'll need a new nose, a lot of beefsteak for black eyes, and perhaps a supporter below"?

3649. What is the average age at which America's presidents have taken office?

3637. Alexander Hamilton.

3638. Polish patriot Thaddeus Kosciusko.

3639. Three—sons Jack (John William), Chip (James Earl), and Jeff (Donnel Jeffrey).

3640. Richard M. Nixon.

3641. Both took place in the year '68—Andrew's in 1868; Lyndon's in 1968.

3642. Harry S. Truman—but Franklin Delano Roosevelt had ordered the change before his death in 1945.

3643. John Tyler, who withdrew his candidacy before the election, Martin Van Buren, Millard Fillmore, and Theodore Roosevelt.

3644. He served a two-year term in the House of Representatives.

3645. "Stolen from the White House."

3646. Patsy.

3647. Five—Lincoln, Grant, Hayes, Garfield and Benjamin Harrison.

3648. A music review that panned daughter Margaret's singing ability. The letter was sent to Washington Post music critic Paul Hume.

3649. 54.

3650. What American president was First Lady Barbara Bush's great-great-great-uncle?

3651. What American president had an electric horse installed in his White House bedroom—and rode it almost daily?

3652. What is former Vice President Dan Quayle's first name?

3653. Who was the only U.S. president not to use the word "I" in his inaugural address?

3654. Who was the first president elected when women nationwide had the right to vote?

3655. How big a raise in his base pay did George Bush receive when he moved up from vice president to president?

3656. Which American president owned dogs named Drunkard, Tipler and Tipsy?

3657. What engraved gift did President Lyndon Johnson give to friends and acquaintances to make sure they thought of him "first thing in the morning and the last at night"?

3658. Who was the last governor to serve as vice president?

3659. Which two members of George Washington's cabinet were redheads?

3660. As a boy, what 20th-century American president was known as Tommy?

3661. Who was the first American president to hold an airplane pilot's license?

3662. Who was the first American president to have an inaugural ball?

3663. Who was the first American to win a Noble Prize?

3664. What was the name of Theodore Roosevelt's dog?

3650. *Democrat Franklin Pierce. Mrs. Bush's maiden name is Pierce.*

3651. *Calvin Coolidge.*

3652. *James.*

3653. *Theodore Roosevelt.*

3654. *Warren G. Harding, in 1920.*

3655. *$85,000—from $115,000 as vice president to $200,000 as president.*

3656. *George Washington. They were foxhounds.*

3657. *Electric toothbrushes.*

3658. *Nelson Rockefeller of New York. Gerald Ford nominated Rockefeller as vice president in August 1974 after Ford vacated the post to become president upon the resignation of Richard Nixon. (Spiro Agnew of Maryland was the last governor elected vice president, in 1972.)*

3659. *His secretary of state, Thomas Jefferson, and his treasury secretary, Alexander Hamilton.*

3660. *Woodrow Wilson, whose given names were Thomas Woodrow. He officially dropped his first name when he was 24.*

3661. *Dwight David Eisenhower, who was issued a license in November 1939. He learned to fly while a lieutenant colonel on Gen. Douglas MacArthur's staff in the Philippines.*

3662. *George Washington. He held his inaugural ball in New York City on May 7, 1789.*

3663. *Theodore Roosevelt. He won the coveted Noble Prize in 1906 for helping end the Russo-Japanese War with the Treaty of Portsmouth.*

3664. *Scamp.*

3665. Who was the first U.S. President born outside the 13 original states?

3666. What was the first moving picture ever to be shown at the White House?

3667. Where was the first Presidential mansion located?

3668. On a 1957 visit to Disneyland, Harry S. Truman refused to ride one of the attractions. Which one was it, and why?

3669. Franklin D. Roosevelt held the office of President of the United States of America for the longest period. Which President holds the record for longevity after leaving office?

3670. What was the nickname of the first official Presidential airplane (a C-45 piloted by Major Henry T. Myers in 1944)?

3671. What famous politician was nicknamed Gloomy Gus when he attended Duke University law school?

3672. What was the nickname of Jimmy Carter's campaign plane in 1976?

3673. Thelma Catherine Ryan is the real name of the wife of one of American's most controversial public figures from the 1970's. Who is she?

3674. Two books written by United States Presidents have been made into television series. What are they?

3675. Which First Lady was edited out of her movie debut?

3676. Who was the first woman Presidential candidate?

3677. Who were the only left-handed Presidents?

3678. President Richard M. Nixon kept a music box in his Oval Office desk. What tune did it play?

3679. Who was the only U.S. President to marry a woman from another country?

3665. *Abraham Lincoln, who was born in Kentucky, the 15th state.*

3666. *"The Birth of a Nation," on February 15, 1916.*

3667. *At 1 Cherry Street in New York City.*

3668. *Dumbo the Elephant, since he considered it the symbol of the Republican Party.*

3669. *John Adams, who was ex-President for 25 years and 4 months (March 1801 to July 1826).*

3670. *Sacred Cow.*

3671. *Richard M. Nixon.*

3672. *Peanut One, piloted by James Carter (no relation).*

3673. *Pat Nixon.*

3674. *"Crusade In Europe" by Dwight D. Eisenhower, and "Profiles In Courage" by John F. Kennedy.*

3675. *Pat Nixon, who had a walk-on in the 1935 film, "Becky Sharp," only to have her scenes end up on the cutting room floor.*

3676. *Victoria Claflin Woodhull, who, on May 10, 1872, was nominated by the Equal Rights Party.*

3677. *James Garfield, Harry Truman and Gerald Ford.*

3678. *"Hail to the Chief."*

3679. *John Quincy Adams, whose wife, Louisa, was born in London.*

3680. Who was the only U.S. president to serve as a member of the Congress of the Confederate States?

3681. What presidential candidate ran his campaign from prison, in 1920?

3682. Both President John Tyler Jr. and his father, John Tyler Sr. served as governor of what state?

3683. What name did George Washington use in addressing his friend the Marquis de Lafayette?

3684. What twentieth-century American president was so obsessed with secrecy that he often wrote "burn this" on personal letters?

3685. What famous American politician coined the phrase "lunatic fringe"?

3686. What crime was the U.S. Secret Service established to combat when it was created in 1865?

3687. How many doors are there in the 132-room White House?

3688. What three successive American presidents were Republicans, Union Army generals and born in Ohio?

3689. Who was the only president born in Illinois, the Land of Lincoln?

3690. What were the Four Freedoms outlined by President Franklin D. Roosevelt in his State of the Union message to Congress in January 1941?

3691. Who was the only American president to graduate from the U.S. Naval Academy?

3692. How many men named Johnson have served as vice president of the United States?

3693. How many presidents did J. Edgar Hoover serve under as chief of the Federal Bureau of Investigation?

3680. *John Tyler.*

3681. *Eugene V. Debs, the Socialist Party candidate. Jailed for sedition, he received nearly one million votes.*

3682. *Virginia.*

3683. *Fayette.*

3684. *Lyndon Baines Johnson.*

3685. *Teddy Roosevelt. He used the term in 1913 to describe people of excessive zeal within the reform groups that supported him.*

3686. *Counterfeiting. It was not until 1901, after the assassinations of Presidents Abraham Lincoln, James A. Garfield and William McKinley, that the Secret Service was given the job of protecting American presidents.*

3687. *412.*

3688. *Ulysses S. Grant, Rutherford B. Hayes and James A. Garfield.*

3689. *Ronald Reagan. He was born in Tampico, Illinois. Lincoln was born in Kentucky.*

3690. *Freedom of speech and worship, and freedom from want and fear.*

3691. *Jimmy Carter, who was in the class of 1946.*

3692. *Three—Richard Mentor Johnson, who served with Martin Van Buren; Andrew Johnson, who served with Abraham Lincoln and succeeded him as president; and Lyndon Baines Johnson, who served with John F. Kennedy and succeeded him as president.*

3693. *Eight—Calvin Coolidge, Herbert Hoover, Franklin D. Roosevelt, Harry S. Truman, Dwight D. Eisenhower, John F. Kennedy, Lyndon B. Johnson and Richard M. Nixon. Hoover headed the agency from 1924 until his death in 1972.*

3694. How many animals did ex-president Theodore Roosevelt bag during his 11-month hunting expedition to Africa after leaving office in 1909?

3695. How many times did Abraham Lincoln and Stephen Douglas debate during their 1858 race for the U.S. Senate?

3696. What president's bid for reelection inspired the opposition slogan, "Let's get another deck"?

3697. What U.S. president was born on the Fourth of July?

3698. After Spiro Agnew resigned from office in disgrace in 1973, what entertainer loaned him $230,000 for living expenses and payment of Internal Revenue Service fines?

3699. What three animals were party symbols in the 1912 presidential race?

3700. What recipe offered by First Lady-to-be Florence Harding in the 1920 presidential race became a symbol of her husband's "return to normalcy" campaign?

3701. What U.S. president appointed the greatest number of Supreme Court justices?

3702. George Washington's second inaugural address was the shortest in U.S. history; what president gave the second-shortest?

3703. Why did President Millard Fillmore turn down a prestigious honorary degree from Oxford University?

3704. What valuables were found hidden in Mary Todd Lincoln's underwear when the president's widow was judged insane in 1875?

3705. According to a book co-authored by Sigmund Freud, what American president suffered from an unresolved Oedipus complex?

3706. What did President Andrew Jackson have installed on the second floor of the White House in 1835 to ensure that he had a steady supply of running water?

3694. *296—including 9 lions, 5 elephants, 13 rhinos and 7 hippos.*

3695. *Seven. They debated in each of Illinois' seven congressional districts. Douglas won the election—and Lincoln gained national prominence.*

3696. *Franklin Delano Roosevelt's—in 1936. The slogan was the Republican party's response to Roosevelt's New Deal.*

3697. *Calvin Coolidge—in 1872. (Three American presidents died on July 4th—Thomas Jefferson and John Adams in 1826, and James Monroe in 1831.)*

3698. *Frank Sinatra.*

3699. *The two old standards, the donkey and the elephant, and the bull moose, for Theodore Roosevelt's independent Bull Moose party.*

3700. *Her waffle recipe. It was the first recipe offered as a campaign tactic in a presidential election. Not coincidentally, 1920 was the year women got the vote.*

3701. *George Washington. He named ten during his eight years in office. The high court was composed of six members at the time.*

3702. *Franklin Delano Roosevelt—his fourth inaugural address was 559 words long. Other inaugural addresses under 1,000 words were Lincoln's second, with 698 words. Theodore Roosevelt's, 985; Zachary Taylor's, 996.*

3703. *Because it was written in Latin, a language he didn't understand. As he explained, "I have not the advantage of a classical education and no man should, in my judgment, accept a degree he cannot read."*

3704. *Bonds worth $56,000.*

3705. *Woodrow Wilson. In the book Thomas Woodrow Wilson, written with William Bullitt, Freud claimed Wilson's two wives served as mother substitutes.*

3706. *Free-standing water hydrants.*

3707. What American president banned Christmas trees in his home—even when he lived in the White House?

3708. What two brothers were nominated for president at the Republican Party convention in 1884?

3709. President Franklin D. Roosevelt appeared in the 1943 romantic comedy *Princess O'Rourke*—as what?

3710. What two rivers, bearing the names of the United States presidents, join the Gallatin River in Montana to form the Missouri?

3711. The campaign slogan of what presidential candidate is on the oldest printed T-shirt in the Smithsonian Institution's extensive T-shirt collection?

3712. Who was the first presidential jogger?

3713. Who was the first divorcée to live in the White House as First Lady of the United States?

3714. What is the minimum age set in the Constitution for the president of the United States?

3715. When all the paint was stripped from the outer walls of the White House for the very first time in the 1980's, how many coats were removed?

3716. How many presidents were among the eight great American leaders profiled by president-to-be John F. Kennedy in his 1956 Pulitzer Prize-winning book *Profiles in Courage*?

3717. How many U.S. presidents were British subjects at birth?

3718. What major American city is named for the man who served as vice president of the United States from 1845 to 1849?

3719. What American president signed an amnesty bill restoring citizenship to Jefferson Davis, retroactive to 1868?

3720. What were the Secret Service code names for Presidents Carter and Nixon?

3707. *Theodore Roosevelt, who was a staunch conservationist. Christmas trees did get into the White Hose during his presidency, though—his children smuggled them into their bedroom.*

3708. *General William Tecumseh Sherman and Senator John Sherman of Ohio. The general got 2 votes on the first ballot; the senator, 30. James G. Blaine won the party's nomination on the fourth ballot and lost the election to Grover Cleveland.*

3709. *Himself. The film featured Olivia de Havilland in the title role.*

3710. *The Jefferson and the Madison.*

3711. *Thomas E. Dewey. The slogan, "DEW-IT with DEWEY," is from his ill-fated 1948 presidential campaign against Harry S. Truman.*

3712. *Theodore Roosevelt. He jogged around the Washington Monument daily.*

3713. *Florence Harding, wife of Warren G. Harding.*

3714. *35—according to Article II, Section 1.*

3715. *42.*

3716. *One—John Quincy Adams. The other seven profiled were Daniel Webster, Thomas Hart Benton, Sam Houston, Edmund G. Ross, Lucius Quintus Cincinnatus Lamar, George Norris and Robert A. Taft.*

3717. *Eight. George Washington, John Adams, Thomas Jefferson, James Madison, James Monroe, John Quincy Adams, Andrew Jackson and William Henry Harrison. The first president born an American was Martin Van Buren, who served between Jackson and Harrison.*

3718. *Dallas, Texas. It was named for Pennsylvanian George M. Dallas, who was vice president under James Polk in 1846 when Big D was laid out.*

3719. *Jimmy Carter.*

3720. *Carter was Deacon; Nixon was Searchlight.*

3721. What historic presidential site was closed in 1985 because visitors balked at having to pass prison gates, gun towers and armed guards to get to it?

3722. What president won election after three unsuccessful bids for the nomination?

3723. Who was honored with the first toast ever made at a White House dinner?

3724. Which U.S. president has the greatest number of American communities named after him?

3725. What president was granted a patent for a device for lifting vessels over shoals?

3726. Presidents Jefferson, Tyler and Nixon played the violin; Truman and Nixon, the piano. What did "Silent" Calvin Coolidge play?

3727. What American president, in a bid to pay back $107,000 in debts, set up a lottery with his house as the prize?

3728. What president-to-be released the trap door on the gallows at two hangings?

3729. Who wrote the words to the American presidential anthem, "Hail to the Chief"?

3730. What jellybean flavors were Ronald Reagan's favorites?

3731. Who posed for the statue of Alexander Hamilton that stands in front of the Treasury Building in Washington, D.C.?

3732. The heads of four U.S. presidents were carved on Mount Rushmore to the scale of a man 465 feet tall. Who are they and how long are each of their noses?

3733. What were the names of Abe Lincoln's four sons?

3734. Which American president was the first to have a phone on his desk in the White House?

3721. The house in Moreau, New York, where Ulysses S. Grant completed his memoirs and died. It's now part of Mt. McGregor Prison.

3722. James Buchanan, who won in 1856 after losing the nomination in 1844, 1848 and 1852.

3723. Lafayette. President John Quincy Adams proposed the toast on September 6, 1825, as the Marine Corps Band played the "Marseillaise."

3724. Thomas Jefferson, with 37. Lincoln and Washington are tied for second with 32 each.

3725. Abraham Lincoln, in 1849.

3726. The harmonica.

3727. Thomas Jefferson, in 1826. There were few takers, however, and the lottery was abandoned shortly before Jefferson's death later that year.

3728. Grover Cleveland, while he was sheriff of Buffalo, New York, in the early 1870s.

3729. Sir Walter Scott. They're from his poem, "The Lady of the Lake." English tunesmith James Sanderson set the words to music and the song was first performed in London in 1811.

3730. Coconut and licorice.

3731. Strongman Charles Atlas. The statue was unveiled on May 17, 1923.

3732. The noses of Washington, Jefferson, Lincoln and Theodore Roosevelt are each 20 feet long.

3733. Robert, Eddie, Willie and Tad. Only Robert lived to maturity.

3734. Herbert Hoover, in 1929. Previous presidents used an enclosed phone booth in the hallway outside the Oval Office.

3735. Who were the five Civil War generals who went on to serve as president of the United States?

3736. Who was President Ronald Reagan quoting when he said "I forgot to duck" after he was shot by John W. HinckleyJr. in 1981?

3737. President Andrew Jackson's political advisers were nicknamed the Kitchen Cabinet. What label was given to President Warren G. Harding's advisers?

3738. Which president modeled winter sportswear for *Look* magazine in 1939?

3739. Which two presidents were Quakers?

3740. Which First Lady was known as Lemonade Lucy?

3741. What was Richard Nixon talking about when he told a TV audience, "I just want to say this, right now, that regardless of what they say about it, we are going to keep it"?

3742. John Quincy Adams, describing the first presidential inaugural ball, wrote: "The crowd was excessive—the heat excessive, and the entertainment bad." Whose ball was it?

3743. Which two presidents are buried at Arlington National Cemetery?

3744. What president installed the first bathtub in the White House?

3745. What was George Washington's shoe size?

3746. What are George Washington' s false teeth—stolen in 1981 from the Smithsonian Institution in Washington, D.C.—composed of?

3747. Why did the general and president we know as Ulysses Grant change his given name, Hiram Ulysses, to Ulysses Hiram?

3748. If the seated figure in the Lincoln Memorial in Washington, D.C., were to stand up, how tall would it be?

3735. In order of their terms of office: Ulysses S. Grant, Rutherford B. Hayes, James A. Garfield, Chester A. Arthur and Benjamin Harrison.

3736. Jack Dempsey, who made the remark after Gene Tunney beat him in a world heavyweight championship bout in 1926.

3737. The Poker Cabinet.

3738. Gerald R. Ford, who was a Yale University law student at the time.

3739. Herbert Hoover and Richard M. Nixon.

3740. Rutherford B. Hayes's teetotaling wife, who permitted only soft drinks in the White House during her husband's term, from 1877 to 1881.

3741. His family dog, Checkers, given to him by a supporter. The TV address was his famous Checkers speech.

3742. James Madison's.

3743. William Howard Taft and John Fitzgerald Kennedy.

3744. Millard Fillmore, our thirteenth president, who served from 1850 until 1853.

3745. Thirteen.

3746. The uppers, gold and hippopotamus teeth; the lowers, elephant and hippopotamus teeth.

3747. He did not want his initials to be H.U.G. He became U.S. Grant when his congressman mistakenly nominated him for West Point as Ulysses Simpson Grant. (Simpson was his mother's maiden name.)

3748. It would be 28 feet tall. Lincoln himself stood 6 feet 4 inches.

3749. Who was the first president to wear long trousers rather than knee breeches to his inauguration?

3750. Which president was the first to visit China?

3751. Who was the first president to have the name of his official residence, the White House, on his stationery?

3752. Into what three major categories did Thomas Jefferson organize the books in his library at Monticello?

3753. How many pages long was John F. Kennedy's will?

3754. Why was Franklin D. Roosevelt chosen to be portrayed on the dime in 1945?

3755. What future American First Lady's display of support helped save the Marquis de Lafayette's wife from the guillotine?

3756. Who was the first U.S. president to die in office?

3757. Who was the first presidential wife to be referred to as FLOTUS—for First Lady of the United States?

3758. What age were four of the first six U.S. presidents—George Washington, Thomas Jefferson, James Madison and John Quincy Adams—when they were inaugurated?

3759. What president's inaugural jacket was woven from the wool of sheep he was raising at home in Virginia?

3760. Which scandal-scarred official in the Nixon administration borrowed $4,850 from the White House safe to pay for his honeymoon?

3761. Which presidential library was the first to be established?

3762. What was the official presidential plane called during Harry S. Truman's presidency?

3763. During whose presidency were the greatest number of states admitted to the Union?

3749. *Our sixth president, John Quincy Adams, in 1825.*

3750. *Ulysses S. Grant, in 1879, two years after he left the White House.*

3751. *Teddy Roosevelt.*

3752. *Memory, reason and imagination. Memory covered history; reason included philosophy, law, science and geography; and imagination included architecture, music, literature and the leisure arts. Within each category, books were arranged according to size.*

3753. *16. In it he set up trusts for his wife and children.*

3754. *Because of his work on behalf of the March of Dimes and its battle against polio, the disease that crippled Roosevelt.*

3755. *Elizabeth Monroe, while James Monroe was serving as U.S. minister to France.*

3756. *William Henry Harrison. He died on April 4, 1841, a month after contracting pneumonia at his inauguration.*

3757. *Mary Todd Lincoln. FLOTUS (pronounced FLOW-tus) and POTUS (President of the United States) have long been acronyms for the First Couple used by White House staff.*

3758. *57. No other presidents have been inaugurated at that age.*

3759. *James Madison. He had imported the Merino sheep from Portugal.*

3760. *John Dean. He paid it all back.*

3761. *The Rutherford B. Hayes Presidential Library in Fremont, Ohio. It was dedicated in 1916.*

3762. *The Independence, after his hometown in Missouri. Truman's predecessor, Franklin D. Roosevelt, was the first White House occupant to have an official presidential plane. His was nicknamed "Sacred Cow" by reporters.*

3763. *Benjamin Harrison's. He served from 1889 to 1893 and saw six states added to the Union: North Dakota, South Dakota, Montana and Washington in 1889; Idaho and Wyoming in 1890.*

3764. Who gave Chelsea Clinton her cat, Socks?

3765. How was Martha Washington formally addressed during her husband's presidency?

3766. Who was the first U.S. presidential nominee to give his acceptance speech in person at his party's convention?

3767. Who piloted Eleanor Roosevelt, in evening dress, to Baltimore, just after she became First Lady?

3768. Who was the first black presidential candidate nominated at a national political convention?

3769. Who was the first rap artist to perform at a presidential inaugural gala? Bonus: Who was the president?

3770. What live trophy from the Lewis and Clark expedition to the American Northwest did President Thomas Jefferson keep on the grounds of the White House?

Bonus Trivia

3771. On his way home from Harvard one day, Robert Todd Lincoln, the son of President Abraham Lincoln, fell off the platform while waiting for his train. He was saved from possible death by Edwin Booth, the actor, and the brother of John Wilkes Booth—the man who, only a few week later, assassinated President Lincoln.

3764. *Her piano teacher, who found Socks and his sister, Midnight, abandoned in a park in Little Rock, Arkansas, in 1990 and took them home. Chelsea fell in love with Socks during a piano lesson and adopted her.*

3765. *As Lady Washington.*

3766. *Franklin D. Roosevelt, in 1932.*

3767. *Amelia Earhart. Mrs. Roosevelt was so enthusiastic about the flight, she wanted Earhart to give her flying lessons, but the president said no.*

3768. *Frederick Douglass, in 1888. He received one vote at the Republican convention in Chicago that ultimately picked Benjamin Harrison as the party candidate. Douglass went on to become U.S. minister to Haiti.*

3769. *The performer was L.L. Cool J; the president, Bill Clinton; the year, 1993.*

3770. *A grizzly bear.*

Science, Nature & Medicine

Questions

3772. If man had a jumping ability proportional to that of the minuscule flea—which can make a horizontal leap of over a foot—how far would one leap take him?

3773. When you cross cattle with buffalo, what do you get?

3774. What is the most plentiful metal in the earth's crust?

3775. An octopus has eight tentacles. How many does its relative the squid have?

3776. What reason did Sigmund Freud give for sitting behind his patients' couch during psychoanalytic sessions?

3777. How fast does lightning travel?

3778. What is the normal body temperature of a horse?

3779. What living creature is believed to enjoy more hours of daylight annually than any other?

3780. What male mammal has the greatest number of mates in a season?

3781. What gives the gemstone turquoise its distinctive color?

Answers

3772. Five city blocks.

3773. Beefalo.

3774. Aluminum, most of which is extracted from bauxite.

3775. Ten.

3776. Freud wrote: "I cannot bear to be gazed at eight hours a day."

3777. It travels 90,000 miles a second—almost half the speed of light (186,000 miles a second).

3778. 100.5°F.

3779. The Arctic tern, which travels twice a year from pole to pole—covering more than 20,000 miles round-trip—to enjoy nearly four months of continuous daylight during the Arctic summer and another four months during the Antarctic summer.

3780. The northern fur seal, which averages 40 to 60 mates a season.

3781. Traces of copper.

3782. How fast do flying fish "fly"?

3783. Who was the first to suggest using contact lenses to improve vision?

3784. How many cubic feet of gas does a cow belch on an average day?

3785. When lions and tigers mate, what do you call their cubs?

3786. What are the seven colors of the rainbow?

3787. How many times a minute does the average adult elephant's heart beat?

3788. What animal always gives birth to identical quadruplets?

3789. How much does the heart of the average man weigh?

3790. How many sides are there to a snow crystal?

3791. Why could we call William Stewart Halsted the "Mr. Clean" of medicine?

3792. How many ribs does man have?

3793. What Nobel Prize winner admitted that he had contributed his sperm to a sperm bank in hopes of producing exceptionally gifted children?

3794. If seedless oranges don't have seeds, how are they propagated?

3795. What vaccine caused more death and illness than the disease it was intended to prevent?

3796. What distinction do the chevrotain (mouse deer) and dik-dik (antelope) share?

3797. What is the hardest part of the normal human body?

3798. What is the maximum lifespan of a goldfish in captivity?

3782. They average 35 mph and have been known to go as fast as 45 mph.

3783. Leonardo da Vinci, in 1508.

3784. Thirty-five.

3785. Ligers when the father is a lion; tigons or tiglons when the father is a tiger.

3786. Red, orange, yellow, green, blue, indigo and violet.

3787. Only 25. In man, the average adult heartbeat is 70 to 80 times per minute.

3788. The nine-banded armadillo, known as Dasypus novemcinctus— the only armadillo native to the U.S.

3789. From 10 to 12 ounces. A woman's heart weighs from 8 to 10 ounces.

3790. Six.

3791. Halsted, developer of local anesthesia, was the first doctor to wear rubber gloves in surgery in 1890.

3792. Twenty-four.

3793. William Shockley, inventor of the transistor.

3794. By grafting. The original seedless orange was a mutant.

3795. The swine flu vaccine, 1976.

3796. They are among the world's tiniest-hoofed animals, reaching only 12 to 16 inches in height.

3797. Tooth enamel.

3798. Twenty-five years.

3799. What did Dr. Alfred Kinsey study before he turned his attention to our sexual behavior?

3800. How many bee trips from flower to hive does it take to make a pound of honey?

3801. A baby kangaroo is called a joey. What are its parents called?

3802. What flower has more varieties than any other—at least 30,000—ranging in size from ¼ inch to 20 feet?

3803. What famous American hero—educated as a mechanical engineer—helped design a germ-proof "artificial heart" in the early 1930s?

3804. The mayfly lives six hours. How long do its eggs take to hatch?

3805. A female black bear weighs about 300 pounds. How much does one of its babies weigh at birth?

3806. What is the largest member of the dolphin family?

3807. How many of the average adult's 32 permanent teeth are molars?

3808. Approximately how many pounds of dung does the average elephant produce daily?

3809. How were the first written messages transmitted by air?

3810. How can you tell the age of a mountain goat?

3811. What is the most plentiful element in seawater?

3812. What device was introduced commercially in 1934 as a "portable superregenerative receiver and transmitter"?

3813. What mammal has the world's shortest sperm?

3814. What color is topaz in its pure state?

3815. Before the barometer was discovered, what animal did German meteorologists use to predict air pressure changes?

3799. *The gall wasp.*

3800. *Forty thousand.*

3801. *Mom's a flyer; Dad, a boomer.*

3802. *The orchid.*

3803. *Charles Lindbergh, working with surgeon Alexis Carrel.*

3804. *Three years.*

3805. *One-half pound.*

3806. *The killer whale.*

3807. *12. There are 3 per quadrant—top and bottom, on each side of the mouth.*

3808. *50.*

3809. *By arrow—in the fifth century B.C., during the siege of Potidaea during the Peloponnesian War.*

3810. *By the number of rings on its small, curved black horns. The first ring develops at age two, and another ring is added every spring thereafter. Both males and females grow horns.*

3811. *Chlorine.*

3812. *The walkie-talkie.*

3813. *The hippopotamus.*

3814. *It's colorless. Topaz takes on a variety of hues from trace elements, radiation and defects in its crystal structure. Pale gold-brown is its most common color.*

3815. *The frog. Frogs croak when the pressure drops.*

3816. How many points must a stag elk have on each of its antlers to be considered mature?

3817. The name of what dog breed, translated from German, means "monkey terrier"?

3818. The giant panda is a member of the bear family. To what family does the much smaller red panda belong?

3819. At what temperature does water boil at the top of Mount Everest?

3820. What dog carries the name of the English minister who first bred it?

3821. What is the most common transplant operation?

3822. What did a National Aeronautics and Space Administration employee buy at a Wal-Mart in 1995 to protect the space shuttle from woodpeckers?

3823. What is the largest rodent in North America?

3824. Where did Leonardo da Vinci advise the adventurous to test his design for a rudimentary helicopter?

3825. What mammal can starve to death, despite a plentiful supply of food, if there are too many cool, cloudy days in a row?

3826. At what standard level above ground—in feet—do meteorologists measure wind speed?

3827. How many eyes does a bee have?

3828. How much does a baby giraffe weigh at birth?

3829. What planet has the greatest number of known satellites?

3830. What is believed to be the largest of all the world's creatures with no backbone?

3831. How many domestic silkworm cocoons does it take to make a man's tie?

3816. *Six. The antlers drop off at the end of each mating season and usually gain a point every time they grow back.*

3817. *The Affenpinscher. In German, affe means "monkey" and pinscher means "terrier."*

3818. *The raccoon family.*

3819. *At 150°F (or 70°C). At sea level, the boiling point of water is 212°F (100°C). As you get higher, the atmospheric pressure drops, and with it the boiling point of water.*

3820. *The Jack Russell. It's named for the Rev. John Russell.*

3821. *The bone graft.*

3822. *Six plastic owls.*

3823. *The beaver. The porcupine is second.*

3824. *Over a body of water. He wrote: "You will experiment with this instrument on a lake, so that in falling you will come to no harm."*

3825. *The sloth, which has to sun itself daily to raise its body temperature so the bacteria in its stomach is warm enough to break down the leaves it eats. It often takes up to 100 hours to digest a stomachful of food.*

3826. *33 feet.*

3827. *Five. The two large compound eyes on either side of its head are complex visual organs; the three ocelli (primitive eyes) on top of its head are believed to primarily detect light intensity.*

3828. *About 150 pounds—and it's about 6 feet tall.*

3829. *Saturn, with 20. Close behind are Jupiter, with 16, and Uranus, with 15.*

3830. *The giant squid.*

3831. *110. It takes 630 to make a blouse.*

3832. What was the original purpose of ENIAC, the world's first "modern" computer?

3833. What gives the mineral turquoise its distinctive color?

3834. What creature was named walckvogel—"disgusting bird"— by the Dutch explorers who first spotted it in 1598?

3835. What percentage of the average human brain is water?

3836. What does eccentricity mean to an astronomer?

3837. What was the first human organ to be successfully transplanted?

3838. What is alloyed with steel to make it stainless?

3839. How long—in feet—is the trunk of the average full-grown elephant?

3840. An average human has 46 chromosomes. How many does a cabbage have?

3841. Which planet weighs over twice as much as all the other known planets combined?

3842. How many inkblots are on the standard Rorschach test?

3843. How many pounds of fish can a pelican hold in its pouch?

3844. On an average day, how many hours does an elephant spend sleeping? How about a giraffe?

3845. How fast—in miles per hour—do the fastest messages transmitted by the human nervous system travel?

3846. Some armadillos give birth to duodecuplets. How many offspring is that?

3847. What parts of the oleander plant are toxic?

3848. On average, how many peas are there in a pod?

3832. *To compute ballistic trajectories for artillery shells. ENIAC—an acronym for Electronic Numerical Integrator and Calculator—was introduced in 1946.*

3833. *Traces of copper.*

3834. *The flightless and now-extinct dodo. The Dutch saw it on the island of Mauritius.*

3835. *80 percent.*

3836. *The degree to which an orbit deviates from a circle. The eccentricity of Earth's orbit is 0.017 (or 0.016722, to be more precise).*

3837. *The kidney. Dr. Richard H. Lawler performed the transplant in 1956 in Chicago. His patient, Ruth Tucker, lived for five years with her new kidney.*

3838. *Chromium.*

3839. *8 feet.*

3840. *18.*

3841. *Jupiter, the largest planet in our solar system.*

3842. *10.*

3843. *About 25 pounds.*

3844. *Four hours for both.*

3845. *180 to 200 mph.*

3846. *12.*

3847. *All parts. The seeds of the ornamental bush are usually the most toxic, the leaves a little less and the flowers least—but still dangerous. Even the stems are toxic.*

3848. *Seven to nine.*

3849. How many frames—or pictures—per second are transmitted over American television?

3850. In years past what was used as transmission oil in Rolls-Royce automobiles?

3851. What breed of dog is particularly distinctive because of a genetic condition called achondroplasia?

3852. How many pointers were there on the first clocks with hands—made in the fourteenth century?

3853. What temperature does the tungsten filament in an electric light reach when the light is turned on?

3854. What bird has been spotted flying at 27,000 feet—higher than any other bird on record?

3855. An estimated five million Americans suffer from a recurring ailment known as SAD. For what is SAD an acronym?

3856. Why did German scientist Wilhelm Roentgen name the invisible rays he discovered X-rays?

3857. How small is a pygmy right whale?

3858. Who, long before Columbus, claimed the world was round, reasoning that if it were flat all the stars would be visible from all points on its surface?

3859. When did American sales of cassette recordings surpass those of long-playing records?

3860. What product was originally called the Soundabout when it was introduced in the U.S. in 1979?

3861. The wild pomegranate is said to contain as many seeds as there are commandments in the Old Testament. How many is that?

3862. What are zygodactyl feet?

3849. *30.*

3850. *Spermaceti oil—from the sperm whale.*

3851. *The dachshund. Achondroplasia causes dwarfism—in the dachshund's case, abnormally short legs.*

3852. *Only one—to tell the hour. Minute and second hands were added in the sixteenth and seventeenth centuries.*

3853. *2,577°C (4,664°F).*

3854. *The whooper swan. A flock of 30 was spotted by a pilot and picked up on radar at that altitude in 1967.*

3855. *Seasonal affective disorder. It's a wintertime syndrome that can be treated with light.*

3856. *Because he had no idea what the mysterious rays were.*

3857. *It's about 16 feet long.*

3858. *Aristotle, who offered as added proof the fact that the earth casts a spherical shadow on the moon during an eclipse.*

3859. *Eight years ago, in 1983.*

3860. *The Sony Walkman. It was called the Stowaway in England.*

3861. *613.*

3862. *Feet with two toes pointing forward and two pointing backward— which birds such as parakeets, parrots and woodpeckers have.*

3863. What do the letters represent in the acronym DNA—the protein substance inside each cell that transmits genetic information from parent to child?

3864. What is the larva of the ant lion called?

3865. How long does a nanosecond last?

3866. What animal is the source of the luxuriously soft wool known as cashmere?

3867. What are the berries that grow on the hawthorn tree called?

3868. What percentage of the world's food crops are pollinated by insects?

3869. What is the difference between a crawfish and a crayfish?

3870. If you're selecting a three-course meal from a menu that offers four appetizers, seven entrées and three desserts, how many different meals can you order?

3871. How many different chemical reactions occur in the normal human brain every second?

3872. Which is larger, a crocodile's egg or a duck's egg?

3873. In mathematics, what is the meaning of the term googol?

3874. What word defines sounds too low for human hearing?

3875. What reptile, according to ancient legend, was able to live in fire?

3876. How many eyes do most spiders have?

3877. Where are the grasshopper's "eardrums" located?

3878. How did the bird known as the Baltimore oriole get its name?

3879. How did the element strontium— also known by the symbol Sr and the atomic number 38—get its name?

3863. *Deoxyribonucleic acid.*

3864. *A doodlebug.*

3865. *One billionth of a second*

3866. *The Kashmir goat, which lives in mountainous regions of Kashmir (in India), China and Iran.*

3867. *Haws.*

3868. *80 percent.*

3869. *Nothing. Both names apply to the same freshwater crustacean.*

3870. *84 (that's 4 × 7 × 3).*

3871. *At least 100,000.*

3872. *They're about the same size—around three inches long.*

3873. *It represents the number 1 followed by 100 zeroes—or 10^{100}.*

3874. *Infrasonic.*

3875. *The salamander.*

3876. *Eight.*

3877. *Either on its forelegs or at the base of its abdomen, depending on the type of grasshopper.*

3878. *From its colors, orange and black—the same as those on the heraldic coat of arms of the House of Baltimore, the family that founded the colony of Maryland and gave the city of Baltimore its name.*

3879. *From Strontian, the Scottish mining village in which it was discovered.*

3880. What reply did newspaper tycoon William Randolph Hearst receive when he sent a telegram to a leading astronomer asking, "Is there life on Mars? Please cable one thousand words"?

3881. How many miles of arteries, capillaries and veins are there in the adult human body?

3882. What do beavers eat?

3883. How many pounds of lunar rock and soil were collected and brought back to Earth from America's six expeditions to the moon?

3884. What is the average lifespan of a human being's tastebud?

3885. What planet is most like earth in size, mass, density and gravity?

3886. Berkshire, Cheshire, Victoria and Poland China are breeds of what animal?

3887. What percentage of its body weight does the average bear lose during hibernation?

3888. What is the name of the computer program developed by the Los Angeles Police Department to help solve homicides?

3889. In the original Hippocratic oath, by whom did the individual doctor swear to uphold the standards of professional behavior?

3890. What do the bacteria Lactobacillus bulgaricus and Streptococcus thermophilus have in common?

3891. What heavenly bodies have astronomers named after Brahms, Beethoven, Bach, the four Beatles and Eric Clapton—among others?

3892. Where are sea horses hatched?

3893. What animal is believed to limit its breeding to Macquarie Island, the rocky crest of a submerged South Pacific mountain?

3894. How many pairs of legs does a shrimp have?

3880. *"Nobody knows"—repeated 500 times.*

3881. *62,000.*

3882. *The bark of hardwood trees, leaves, and aquatic and shore plants. Beavers are vegetarians—and do not eat fish, as is widely believed.*

3883. *841.6.*

3884. *From 7 to 10 days.*

3885. *Venus.*

3886. *The pig.*

3887. *Up to 25 percent.*

3888. *HITMAN—for Homicide Information Tracking Management Automation Network.*

3889. *Apollo.*

3890. *Both must be present in a product for it to be labeled yogurt under U.S. Food and Drug Administration regulations.*

3891. *Asteroids.*

3892. *In a pouch on the male parent's belly. Eggs are deposited there by the female.*

3893. *The royal penguin.*

3894. *Five.*

3895. What is the difference between poultry and fowl?

3896. The winter sleep of bears and other animals in cold climates is known as hibernation. What do we call the summer sleep of desert snails and other creatures in excessively warm or dry climates?

3897. How many eyes—or eye spots—do most starfish have?

3898. Fish travel in schools; what about whales?

3899. How many muscles are there in an elephant's trunk?

3900. How many beats per second does a bumblebce flap its wings?

3901. How long is a day on Mars?

3902. What distance can the average healthy slug cover in a day?

3903. Even with leap year, the average year is about 26 seconds longer than Earth's orbital period. How many years will it take for those seconds to build up into a single day?

3904. How many watts are there in one horsepower of energy?

3905. How many calories are consumed during an hour of typing?

3906. What bird is the only one to have nostrils at the tip of its bill?

3907. How many hairs does the average human scalp contain?

3908. Which celebrated chemist-inventor is credited with developing plywood?

3909. Do peacocks give birth to their young or do they lay eggs?

3910. What is the only food a koala bear will eat?

3911. What is cosmology?

3912. In the days when British sailors were given lime or lemon juice to prevent scurvy, what were Dutch sailors given?

3895. *Poultry is domesticated fowl.*

3896. *Estivation.*

3897. *Five—one at the tip of each of its arms.*

3898. *They get together in gams, or pods.*

3899. *100,000.*

3900. *160.*

3901. *24 hours, 37 minutes and 22 seconds.*

3902. *50 yards. Slug races generally are held on a 1-yard course.*

3903. *3,323.*

3904. *746.*

3905. *110—just 30 more an hour than the number consumed while sleeping.*

3906. *The kiwi.*

3907. *Between 120,000 and 150,000.*

3908. *Alfred Nobel, the inventor of dynamite and subsequent founder of the Nobel Prize.*

3909. *Neither—a peacock is male, but a peahen lays eggs.*

3910. *The leaves of the eucalyptus tree.*

3911. *The study of the origin and structure of the universe.*

3912. *Sauerkraut—or zourkool, as they called it.*

3913. How many milligrams of sodium are there in a teaspoon of salt?

3914. How many bones are there in the human wrist?

3915. To what plant family do the radish and turnip belong?

3916. What part of the poison hemlock plant is deadly?

3917. What are the colors of a primary rainbow, from inside to outside?

3918. In the world of fruit, what is the rag?

3919. What famous scientist was the first to figure out how to gauge the tidal effects of the moon and sun and how to calculate the exact path of a comet?

3920. How many toes does a rhinoceros have on each foot?

3921. What are the durian, cherimoya and mangosteen?

3922. To what plant family do rosemary, oregano, thyme and marjoram belong?

3923. A group of lions is a pride; a group of elephants, a herd; what is a group of leopards?

3924. What poisonous weed gets it name from a historic American village?

3925. What is a scalene triangle?

3926. How many miles of nerves are there in the adult human body?

3927. What diameter does a drop of liquid precipitation have to reach to graduate from drizzle to rain?

3928. How fast do microwaves travel?

3929. How many pints of air per minute does the average adult use during normal quiet breathing?

3913. *Approximately 2,000.*

3914. *Eight.*

3915. *The mustard family.*

3916. *All parts—the flowers, seeds, leaves, stem and roots.*

3917. *Violet, indigo, blue, green, yellow, orange and red.*

3918. *The white fibrous membrane inside the skin and around the sections of citrus fruit.*

3919. *Sir Isaac Newton.*

3920. *Three—encased in a hoof.*

3921. *Exotic fruits.*

3922. *The mint family.*

3923. *A leap.*

3924. *Jimson weed—which is a corruption of its original name, Jamestown weed, which was named for Jamestown, Virginia.*

3925. *A triangle with unequal sides and angles.*

3926. *45.*

3927. *It's a raindrop if it's over .02 inch in diameter.*

3928. *186,282 miles per second—the speed of light—as do all kinds of electromagnetic radiation including radio waves, infrared rays, visible light, ultraviolet light and X-rays.*

3929. *Almost 13 pints, or 6 liters.*

3930. For what therapeutic purpose have physicians used green blowfly maggots?

3931. How much farther from Earth does the moon's orbit move every year?

3932. What word was spelled out in the first neon sign?

3933. By definition, what is the lifting capacity of one unit of horsepower?

3934. What earthly creature has four "noses" and 3,000 tiny teeth?

3935. A beehive produces between 100 and 200 pounds of honey a year. How much does a single worker honeybee manufacture in its lifetime?

3936. How long does it take a whole fingernail to replace itself?

3937. How fast per second does Earth travel in its orbit around the sun?

3938. What is on the daily menu for an adult hippopotamus at the National Zoo in Washington, D.C.?

3939. How many toes does an ostrich have?

3940. What do you call the little bits of paper left over when holes are punched in data cards or tape?

3941. What part of the human body is named for its resemblance to the sea horse?

3942. How many eggs at a time do the most productive starfish release?

3943. How fast does the sound of thunder travel per second?

3944. How did the fish known as the guppy get its name?

3945. How many meteorites hit the earth each year?

3930. *To cleanse wounds. The maggots eat decaying flesh and release a natural antibiotic. This practice was most widely used during World War I.*

3931. *About 1.5 inches. Scientists believe the moon has been inching away from Earth for billions of years.*

3932. *Neon. The small bright red sign was created by Dr. Perley G. Nutting, a government scientist, and exhibited at the 1904 Louisiana Purchase Exposition in St. Louis, Missouri—15 years before neon signs became widely used commercially.*

3933. *The ability to raise 33,000 pounds one foot high in one minute.*

3934. *The slug.*

3935. *¹/₁₂ teaspoon.*

3936. *About three months. Our nails grow about 0.1 mm (.004 inch) per day.*

3937. *18.5 miles per second.*

3938. *About 10 pounds of kale, 3 gallons of high-protein cereal pellets and ¾ bale of alfalfa hay.*

3939. *Four—two on each of its feet.*

3940. *Chad.*

3941. *The hippocampus—the ridge along each lateral ventricle of the brain. Hippocampus is Latin for "sea horse."*

3942. *Up to 2.5 million.*

3943. *About 1,100 feet.*

3944. *From the man who discovered it and presented specimens to the British Museum—naturalist R . J .L. Guppy of Trinidad.*

3945. *About 500—most of them go unrecorded, falling into oceans, deserts and other uninhabited areas.*

3946. How often does the epidermis, the outer layer of our skin, replace itself?

3947. Modern computer chips consist of millions of transistors. How many transistors were on the first chips made in 1958?

3948. In 1988 what did a panel of 10 international design experts pick as the best-designed product costing less than $5?

3949. In computerese, what does wysiwyg mean?

3950. Before surgical dressings of gauze and cotton were introduced, what was commonly used to cover wounds in American hospitals?

3951. How did the magnolia get its name?

3952. To what plant family does the asparagus belong?

3953. What is a group of rhinoceroses called?

3954. What is the only member of the cat family that does not have retractable claws?

3955. Noble Prize-winning missionary Dr. Albert Schweitzer had a pet named Parsifal. What kind of animal was it?

3956. There are an estimated 10 trillion stars in our galaxy, the Milky Way. How many are visible to the naked eye from the earth?

3957. What is a geoduck?

3958. How can you tell the sex of a horse by its teeth?

3959. What animal is believed to have the best hearing?

3960. From what language do we get the two scientific terms used to describe hardened lava fields: aa and pahoehoe?

3961. What was the first human organ to be successfully transplanted?

3946. About once every four weeks.

3947. Just two.

3948. The eightpenny finishing nail.

3949. It's shorthand for what you see is what you get.

3950. Pressed sawdust.

3951. From French botanist Pierre Magnol, who introduced it.

3952. It's a member of the lily family—as are the onion and garlic.

3953. A crash.

3954. The cheetah.

3955. A pelican.

3956. About 6,000.

3957. A large clam.

3958. Most males have 40 teeth; most females 36.

3959. The barn owl—even though its ears can't be seen. Its face is dish-shaped, enabling the owl to receive sounds like sonar.

3960. Hawaiian. Aa is lava that is rough and jumbled; pahoehoe is lava that is smooth and wavy.

3961. The kidney. Dr. Richard H. Lawler performed the transplant in 1956 in Chicago. His patient, Ruth Tucker, lived for five years with her new kidney.

3962. How many pounds per day does a baby blue whale gain during its first seven months of life?

3963. What is the "lead" in a lead pencil?

3964. Why is the small shorebird Americans know as the red phalarope called the grey phalarope in England?

3965. By what popular name do we know the fluorine-based compound polytetrafluoro-ethylene, or PTFE?

3966. How many toes does a giraffe have on each foot?

3967. Where are a butterfly's tastebuds located?

3968. What popular dog was originally known as a waterside terrier?

3969. How long is the tongue of the giant anteater of South America?

3970. What is a horse called before it reaches age one and becomes a yearling?

3971. How long is the average adult's spinal cord?

3972. What bacterium is named for German pediatrician Theodor Escherich?

3973. What six elements make up over 95 percent of all living material?

3974. If a carnivore is a meat-eating animal, what's a frugivore?

3975. At what wind speed does a snowstorm become a blizzard?

3976. What part of a horse's anatomy is known as a stifle?

3977. Which is the largest order of mammals, with about 1,700 species?

3962.   *At least 200 pounds. A baby blue whale—which is about 22 feet long at birth—grows 29 feet longer in its first seven months.*

3963.   *Graphite and clay. Lead pencils never contained lead—but graphite was originally thought to be a type of lead.*

3964.   *The bird is named for its summer plummage in America; for its winter plummage in England.*

3965.   *Teflon.*

3966.   *Two.*

3967.   *On its legs. They are microscopic hairs, called sensilla, on the terminal part of the butterfly's legs.*

3968.   *The airdale. It was renamed when a judge at the Airdale Agriculture Society Show in Bingley, Yorkshire—in the valley of the Aire River— suggested another name be found for the locally bred dog.*

3969.   *22 to 24 inches. It uses its tongue to lap up ants—about 35,000 a day.*

3970.   *A weanling. It remains a weanling until its first birthday, which is always on January 1.*

3971.   *From 17 to 18 inches. It weight, minus membranes and nerves, is about 1½ ounces.*

3972. **E.** *coli. The E is for Escherichia, after its discoverer, who first identified the bacteria in 1885 and called it Bacterium coli commune. It was give its current name in 1919.*

3973.   *Carbon, hydrogen, nitrogen, oxygen, phosphorus and sulfur.*

3974.   *A fruit eater.*

3975.   *In excess of 35 miles an hour.*

3976.   *The joint on the hind leg—between the femur and the tibia—that corresponds anatomically to a human's knee. It's also know as the stifle joint.*

3977.   *Rodents. Bats are second, with about 950 species.*

3978. How many vertebrae does a human being have?

3979. What is the body's largest organ—by weight?

3980. In the world of horses, what's a palomilla?

3981. What are the only two types of mammals that are poisonous?

3982. How many seeds from the giant sequoia tree—the most massive of all living things—are there in an ounce?

3983. Which is the longest muscle in the human body?

3984. How many mosquito-size insects is the one-ounce brown bat—the most common bat in North America—capable of eating in an hour of nighttime dining?

3985. What form of precipitation generally falls only from cumulonimbus clouds?

3986. What part of the body is the Brannock device used to measure?

3987. How wide an angle is the average person's field of vision?

3988. In what country did the French poodle originate?

3989. What mammal has the heaviest brain?

3990. What is your buccal cavity?

3991. How fast—in miles per hour—can a crocodile move on land? How about in water?

3992. How many times brighter is a full moon than a half moon?

3993. What does a mellivorous bird eat?

3994. With the exception of the whale, what animal has the largest mouth?

3978. *33—7 cervical, 12 thoracic (or dorsal), 5 lumbar, 5 sacral, and 4 caudal (or coccygeal).*

3979. *The lungs. Together they weigh about 42 ounces. The right lung is two ounces heavier than the left, and the male's lungs are heavier than the female's.*

3980. *A milk-white horse with white mane and tail.*

3981. *Shrews and platypuses. Some shrews have slightly poisonous bites, and male platypuses have poisonous spurs on their hind legs.*

3982. *8,000. The seeds are ¼ inch long. The largest giant sequoia in existence, the General Sherman, is in California's Sequoia National Park.*

3983. *The sartorius, which runs from the pelvis across the front of the thigh to the top of the tibia below the knee.*

3984. *About 500.*

3985. *Hail. Cumulonimbus clouds are heavy, swelling, vertically developed clouds.*

3986. *The foot. It's the device used in shoe stores to determine your shoe size.*

3987. *About 200 degrees.*

3988. *In Germany, where it was known as the pudel, from a word meaning "to splash in the water." In France, it's known as the caniche, which is derived from "duck dog." Its Latin name is canis familiaris aquatius.*

3989. *The sperm whale. Its brain weighs up to 20 pounds—six times heavier than a human's.*

3990. *The inside of your mouth.*

3991. *On land, up to 30 mph; in water, 20.*

3992. *10 times.*

3993. *Honey. Mell comes from a Greek word for "honey."*

3994. *The hippopotamus.*

3995. How much does the skeleton of the average 160-pound body weigh?

3996. Pine wood ignites at 800°F. At what temperature does charcoal ignite?

3997. What creature produces sperm that are ⅔ inch long—the longest in the world?

3998. What planet's moon is the largest satellite in our solar system?

3999. How did scientist Louis Pasteur make sure the food he was served at the homes of his friends was safe to eat?

4000. Where in the human body is the only bone that is not connected to another bone?

4001. How can you tell a fish's age?

4002. What is the first bird mentioned in the Bible?

4003. What animal's skin is the source of true moroccan leather?

4004. How did the skeleton of the more than-three-million-year-old female hominid discovered in Ethiopia in 1974 come to be called Lucy?

4005. What unpopular bird's Latin name is Sturnus vulgaris?

4006. What mammal is the only living member of its order?

4007. What two types of dogs were crossed to create the whippet?

4008. What is the only land mammal native to New Zealand?

4009. How fast can a sailfish swim—in miles per hour?

3995. *About 29 pounds.*

3996. *580°F.*

3997. *Some fruit flies of the genus Drosophila. Their sperm, more than 300 times longer than human sperm, are six times longer than the fly itself—but hair-thin and all balled up.*

3998. *Jupiter's moon Ganymede.*

3999. *He checked it with a portable microscope he carried with him.*

4000. *In the throat, at the back of the tongue. It's the horseshoe-shaped hyoid bone, which supports the tongue and its muscles. Also known as the lingual bone, it is suspended by ligaments from the base of the skull.*

4001. *From the number of growth rings on each of its scales. Each pair of rings represents a year—the dark narrow rings represent winter; the wider, lighter rings represent summer.*

4002. *The raven. It appears in Genesis 8:7, when it is sent out from the ark by Noah to see if the flood waters have abated.*

4003. *The goat.*

4004. *Donald Johanson, the anthropologist who found the skeleton, and his colleagues were listening to the Beatles' song "Lucy in the Sky with Diamonds" while they were discussing and celebrating the discovery—and they started referring to the skeleton by that name.*

4005. *The common, or European, starling, which is held in low esteem by bird-watchers because it takes the nest of domestic songbirds, and by farmers because it often damages fruit and grain crops.*

4006. *The aardvark. Its order is Tubulidentata*

4007. *The greyhound and the terrier.*

4008. *The bat.*

4009. *More than 60 mph, faster than any other known fish. Humans have been recorded swimming up to 5.19 mph.*

4010. What is the main food of mosquitoes?

4011. What wind speed does a storm have to exceed to be given a name by the National Hurricane Center?

4012. What plant's name—derived from the French—means "lion's tooth"?

4013. How many times per second does a mosquito beat its wings?

4014. What is the only female deer to grow antlers?

4015. What physical symptom is exhibited by those who suffer from blepharospasms?

4016. What does the chemical symbol Fe2O3 represent?

4017. A female pig is called a sow; what is a male pig called?

4018. How many legs does a spider have?

4019. How many true vocal cords does a normal person have?

4020. What is the wrinkled flesh that hangs from the neck of a turkey called?

4021. If the angles of a pentagon are equal, what are they—in degrees?

4022. Where in the world are you most likely to find lemurs in the wild?

4023. Where on the human face is there a muscle know as the corrugator?

4024. Before the advent of electricity, how did theatrical companies put their stars in the spotlight?

4025. What was the "dephlogisticated air" discovered by English scientist Joseph Priestley in 1774?

4026. What is the average minimum speed in miles per hour needed for a bird to remain aloft?

4010. Nectar from flowers, not your blood. The blood we lose to mosquitoes—females only—is needed for protein to help them lay their eggs.

4011. 39 mph.

4012. The dandelion. In French it's called dente de lion, for the toothlike points on its leaves.

4013. Up to 600.

4014. The reindeer.

4015. Uncontrollable winking.

4016. Rust.

4017. A boar. A baby is a piglet.

4018. Eight—four pairs, which is one of the features that distinguishes a spider from an insect, which has three pairs of legs.

4019. Two. They are called true (or inferior) vocal cords and are involved in the production of sound. We also have a pair of false (or superior) vocal cords that have no direct role in producing the voice.

4020. The wattle.

4021. 108 degrees. Such a pentagon is called a regular pentagon.

4022. In Madagascar.

4023. On the forehead. It's the muscle that contract the forehead into wrinkles and pulls the eyebrows together.

4024. Lime was burned in a lamp, creating an intense white light that was directed at featured performers—and giving us the word limelight.

4025. Oxygen. At the time phlogiston was believed to be a chemical released during combustion.

4026. 11 mph—or 16½ feet per second.

4027. What planet has surface winds that have been measured at 1,500 mph—the strongest in the solar system?

4028. How many of an adult domestic cat's 30 teeth are canines?

4029. How much coal does it take to get the same amount of energy provided by burning one full cord of seasoned firewood?

4030. How tall is a baby giraffe at birth?

4031. How are all the workers of an African driver ant colony, numbering around 22 million, related?

4032. On what planet is the largest known mountain in the solar system?

4033. How fast can an ostrich run?

4034. How was the Tonkinese breed of cat developed?

4035. What animal's name means "earth pig"?

4036. If you hear thunder 10 seconds after you see lightning, how far away was the lightning?

4037. What was Sigmund Freud's fee—in U.S. dollars—for one session of psychoanalysis in 1925?

4038. How many bones are there in the human skull?

4039. How much does an adult giraffe's heart weigh?

4040. How many newborn opossums can fit in a teaspoon?

4041. How many constellations are there?

4042. The name of what flower means "fleshlike"?

4043. What part of the human body is the axilla?

4044. What is a diadromous fish?

4027. *Neptune.*

4028. *4. The cat also has 12 incisors, 10 premolars and 4 molars.*

4029. *One ton.*

4030. *About 6 feet.*

4031. *They're all sisters—although they have different fathers.*

4032. *On Mars. Called Olympus Mons, it's a volcano more than three times the height of Mount Everest.*

4033. *About 40 miles per hour—taking strides of 12 to 15 feet.*

4034. *By crossing a Burmese with a Siamese.*

4035. *The aardvark's—in the Afrikaans language.*

4036. *2 miles away. Sound travels about a mile in 5 seconds.*

4037. *$25—adjusted for inflation, that would be about $160 today.*

4038. *29—the cranium has 8; the face, 15 (including the lower jaw); the ears, 6.*

4039. *About 25 pounds. It's 2 feet long, with walls up to 3 inches thick. It has quite a job pumping blood to the brain—which is sometimes 12 feet above the heart.*

4040. *About 24. They're very small—about .07 ounce each—at birth.*

4041. *100,000.*

4042. *The carnation, which was named for a rosy pink color developed by artists during the sixteenth century. The first carnations were that color. In Latin, carnis means "flesh."*

4043. *The armpit.*

4044. *A fish—such as salmon or sturgeon—that can exist in both salt water and fresh water.*

4045. How many sweat glands are there on the skin of the average adult human being?

4046. How many toes does a pig have on each of its feet?

4047. The average adult takes 14 breaths a minute; how many does an infant take?

4048. How much horsepower does the typical horse provide?

4049. How fast can a swordfish swim?

4050. What animal has the largest eyes—each a foot or more in diameter?

4051. What contribution did Sarah Nelmes make to medicine in 1796?

4052. What are the odds of having an ear of corn with an odd number of rows of kernels?

4053. What is the gestation period for an elephant?

4054. What is the largest deer in the world?

4055. From where in nature do we get quinine, the medicine used to treat and prevent malaria?

4056. How much syrup does the average sugar maple tree yield each season?

4057. What animal, traveling at an average ground speed of six to eight feet per minute, is the slowest moving land mammal?

4058. In Space Age lingo, what is LOX?

4059. Which has more cervical vertebrae—a mouse, a man or a giraffe?

4060. How many average-size houses can you make from one giant sequoia—the biggest living thing on earth today?

4061. What bird strays as far as 2,500 miles from its nest to find food for its young?

4045. *More than 2 million—an estimated 2,381,248, according to Gray's Anatomy.*

4046. *Four—two of which touch the ground.*

4047. *33.*

4048. *About 24. Horsepower is the power needed to lift 33,000 pounds 1 foot in 1 minute. Scientists came up with the 24 horsepower figure based on a horse weighing about 1,320 pounds.*

4049. *More than 60 miles an hour. It and the sailfish are the fastest swimming fish.*

4050. *The giant squid. The largest creature without a backbone, it weighs up to 2.5 tons and grows up to 55 feet long.*

4051. *Edward Jenner used her cowpox lesions for the first smallpox vaccination.*

4052. *Zero. There are always an even number of rows.*

4053. *From 20 to 22 months. Baby weighs in at about 200 pounds.*

4054. *The Alaska bull moose, which has been known to reach a shoulder height of 7½ feet and a weight of up to 1,800 pounds.*

4055. *From the bark of the cinchona tree, a South American evergreen.*

4056. *One to one and a quarter quarts.*

4057. *The three-toed sloth, which spends 18 hours of every day sleeping.*

4058. *Liquid oxygen, a component of rocket fuel.*

4059. *All have the same number, seven.*

4060. *Fifty. The sequoia often exceeds 300 feet in height and 25 feet in diameter. Its seed weighs only ¹⁄₆₀₀₀ ounce.*

4061. *The albatross, which has the largest wingspan of any living bird—over 11 feet.*

4062. How old is the average 1½-pound lobster?

4063. What is the lightest substance known to science?

4064. What makes flamingos pink?

4065. How many muscles does a caterpillar have?

4066. The swallows traditionally return to San Juan Capistrano, California, on March 19. What birds return to Hinckley, Ohio, four days earlier?

4067. How did a Nebraska mule named Krause make news, first in 1984 and again in 1985?

4068. How many times a day does the average human heart beat?

4069. How many bones does the average human adult have?

4070. How many muscles do we use when we smile broadly?

4071. You get a geep when you cross what two animals?

4072. What is the world's tallest grass, which sometimes grows 130 feet or more?

4073. What is the only pouched animal found in North America—and the only one not found in Australia?

4074. In what direction do most cyclones whirl?

4075. What is the ermine known as during its off-seasons, when its fur isn't white?

4076. How many leaves does the average mature oak tree shed in the fall?

4077. What part of the human body is called the atlas?

4078. Who was the first person known to have died of radiation poisoning?

4079. What is the only breed of dog to have a black, rather than pink, tongue?

4062. *About 8 years old. If it avoids the lobster trap, it can live to about 50 and weigh up to 35 pounds.*

4063. *The element hydrogen, with a specific gravity of 0.0695 compared to air. Helium is the second lightest with a specific gravity of 0.139.*

4064. *Canthaxantin, a Vitamin A-like chemical found in the soda lakes where they feed. Away from the lakes, flamingos turn white.*

4065. *Four thousand—more than five times as many as a human.*

4066. *The turkey buzzards.*

4067. *Although mules are almost always infertile, Krause gave birth to baby mules in both years. Each birth was a billion-to-one shot.*

4068. *About 100,000—to pump five quarts of blood every minute.*

4069. *Two hundred and six.*

4070. *Seventeen.*

4071. *A sheep and a goat. Some prefer to call it a shoat.*

4072. *Bamboo.*

4073. *The opossum.*

4074. *Clockwise in the Southern Hemisphere; counterclockwise in the Northern Hemisphere.*

4075. *The short-tailed weasel, also known as a stoat.*

4076. *About 700,000.*

4077. *The first vertebra of the neck, which holds up your head—just as Atlas held up the world.*

4078. *Two-time Nobel Prize-winner Marie Curie.*

4079. *The chow.*

4080. What expensive fur do we get from an aquatic cat-sized rodent with orange teeth called the coypu?

4081. What element is named after a state?

4082. How long does it take light from the sun to travel to earth, a distance of about 93,000,000 miles?

4083. What part of the human body has the thinnest skin?

4084. Which is the only bird that can fly backward?

4085. An animal named Louise has helped West German police sniff out narcotics, explosives and other contraband. What kind of animal is she?

4086. What temperature do honey bees maintain in their hives year-round?

4087. How many bones are there in your big toe?

4088. What are the only two mammals that lay eggs rather than give birth to live offspring?

4089. How many teeth are there in our first set of teeth—our baby teeth?

4090. What important point did Scottish mathematician John Napier come up with in the early seventeenth century?

4091. What was the name of the first computer used for weather research?

4092. When is Halley's comet, first observed in 240 B.C. and last seen in 1986, expected to appear again?

4093. How much does the blue whale, the world's largest mammal, weigh at birth?

4094. For what operation was Antonio de Egas Moniz of Portugal awarded the Nobel Prize in medicine in 1949?

4095. How tall is a newborn giraffe?

4080. Nutria.

4081. Californium, first produced in 1950 by scientists at the University of California at Berkeley.

4082. About eight minutes.

4083. The eyelid—it's less than ¹⁄₅₀₀ inch thick.

4084. The tiny hummingbird.

4085. A wild boar.

4086. An even 94 °F.

4087. Fourteen, the same as in your other toes.

4088. The duck-billed platypus and the spiny anteater.

4089. Twenty. Our second set has 32.

4090. The decimal point.

4091. MANIAC—an acronym for Mathematical Analyzer, Numerical Integrator and Computer.

4092. In the year 2061.

4093. Two tons. Fully grown, it will weigh as much as 150 tons.

4094. The now-discredited prefrontal lobotomy.

4095. Five and a half feet, head to hoof.

4096. Do identical twins have identical fingerprints?

4097. What bird has the longest nestling life—taking up to nine months to fly?

4098. In geology, what is calving?

4099. What common chemical compound is represented by the formula NH3?

4100. In the animal kingdom, what is a glutton?

4101. How did the tarantula get its name?

4102. What is the name of the protein—the most abundant in the human body—that holds our skin together?

4103. How much saliva does the average human produce daily?

4104. How long are the antlers of the pudu, the smallest deer in the world?

4105. How many muscles are there in the human ear?

4106. What kind of creature do Australians call the tasseled wobbegong?

4107. How many teeth does a turtle have?

4108. What color are the eggs laid by the flightless emu, the largest bird alive today after the ostrich?

4109. What is the world's largest living fish?

4110. How many calories do hibernating bears burn daily?

4111. What is the average lifespan of a red blood cell in the normal human body?

4112. How many bones are there in the human hand?

4113. What is N2O—nitrous oxide—more commonly called?

4096. *No. No two sets of prints are alike, including those of identical twins.*

4097. *The wandering albatross.*

4098. *The breaking off or detachment of an iceberg from a glacier that has reached the sea, or the separation of a portion of a floating iceberg.*

4099. *Ammonia.*

4100. *A wolverine.*

4101. *From the Italian seaport city of Taranto, where the hairy, venomous wolf spider once abounded.*

4102. *Collagen.*

4103. *One quart.*

4104. *They grow to 3 inches long. The pudu, found in northwest and southwest South America, is about 14 inches tall to the shoulders and weighs about 20 pounds.*

4105. *Six.*

4106. *A shark found near Australia's Great Barrier Reef.*

4107. *None—turtles are toothless, although some have sharp, jagged edges on their horny jaws that function as teeth.*

4108. *Green.*

4109. *The harmless whale shark, which reaches up to 50 or more feet in length and weighs up to 20 tons.*

4110. *About 4,000.*

4111. *Four months.*

4112. *27.*

4113. *Laughing gas.*

4114. In what order do most pigs move their legs when walking normally?

4115. How many miles of blood vessels are there in the average human body?

4116. What is the softest mineral known?

4117. What is the largest living invertebrate?

4118. What color is the blood of an octopus?

4119. What is unique about the food-catching technique of the anhinga—also known as the snakebird, darter or water turkey?

4120. What were the first objects in the solar system discovered by means of a telescope?

4121. How many teeth does a normal adult dog have?

4122. How long is a Martian year in Earth days—a year being the length of time it takes the planet to revolve once around the Sun?

4123. How did the quarter horse get its name?

4124. What animal has more teeth than any other North American land mammal?

4125. What two elements comprise almost 100 percent of the matter in the universe?

4126. In the American system of mathematical progressions, what five denominations come after million, billion and trillion?

4127. In costume jewelry, when gold is electroplated to metal, how thick must the layer of gold be?

4128. What is present in the variety of quartz stone known as cat's-eye that gives it its unique glowing appearance?

4129. In what direction does the jet stream flow?

4130. What is the most abundant metallic element in the earth's surface?

4114. *Left front foot first, then right rear foot, right front foot, left rear foot.*

4115. *About 62,000.*

4116. *Talc.*

4117. *The giant squid, which achieves a length of more than 60 feet—tentacles included.*

4118. *Pale bluish-green.*

4119. *It spears fish with its long, straight, sharp bill—the only bird to do so. It has extra cervical vertebrae, which enable it to coil its neck and then release it with viper-like speed.*

4120. *The four largest satellites of Jupiter—Ganymede, Io, Callisto and Europa.*

4121. *42—that's 20 on the upper jaw and 22 on the lower jaw. The adult human has 32, evenly divided between upper and lower jaws.*

4122. *687 days.*

4123. *From its speed in running the quarter mile.*

4124. *The opossum, the only marsupial native to North America. It has 50 teeth.*

4125. *Hydrogen (approximately 75 percent) and helium (approximately 25 percent). The remaining, heavier elements constitute a mere fraction of existence.*

4126. *Quadrillion, quintillion, sextillion, septillion and octillion.*

4127. *At least seven millionths of an inch thick—and the gold must be at least 10-karat.*

4128. *Asbestos fibers. The glow is known as chatoyancy.*

4129. *From west to east.*

4130. *Aluminum—it accounts for an estimated 8 percent of the solid portion of the earth's crust.*

4131. What are the ornamental plumes of the male egret called?

4132. If you traveled at a snail's pace, how much ground would you cover in an hour?

4133. How many fat cells does the average adult have?

4134. Where are the pyramids of Malpighi and the pyramids of Ferrein?

4135. Bovine means cow-like. What does murine mean?

4136. What is a group of foxes called?

4137. A cob is a male swan; a cygnet is a baby. What is the female called?

4138. What is a female rabbit called?

4139. How did the horse chestnut tree get its name?

4140. What tree's name contains all five vowels?

4141. What are amberjack, cusk and pout?

4142. What are Shaggy Mane, Slimy Gomphidius, Inky Cap, Sulphur Top and Pig's Ears?

4143. What is the skin that peels off after a bad sunburn?

4144. What word best describes the snout of a pig?

4145. What is a group of owls called?

4146. What are baby beavers called?

4147. What is a perfusionist's role in a hospital operating room?

4148. There are two atria in the human body—where are they?

4149. What do the letters CAT represent in CAT scan—the three-dimensional composite image that can be taken of body, brain or lungs?

4131. *Aigrettes.*

4132. *25 feet—for a great many species.*

4133. *Between 40 and 50 billion.*

4134. *In the human body—in the kidneys.*

4135. *Mouse-like.*

4136. *A skulk.*

4137. *A pen.*

4138. *A doe. A male is a buck; a baby, a kit or kitten. The act of giving birth is known as kindling.*

4139. *From the early use of its chestnuts as a medicine for horses.*

4140. *The sequoia's.*

4141. *Fish.*

4142. *Mushrooms.*

4143. *Blype.*

4144. *Gruntle.*

4145. *A parliament.*

4146. *Kits or kittens.*

4147. *Running the heart-lung machine during open-heart surgery. The machine keeps the patient's heart pumping while it removes carbon dioxide from the blood and adds oxygen to it.*

4148. *In the heart. They are the two upper chambers (auricles) that receive the blood from the veins and pump it into the two lower chambers (ventricles).*

4149. *Computerized axial tomography.*

4150. What belief was Galileo forced to recant by the Inquisition in 1633?

4151. In astronomy, what is a white dwarf?

4152. Wild turkeys can run at speeds of at least 12 miles an hour. How fast can they fly?

4153. What does the acronym DSB mean to a hospital worker?

4154. What famous naturalist penned a book entitled, *The Formation of Vegetable Mold, Through the Action of Worms, With Observations on Their Habits?*

4155. What was the Calypso, Jacques-Yves Cousteau's ship, before he converted it into an oceanographic research vessel?

4156. Who was the first person to record that the number of rings in the cross section of a tree trunk reveals its age?

4157. What is the meaning of the word "lore" when it's used by an ornithologist?

4158. What's a winkle?

4159. In the world of living things, what are zebus? How about zebubs?

4160. What celestial body got its name from a Greek word meaning "long-haired"?

4161. How many compartments does a normal cow's stomach have?

4162. The discovery of what semiprecious stone often indicates that diamonds are nearby?

4163. To what animal family does the wolverine belong—as its largest member?

4164. Why are Mercury and Venus known as inferior planets?

4150. *That the earth revolved around a stationary sun. He was kept under house arrest for the last eight years of his life for debunking the traditional belief that the earth was the center of the universe.*

4151. *The dense, burned-out remains of a star; a stellar corpse.*

4152. *Up to 55 miles an hour.*

4153. *Drug-seeking behavior. The designation is used for a patient or wannabe patient who is complaining of a bogus ailment in an attempt to get narcotics.*

4154. *Charles Darwin, who is better known for his revolutionary tome,* Origin of the Species. *His book on worms, a pioneering work in the field of quantitative ecology published in 1881, was his last.*

4155. *A minesweeper.*

4156. *Leonardo da Vinci. He also discovered that the width between the rings indicates annual moisture.*

4157. *The space between a bird's eye and its bill.*

4158. *An edible sea snail.*

4159. *Zebus are humped cattle found in India, China and northern Africa; zebubs are tsetse-like flies found in Ethiopia.*

4160. *Comet. The name comes from the Greek kom(t(s, an adjective formed from the verb koman, "to wear long hair."*

4161. *Four. The rumen, reticulum (storage area), omasum (where water is absorbed), and abomasum (the only compartment with digestive juices).*

4162. *Garnet.*

4163. *The weasel family, Mustelidae.*

4164. *Their orbits are closer to the sun than Earth's orbit. Planets orbiting the sun beyond Earth are referred to as superior planets.*

4165. How much silver must an item contain to be considered sterling?

4166. What system of healing did Canadian-born grocer Daniel David Palmer formally introduce in Davenport, Iowa, in September 1895?

4167. What part of a horse is the pastern?

4168. What is unusual about the tail of the flightless kiwi bird?

4169. What is silviculture?

4170. How many times its own body weight can a worker ant carry?

4171. In Web site addresses on the Internet, what does http stand for?

4172. How many degrees can a great horned owl turn its head?

4165. *92.5 percent.*

4166. *Chiropractic medicine. Although new at the time, the principles upon which chiropractic medicine was based can be traced back to the earliest physicians—including Hippocrates (460-370 B.C.). Palmer created the name "chiropractic" by combining the Greek words for hand, cheir, and practical (or efficient), praktikos.*

4167. *The part of the foot between the fetlock and the hoof.*

4168. *It doesn't exist. The kiwi has no tail feathers.*

4169. *Forestry—the planting of trees for the preservation of forests. The Latin word silva means "forest."*

4170. *Up to 50 times its weight. Worker ants are always female.*

4171. *Hypertext transfer protocol.*

4172. *270 degrees.*

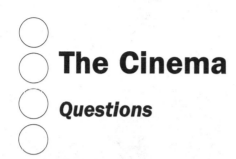

The Cinema

Questions

4173. What well-known Tasmanian-born leading lady launched her entertainment career under the name Queenie O'Brien?

4174. In what country was famous French actor Yves Montand born?

4175. What were the real first names of Beau Brummell and Beau Geste?

4176. What famous character actor prepared for a career in psychiatry—studying and working with pioneer psychoanalysts Sigmund Freud and Alfred Adler—before he turned to performing?

4177. In a charity pantomime performance in 1984, rocker Elton John was featured as "Mother Goose." Who co-starred as the "Egg Yolk"?

4178. Bob Hope and Bing Crosby took movie "roads" to seven destinations. How many can you name?

4179. Who wrote the scripts for his own films under pseudonyms that included Otis T. Criblecoblis and Mahatma Kane Jeeves?

Answers

4173. *Merle Oberon. Born Estelle Merle O'Brien Thompson, she went on to use a variation of her middle names for her professional name.*

4174. *In Italy, as Yvo Livi.*

4175. *Brummell was George; Geste, Michael.*

4176. *Peter Lorre.*

4177. *Sir John Gielgud.*

4178. *Singapore, Zanzibar, Morocco, Utopia, Rio, Bali, and Hong Kong.*

4179. *W. C. Fields.*

4180. What actor—and one-time New York Yankee batboy—portrayed Babe Ruth in the 1948 movie biography of the Sultan of Swat?

4181. What actor's profile was once compared to "the steely prehensile outline of an invariably victorious bottle opener"?

4182. Who provided Mickey Mouse's high-pitched voice in the early Walt Disney films starring the animated mouse?

4183. For what two films did Elizabeth Taylor win best actress Oscars?

4184. Who dubbed Miss Piggy's singing voice in "The Muppet Movie"?

4185. When British film companies buy a product called Kensington Gore, what are they purchasing?

4186. What American actress once described herself as "pure as the driven slush"?

4187. What was the name of the popular Broadway musical that was turned into the 1934 movie *The Gay Divorcée*?

4188. Who said: "A man in love is incomplete until he is married. Then he is finished"?

4189. What film did Ingrid Bergman make twice—first in Swedish and then in English for her Hollywood debut?

4190. What was the only horror film in which Humphrey Bogart appeared?

4191. What color was actor Yul Brynner's hair—when he had hair?

4192. Who was Gene Kelly's unusual dancing partner in an imaginative pas de deux in the 1945 film *Anchors Aweigh*?

4193. What entertainer boxed under the name Kid Crochet as a teenager?

4180. *William Bendix.*

4181. *George C. Scott's. Critic Kenneth Tynan made the comparison.*

4182. *Walt Disney, himself.*

4183. Butterfield 8, *in 1960;* Who's Afraid of Virginia Woolf, *in 1966.*

4184. *Johnny Matthis.*

4185. *Artificial blood, used for special effects.*

4186. *Tallulah Bankhead.*

4187. The Gay Divorce. *The Hollywood censors nixed that title, however, apparently finding it inappropriate to call a divorce happy.*

4188. *Oft-married Zsa Zsa Gabor.*

4189. Intermezzo: A Love Story.

4190. The Return of Dr. X. *Bogart played a zombie in the 1939 film.*

4191. *Dark brown.*

4192. *Jerry, the animated mouse from the* Tom and Jerry *cartoon.*

4193. *Dean Martin, was born Dino Crocetti.*

4194. How old was Shirley Temple when she appeared in her first film, *The Red-Haired Alibi* ?

4195. For what offense was Australian-born *Million Dollar Mermaid* Annette Kellerman, the first aquatic glamour girl, arrested in 1909?

4196. Who played Scorpio, the sadistic killer, in Clint Eastwood's 1971 film, *Dirty Harry* ?

4197. What British actor made his screen debut as a Mexican wearing a blanket in the very first Hopalong Cassidy movie?

4198. Who wrote the screenplay for *The Misfits*, the 1961 film that marked the last screen appearances of both Clark Gable and Marilyn Monroe?

4199. What 1977 movie was originally going to be called *Anhedonia*—a word that means the psychological inability to experience pleasure?

4200. Whose lengthy Oscar acceptance speech prompted the Academy of Motion Picture Arts and Sciences to set a time limit at later award ceremonies?

4201. What was the name of the dolphin that played Flipper in the movies?

4202. What famous American actress made her stage debut in 1966 as a silent Helen of Troy in *Dr. Faustus* ?

4203. In what film did tough guy actor Clint Eastwood first deliver his trademark line, "Make my day"?

4204. What was the first R-rated film produced by the Walt Disney studio?

4205. What was used to simulate blood in the famous shower scene in the 1960 Alfred Hitchcock chiller *Psycho* ?

4206. Comedian W.C. Fields' waterfront summer home in New York City was sold in 1980 so that an existing business could expand. What was the business?

4194. *Three years old.*

4195. *Indecent exposure—for wearing one of her newly created, one-piece bathing suits. The skirtless creation covered her legs all the way down to the calf.*

4196. *Andy Robinson, son of Edward G. Robinson.*

4197. *David Niven, who noted, "Of course they daren't let me open my mouth."*

4198. *Monroe's ex-husband, Pulitzer Prize-winning playwright Arthur Miller.*

4199. *Woody Allen's* Annie Hall.

4200. *Greer Garson's. She said her thanks for 5½ minutes at the 1943 ceremonies when she was honored for her starring role in* Mrs. Miniver.

4201. *Mitzi. For the TV series she was replaced by two other dolphins, Suzy and Cathy.*

4202. *Elizabeth Taylor. Her first speaking role in the theater came 15 years later when she appeared on Broadway in Lillian Hellman's* The Little Foxes.

4203. *In* Sudden Impact, *during his fourth appearance as Inspector "Dirty Harry" Callahan.*

4204. Down and Out in Beverly Hills, *starring Richard Dreyfuss, Bette Midler and Nick Nolte, in 1985.*

4205. *Hershey's chocolate syrup.*

4206. *The home of the man who reportedly once said, "Any man who hates children and dogs can't be all bad," was purchased by a nursery school.*

4207. In the 1952 hit musical *Singin' in the Rain,* who dubbed the splash dancing heard while Gene Kelly does his celebrated tap dance in the rain?

4208. What do Rudolf Nureyev's legs, Bette Davis' waistline and Jimmy Durante's nose have in common?

4209. What song was the musical theme of James Cagney's 1931 gangster classic *Public Enemy* ?

4210. What great American actor's first stage appearance was as a chorus girl in a show called *Every Sailor* ?

4211. What was Boris Karloff's real name?

4212. What was the real name of the elderly British schoolteacher in the James Hilton novel *Goodbye, Mr. Chips,* portrayed on the silver screen by Robert Donat?

4213. What famous Hollywood leading man appeared as Pinkerton in the 1932 non-musical film version of the Giacomo Puccini opera *Madame Butterfly* ?

4214. Actresses Mary Pickford and Alexis Smith were both born with the same name—and changed it for Hollywood. What was it?

4215. How many costume changes did Elizabeth Taylor make in the $37 million, 1963 motion picture extravaganza *Cleopatra* ?

4216. What were the first words spoken by Greta Garbo in a movie?

4217. What unusual pet did actor John Barrymore have?

4218. What 1939 James Stewart movie classic aroused Congressional threats against Hollywood and attempts to block its European release by U.S. Ambassador to England Joseph P. Kennedy?

4219. What actress changed her name from Edda van Heemstra for Hollywood?

4207. *Then-unknowns Gwen Verdon and Carol Haney.*

4208. *All were insured by Lloyd's of London.*

4209. *"I'm Forever Blowing Bubbles."*

4210. *James Cagney's, in 1920.*

4211. *William Henry Pratt.*

4212. *Mr. Chipping.*

4213. *Cary Grant. Sylvia Sidney was his Madame Butterfly.*

4214. *Gladys Smith.*

4215. *Sixty-five.*

4216. *"Gimme a whiskey. Ginger ale on the side. An' don' be stingy, baby."* *The film was* Anna Christie; *the year, 1930.*

4217. *A vulture named Maloney. It would sit on his knee and hiss.*

4218. *Frank Capra's* Mr. Smith Goes To Washington.

4219. *Belgian-born Audrey Hepburn.*

4220. What starring role did film stars Robert Redford, Steve McQueen and Paul Newman all turn down, despite a contract offer of $4 million?

4221. What was the nationality of Warner Oland, the actor who appeared as Charlie Chan in dozens of films?

4222. What 1935 movie was the silver screen's first Technicolor offering?

4223. Who dressed in Greta Garbo's clothes and doubled for her in a horseback-riding scene in her first American movie, the 1926 silent film *Torrent*?

4224. In the 1968 film *2001: A Space Odyssey*, what song did HAL, the computer, learn to sing?

4225. Who dubbed the voice of Darth Vader in the movies *Star Wars* and *The Empire Strikes Back*?

4226. What was the name of the Good Witch portrayed by Billie Burke in the 1939 film classic *The Wizard of Oz*?

4227. Who was Fred Astaire's first silver screen dancing partner?

4228. What was the name of the mechanical shark in the 1975 hit movie *Jaws*?

4229. What 1960 film classic is based on the Edward Gein murder case?

4230. What famous American playwright wrote the script for *The Cocoanuts* and several other Marx Brothers movies?

4231. What American actress was the first to have a theater named after her?

4232. What unusual insurance policy did silent-film slapstick comedian Ben Turpin take out?

4233. For starring roles in what two films did Jane Fonda win Oscars?

4220. Superman. *Christopher Reeve took the part—for $250,000.*

4221. *He was Swedish.*

4222. Becky Sharp, *a film adaptation of the William Makepeace Thackeray novel* Vanity Fair.

4223. *Actor Joel McCrea.*

4224. *"A Bicycle Built For Two."*

4225. *James Earl Jones.*

4226. *Glinda.*

4227. *Joan Crawford, in* Dancing Lady *in 1933. Later that year he teamed up with Ginger Rogers in* Flying Down to Rio.

4228. *Bruce.*

4229. *Alfred Hitchcock's* Psycho.

4230. *George S. Kaufman.*

4231. *Ethel Barrymore. The theater, in New York, opened in 1928.*

4232. *A $100,000 policy against the possibility that his trademark crossed eyes would straighten out.*

4233. Klute, *in 1971, and* Coming Home, *in 1978.*

4234. Who played Vincent Price's menacing mute assistant in the 3-D horror film *House of Wax* ?

4235. What Oscar-winning 1971 movie was based on the 1951 Broadway play *I Am a Camera* ?

4236. Robert Redford was paid $6 million for his role in the 1985 film *Out of Africa*. How much was leading lady Meryl Streep paid?

4237. A process called Smell-O-Vision was used in 1960 for one film and then abandoned forever. What was the odorous offering?

4238. How did Charlie Chaplin place when he entered a Charlie Chaplin lookalike contest in Monte Carlo?

4239. What movie's cast included 124 midgets?

4240. What movie series did Johnny Weissmuller star in after he outgrew his *Tarzan* loincloth?

4241. Who replaced Dorothy Lamour as the female lead in the last of the seven Bing Crosby-Bob Hope "Road movies?

4242. What famous American movie star's ashes are in an urn that also contains a small gold whistle?

4243. Rudolph Valentino, the great lover, was married twice. How did he spend his wedding nights?

4244. What film star represented Scotland in the 1952 Mr. Universe contest?

4245. What was movie mogul Samuel Goldwyn's real name?

4246. How much was Marlon Brando paid for his brief appearance as Jor-el in the movie "Superman"?

4247. What is Dolly Parton's CB "handle"?

4248. What actress in what movie said, "How dare he make love to me and not be a married man"?

4234. *Charles Bronson, in 1953, before he changed his name from Charles Buchinski.*

4235. Cabaret, *starring Liza Minnelli and Joel Grey.*

4236. *She received $3 million.*

4237. Scent of Mystery, *produced by Mike Todd Jr.*

4238. *He came in third.*

4239. *The 1939 version of* The Wizard of Oz *starring Judy Garland. The midgets played Munchkins.*

4240. Jungle Jim, *in which he wore a bush jacket to cover his added weight.*

4241. *Joan Collins. Lamour, however, did make a cameo appearance in the 1962 film,* The Road to Hong Kong.

4242. *Humphrey Bogart's. His actress wife Lauren Bacall had the whistle inscribed, "If you need anything, just whistle"—words she spoke to him in their first film together,* To Have and Have Not.

4243. *His first, locked out by wife Jean Acker; his second, in jail for bigamy, unable to be with wife Natacha Rambova.*

4244. *Sean Connery.*

4245. *Samuel Goldfish. He took his new name from the company he formed with the Selwyn brothers.*

4246. *He received a reported $3.7 million, as well as another $15 million after suing for a share of the box-office take.*

4247. *Booby Trap.*

4248. *Ingrid Berman, speaking of Cary Grant in* Indiscreet.

4249. How much does the 13½-inch-tall Academy Award Oscar weigh?

4250. What famous passenger ship was sunk to provide the dramatic climax of the 1960 film, *The Last Voyage* ?

4251. What actor claims he is never without his emerald-green socks?

4252. Can you name the three boxers Sylvester Stallone faced in the climactic scenes of his first four *Rocky* movies?

4253. What actress was the granddaughter of famed architect Frank Lloyd Wright?

4254. Who dubbed Lauren Bacall's singing voice in *To Have and Have Not,* her screen debut and first pairing with future husband Humphrey Bogart?

4255. In what three films did Doris Day sing "Que Sera Sera"?

4256. What two film classics did Victor Fleming direct in 1939?

4257. In what film did the star propose by saying, "Marry me and I'll never look at another horse"?

4258. What screen role did Telly Savalas, Donald Pleasance, Max Von Sydow and Charles Gray have in common?

4259. For her role of Rosie in the 1951 film classic *The African Queen,* who was Katharine Hepburn told to use as a model?

4260. In what film classic was the heroine advised: "You can't show your bosom 'fore three o'clock"?

4261. What was the first British sound film?

4262. What comedienne is a direct descendant of Edward Rutledge, the youngest signer of the Declaration of Independence?

4249. *The statuette weighs eight and a half pounds.*

4250. *The Ile de France, which was renamed Faransu Maru ("French Ship" in Japanese) for the occasion.*

4251. *Irish-born Peter O'Toole.*

4252. *Apollo Creed (Carl Weathers) in* Rocky *and* Rocky II*; Clubber Lang (Mr. T) in* Rocky III*; and Drago (Dolph Ludgren) in* Rocky IV.

4253. *Anne Baxter.*

4254. *A teenage Andy Williams.*

4255. The Man Who Knew Too Much *in 1956;* Please Don't Eat the Daisies *in 1960; and* The Glass Bottom Boat *in 1966.*

4256. Gone With the Wind *and* The Wizard of Oz.

4257. A Day at the Races. *Groucho Marx was popping the question to Margaret Dumont.*

4258. *All played SPECTRE chief Ernst Stavro Blofeld in James Bond films.*

4259. *Eleanor Roosevelt.*

4260. Gone With the Wind. *Hattie McDaniels gave the etiquette tip to Vivien Leigh.*

4261. Blackmail, *Alfred Hitchcock's 1929 masterpiece.*

4262. *Goldie Hawn.*

4263. At an MGM auction in 1970, two items went for the top price of $1,500. One was the full-sized boat used in the musical *Showboat*. What was the other?

4264. Clark Gable starred in the 1932 film *Red Dust* with Jean Harlow and Mary Astor. What was the name of the 1953 remake, featuring Gable in the same role with costars Ava Gardner and Grace Kelly?

4265. What filmmaker made a cameo appearance in *Close Encounters of the Third Kind*?

4266. What famous actor starred in two classic "Bridge" movies?

4267. Who appeared as a character named Alias in the 1973 Sam Peckinpah film *Pat Garrett and Billy the Kid*?

4268. What famous performer appeared in a movie riding Trigger before Roy Rogers rode him to silver-screen stardom?

4269. Who subbed for Claire Bloom in the dance sequences in the 1952 film *Limelight*, which also starred Charlie Chaplin?

4270. Who portrayed Snow White in a live-action movie to help Walt Disney's animators achieve realism in their cartoon feature film?

4271. What actress once sued a California animal breeder for naming a two-headed goat after her?

4272. Who was William Claude Dukenfield?

4273. What film did Alfred Hitchcock make twice?

4274. Where were the disco scenes in *Saturday Night Fever* shot?

4275. Who played *The Great Gatsby* in the 1949 film version of the F. Scott Fitzgerald novel?

4276. What film star won a special Oscar as "the most outstanding personality of 1934"?

4263. *Judy Garland's size-4½ red shoes from* The Wizard of Oz.

4264. Mogambo.

4265. *FranÁois Truffaut. He appeared as a UFO expert.*

4266. *William Holden. He was in* The Bridge on the River Kwai *and* The Bridges at Toko-ri.

4267. *Singer Bob Dylan.*

4268. *Olivia de Havilland, in* The Adventures of Robin Hood *in 1938. At the time, Trigger was known as Golden Cloud.*

4269. *Ballerina Melissa Hayden.*

4270. *Dancer Marge Champion, who was married to a Disney animator at the time. She also was the model for the Blue Fairy in* Pinocchio.

4271. *Hedy Lamarr.*

4272. *Comedian W.C. Fields.*

4273. The Man Who Knew Too Much—*in 1934 with Leslie Banks and Edna Best, and in 1956 with James Stewart and Doris Day.*

4274. *At the 2001 Odyssey Disco in Bay Ridge, Brooklyn.*

4275. *Alan Ladd. Robert Redford starred in the same role 25 years later.*

4276. *America's dimpled darling Shirley Temple, who was Hollywood's top box-office attraction from 1935 through 1938.*

4277. What actor launched his performing career as a public-address announcer for the Brooklyn Dodgers at Ebbets Field in 1938?

4278. In his first starring role in the 1935 film *The Phantom Empire,* what horse did Gene Autry ride?

4279. In what film did the heroine declare, "I've met the most wonderful man. Of course, he's fictional. But you can't have everything"?

4280. Who launched her film career at age 10 in a low-brow comedy called *There's One Born Every Minute,* which also featured former Our Gang star Carl "Alfalfa" Switzer?

4281. In the Walk Disney film, what was the profession of Snow White's friends, the seven dwarfs?

4282. Who paid $300 for 32 cotton sheets and 35 pillow cases—worth $50 new—at an auction of actor John Gilbert's personal effects following his death in 1936?

4283. Who was scheduled to star in the 1984 film *Beverly Hills Cop* before the role went to Eddie Murphy?

4284. Which of his almost 100 movies was Roy Rogers' favorite?

4285. For which Alfred Hitchcock film did artist Salvadore Dali design the graphics?

4286. Which profile did actor John Barrymore consider "the moneymaking side" of his face?

4287. What famous American author appeared in the 1976 movie comedy *Murder by Death* ?

4288. In Walt Disney's 1938 cartoon short *Mother Goose Goes Hollywood,* what star was caricaturized as Little Bo-Peep?

4289. Who starred in the title role in the 1977 film *Valentino* ?

4290. Two movies were named after the song "Red River Valley." Who starred in them?

4277. John Forsythe.

4278. Tom Mix's horse Tony Jr.—not Champion.

4279. The Purple Rose of Cairo, *starring Mia Farrow.*

4280. Elizabeth Taylor.

4281. Bashful, Doc, Dopey, Grumpy, Happy, Sleepy and Sneezy were jewel miners.

4282. Marlene Dietrich.

4283. Sylvester Stallone, in a much more macho version written by Rocky-Rambo himself. And before Stallone, Mickey Rourke had been slated for the part.

4284. My Pal Trigger.

4285. Spellbound, *in 1945. Dali created the graphics for amnesiac Gregory Peck's Freudian dreams.*

4286. The left.

4287. Truman Capote.

4288. Katherine Hepburn.

4289. Another Rudolph—Rudolf Nureyev.

4290. Gene Autry in 1936; Roy Rogers in 1941. The song originated in New York at the turn of the century as "In the Bright Mohawk Valley."

4291. Who said, "If I had as many love affairs as you have given me credit for, I would now be speaking to you from a jar in the Harvard Medical School"?

4292. When Eddie Cantor ducks to avoid a handful of mud in the 1932 film *Roman Scandals*, what Goldwyn girl gets it right in the face?

4293. Who coined the phrase "cameo role" to describe the appearance of a top movie star in a bit part?

4294. In what film did Jean Arthur make her last screen appearance?

4295. What Hollywood movie star's contract included a morals clause that forbade "adulterous conduct or immoral relations" with men other than her husband?

4296. Paul Newman took an ad in a newspaper to apologize for what movie, when the film was shown on TV?

4297. Whom did Fred Astaire name as his favorite dance partner?

4298. What American film classic did actor John Wayne call "the most un-American thing I've ever seen in my whole life"?

4299. Whom did actor Richard Dreyfuss portray in his first important film role—in the 1973 movie Dillinger?

4300. How old was actress Joan Collins when she posed semi-nude for Playboy in 1983?

4301. Italian film producer Carlo Ponti was considered for the title role of what 1972 blockbuster movie?

4302. Who played Watergate cover-up informant Deep Throat in the 1976 film *All The President's Men*?

4303. What struggling movie cowboy served as Gary Cooper's dialogue coach for his first all-talkie, the 1929 western classic *The Virginian*?

4291. *Frank Sinatra.*

4292. *Lucille Ball.*

4293. *Showman Mike Todd, when he produced his Oscar-winning* Around the World in 80 Days *in 1955. It featured Frank Sinatra, Marlene Dietrich, Buster Keaton, Noel Coward, Ronald Colman, Beatrice Lillie and others in unexpected walk-ons.*

4294. *In* Shane, *in 1953.*

4295. *Gloria Swanson's.*

4296. *His 1954 screen debut,* The Silver Chalice.

4297. *Gene Kelly.*

4298. *The 1952 Gary Cooper western* High Noon. *Wayne's objection: "The last thing in the picture is ole Coop putting the United States marshal's badge under his foot and stepping on it."*

4299. *George "Baby Face" Nelson. Warren Oates was featured in the title role.*

4300. *50. The issue sold out.*

4301. The Godfather. *Marlon Brando, the actor who finally got the role of Don Vito Corleone, won an Oscar for his performance.*

4302. *Hal Holbrook.*

4303. *Randolph Scott. Scott, a native Virginian, had a bit part in the film.*

4304. What did actor Jack Lemmon use to strain spaghetti in the 1960 comedy classic *The Apartment*?

4305. What 1959 film ends with the heroine saying, "In spite of everything, I still believe that people are good at heart"?

4306. Actor Peter Fonda was once arrested and charged with disturbing the peace and destroying private property for slashing a sign. What did the sign say?

4307. What was the name of actress Elizabeth Taylor's childhood pet chipmunk, which she immortalized in a book written in 1946?

4308. A life-size statue of what Hollywood filmmaker has been erected in Puerto Vallarta, Mexico?

4309. What two tough-guy actors turned down the role of the avenging "Man with No Name" in Sergio Leone's spaghetti western *A Fistful of Dollars* before Clint Eastwood was offered the part?

4310. What popular movie was remade in 1981 under the title *Outland*, with Sean Connery in the lead role and the setting shifted from the Old West to the third moon of Jupiter?

4311. How many frames per second are projected in most animated films?

4312. Who dubbed the voice of the Beast in the animated 1991 Disney version of *Beauty and the Beast*?

4313. What famous actor's brother enjoyed a brief movie career as a child, appearing in a bit part in the 1939 Frank Capra classic *Mr. Smith Goes to Washington*?

4314. What was the name of the stray alley cat adopted by Holly Golightly, portrayed by Audrey Hepburn, in the 1961 movie *Breakfast at Tiffany's*?

4315. What 1977 R-rated hit movie was later re-released with a PG rating after seven minutes of footage had been removed?

4304. *A tennis racquet.*

4305. The Diary of Anne Frank.

4306. *"Feed Jane Fonda to the Whales." Charges against Fonda were dropped when two key witnesses to the 1981 incident at Denver's Stapleton International Airport failed to appear at his trial.*

4307. *Nibbles. Taylor wrote and illustrated the book Nibbles and Me when she was 14.*

4308. *Director John Huston—because of the number of tourists drawn to the picturesque seaside village by his 1964 hit The Night of the Iguana.*

4309. *James Coburn and Charles Bronson. Henry Fonda was the first choice, but he was too expensive.*

4310. High Noon.

4311. 24.

4312. *Robby Benson.*

4313. *Dustin Hoffman's older brother Ronald.*

4314. *It had no name—she called it "cat."*

4315. Saturday Night Fever, *starring John Travolta. The cut footage featured some sex scenes and blue language.*

4316. What was the first name of Lt. Bullitt, the down-and-dirty San Francisco detective portrayed by Steve McQueen in the 1968 hit movie *Bullitt*?

4317. In what year did Hollywood start keeping the names of Oscar winners sealed and secret?

4318. What unusual message did actress Joan Hackett have inscribed on her grave marker?

4319. In what roles did Francis Ford Coppola's daughter, Sofia, appear in each of the Godfather movies?

4320. Which is the only airline "Rain Man" Dustin Hoffman says he would be willing to fly in the 1988 Academy Award-winning film?

4321. Under what pseudonym did strongman Arnold Schwarzenegger make his screen debut?

4322. Who wrote the 1975 Academy Award-winning song "I'm Easy" for the movie *Nashville*?

4323. What is comedian Chevy Chase's real first name?

4324. What movie star's trademark telephone greeting became the title of a popular 1965 movie comedy?

4325. What Cecil B. DeMille film was the first movie to include screen credits?

4326. By what name do we know the play and cult movie that was originally going to be called *They Came From Denton High*?

4327. What were the names of mad scientist Dr. Emmett Brown's dogs in *Back to the Future* and *Back to the Future II*?

4328. Who wrote and directed the 1984 "rockumentary" satire *This Is Spinal Tap* and the 1986 hit *Stand By Me*?

4329. In the 1953 film *Mogambo*, what did Clark Gable reply when Grace Kelly asked, "Who is this man Thomson that gazelles should be called after him?"

4316. *Frank.*

4317. *1940—the year after the Los Angeles Times broke its promise and published the names of the winners before they had been officially announced.*

4318. *"Go Away! I'm Sleeping."*

4319. *In* The Godfather *she was a baby; in* The Godfather, Part II, *she was a child immigrant; and in* The Godfather, Part III, *in her first speaking part, she played Godfather Michael Corleone's daughter, Mary.*

4320. *Qantas, because of its safety record.*

4321. *Arnold Strong. He starred in the 1970 Italian-TV film Hercules in New York.*

4322. *Actor Keith Carradine, who sang the song in the film and at the Oscar ceremonies.*

4323. *Cornelius.*

4324. *Warren Beatty's line "What's new, pussycat."*

4325. *His 1913 silent version of* Squaw Man—*the first of three versions DeMille made of the story.*

4326. The Rocky Horror Picture Show.

4327. *Einstein and Copernicus.*

4328. *Rob Reiner, who once played Mike "Meathead" Stivic on TV's* All in the Family.

4329. *Gable said: "He's a third baseman for the Giants who got a home run against the Dodgers once." Actually, the Thomson's gazelle is named for nineteenth-century Scottish explorer Joseph Thomson, who was the first European to visit many regions of East Africa.*

4330. Who were the only consecutive Best Actress Oscar winners to appear together in the first movie both made after receiving their awards?

4331. What movie introduced the song "Some Day My Prince Will Come"?

4332. What film star early in his career appeared in a series of movies as Singin' Sam, the silver screen's first singing cowboy?

4333. What Oscar-winning title role, rejected by both Marlon Brando and Albert Finney, brought stardom to the little-known actor who signed for the part?

4334. What was the name of Baby Jane's wheelchair-bound sister in the 1962 chiller *Whatever Happened to Baby Jane?*, starring Bette Davis and Joan Crawford?

4335. What four 1939 Hollywood classics were honored on 25-cent stamps issued by the U.S. Postal Service in celebration of their 50th anniversaries?

4336. What movie star couple, in a bid to discourage sightseers, once put a hand-painted sign in front of their Beverly Hills home that said "Please—They have Moved!—The Piersons"?

4337. Who appeared as God in the 1968 Otto Preminger film *Skidoo?*

4338. According to his Nazi dossier in the 1942 film classic *Casablanca*, what color are Rick's eyes?

4339. Who turned down the role of Bonnie in the 1967 hit movie *Bonnie and Clyde* before Faye Dunaway got the part?

4340. What unique money-saving attachments did Greta Garbo have installed in her Duesenberg automobile?

4341. How many films had Humphrey Bogart made when he co-starred with wife-to-be Lauren Bacall in her first movie, *To Have and Have Not*, in 1945?

4330. Jessica Tandy, who won the Oscar in 1989 for Driving Miss Daisy, *and Kathy Bates, who won it in 1990 for* Misery. *Their joint project was the 1992 film* Fried Green Tomatoes.

4331. Walt Disney's 1937 Snow White and the Seven Dwarfs. *The song was written for the film by Frank Churchill and Larry Morey.*

4332. John Wayne. He gave up the role because his singing and guitar-playing were dubbed, making personal appearances difficult if not impossible.

4333. Lawrence of Arabia. *The role, of course, went to Peter O'Toole.*

4334. Blanche. Davis played Jane; Crawford, Blanche.

4335. Gone With the Wind, Beau Geste, Stagecoach *and* The Wizard of Oz.

4336. Paul Newman and Joanne Woodward.

4337. Groucho Marx.

4338. Brown. In the film, Rick—played by brown-eyed Humphrey Bogart—asks Major Strasser, "Are my eyes really brown?" when he's handed a copy of his dossier.

4339. Jane Fonda.

4340. Safes—six of them.

4341. 50.

4342. Who played the parole officer of elderly ex-con train robbers Burt Lancaster and Kirk Douglas in the 1986 film comedy *Tough Guys?*

4343. Why has actor Robert Duvall named several of his pet dogs Boo Radley?

4344. What 1987 chiller was an expanded version of a 45-minute 1979 British film called *Diversion?*

4345. What line, delivered by Carole Lombard to William Powell in the 1936 comedy *My Man Godfrey*, inspired the trademark greeting of a popular cartoon character?

4346. What actress, asked to audition for a supporting role in a 1990 Hollywood movie, sat down at the casting director's desk, pulled two Oscars from a satchel and demanded, "Do you still want me to read for this part?"

4347. Who was listed as "Shakespearean Tutor to Mr. Newman" in the credits for the 1990 Paul Newman—Joanne Woodward film *Mr. and Mrs. Bridge?*

4348. What did Marilyn Monroe reply when a journalist asked her what she wore to bed?

4349. What famous actor worked at New York's Central Park Zoo—sweeping out the lion cages—to support himself while trying to make it in show biz?

4350. What hairy covering was used to make a 40-foot-high, 6 ½-ton mechanical ape look lifelike in the 1976 remake of the 1933 film classic *King Kong?*

4351. What do the initials RKO stand for in the theater company's name?

4352. In 1980, who were the Top 10 box-office stars in Hollywood, according to the nation's film exhibitors?

4342. *Comedian Dana Carvey, best known as the Church Lady on TV's* Saturday Night Live, *and as Garth Algar in the 1992 film* Wayne's World

4343. *In honor of his breakthrough film role as Boo Radley, the reclusive, retarded neighbor in the 1962 movie* To Kill a Mockingbird.

4344. Fatal Attraction. *The screenplays of both were written by James Dearden.*

4345. *"What's up, Duke?"—which Bugs Bunny's creator Bob Clampett borrowed and turned into "What's up, Doc?"*

4346. *Shelley Winters. The film was* ß. *The part she auditioned for—Robert De Niro's mother—went to actress Ruth Nelson.*

4347. *Senator Bob Dole. Newman, who played a Kansas lawyer in the film, had asked the Kansas senator to help him get the accent right by tape-recording part of the balcony scene from Romeo and Juliet (which Newman recites in the film).*

4348. *"Chanel No. 5."*

4349. *Sylvester Stallone.*

4350. *Argentine horse tails—2 tons of them.*

4351. *Radio-Keith-Orpheum. It was formed by the merger of the Radio Corporation of America (RCA) and the Keith-Orpheum theater chain in 1921.*

4352. *From 1 to 10: Burt Reynolds, Robert Redford, Clint Eastwood, Jane Fonda, Dustin Hoffman, John Travolta, Sally Field, Sissy Spacek, Barbra Streisand and Steve Martin.*

4353. Who played Nicky Jr., son of Nick and Nora Charles, in the last of the six films in the Thin Man series, *Song of the Thin Man*?

4354. Under the motion picture censorship code in effect from 1934 to 1968, how long did a screen kiss have to last to be judged "indecent"?

4355. What film role did actresses Theda Bara, Claudette Colbert and Elizabeth Taylor have in common?

4356. What did writer Somerset Maugham ask about Spencer Tracy's performance during a visit to the set of the 1941 film *Dr. Jekyll and Mr. Hyde*?

4357. On a movie set, what is the job of the "best boy"?

4358. Who was the youngest performer in history to win an Oscar?

4359. What was Sleeping Beauty's name in the 1959 Walt Disney film?

4360. What famous American actor made his screen debut portraying a paraplegic war veteran struggling to overcome his handicap?

4361. Jack Palance portrayed Cuban dictator Fidel Castro in the 1969 movie *Che!* Who appeared in the title role as revolutionary leader Che Guevara?

4362. Where did actress Sigourney Weaver—whose given name was Susan—find her unusual adopted first name?

4363. What line did Jean Arthur deliver to Cary Grant in *Only Angels Have Wings* that Lauren Bacall repeated to Humphrey Bogart in *To Have and Have Not* and Angie Dickinson said to John Wayne in *Rio Bravo*?

4364. Who once said, "I always wanted to do what my mother did—get all dressed up, shoot people, fall in the mud. I never considered doing anything else"?

4353. Dean Stockwell.

4354. More than thirty seconds.

4355. Cleopatra. Each starred in a film entitled Cleopatra—*Bara in 1917; Colbert in 1934; Taylor in 1963. Others who appeared as the Egyptian queen include Vivien Leigh, in* Caesar and Cleopatra, *1945; Rhonda Fleming, in* Serpent of the Nile, *1953; and Hedy Lamarr, in* The Story of Mankind, *1957.*

4356. "Which one is he playing now?"

4357. Assisting the "gaffer," or chief electrician.

4358. Tatum O'Neal, who was 10 when she won an Oscar for best supporting actress as a chain-smoking, foul-mouthed young con artist in the 1973 film Paper Moon.

4359. Princess Aurora. The Good Fairies, however, called her Briar Rose.

4360. Marlon Brandon, in the 1950 film The Men.

4361. Egyptian-born Omar Sharif.

4362. In The Great Gatsby *by F. Scott Fitzgerald. Sigourney is a minor character in the book.*

4363. "I'm hard to get—all you have to do is ask me." All three films were directed by Howard Hawks.

4364. Actress Carrie Fisher, daughter of Debbie Reynolds.

4365. Can you name Hollywood's Top 10 box-office stars of 1965—according to the nation's film exhibitors?

4366. What were the names of Bambi's rabbit and skunk friends in the 1942 Walt Disney film *Bambi*?

4367. What top Hollywood star co-scripted and co-produced *Head*, a 1968 psychedelic musical fantasy that starred the rock group the Monkees?

4368. By what stage names do we know father and son actors Ramon and Carlos Estevez?

4369. Three stars appearing in the 1953 Academy Award-winning film *From Here to Eternity* were nominated for best actor or best actress Oscars. How many won?

4370. Who won a job in Hollywood after appearing in a screen test wearing only a loincloth and sporting a rose behind his left ear?

4371. Russia permitted the 1940 American film classic *The Grapes of Wrath* to be shown because of the grim picture it painted of the American depression. Why was it later banned?

4372. Who played the tyrannical king in the movie *Anna and the King of Siam*—10 years before Yul Brynner starred in the musical version, *The King and I*?

4373. What was the name of the hard-nosed paratrooper colonel who blasted apart a Coca-Cola vending machine in Stanley Kubrick's 1964 film satire *Dr. Strangelove*?

4374. What distinguished English actor appeared as pirate William Kidd in the 1952 film *Abbott and Costello Meet Captain Kidd*?

4375. Can you name the four "Lucky H" movies that actor Paul Newman starred in during the 1960s?

4376. What unusual insurance policy did Anthony Quinn take out when he agreed to appear in the 1968 film *The Magus*?

4377. In 1940, what Hollywood stars were voted the Top 10 box-office attractions in the land by the nation's film exhibitors?

4365. From 1 to 10: Sean Connery, John Wayne, Doris Day, Julie Andrews, Jack Lemmon, Elvis Presley, Cary Grant, James Stewart, Elizabeth Taylor and Richard Burton.

4366. The rabbit was Thumper; the skunk, Flower.

4367. Jack Nicholson.

4368. Ramon is Martin Sheen; Carlos is his son Charlie Sheen. The name was inspired by Roman Catholic Bishop Fulton J. Sheen.

4369. None. Burt Lancaster and Montgomery Clift lost to William Holden (Stalag 17) for best actor, and Deborah Kerr lost to Audrey Hepburn (Roman Holiday) for best actress. But Frank Sinatra won an Oscar for best supporting actor, and Donna Reed won one for best supporting actress.

4370. Clark Gable.

4371. Because Russian audiences were impressed that the poor, struggling Dust Bowl family depicted in the film was able to own an automobile.

4372. Rex Harrison, in 1946. His co-star was Irene Dunne.

4373. Bat Guano, who was portrayed by Keenan Wynn.

4374. Charles Laughton.

4375. The Hustler, 1961; , 1963; Harper, 1966; and Hombre, 1967.

4376. Quinn, who shaved his head for his role, was insured against failing to grow back a healthy head of hair.

4377. From 1 to 10: Mickey Rooney, Spencer Tracy, Clark Gable, Gene Autry, Tyrone Power, James Cagney, Bing Crosby, Wallace Beery, Bette Davis and Judy Garland.

4378. What comedy team appeared in more movies than any other in U.S. film history?

4379. In what film did Julie Andrews make her first appearance in a non-singing role?

4380. What historic figure has been portrayed on the silver screen by actors Errol Flynn, Clark Gable, Marlon Brando and Mel Gibson?

4381. Who played Mr. Smith in the 1937 Irene Dunne-Cary Grant comedy *The Awful Truth* and George in the 1938 Katherine Hepburn-Cary Grant comedy *Bringing Up Baby*?

4382. What was Marion Michael Morrison's screen name before he sought stardom as John Wayne?

4383. Rotund comedian Billy Gilbert, famous for his repertoire of violent sneezes, dubbed the voice of Sneezy in Walt Disney's *Snow White and the Seven Dwarfs*. Whose voice was used for Dopey in the 1937 cartoon classic?

4384. What cameo role did Charlie Chaplain play in his last movie, *A Countess from Hong Kong*, in 1967?

4385. What famous Hollywood star was married to Avrom Goldbogen?

4386. Who appeared in the 1957 Elvis Presley film *Loving You* as members of an enthusiastic audience?

4387. In the 1954 film *Her Twelve Men*, Greer Garson portrays a dedicated school teacher at a boys' school. How many boys were in her class?

4388. Who were the four artists of the silver screen who founded the United Artists film company in 1919?

4389. What Academy Award-winning title role was turned down by Hollywood heavy-hitters Burt Lancaster, John Wayne, Robert Mitchum, Lee Marvin and Rod Steiger?

4378. *The Three Stooges.*

4379. *In* The Americanization of Emily, *in 1964.*

4380. *Fletcher Christian, first mate on the Bounty. Flynn in* In the Wake of the Bounty, *in 1933; Gable in* Mutiny on the Bounty, *in 1935; Brando in* Mutiny on the Bounty, *in 1962; and Gibson in* The Bounty,*in 1984.*

4381. *Asta, the terrier who became a star in the Thin Man series.*

4382. *Duke Morrison.*

4383. *No one's—Dopey was a mute in the movie.*

4384. *He appeared as an elderly, seasick ship's steward in the film, which starred Marlon Brando and Sophia Loren.*

4385. *Elizabeth Taylor—long after Goldbrogen had changed his name to Mike Todd.*

4386. *Elvis' parents, Gladys and Vernon.*

4387. *Thirteen.*

4388. *Douglas Fairbanks, Mary Pickford, Charlie Chaplain and D. W. Griffith.*

4389. Patton, *in 1970. George C. Scott got the role.*

4390. Producer-director Otto Preminger paid Columbia Pictures $100,000 to use Kim Novak in the 1956 film *The Man with the Golden Arm*. How much was Novak paid?

4391. Why was popcorn banned at most movie theaters in the 1920s?

4392. Why was Mike Nichols fired as a busboy at a Howard Johnson's restaurant in New York, where he worked while taking drama lessons in the early 1950s?

4393. Under what name did a family named Blythe gain fame on stage and screen?

4394. On what planet did Abbott and Costello land in their 1953 film *Abbott and Costello Go to Mars* ?

4395. How much were Spencer Tracy and Katharine Hepburn paid for their last joint film appearance—in the 1967 film *Guess Who's Coming to Dinner* ?

4396. How much was paid at a 1987 auction for Charlie Chaplin's famous bowler hat and cane?

4397. What 1955 American movie was shown in Hong Kong under the title *The Heart of a Lady as Pure as a Full Moon Over the Place of Medical Salvation* ?

4398. What Hollywood great started his show business career on Broadway dancing in the background in Eskimo clothes as Mary Martin sang "My Heart Belongs to Daddy"?

4399. What now-famous actress had a bit part as Woody Allen's date at the end of his 1977 film *Annie Hall* ?

4400. What famous actor's Oscar was on display in the front window of his father's hardware store for 20 years?

4401. What symbol did Charlie Chaplin wear as a parody of the swastika in his 1940 film satire *The Great Dictator* ?

4402. What comic strip character does Whoopi Goldberg have tattooed above her left breast?

4390. *Her salary was $100 a week.*

4391. *It was considered too noisy.*

4392. *He claims he was canned "when somebody asked me the ice cream flavor of the week and I said, 'Chicken.'"*

4393. *Barrymore—as in John, Ethel and Lionel. Founding father Maurice, who had been disowned by his family in England for boxing professionally, took the name Barrymore from an aging poster on an old English vaudeville house in London before leaving for America to launch his acting career.*

4394. *Venus.*

4395. *Tracy was paid $300,000; Oscar-winner Hepburn, $200,000.*

4396. *$151,800.*

4397. Not as a Stranger, *starring Robert Mitchum as a young doctor and Olivia de Havilland as his nurse-wife.*

4398. *Gene Kelly. The year was 1938; the show, the Cole Porter hit* Leave It to Me.

4399. *Sigourney Weaver.*

4400. *James Stewart's. The Oscar was for his performance in the 1940 film* The Philadelphia Story; *the hardware store, founded by his grandfather in 1853, was in Indiana, Pennsylvania.*

4401. *Two "x" marks—the sing of the double cross.*

4402. *Woodstock, Snoopy's bird-buddy in the* Peanuts *comic strip.*

4403. Who made a cameo appearance as a man who thinks he's singer Ethel Merman in the 1980 film *Airplane!*?

4404. In the 1939 film classic *The Wizard of Oz*, what did the scarecrow, played by Ray Bolger, recite to prove he had a brain?

4405. What was actor Michael Keaton's name at birth?

4406. What popular actress once greeted Lauren Bacall by saying, "Hi, I'm the young you"?

4407. What famous Hollywood husband and wife once took out a half-page ad in *The Los Angeles Times* to deny rumors that they were splitting up?

4408. What famous actress helped pay her college tuition by modeling for a brochure promoting Washington's Watergate Hotel?

4409. Japanese filmmaker Akira Kurosawa's movies *The Seven Samurai* and *Yojimbo* were remade as the westerns *The Magnificent Seven* and *A Fistful of Dollars,* respectively. What American classic did his 1958 offering *The Hidden Fortress* inspire?

4410. In what popular 1975 film did teenager Carrie Fisher make her screen debut?

4411. Who dubbed the voice of the late Laurence Olivier when his previously cut, sexually suggestive Roman bathhouse scene with Tony Curtis was restored for the 1991 re-release of the 1960 biblical epic *Spartacus*?

4412. What vehicle did Arnold Schwarzenegger receive as partial payment for starring in *Terminator 2: Judgement Day*?

4413. What film star lives in a house that once served as a hideaway for gangster Al Capone?

4414. What role did director John Landis have his mother, Shirley Levine, play in his 1983 Eddie Murphy-Dan Akroyd comedy *Trading Places*?

4403. *Ethel Merman.*

4404. *The Pythagorean theorum: The square of the hypotenuse of a right-angled triangle is equal to the sum of the squares of the other two sides.*

4405. *Michael Douglas.*

4406. *Kathleen Turner.*

4407. *Joanne Woodward and Paul Newman. The ad cost $2,000.*

4408. *Susan Sarandon, who at the time was known as Susan Tomalin.*

4409. Star Wars, *in 1977.*

4410. Shampoo—*in which she seduces Warren Beatty.*

4411. *Anthony Hopkins.*

4412. *A Gulfstream G-III jet.*

4413. *Burt Reynolds—in Jupiter, Florida.*

4414. *A bag lady.*

4415. Who played John Wayne's young niece—orphaned, kidnapped and raised by Indians— in the great 1956 western saga *The Searchers*?

4416. Who portrayed artist Paul Gauguin in *Lust for Life*, the 1956 film biography of Vincent van Gogh?

4417. When the pedigree spaniel Lady had four puppies in the 1955 Disney film *Lady and the Tramp*, what name was given to the only one resembling papa-mutt Tramp?

4418. Who was originally cast as the bumbling Inspector Jacques Clouseau before Peter Sellers got the role in the 1963 film comedy *The Pink Panther*?

4419. What famous director featured his teenage daughter in a 1969 film, to the great dismay of reviewers, one of whom described her as having the face of "an exhausted gnu, the voice of an unstrung tennis racket, and a figure of no describable shape"?

4420. What was the wet stuff raining down on Gene Kelly in his famous splash-dance scene in the 1952 musical *Singing' in the Rain*?

4421. What was the most expensive silent film ever made?

4422. What popular 1973 movie was almost renamed *Another* Slow *Night in Modesto* because a studio executive feared the planned title would mislead filmgoers into believing it was an Italian movie?

4423. What is the only thing shown in color in Francis Ford Coppola's 1983 film *Rumble Fish*?

4424. Who is the only movie star to win the best actor Academy Award two years in a row?

4425. What does R2-D2—the name of the robot in the movie *Star Wars*—mean in film editing lingo?

4426. As a child, what famous actress shaved her head, wore pants and called herself "Jimmy" because she wanted to be a boy?

4415. *Natalie Wood.*

4416. *Anthony Quinn, who won an Oscar as best supporting actor for his performance. Van Gogh was played by Kirk Douglas.*

4417. *Scamp.*

4418. *Peter Ustinov. He bowed out at the last minute.*

4419. *John Huston—who cast his daughter, Anjelica, in a leading role in* A Walk with Love and Death. *It was her film debut.*

4420. *A mixture of water and milk. The milk was added to make the rain more visible.*

4421. Ben Hur. *The 1926 epic, which starred Ramon Novarro and Francis X. Bushman, cost $3.9 million.*

4422. American Graffiti.

4423. *Mickey Rourke's Siamese fighting fish.*

4424. *Spencer Tracy, in 1937 and 1938, for his performances in* Captains Courageous *and* Boy's Town.

4425. *Reel 2, dialogue 2.*

4426. *Katherine Hepburn.*

4427. What actress, using the name Rainbo, recorded a song entitled "John, You've Gone Too Far This Time," which gently chided John Lennon for appearing nude with wife Yoko Ono on the cover of the album *Two Virgins*?

4428. What was served in the 1981 film *My Dinner with Andre*?

4429. In what actress's marital split was Warren Beatty named corespondent and ordered to pay the divorce costs?

4430. What role did Dennis Hopper play in the 1957 western classic *The Gunfight at the O.K. Corral*?

4431. What was the name of singing cowboy Gene Autry's ranch in Placerita Canyon, northwest of downtown Los Angeles?

4432. Who turned down the role of the seductive and vindictive Mrs. Robinson in *The Graduate* before Anne Bancroft was offered the part in the 1967 hit film?

4433. What popular leading man dropped out of college to tour as Snow White's Prince Charming in the *Disney on Parade* ice show?

4434. How old was actor Jeff Bridges when he made his screen debut?

4435. How much was producer David O. Selznick fined by the Motion Picture Association of America for letting the word "damn" be used in *Gone With the Wind*?

4436. Before actor Clint Eastwood spent a record $25,000 on his winning 1986 campaign for mayor of Carmel, California, what had been the previous high for that town?

4437. How many doggie spots did Walt Disney animation artists draw for the 1961 cartoon feature *One Hundred and One Dalmations*?

4438. What now-famous entertainer's big break came when she jumped from the Broadway chorus of Zero Mostel's *Fiddler on the Roof* to the principal role of Tzeitel, the fiddler's eldest daughter?

4427. *Sissy Spacek. The record was a flop and Spacek turned her attention to acting.*

4428. *Potato soup, fish pâté and roast quail.*

4429. *Leslie Caron's, in 1965. British stage director Peter Hall obtained the divorce in London.*

4430. *Billy Clanton, the youngest of the outlaw Clanton gang.*

4431. *The Melody Ranch. Autry sold it in 1991 after the death of his horse Champion at age 41.*

4432. *Doris Day, who explained that she rejected the part because: "I can't picture myself in bed with someone, all the crew around us, doing what I consider so exciting and exalting when it is very personal and private."*

4433. *Patrick Swayze.*

4434. *Four months. He appeared as a crying baby in the 1950 film* The Company She Keeps.

4435. *$5,000.*

4436. *$750.*

4437. *6,469,952.*

4438. *Bette Midler.*

4439. What famous entertainer once told an interviewer, "I patterned my look after Cinderella, Mother Goose and the local hooker"?

4440. What was the name of the school that murderous teenager Carrie attended in the 1976 movie shocker *Carrie*?

4441. Who was originally slated to play paraplegic Vietnam War veteran Ron Kovic in the anti-war epic *Born on the Fourth of July*?

4442. What does actor E.G. Marshall reply when asked what his initials stand for?

4443. What leg did James Stewart have in a cast in the 1954 Alfred Hitchcock thriller *Rear Window*?

4444. What famous actor won a part in the 1937 Cecil B. DeMille western *The Plainsman* by pretending to be a Cheyenne Indian with little knowledge of the English language?

4445. What was the name of the machine that replaced sex in Woody Allen's 1973 comedy *Sleeper*?

4446. Why did *Cleopatra*, the 1963 film extravaganza starring Elizabeth Taylor, Richard Burton and Rex Harrison, have to be color-corrected before its release?

4447. What did Nick and Nora Charles give their dog Asta as a Christmas present in the 1934 comedy classic *The Thin Man*?

4448. When did former child screen star Shirley Temple stop believing in Santa Claus?

4449. What is the French equivalent of the Oscar?

4450. In 1928, what was the only word of dialogue in MGM's first picture with sound, *White Shadows in the South Seas*?

4451. What unique weapon was featured in the movies *The Tenth Victim*, starring Marcello Mastroianni and Ursula Andress, and *The Ambushers*, with Dean Martin and Janice Rule?

4452. In what film did Brooke Shields make her screen debut?

4439. *Dolly Parton.*

4440. *Bates High—in homage to Alfred Hitchcock and his "Psycho" killer Norman Bates.*

4441. *Al Pacino, in 1978, but the financing fell through. The film was finally made in 1989 with Tom Cruise.*

4442. *"Everyone's Guess." Marshall generally refuses to reveal his given names—but has acknowledged that the initials stand for Edda Gunther, a name that reflects his Norwegian ancestry.*

4443. *Both. Most of the time, it was on the left leg. But in one scene with co-star Grace Kelly, the cast shifted to the right leg. And at the end of the movie, both legs were in casts at the same time.*

4444. *Anthony Quinn, who answered a casting call for an Indian who could do a war chant in native Cheyenne.*

4445. *The Orgasmatron.*

4446. *Because Taylor sunbathed while outdoor scenes were being shot in Italy and her skintones in those scenes didn't match those in footage shot earlier indoors.*

4447. *A toy fire hydrant.*

4448. *As she tells it: "When my mother took me to see him in a department store and he asked for my autograph."*

4449. *The César.*

4450. *"Hello." (It was also the first film to feature Leo the Lion's roar.)*

4451. *A shooting bra.*

4452. Holy Terror, *a 1977 horror movie also known as* Alice, Sweet Alice.

4453. What was Citizen Kane's full name in the 1941 Orson Welles film classic?

4454. The first film documentary was screened in 1922 and given a sound track in 1939. What was it?

4455. What is the "Tech" in Technicolor—the color process introduced in the Disney film *Flowers and Trees* in 1932?

4456. What role did Patty Duke play in *The Miracle Worker*?

4457. Leonard Slye and Frances Octavia Smith rode to fame under what show business names?

4458. Who portrayed Mighty Joe Young's mistress in the movie about the giant gorilla?

4459. In the film *The Day the Earth Stood Still*, what words did Patricia Neal utter to stop the robot Gort from destroying the world?

4460. Movie mogul Sam Goldwyn spent $20,000 to reshoot a scene in his first all-talking film, "Bulldog Drummond," because he didn't understand what word?

4461. In 1968, two movie stars won the Oscar for Best Actress. Who were they?

4462. The PATSY—Picture Animal Top Star of the Year—award was first given in 1951. Who won it?

4463. Who was the first actor to have a pie thrown in his face in a movie?

4464. Jack Nicholson played the title role in his first movie. What was it?

4465. What actress once confessed, "I used to be Snow White, but I drifted"?

4466. Buddy Ebsen was originally cast as the Tin Man in the movie *The Wizard of Oz*. Why did Jack Haley replace him?

4453. *Charles Foster Kane*—*who was modeled after publishing tycoon William Randolph Hearst.*

4454. *The Eskimo saga* Nanook of the North.

4455. *Inventor Herbert Kalmus's tribute to his alma mater, the Massachusetts Institute of Technology.*

4456. *She played Helen Keller, in the 1962 movie, and Keller's teacher-companion Annie Sullivan, in the 1979 made-for-TV movie.*

4457. *Roy Rogers and Dale Evans.*

4458. *Terry Moore.*

4459. *Klaatu barada nikto.*

4460. *"Din." He had it changed to "noise".*

4461. *Katherine Hepburn, for* The Lion in Winter, *and Barbra Streisand, for* Funny Girl.

4462. *Francis the Talking Mule.*

4463. *Cross-eyed comic Ben Turpin, in an early Keystone Kop film. Mabel Normand threw it.*

4464. The Crybaby Killer, *in 1958.*

4465. *Mae West.*

4466. *Ebsen's aluminum-dust makeup turned him bright blue and sent him to the hospital with serious respiratory problems. Different makeup was devised for Haley.*

4467. Where was King Kong's home?

4468. Gangster Al Capone enjoyed the 1932 film *Scarface* so much that he gave director Howard Hawkes a gift. What was it?

4469. In what movie did long-time Superman George Reeves make his screen debut?

4470. In the saucy 1953 comedy *The Moon is Blue*, starring William Holden, David Niven, and Maggie McNamara, what word made its movie debut and caused the film to be banned in several parts of the country?

4471. To whom did actor Ryan O'Neal mail a live tarantula?

4472. What was the name of the general played by Sterling Hayden in the movie *Dr. Strangelove* ?

4473. Who played the title role in *Marty* when it was presented as a TV movie in 1953—three years before the Oscar-winning film starring Ernest Borgnine?

4474. Who starred in: *The Black Camel, Black Dragons, Black Friday, The Black Sheep,* and two films entitled *The Black Cat* ?

4475. In the movie *Bananas,* who did the play-by-play on Woody Allen's wedding night with Louise Lasser?

4476. What British actress made her stage debut at age 33, when she appeared as a fairy with a long nose in a pantomime play called *Little Jack Horner* ?

4477. What was the name of the sewer worker attacked by a 36-foot alligator in the 1980 monster movie, *Alligator* ?

4478. Where did John Wayne get his nickname Duke?

4479. Who portrayed the dying sea captain who delivered the *Maltese Falcon* in the 1941 John Huston film classic?

4480. What actor started his career on Broadway in 1922 as one of the robots in Karel Capek's *R.U.R.*?

4467. *Skull Island.*

4468. *A miniature machine gun.*

4469. Gone With the Wind. *He played Brent Tarleton, one of the redheaded twins who wooed Scarlett O'Hara.*

4470. *"Virgin."*

4471. *Gossip commentator Rona Barrett.*

4472. *Gen. Jack D. Ripper.*

4473. *Rod Steiger.*

4474. *Bela Lugosi.*

4475. *Sportscaster Howard Cosell.*

4476. *Margaret Rutherford, who was 71 when she made her first Miss Marple movie and 80 when she died.*

4477. *Ed Norton, undoubtedly in deference to the character created by Art Carney in TV's* The Honeymooners.

4478. *From his favorite childhood dog, an Airedale called Duke.* **4479.** *John Huston's actor-father, Walter.*

4480. *Spencer Tracy.*

4481. What foreign actress once earned a living as a model, working under the name Diana Loris?

4482. What actress once said, "Sometimes I'm so sweet, even I can't stand it"?

4483. Who played wise-guy dragster Bob Falfa in the movie *American Graffiti*?

4484. There were 291 words spoken in *The Jazz Singer*, the first motion picture feature with a sound track. What six are the most famous?

4485. What two people involved in the 1956 movie *The Invasion of the Body Snatcher*s had cameo roles in the 1978 remake?

4486. What actress had a daughter by Marcello Mastroianni and a son by Roger Vadim but married neither of them?

4487. How did HAL, the computer in *2001: A Space Odyssey*, get its name?

4488. What country was *The Mouse That Roared* in the Peter Sellers movie of that name?

4489. Who played the ancient lama in the 1937 movie *Lost Horizon*?

4490. What actress performed topless in Las Vegas before breaking into the movies as an outer space sex siren?

4491. Robert Mitchum launched his film career playing bad guy bit parts in whose cowboy movies?

4492. What actor first went to Hollywood as a chaperon-bodyguard for a gangster's girlfriend?

4493. Who made her film debut in the 1948 film *Scudda-Hoo! Scudda-Hay!*?

4494. What two Brooklyn comedians named Kaminsky gained fame under other names?

4481. *Gina Lollobrigida.*

4482. *Julie Andrews.*

4483. *Harrison Ford.*

4484. *Al Jolson's first: "You ain't heard nothing yet, folks!"*

4485. *Star Kevin McCarthy and director Don Siegel.*

4486. *Catherine Deneuve.*

4487. *Advance each letter by one and you have the answer—IBM.*

4488. *The Grand Duchy of Fenwick.*

4489. *Sam Jaffe.*

4490. *Valerie Perrine. Her film debut was as Montana Wildhack in* Slaughterhouse Five.

4491. *Hopalong Cassidy's.*

4492. *George Raft, who watched over nightclub singer Texas Guinan for his buddy Owney "the Killer" Madden.*

4493. *Marilyn Monroe. She was in the distant background rowing a boat.*

4494. *David Daniel Kaminsky, who became Danny Kaye; and Melvin Kaminsky, who became Mel Brooks. They are not related.*

4495. When Janet Gaynor won the first Academy Award for Best Actress in 1928, who won for Best Actor?

4496. What actor has to cover his arm with make-up when he performs in order to mask tattoos proclaiming his love for Mom and Dad and Scotland?

4497. Where was Francis Ford Coppola's Vietnam epic *Apocalypse Now* filmed?

4498. Who played Humpty Dumpty in the 1933 movie *Alice in Wonderland*?

4499. In what 1968 film did Marlon Brando play a long-haired Jewish guru; Ringo Starr, a Mexican gardener; Charles Aznavour, a hunchback; and Richard Burton, an alcoholic Welsh poet?

4500. What famous comedian played the Tin Woodman in the 1925 silent-movie version of *The Wizard of Oz*?

4501. Who was the first black performer signed to a long-term contract by a major Hollywood studio?

4502. Where did the Warner Brothers—Jack, Harry, Sam and Albert—get the 99 chairs they used in the first theater they opened in 1903 in New Castle, Pennsylvania?

4503. Where was Anthony "Zorba the Greek" Quinn born?

4504. Whose ashes does actor Marlon Brando keep in his home in Tahiti?

4505. What was the name of Hollywood's first 3-D movie, released in 1952?

4506. Who portrayed Mia Farrow's sister in Woody Allen's *Zelig* and *The Purple Rose of Cairo*?

4507. What famous funnyman co-authored the 1974 film comedy *Blazing Saddles* with actor-director Mel Brooks?

4508. In what film did actress Dorothy Lamour first don a sarong?

4495. *Emil Jannings.*

4496. *Sean Connery, best known for his James Bond portrayal.*

4497. *In the Philippines.*

4498. *W. C. Fields.*

4499. Candy, *based on Terry Southern's novel.*

4500. *Oliver Hardy, of Laurel and Hardy fame.*

4501. *Singer Lena Horne, in 1942. The studio was Metro-Goldwyn-Mayer.*

4502. *From the local undertaker. The chairs had to be returned whenever there was a funeral.*

4503. *In Chihuahua, Mexico.*

4504. *Those of his childhood friend, comedian Wally Cox, who died in 1973.*

4505. Bwana Devil.

4506. *Mia's sister, Stephanie Farrow.*

4507. *Richard Pryor.*

4508. *In her very first movie,* The Jungle Princess, *in 1936—four years before her first "Road" movie with Bob Hope and Bing Crosby.*

4509. What famous leading man turned down the role of Rhett Butler in *Gone With the Wind* and predicted it would be "the biggest flop in Hollywood history"?

4510. On what day of the week was actress Tuesday Weld born?

4511. Which two top Hollywood stars turned down the role of Professor Henry Higgins in the film version of *My Fair Lady* before Rex Harrison was offered the part?

4512. From what earlier stage name did actress-comedienne Whoopi Goldberg derive her current name?

4513. What two Frank Sinatra movie thrillers did Ole Blue Eyes own and order shelved for years because of their frightening political themes?

4514. Who played Robert Redford's laid-back rodeo pal and manager in the 1979 film *The Electric Horseman*?

4515. What actor was dropped by Universal Studios in the early 1950s because of his protruding Adam's apple and slow speech?

4516. What star—seven months pregnant with her first child— sang the Oscar-winning song "Once I Had a Secret Love" at the 1953 Academy Awards show?

4517. Ronald Reagan used a famous line from one of his movies as the title of his 1965 autobiography. What's the line?

4518. The family name of what famous fictional sleuth was Charalambides before it was anglicized by an immigration official on Ellis Island?

4519. What unusual stipulation was included in funnyman Buster Keaton's contract with MGM?

4520. What song does Kate Capshaw sing in broken Chinese in the opening scene of the 1984 film Indiana Jones and the *Temple of Doom*?

4509. *Gary Cooper.*

4510. *Friday—August 27, 1943.*

4511. *Cary Grant and James Cagney.*

4512. *Whoopi Cushion.*

4513. The Manchurian Candidate, *made in 1962, and* Suddenly, *made in 1954—both of which dealt with political assassinations.*

4514. *Country singer Willie Nelson.*

4515. *Clint Eastwood.*

4516. *Ann Blyth sang the song, which was from the movie* Calamity Jane.

4517. *"Where's the rest of me?"—words he delivered in the 1941 film "King's Row" when he woke up and discovered both his legs had been amputated.*

4518. *"The Thin Man" Nick Charles.*

4519. *He was not to smile in public.*

4520. *The Cole Porter classic* Anything Goes.

4521. Robert Redford turned down the lead role in *The Graduate* because he considered himself too old. How old was Dustin Hoffman when he took the part?

4522. The mother of what famous European actress once won a Great Garbo look-alike contest and a trip to Hollywood to work as Garbo's double?

4523. What actress changed her name to avoid seeking fame and fortune as Sarah Jane Fulks?

4524. Who played Gypsy Rose Lee's younger sister June in the 1962 movie *Gypsy* ?

4525. What Alfred Hitchcock classic was filmed but not released in 3-D?

4526. What was the last Hollywood film made by silver-screen legend Cary Grant?

4527. With whom did Dorothy live in the film classic *The Wizard of Oz* ?

4528. What was the name of the killer whale movie made in 1977 in a bid to cash in on the popularity of the killer shark shocker *Jaws* ?

4529. What actor, following his 1966 film debut as a bellboy in *Dead Heat on a Merry-Go-Round*, was told, "Kid, you ain't got it"?

4530. What was the name of the chimpanzee that starred with Ronald Reagan in the 1951 film *Bedtime for Bonzo* ?

4531. What popular 1982 film was banned in Sweden because it showed parents acting hostilely toward their children?

4532. What film so embarrassed star Katharine Hepburn that she offered to make another movie without salary if RKO withheld its release?

4533. How much was Jacqueline Onassis reportedly offered to portray herself in the 1978 film *The Greek Tycoon* ?

4521. *Thirty—the same age as Redford.*

4522. *Sophia Loren. But her mother never made the trip because her own mother (Sophia's grandmother) wouldn't let her.*

4523. *Jane Wyman.*

4524. *Ann Jillian.*

4525. *His 1954 chiller,* Dial M for Murder.

4526. Walk, Don't Run, *in 1966.*

4527. *Her Auntie Em and Uncle Henry.*

4528. Orca.

4529. *Harrison Ford.*

4530. *Peggy. The talented chimp also appeared in Johnny Weissmuller's* Jungle Jim *movies.*

4531. E.T

4532. Sylvia Scarlett. *Hepburn plays a young woman who dresses like a boy in the film, which was released in 1935. Her co-star was Cary Grant.*

4533. *$1 million. Jacqueline Bisset took the role for half that amount.*

4534. For what 1969 film did poet Rod McKuen write the popular Oscar-nominated ballad "Jean"?

4535. In what 1950 film classic did Cecil B. DeMille, Buster Keaton and Hedda Hopper all play themselves?

4536. The film version of what great novel had its title changed to *Lost Child in Foggy City* when it was shown in China?

4537. What condition does Roger Moore include in all his film contracts?

4538. Who played Major Major, the timid squadron leader, in the 1970 film *Catch 22* ?

4539. Under what title was the 1978 hit movie *Grease* released in Venezuela?

4540. Who was the highest paid star in the 1943 film classic *Casablanca* ?

4541. Who played Dirty Harry Callahan's cute rookie partner in Clint Eastwood's 1976 film *The Enforcer* ?

4542. Who played the female lead in *Satan Met a Lady*, the 1936 film version of Dashiell Hammett's *The Maltese Falcon* ?

4543. Who spoke only Sioux in portraying an Indian named Buffalo Cow Head in the 1970 film *A Man Called Horse* ?

4544. Who played the role of Jack Nicholson's bowling alley pickup in *Five Easy Pieces* ?

4545. What actor appeared in more Alfred Hitchcock thrillers than any other?

4546. What 1977 film included "first aid" in its list of credits?

4547. Who was the only female to appear in the 1954 film classic *Bad Day at Black Rock* ?

4548. What famous child star failed her screen test for a part in the *Our Gang movie comedies*?

4534. The Prime of Miss Jean Brodie.

4535. Sunset Boulevard, *starring Gloria Swanson and William Holden.*

4536. Oliver Twist, *by Charles Dickens.*

4537. *That he be provided with an unlimited supply of hand-rolled Cuban cigars while on location.*

4538. *Bob Newhart.*

4539. Vaselina.

4540. *Not Bogart, Bergman, Greenstreet, Raines, or Lorre—but Conrad Veidt. He was paid $5,000 a week to portray Major Strasser.*

4541. *Tyne Daly, who went on to become veteran cop Mary Beth Lacey on TV's* Cagney & Lacey.

4542. *Bette Davis.*

4543. *Dame Judith Anderson.*

4544. *Sally Struthers.*

4545. *Leo G. Carroll. He was in five—*Suspicion, Spellbound, The Paradine Case, Strangers on a Train *and* North by Northwest.

4546. The Gauntlet, *a chase film starring Clint Eastwood.*

4547. *Anne Francis, who played the young gas station operator who was one of the 37 residents of Black Rock. The male cast included Spencer Tracy, Robert Ryan, Dean Jagger, Walter Brennan, John Ericson, Ernest Borgnine and Lee Marvin.*

4548. *Shirley Temple.*

4549. Who was the first American movie star to headline in a film directed by Sweden's Ingmar Bergman?

4550. Who won the Oscar for best supporting actress in 1983— for her portrayal of a man?

4551. How old was actor Sydney Greenstreet when he made his screen debut?

4552. What actor appeared as a fig leaf in a Fruit of the Loom television commercial before he landed an Oscar-winning role?

4553. Can you name the four sets of brothers featured in *The Long Riders*, a 1980 film about the James gang?

4554. What size bra did Dustin Hoffman wear in the 1982 film *Tootsie* ?

4555. What Oscar-winning actress placed a three-page thank you note in a movie trade paper listing all the people she had forgotten to mention in her 1987 acceptance speech?

4556. Who did James Cagney want to play the lead role in his life story?

4557. What was the name of the prince who woke up Sleeping Beauty with a kiss in the Walt Disney version of the popular fairy tale?

4558. Dudley Moore appeared in the 1984 film *Unfaithfully Yours*, about a conductor who suspects his wife is cheating on him. Who appeared in the same role in the 1948 film of the same name?

4559. Caryn Johnson is a well-known comedienne, but she performs under another name. What is it?

4560. What comic-to-be made his movie debut at age five as a little boy thrown from a moving train in the cliff-hanger serial *The Perils of Pauline* ?

4561. What late Broadway and Hollywood entertainer is known by a grade school nickname he acquired because of his poor marks?

4549. *Elliott Gould, in 1971. The film was* The Touch.

4550. *Linda Hunt. The film was* The Year of Living Dangerously.

4551. *He was 62. The movie was John Huston's* The Maltese Falcon; *the year, 1941.*

4552. *Murray Abraham, who won a best actor Academy Award in 1984 for his portrayal of Salieri in* Amadeus.

4553. *Stacy and James Keach as the James brothers; David, Keith and Robert Carradine as the Younger brothers; Randy and Dennis Quaid as the Miller brothers; and Nicholas and Christopher Guest as the Ford brothers.*

4554. *Size 36C.*

4555. *Cher, who won the best actress Oscar for her performance in* Moonstruck.

4556. *Michael J. Fox.*

4557. *Prince Philip. (Sleeping Beauty's name was Princess Aurora.)*

4558. *Rex Harrison.*

4559. *Whoopi Goldberg.*

4560. *Milton Berle.*

4561. *Zero Mostel, who was born Samuel Mostel.*

4562. Who is seen hitting the jackpot at a slot machine in a brief cameo appearance in the 1956 film *Meet Me in Las Vegas*?

4563. Can you name the two students Actors Studio guru Lee Strasberg said stood out "way above the rest"?

4564. What was distinctive about the line of towels introduced as a commercial tie-in to the 1939 film extravaganza *Ben Hur*?

4565. How many rats were specifically bred for the film *Indiana Jones and the Last Crusade*?

4566. What famous comic once doubled for actress Dolores Del Rio by jumping from the second-story window of a Klondike saloon in a flowing black wig and can-can dress?

4567. Who appeared at the 1968 Academy Awards celebration in a see-through pants suit?

4568. What famous Hollywood husband and wife met when both were working as understudies for the 1953 Broadway production of *Picnic*?

4569. By what name is S.P. Eagle, the producer of *The African Queen*, better known?

4570. What woman sports figure appeared as a maid in John Ford's 1959 film classic *The Horse Soldiers*?

4571. What was the last line ever spoken by Marilyn Monroe on the silver screen?

4572. What famous American acting family has a town in New York named after it—thanks to an ancestor who settled there in the seventeenth century?

4573. What famous actress once said, "The less I behave like Whistler's mother the night before, the more I look like her the morning after"?

4574. What Steve Martin movie was shown in Spanish-speaking countries under the title *Better Alone Than Badly Accompanied*?

4562. *Frank Sinatra.*

4563. *Marlon Brando and Marilyn Monroe.*

4564. *They were marked "Ben-His" and "Ben-Hers."*

4565. *3,000.*

4566. *Lou Costello, the hefty half of the Abbott and Costello team. The silent movie was* The Trail of '98.

4567. *Barbra Streisand. The following year she showed up in what one writer described as a "nice pink bar-mitzvah mother dress."*

4568. *Joanne Woodward and Paul Newman.*

4569. *Sam Spiegel. The Polish-born producer of* The Bridge on the River Kwai, Lawrence of Arabia, *and* On the Waterfront *used the pseudonym S.P. Eagle until 1954.*

4570. *Tennis star Althea Gibson.*

4571. *"How do you find your way back in the dark?" The line, said to Clark Gable, came at the end of the 1961 film* The Misfits. *She died in 1962.*

4572. *The Fondas. Their ancestors emigrated from Italy to the Netherlands in the fifteenth century, and two centuries later one of their descendants— Douw Fonda—sailed to America and settled in upstate New York.*

4573. *Tallulah Bankhead.*

4574. Planes, Trains and Automobiles, *the wacky 1987 comedy in which he co-starred with John Candy.*

4575. What actor turned down the roles played by Humphrey Bogart in the movies *High Sierra*, *The Maltese Falcon* and *Dead End*?

4576. On what cliffs did silent film serial queen Pearl ("Perils of Pauline") White do her famous cliff-hanging?

4577. What African political leader portrayed a tribal chief in the 1935 British adventure film *Sanders of the River*?

4578. In Japan, they called this 1962 movie thriller *We Don't Want a Doctor*. What was its title in the United States?

4579. What famous playwright wrote the Oscar-winning screenplay for the 1976 movie *Network*?

4580. What Hollywood legend spent three days in jail in 1916 after being arrested by New York vice squad detectives on charges of blackmail?

4581. In what film do the two main characters meet when one asks the other, "Hey, boy, what you doin' with my momma's car?"

4582. What 1954 film classic was based on a series of prize-winning exposés published in a New York newspaper?

4583. In the 1939 Hollywood classic *The Wizard of Oz*, what directions did Glinda, the good witch, give Dorothy for getting back home to Kansas?

4584. How much was Dustin Hoffman paid for appearing in the title role of the 1967 hit *The Graduate*, which grossed $80 million?

4585. Why was famed opera singer Enrico Caruso's first film, *My Cousin*, a big flop and his second film, *The Splendid Romance*, never released?

4586. What 1957 film was based on the life of Christine Sizemore? Hint: an actress won an Oscar for her performance in the title role.

4587. Where did director Elia Kazan shoot *Splendor in the Grass*, the 1961 Natalie Wood-Warren Beatty hit film about hot-blooded teenage love in Kansas in the late 1920s?

4575. *George Raft.*

4576. *On the Pallisades—on the western shore of the Hudson River, across from New York City.*

4577. *Jomo Kenyatta, who went on to become president of Kenya.*

4578. Doctor No. *It was the first of the James Bond film series.*

4579. *Paddy Chayefsky, who earlier gave us* Marty.

4580. *Rudolph Valentino.*

4581. Bonnie and Clyde. *Bonnie (Faye Dunaway) asks the question of Clyde (Warren Beatty) as he's about to drive off with her mother's car.*

4582. On the Waterfront. *The articles, by Malcolm Johnson of the* New York Sun, *exposed waterfront crime.*

4583. *"Close your eyes and tap your heels together three times. And think to yourself, there's no place like home."*

4584. *He got $750 a week—for a total of about $20,000—and graduated to the big time.*

4585. *Both were silent movies—not a big box-office draw for a professional singer.*

4586. *The film was* The Three Faces of Eve; *the actress, Joanne Woodward.*

4587. *On Staten Island, the least populated of New York City's five boroughs.*

4588. Who created the role of finicky Felix Ungar in 1965 in the original Broadway production of *The Odd Couple* ?

4589. What aspiring actor changed his name in 1938 after a movie executive told him, "Beedle! It sounds like an insect!"

4590. John Wayne wore a variety of studio-issued military uniforms in the movies. Which did he wear in real life?

4591. What Alfred Hitchcock spy thriller was almost called *The Man on Lincoln's Nose* ?

4592. Who was crowned the first Artichoke Queen in Castroville, California, the self-proclaimed "artichoke capital of the world"?

4593. Who played Santini, the mentally retarded student, in the 1955 film classic *The Blackboard Jungle* ?

4594. Who turned down the movie role of Eliza's father, Alfred P. Doolittle, in *My Fair Lady* before Stanley Holloway got the part?

4595. In the 1961 film *Breakfast at Tiffany's,* what are stars Audrey Hepburn and George Peppard shown when they ask a Tiffany salesman for something in the $10 range?

4596. Why were 30 acres of old movie sets in Culver City, California, put to the torch in 1938?

4597. Jack Nicholson won an Oscar for his portrayal of Randle P. McMurphy in the 1975 film *One Flew Over the Cuckoo's Nest.* Who starred in the same role on Broadway in 1963?

4598. What performers were originally sought as co-stars for *The Road to Singapore,* the first of the popular "Road" films that featured Bing Crosby and Bob Hope?

4599. What popular actor worked as an efficiency expert for the Connecticut State Budget Bureau before pursuing his acting career?

4600. What was the name of Mickey Rooney's mythical hometown in the "Andy Hardy" film series?

4588. *Art Carney, best known for his portrayal of far-from-finicky sewer worker Ed Norton on Jackie Gleason's* The Honeymooners. *Walter Matthau played Oscar Madison.*

4589. *William Holden, who was named William Beedle at birth.*

4590. *None. He was granted an exemption from military duty during World War II as a father of four and the sole support of his widowed mother.*

4591. North by Northwest, *starring Cary Grant and Eva Marie Saint. The title that didn't make it referred to a key scene that takes place on Mount Rushmore in the 1959 film.*

4592. *Marilyn Monroe. The year was 1947 and Monroe was then a little-known Hollywood starlet.*

4593. *Jamie Farr, best known for his portrayal of nutty, cross-dressing corporal Maxwell Klinger on TV's* M*A*S*H. *He is listed in the movie credits under his given name, Jameel Farah.*

4594. *James Cagney.*

4595. *A sterling silver telephone dialer for $6.75. They don't buy it.*

4596. *To recreate blazing, battle-torn Atlanta for the 1939 film classic* Gone With the Wind.

4597. *Kirk Douglas.*

4598. *George Burns and Fred MacMurray. Hope and Crosby were signed up after MacMurray turned down the project.*

4599. *Peter Falk.*

4600. *Carvel.*

4601. What film star launched his Hollywood career as a $5-a-day extra, portraying a swarthy Mexican soldier in Douglas Fairbanks Sr.'s film "His Majesty, the American"?

4602. What famous character actor—best known for his sinister screen roles—was a tea planter in Ceylon before he turned thespian?

4603. What famous actress made her stage debut portraying a boy in Henrik Ibsen's *A Doll's House*?

4604. What star-to-be appeared on Broadway in 1954 as the insolent homosexual Arab houseboy in André Gide's *The Immoralist*?

4605. Who was the first movie star to deliver the oft-repeated line, "We could have made beautiful music together"?

4606. Who won the Oscar for best actress in 1950—beating out Bette Davis, who starred in *All About Eve*, and Gloria Swanson, who appeared in *Sunset Boulevard*?

4607. Who sang the role of Prince Charming in the 1937 Walt Disney classic *Snow White and the Seven Dwarfs*?

4608. What is the "Oscar" of the saddle-and-spurs set—the award given to entertainers branded the best in the world of movie and TV westerns?

4609. What were the names of the three good fairies in Walt Disney's 1959 movie *Sleeping Beauty*?

4610. What voice do the movies *The King and I, My Fair Lady* and *West Side Story* have in common?

4611. What film star would have been known as Lucille Le Sueur if Hollywood hadn't changed her name after she was discovered in a Broadway chorus?

4612. Actor Sylvester Stallone appeared in a Japanese television commercial in 1989. What was he promoting?

4601. *Boris Karloff, in 1919.*

4602. *Sydney Greenstreet.*

4603. *Joan Collins.*

4604. *James Dean.*

4605. *Gary Cooper, in the 1936 film* The General Died at Dawn. *The line was delivered to Madeleine Carroll.*

4606. *Judy Holliday, for her performance in* Born Yesterday.

4607. *Harry Stockwell, actor-singer father of Dean Stockwell.*

4608. *The Golden Boot.*

4609. *Fauna, the fairy of song; Flora, the fairy of beauty; and Merryweather, the fairy of happiness.*

4610. *That of Marni Nixon. She dubbed the singing for Deborah Kerr, Audrey Hepburn and Natalie Wood.*

4611. *Joan Crawford.*

4612. *Processed ham. There was a stipulation in his contract that the commercial not be shown in the U.S.*

4613. Sales of what part of the male wardrobe dropped sharply after Clark Gable appeared in the romantic comedy *It Happened One Night* in 1934?

4614. Whose family planned to erect a headstone that was a two-ton, nine-foot-tall marble replica of the Oscar—until the Academy of Motion Picture Arts and Sciences complained that it would be a copyright infringement?

4615. In how many films did Katharine Hepburn and Spencer Tracy appear together?

4616. What actor was the first man to appear on the cover of *Playboy* magazine?

4617. Who cursed more—Elizabeth Taylor or Richard Burton—and by how much in the 1966 film *Who's Afraid of Virginia Woolf?*

4618. In how many of his 200 films did Hollywood legend John Wayne die?

4619. What Hollywood great was originally cast in the title role *The Adventures of Robin Hood*—the 1938 film that starred the dashing Errol Flynn?

4620. Who dubbed gagging noises for actress Vivien Leigh in the 1939 film classic *Gone With the Wind*?

4621. What all-American Hollywood leading man appeared in the movies *Arizona Bound, Nevada, The Virginian, The Texan* and *A Man from Wyoming*?

4622. Who portrayed Vito Corleone as a young man in the 1974 film *The Godfather II*?

4623. What 1972 movie won an Oscar for its theme song, "The Morning After"—a song that earned singer Maureen McGovern a gold record?

4624. For what film did Cary Grant delay his honeymoon with his second wife, Woolworth heiress Barbara Hutton, in 1942?

4613. *The undershirt. Gable didn't wear one in the film.*

4614. *Showman Mike Todd's.*

4615. *Nine*—Woman of the Year, Keeper of the Flame, Without Love, Sea of Grass, State of the Union, Adam's Rib, Pat and Mike, The Desk Set and Guess Who's Coming to Dinner?

4616. *Peter Sellers, in 1964.*

4617. *Burton, by two. It was Burton, 24; Taylor, 22.*

4618. *In eight*—Reap the Wild Wind, The Fighting Seabees, The Wake of the Red Witch, Sands of Iwo Jima, The Alamo, The Man Who Shot Liberty Valance, The Cowboys and The Shootist.

4619. *James Cagney. He quit the movie in a contract dispute with Warner Brothers.*

4620. *Actress Olivia de Havilland, who played Melanie in the movie. Leigh, in the starring role of Scarlett O'Hara, refused to make the unladylike sounds when she choked on a radish in her vegetable-garden scene.*

4621. *Gary Cooper—who also starred in* It's a Big Country.

4622. *Robert De Niro.*

4623. The Poseidon Adventure.

4624. Once Upon a Honeymoon, *in which he co-starred with Ginger Rogers.*

4625. Actor Matthew Broderick was offered the lead in the 1983 film *War Games* after Kevin Costner turned it down to take a lesser role in what other film?

4626. Who played Moses as a baby in the 1956 film spectacular *The Ten Commandments*, which starred Charlton Heston?

4627. What famous leading man appeared in drag in two Marlene Dietrich movies?

4628. What substance was used as fuel for the time-traveling car in *Back to the Future Part II* ?

4629. What famous entertainer turned down the role of Romeo in Franco Zeffirelli's 1968 version of Shakespeare's *Romeo and Juliet* before the part was given to teen unknown Leonard Whiting?

4630. According to Hollywood legend, what famous tradition was started in 1927 after actress Norma Talmadge tripped while walking along the street with Douglas Fairbanks Jr. and Mary Pickford?

4631. What was the name of the motorcycle gang led by Lee Marvin in the 1954 Marlon Brando biker movie *The Wild One* ?

4632. What 1937 film starring Humphrey Bogart, Edward G. Robinson, Bette Davis and Wayne Morris is shown on television under the title *Battling Bellhop* to avoid confusion with a 1962 Elvis Presley musical remake?

4633. Who did actor Steve McQueen replace when he was hired to appear in Frank Sinatra's 1959 war film *Never So Few*?

4634. How much per hour did Paramount Pictures pay the U.S. Defense Department for each of the $37 million F-14 jets used in the 1986 Tom Cruise film *Top Gun*?

4635. How much was actor Burt Reynolds paid for posing as *Cosmopolitan* magazine's first nude centerfold in April 1972?

4636. What physical feature did both Rudolph Valentino and George Raft have changed with plastic surgery?

4625. The Big Chill. *Costner signed up to play Alex, the character whose suicide leads to the reunion that provides the movie's setting, but he's not seen in the film. His part—a 15-minute flashback scene—ended up on the cutting room floor.*

4626. *Heston's son Fraser, who grew up to become a screenwriter and motion picture producer.*

4627. *John Wayne—in* Seven Sinners *in 1940 and* The Spoilers *in 1942.*

4628. *Miller beer. The car was a DeLorean.*

4629. *Paul McCartney.*

4630. *Having movie stars leave hand- or footprints on the sidewalk outside Grauman's Chinese Theatre. That's where Talmadge tripped and fell into wet cement.*

4631. *The Beetles.*

4632. Kid Galahad.

4633. *Sinatra's "rat pack" buddy Sammy Davis Jr., who was dropped from the cast following a quarrel with Sinatra.*

4634. *$7,600. The total paid to the Defense Department for equipment and assistance was $1.2 million.*

4635. *He got what he was wearing—absolutely nothing. He posed for free.*

4636. *Their bat ears.*

4637. What common location was used in filming the movies *The Graduate*, *Cocoon*, *Gross Anatomy*, *Shocker*, *The Paper Chase* and both the 1939 and 1982 versions of *The Hunchback of Notre Dame*?

4638. Child actress Shirley Temple was famous for her long curls. How many did she have?

4639. What famous Hollywood character actor portrayed the evil ex-con Gruesome in a 1947 Dick Tracy film?

4640. What film did Notre Dame try to keep off the silver screen in 1965 by going to court?

4641. How did Elizabeth Taylor's rebellious brother, Howard, get out of the screen test—and acting career—his stagestruck mother had set up for him?

4642. What movie star was one of both *The Magnificent Seven* and *The Dirty Dozen*?

4643. What well-known Hollywood producer is the grandson of the man who developed a popular vegetable?

4644. The summer of 1989 was dubbed the "Summer of Sequels." Can you name the eight film sequels that were responsible for this?

4645. What Oscar-winning actor appeared on Broadway in the early 1960s as Rolf, the youth who sings "You Are Sixteen," in the Rodgers and Hammerstein hit musical *The Sound of Music*?

4646. What actors represented *The Good, the Bad and the Ugly* in the 1966 Sergio Leone epic about three drifters in search of a treasure?

4647. What is the name of the actress daughter of Jessica Tandy and Hume Cronyn?

4648. In what film did former television talk-show host Arsenio Hall make his movie debut?

4649. What is actor Michael J. Fox's real middle initial?

4637. *The campus of the University of Southern California, in Los Angeles.*

4638. *55—not counting the spit curl on her forehead.*

4639. *Boris Karloff.*

4640. John Goldfarb, Please Come Home. *In the movie, Richard Crenna plays a Jew forced by an Arab king to coach an Arab football team to beat Notre Dame because the king's son had been cut from its team.*

4641. *He shaved his head on the eve of the scheduled screen test.*

4642. *Charles Bronson.*

4643. *Albert "Cubby" Broccoli, whose grandfather developed the broccoli in Italy. The vegetable was introduced to America in the 1870s by Broccoli's uncle, Pasquale de Cicco.*

4644. Friday the 13th Part VIII: Jason Takes Manhattan*;* Ghostbusters I *;* Indiana Jones and the Last Crusade*;* The Karate Kid III*;* Lethal Weapon II; License to Kill *(in the James Bond series);* Nightmare on Elm Street V: The Dream Child*; and* Star Trek V: The Final Frontier.

4645. *Jon Voight.*

4646. *Clint Eastwood was the Good; Lee Van Cleef, the Bad; and Eli Wallach, the Ugly.*

4647. *Tandy Cronyn.*

4648. Amazon Women on the Moon, *in 1987.*

4649. *A, for Andrew. He had to use an initial under Screen Actors Guild regulations because there was already an actor named Michael Fox, but he didn't want to use A. because of the word play it suggested. He opted for J. out of admiration for character actor Michael J. Pollard.*

4650. What actress once performed as a singer and keyboard player with an all-girl band known as Psychotic Kindergarten?

4651. What was the theme song of comics Laurel and Hardy?

4652. Who was the first American movie director to be paid $1 million to direct a single film?

4653. What did the makeup people do to actress Lana Turner during the filming of *The Adventures of Marco Polo* in 1938 that permanently altered her features?

4654. What is the name of the friendly skunk in Walt Disney's *Bambi*?

4655. The 1987 film *Three Men and a Baby*, starring Tom Selleck, Steve Guttenberg and Ted Danson, is the American version of what very successful French film that came out a year earlier?

4656. What two-time Oscar-winning actress played young Jane Eyre's saintly, consumptive friend in the 1944 film that featured Joan Fontaine in the title role?

4657. What was Pluto's name when he made his debut in 1930 in a Mickey Mouse film?

4658. How old was Orson Welles when he co-wrote, produced, directed and starred in the 1941 film classic *Citizen Kane*?

4659. As a toddler, what famous movie-star-to-be had his picture on packages of baby food?

4660. What popular actor is married to Melissa Mathison, the writer who provided the screenplay for *E.T.*?

4661. What actress appeared on a magazine cover in the late 1970s with director Louis Malle's name tattooed on her breast?

4662. In how many Alfred Hitchcock movies did James Stewart appear? What were they?

4663. Actor Gary Cooper's given name at birth was Frank. What inspired an agent to change it to Gary?

4650. *Daryl Hannah.*

4651. *"The Dancing Cuckoos."*

4652. *Mike Nichols, in 1967, for "The Graduate."*

4653. *For her role as a Eurasian handmaiden, they shaved off her eyebrows regularly for three weeks and replaced them with false slanting eyebrows. As a result, her eyebrows never grew back and she had to either draw them in or paste them on ever after.*

4654. *Flower.*

4655. Three Men and a Cradle.

4656. *Elizabeth Taylor, who was 12 at the time.*

4657. *Rover. The film was* Chain Gang, *a short, in which he had a small role as Minnie Mouse's dog.*

4658. *25.*

4659. *Humphrey Bogart. His mother, a commercial artist, used him as the model for a picture that was used on packages of Mellins baby food.*

4660. *Harrison Ford.*

4661. *Susan Sarandon. Malle was her boyfriend at the time.*

4662. *Four—*Rope *(1948),* Rear Window *(1954),*The Man Who Knew Too Much *(1956) and* Vertigo *(1958).*

4663. *The agent's hometown—Gary, Indiana.*

4664. Who was Thomas "Pop" Dennehy, the prototype for the unseen "Mr. Dennehy" in comedian Jackie Gleason's "Joe the Bartender" skits?

4665. What actor operated a hot-dog stand known as "Tiny's" before making it big in films?

4666. What Hollywood leading man was once a dancer with the Eliot Feld Ballet company?

4667. What Hollywood star turned down the Jack Nicholson role in *The Witches of Eastwick*, the Dustin Hoffman role in *Rain Man* and the title role in *Batman*?

4668. In the 1988 Oscar-winning movie *Rain Man*, the character portrayed by Dustin Hoffman memorizes a telephone book up to the names Marsha and William Gottsegen. Who are they?

4669. What film role was James Dean next scheduled to play when he died in 1955?

4670. Who accepted the Academy Award for best actress in a gown she made herself out of $100 worth of fabric?

4671. For what film did Hollywood hold its first nude screen tests?

4672. What are the names of the young husband and wife who own Lady in Walt Disney's 1955 animated classic *Lady and the Tramp*?

4673. How many years passed between Paul Newman's making of *The Hustler* and its sequel, *The Color of Money*?

4674. What was the size of Scarlett O'Hara's waist in the Margaret Mitchell classic *Gone With the Wind*?

4675. What Oscar-winning actress dubbed the hair-raising voice of the devil in the 1973 chiller *The Exorcist*?

4676. Why did actor Gary Cooper dress in a Yankee uniform with New York spelled backward during the filming of *The Pride of the Yankees*, the story of Lou Gehrig?

4664. *The superintendent of the apartment building Gleason lived in when he was growing up in Brooklyn, New York.*

4665. *Actor Alan Ladd, who was about 5 feet 6 inches tall.*

4666. *Patrick Swayze, who dazzled us with his dancing in the 1987 film* Dirty Dancing.

4667. *Bill Murray.*

4668. *Hoffman's mother- and father-in-law.*

4669. *Boxer Rocky Graziano, in* Somebody Up There Likes Me—*the role that set Paul Newman on the road to stardom.*

4670. *Joanne Woodward. She won her Oscar for* The Three Faces of Eve *in 1957.*

4671. Four for Texas, *a 1963 Western comedy starring Anita Ekberg and Ursula Andress, along with Frank Sinatra and Dean Martin. The screen tests proved unnecessary—censors cut all the nude scenes.*

4672. *He's "Jim, Dear"; she's "Darling."*

4673. *25.* The Hustler *was filmed in 1961;* The Color of Money *in 1986.*

4674. *13 inches.*

4675. *Mercedes McCambridge.*

4676. *Because Gehrig was a lefty and Cooper was a righty. Cooper had tried to bat and field lefty for the part, but looked too awkward. So he was filmed batting righty and fielding righty from third base. Then the negative was reversed to make it look like he was playing lefty. In reversing the negative, New York was no longer spelled backward.*

4677. What was actor Willem Dafoe's name at birth?

4678. What was the only film directed by Marlon Brando?

4679. What did costume designer Edith Head say she was going to do with her Oscar when she accepted the coveted award for her contribution to the 1953 film *Roman Holiday*?

4680. What two Oscar-winning movie stars tied as "least likely to succeed" when they were students at the Pasadena Playhouse acting school?

4681. Joanne Woodward won an Oscar for her first film, The Three Faces of Eve. How many films did her husband Paul Newman appear in before he won an Oscar?

4682. In what city were scenes of the Brooklyn waterfront filmed for the 1954 Academy Award-winning movie *On the Waterfront*?

4683. What was movie hero Indiana Jones's first name?

4684. What famous entertainer's 1980 autobiography is entitled *A View from a Broad*.

4685. Robert De Niro sported 37 tattoos as a vengeful ex-con in the 1991 remake of the thriller *Cape Fear*. How many were his own?

4686. In how many films did Alan Hale play Robin Hood's strapping sidekick Little John?

4687. In the 1974 film *Alice Doesn't Live Here Any More*, what now-famous actress played Audrey, the street urchin who tried to get Alice's son to drink Ripple?

4688. Whom did author Ian Fleming suggest for the role of Agent 007 in the 1962 movie *Dr. No*, the first of Hollywood's James Bond films?

4689. What famous actor once portrayed a character named Badass Buddusky?

4677. *William Dafoe. Willem is the name he adopted in high school to avoid being called Billy.*

4678. *The 1961 movie* One Eyed Jacks.

4679. *She said, "I'm going to take it home and design a dress for it."*

4680. *Dustin Hoffman and Gene Hackman.*

4681. *46. Newman, a frequent nominee, won the Best Actor Oscar for The* Color of Money *in 1986. (Two years earlier, he had been given the Cecil B. DeMille Award for "outstanding contributions to the entertainment field.")*

4682. *Hoboken, New Jersey.*

4683. *Henry.*

4684. *Bette Middler's.*

4685. *Only one—the black panther on his right shoulder.*

4686. *Three—in the 1922 silent film Robin Hood, starring Douglas Fairbanks; in the 1938 film* The Adventures of Robin Hood, *with Errol Flynn in the title role; and in the 1950 film* Rogues of Sherwood Forest, *featuring John Derek as the son of Robin Hood.*

4687. *Jodie Foster.*

4688. *Composer-entertainer Hoagy Carmichael. The role, of course, went to Sean Connery.*

4689. *Jack Nicholson, in the 1973 film* The Last Detail.

4690. How many purebred Large White piglets appeared in the title role of *Babe*, the 1995 movie about a piglet that yearns to be a sheepdog?

4691. In what two films did Peter O'Toole portray England's King Henry II?

4692. What popular actor did poet Carl Sandburg describe as "one of the most beloved illiterates this country has ever known"?

4693. Who dubbed the voice of Draco, the dragon hero, in the 1996 film *Dragonheart*?

4694. What is writer-director-actor Woody Allen's legal name?

4695. What are the names of actor River Phoenix's four siblings?

4696. What two-time Academy Award-winning actress announced her retirement from the movies in 1992 after she was elected to Parliament in England?

4690. *48—all 11 weeks old. It was necessary to change piglets regularly because pigs grow fast and the film took 5 months to shoot. The film also used one "animatronic" robot pig.*

4691. Becket, *in 1964, and* The Lion in Winter, *in 1968.*

4692. *Gary Cooper.*

4693. *Sean Connery.*

4694. *Heywood Allen. He changed it from his birth name, Allen Stewart Konigsberg.*

4695. *Summer, Rainbow, Liberty and Joaquin (once known as Leaf).*

4696. *Glenda Jackson. She won Best Actress Oscars for* Women in Love *in 1970 and* A Touch of Class *in 1973.*

4697. In what two pictures did British comic actor Peter Sellers play three roles?

4698. What actress's father was the first American to be ordained a Tibetan Buddhist monk?

4699. What actress thanked 27 people in her Oscar acceptance speech—more than anyone else ever has?

4700. Who is the only entertainer to have five stars on Hollywood's Walk of Fame, one in each of the walk's five categories—film, TV, recording, radio and theater?

4701. What was the name of the 1970 sequel to the 1966 movie Hawaii?

4702. What actress sisters starred in the 1991 TV remake of the 1962 film *Whatever Happened to Baby Jane?*, which starred Joan Crawford and Bette Davis?

4703. What role did director John Huston play in his 1966 film epic *The Bible?*

4704. In what field of study did actor James Stewart earn a degree at Princeton University?

4705. Who played Beau Geste as a boy in the 1938 film *Sons of the Legion,* which featured Gary Cooper in the adult role?

4706. What is the entertainment publication *Variety* referring to when it uses the word helmer?

4707. Who dubbed James Dean's voice for his climactic "last supper" monologue in the 1956 film *Giant?*

4708. What was the name of the white mongrel with a brown spot over one eye that appeared with Charlie Chaplin in *It's a Dog's Life* and scores of other films?

4709. What does actor Keanu Reeves's first name mean in Hawaiian?

4697. The Mouse That Roared *in 1959 and* Dr. Strangelove, or How I learned to Stop Worrying and Love the Bomb *in 1963.*

4698. *Uma Thurman's. Her father, Robert, later renounced the monastic life.*

4699. *Olivia de Havilland, when she accepted the Oscar for Best Actress for her performance in the 1946 film* To Each His Own.

4700. *Gene Autry.*

4701. *The Hawaiians. Both films were drawn from the James Michener novel* Hawaii.

4702. *Lynn and Vanessa Redgrave.*

4703. *Noah.*

4704. *He received a B.S. in architecture in 1932, but never practiced.*

4705. *Donald O'Connor, who is perhaps best known for his comic dancing in* Singin' in the Rain. *He was 13 years old when he played young Beau.*

4706. *A director.*

4707. *Nick Adams. Shooting of the scene was finished just three days before Dean died.*

4708. *Scraps.*

4709. *"Cool breeze over the mountains." Reeves's father, who is of Chinese-Hawaiian ancestry, named his son after his own father.*

4710. What top film star made an unbilled cameo appearance as a TV news anchor in the 1987 film *Broadcast News*?

4711. In the 1983 film *The Man With Two Brains*, what actress provided the voice of the brain that Steve Martin loves and wants to transplant into his wife's body?

4712. Which Woody Allen movie was the first in which neither the filmmaker nor one of his real-life romantic partners appeared?

4713. What is the entertainment publication *Variety* referring to when it uses the word chopsocky?

4714. What movie and its sequel both won Academy Awards for Best Picture?

4715. Barry Fitzgerald appeared as matchmaker Michaleen Flynn in the 1952 John Ford comedy classic *The Quiet Man*. What role was played by his younger brother, Arthur Shields?

4716. What actress wrote her autobiography, *Little Girl Lost,* when she was just 14 years old?

4717. What well-known movie critic wrote the screenplay for the widely panned 1970 film *Beyond the Valley of the Dolls*?

4718. What is Demi Moore's full first name?

4719. What popular actor, while a student at Oxford, sought but did not get the role of Tarzan in the 1984 movie *Greystoke: The Legend of Tarzan, Lord of the Apes*?

4720. What line did a survey find had been spoken in 81 percent of the Hollywood films produced between 1938 and 1985?

4721. What was the name of the movie Marilyn Monroe was making when she died, and who was her co-star?

4722. What record-breaking hit movie used "A Boy's Life" as a working title to conceal its real subject until the release date?

4723. Artanis was the movie/television production company of which entertainer?

4710. *Jack Nicholson.*

4711. *Sissy Spacek.*

4712. Bullets Over Broadway, *in 1994.*

4713. *A martial arts film.*

4714. The Godfather *(1972) and* The Godfather, Part II *(1974).*

4715. *Rev. Cyril Playfair, the Protestant minister with a dwindling congregation. Irish-born Fitzgerald was born William Joseph Shields but adopted a stage name for fear of losing his civil service job.*

4716. *Drew Barrymore.*

4717. *Roger Ebert.*

4718. *Demetria. Her name at birth was Demetria Guynes. Moore was her first husband's surname.*

4719. *Hugh Grant.*

4720. *"Let's get outta here."*

4721. Something's Got to Give, *with Dean Martin. The movie was later remade as* Move Over Darling, *with Doris Day and James Garner.*

4722. E.T.- the Extra-Terrestrial.

4723. *Frank Sinatra. "Artanis" is "Sinatra" spelled backwards.*

4724. What was the original title of Elvis Presley's 1956 movie debut, *Love Me Tender*?

4725. On what ship did Dr. Doolittle and his friends sail in the 1967 film, *Dr. Doolittle*?

4726. Who are the youngest male and female performers to win Oscars for acting?

4727. Susan Hayward was nominated for an Oscar for three movies in which she played an alcoholic. What were the films?

4728. Henry Winkler and Susan Dey both turned down leading roles in the 1978 film version of a Broadway play that went on to become a huge success—both at the box office and for the people who ultimately took the parts. What was the film?

4729. What bleak, futuristic 1982 movie was based on Philip K. Dick's story, *Do Androids Dream of Electric Sheep?*?

4730. What do Marilyn Monroe, Elizabeth Taylor, Grace Kelly and Brooke Shields have in common, besides their obvious charms?

4731. For what film was the admission price to a movie first raised to $1.00?

4732. Which well known actress provided part of the speaking voice for the loveable alien, in the 1982 movie, *E.T.—The Extra-Terrestrial*?

4733. In what movie did ex-football player Alex Karras play Squash?

4734. Who was the lowest-paid contract player in Hollywood's history?

4735. Other than being film stars, what do Doris Day and Marlon Brando have in common?

4736. In 1965, John Wayne made a brief appearance in a movie, his only line being, "Truly, this was the Son of God." Name the film.

4724. The Reno Brothers.

4725. *The Flounder.*

4726. *Timothy Hutton, who won Best Supporting Actor for Taps at the age of 20; and Tatum O'Neal, who was awarded Best Supporting Actress for Paper Moon at the age of 10.*

4727. Smash-Up, the Story of a Woman *(1947),* My Foolish Heart *(1950), and* I'll Cry Tomorrow *(1956).*

4728. Grease, *starring John Travolta and Olivia Newton-John.*

4729. Blade Runner.

4730. *They have all had dolls modeled after them.*

4731. *For the silent film,* Quo Vadis, *in 1913.*

4732. *Debra Winger.*

4733. Victor/Victoria, *in 1982. Squash was his character's name.*

4734. *Robert Taylor, who signed a seven-year contract in 1934 for $35 a week.*

4735. *They were both born on April 3, 1924.*

4736. The Greatest Story Ever Told.

4737. The Oscar winners of Best Supporting Actress from 1978 to 1981 all had the same initials—M.S. Name all four of these talented ladies.

4738. What is Johnny Carson's only movie acting credit?

4739. Who is the only performer to have won Best Actor Oscars in consecutive years?

4740. In July 1978, what actor became the first male to appear on the cover of *McCall's* magazine in its 100-year-plus history?

4741. What popular 1965 comedy film was subtitled "Or: How I Flew From London To Paris In 25 Hours and 11 Minutes"?

4742. Who was the first child nominated for an Oscar?

4743. What 1977 hit movie featured a frantic search for Devil's Tower, Wyo., America's first national monument?

4744. During the shooting of what film did Grace Kelly meet her future husband, Prince Rainier of Monaco?

4745. Whose screen test was assessed as, "Can't act, can't sing, slightly bald, can dance a little"?

4746. Who was the butt of Constance Bennett's quip, "Now there's a broad with her future behind her"?

4747. What was the only word spoken in the 1976 Mel Brooks film, *Silent Movie*, and who said it?

4748. What was the only song from an Alfred Hitchcock movie ever to win an Oscar for Best Song?

4749. What future world leader appeared as an extra in the 1944 Esther Williams film, *Bathing Beauty*?

4750. Which actor turned down the role of Dr. Indiana Jones in the 1981 movie, *Raiders of the Lost Ark*?

4751. Who was the first American actress to be depicted on a postage stamp?

4737. *Maggie Smith (for* California Suite *in 1978), Meryl Streep (for* Kramer vs. Kramer *in 1979), Mary Steenburgen (for* Melvin and Howard *in 1980) and Maureen Stapleton (for* Reds *in 1981).*

4738. Looking for Love, *with Connie Francis, in 1965.*

4739. *Spencer Tracy, for* Captains Courageous *in 1937, and* Boy's Town *in 1938.*

4740. *John Travolta.*

4741. Those Magnificent Men In Their Flying Machines.

4742. *Jackie Cooper, nominated for Best Actor in 1930 for* Skippy.

4743. Close Encounters of the Third Kind.

4744. To Catch a Thief, *directed by Alfred Hitchcock, in 1955.*

4745. *Fred Astaire's.*

4746. *The young Marilyn Monroe.*

4747. *"No," spoken by mime Marcel Marceau.*

4748. *"Que Sera Sera" ("Whatever Will Be, Will Be") sung by Doris Day in the 1956 film,* The Man Who Knew Too Much.

4749. *Fidel Castro.*

4750. *Tom Selleck, citing his commitment to his TV series,* Magnum, P.I.

4751. *Grace Kelly, on a stamp in Monaco, (1956).*

4752. Who won an Oscar for Best Actor for portraying George M. Cohan, the composer of many patriotic tunes, including "You're a Grand Old Flag"?

4753. Which daughter of a U.S. President appeared with Elvis Presley in the 1964 film, *Kissin' Cousins*?

4754. Within five years of the 1961 release of the film *The Misfits*, three of its stars were dead. Who were they?

4755. From what monolithic building did the giant ape fall in the 1976 remake of the movie, *King Kong*?

4756. Who dubbed the speaking voices of the late actors Peter Sellers and David Niven in the 1983 movie, *The Curse of the Pink Panther*?

4757. Who narrated the 1943 World War II film, *Gung Ho*?

4758. Whose body was used as the model for Tinker Bell in Walt Disney's film, *Peter Pan* ?

4759. In what 1931 film did James Cagney push half a grapefruit into the face of Mae Clarke?

4760. What was the name of Luke Skywalker's home planet in the 1977 film, *Star Wars*?

4761. Who was the only performer in the sound era to win an Oscar for Best Actress without having uttered a word in the film for which she was nominated?

4762. Who was the first actor to appear on the cover of *Time* magazine?

4763. What was actor Stewart Granger's real name?

4764. What is the only X-rated film to win the Academy Award for Best Picture?

4765. Who is the only woman James Bond ever married?

4752. *James Cagney, for* Yankee Doodle Dandy, *in 1942.*

4753. *Maureen Reagan.*

4754. *Clark Gable, Marilyn Monroe and Montgomery Clift.*

4755. *From one of the twin towers of the World Trade Center.*

4756. *Rich Little.*

4757. *Newsman Chet Huntley.*

4758. *Marilyn Monroe's.*

4759. The Public Enemy.

4760. *Tatooine.*

4761. *Jane Wyman, as the deaf-mute in* Johnny Belinda, *in 1948.*

4762. *Charlie Chaplin, on July 6, 1925.*

4763. *James Stewart.*

4764. Midnight Cowboy, *in 1969 (the rating was later reduced to R).*

4765. *Teresa Draco in* On Her Majesty's Secret Service. *Miss Draco was killed soon after their marriage.*

4766. What was the first movie sequel to be filmed in the same year as the original?

4767. What movie record was set in the 1952 film, *Scaramouche*?

4768. James Cagney directed only one film. Name it.

4769. *Joliet Jake* was the working title of what 1980 film?

4770. Who was the only one of Snow White's seven dwarfs not to have a beard?

4771. Who is Ginger Rogers' famous red-headed cousin?

4772. For what 1959 film were some theater seats wired to give a mild shock to the audience?

4773. After the formation of their comedy team, what was the only film made by Lou Costello without Bud Abbott?

4774. Johnny Weismuller and Buster Crabbe, who both were Olympic swimming champions and played Tarzan in the movies, made only one film together. What was it?

4775. The famous advertisement, "Gable's back and Garson's got him," was used for what 1945 Clark Gable-Greer Garson film?

4776. Who was Barbra Streisand's first choice as her co-star in the 1976 remake of the movie, *A Star Is Born*?

4777. For what crime was Lucas Jackson (played by Paul Newman) convicted in the 1967 movie, *Cool Hand Luke*?

4778. Who is the only actor to win an Oscar for playing Santa Claus?

4779. The 1954 film *White Christmas*, starring Bing Crosby, was a remake of an earlier film in which he also starred, and which introduced the famous song. What was the title of the original film?

4780. What popular Hollywood actor calls his production company Oak Productions because of an early nickname?

4766. Son of Kong, *the sequel to* King Kong. *Both were filmed in 1933.*

4767. *The longest sword fight: Stewart Granger and Mel Ferrer dueled for six and a half nerve-racking minutes.*

4768. Short Cut To Hell, *in 1957.*

4769. The Blues Brothers.

4770. Dopey.

4771. *Rita Hayworth; their mothers were sisters.*

4772. The Tingler.

4773. The Thirty-Foot Bride Of Candy Rock, *in 1959.*

4774. Captive Girl, *in 1950.*

4775. Adventure.

4776. *Elvis Presley. (Kris Kristoferson got the part when Miss Streisand and Col. Tom Parker, Elvis's manager, couldn't agree on terms.)*

4777. *Cutting the heads off parking meters.*

4778. *Edmund Gwenn, who won the Best Supporting Actor award for his role as Kris Kringle in* Miracle on 34th Street, *in 1947.*

4779. Holiday Inn, *made in 1942, was the original vehicle for the song, "White Christmas."*

4780. *Muscleman Arnold Schwarzenegger, who was known as the Austrian Oak in his body-building days.*

4781. In Lugos, Hungary—as Bëla Blasko. He took his stage name from his hometown.

4782. He was listed under his real name—Walter Matuschanskayasky.

4783. Gregory Peck. Marlon Brando and Montgomery Clift also were considered for the part by producer Stanley Kramer, but his backer insisted on Cooper.

4784. Hall of Fame pitcher Grover Cleveland Alexander.

4785. Debra Winger, who agreed to take the role as long as she was not identified or listed in the credits.

4786. James Garner—whose name was originally James Bumgarner.

4787. The Third Man.

4788. Seaweed.

4789. Three. The judge also ordered Gabor to put her true age on her driver's license.

4790. Taco Bell, which won the "franchise wars" in the early 21st sentury. In copies of the film distributed in Europe, Taco Bell was replaced by Pizza Hut.

4791. Kim Bassinger.

4792. Only one—Smart Money, in 1931.

4793. The Cotton Club.

4781. Where was horror-film star Bela Lugosi born?

4782. How was actor Walter Matthau listed in the credits fc 1974 film *Earthquake*, in which he had a recurring cameo role drunk?

4783. Who turned down the role of the marshal in the 1! Western classic *High Noon* before Gary Cooper was offered t part?

4784. What baseball great did Ronald Reagan portray in the 195. biopic *The Winning Team*?

4785. What actress appeared in the 1987 film *Made in Heaven* as Emmett, a red-headed male archangel who served as head administrator of heaven?

4786. What popular TV and movie star cut the first syllable— Bum—from his last name when he launched his acting career?

4787. The plaintive musical score of what British motion picture classic was performed on a zither?

4788. What are Captain Nemo's cigars made of in the 1954 Walt Disney version of Jules Verne's *20,000 Leagues Under the Sea*?

4789. How many days in jail did Zsa Zsa Gabor serve in 1989 for slapping a Beverly Hills policeman?

4790. What is the only fast-food chain left on the planet in Sylvester Stallone's 1993 film *Demolition Man*, which takes place in the year 2032?

4791. What top cover girl first came to the attention of American moviegoers as an enemy agent in the 1983 James Bond film *Never Say Never Again*?

4792. How many movies did tough-guy actors James Cagney and Edward G. Robinson appear in together?

4793. What 1984 film was involved in so much litigation before its release that its closing credits include the name of the winning law firm?

4794. In the 1966 remake of *Stagecoach*, what famous entertainer made his last film appearance as the drunken doctor—the role created by Thomas Mitchell in the 1939 John Wayne classic?

4795. What is the name of Bacchus's donkey-unicorn in Fantasia, Walt Disney's 1940 animated spectacular?

4796. What popular actor's first film role was that of an accident-prone young man in a half-hour Army training film?

4797. The 1932 film *What Price Hollywood* was remade three times—under what much better known title?

4798. What famous actress dubbed the dialogue for Andie MacDowell when she appeared as Jane Porter in the 1984 film *Greystoke: The Legend of Tarzan, Lord of the Apes*?

4799. What 1990 movie was the first film released with an NC-17 rating?

4800. What 1963 movie Western starring John Wayne and Maureen O'Hara was based on William Shakespeare's *The Taming of the Shrew*?

4801. What famous film director invented false eyelashes?

4802. As a young man, what cowboy star was offered $100 a month to play shortstop for a professional baseball team?

4803. What film role did Eli Wallach give up in 1953—making way for a famous Oscar-winning performance by an entertainment world legend?

4804. What was the name of the jeep driven by Pat Brady, Roy Rogers's comic sidekick both in the movies and on television?

4805. What restaurant chain had a branch in the space station in the 1968 film *2001: A Space Odyssey*?

4806. In what film does actor Marlon Brando appear on ice skates?

4794. *Bing Crosby.*

4795. *Jacchus.*

4796. *Jack Lemmon.*

4797. A Star Is Born.

4798. *Glenn Close. MacDowell's Southern accent made her a very unconvincing British Jane.*

4799. Henry and June. *NC-17, which means "no children under 17," was created to replace the X rating.*

4800. *McLintock!*

4801. *D.W Griffith, in 1916. He wanted one of the actresses in his film* Intolerance *to have eyelashes that brushed her cheeks.*

4802. *Gene Autry. He turned down an offer from the Cardinal organization to play with its Tulsa farm team and kept his $150-a-month job as a railroad telegraph operator. Years later, Autry became the owner of the California Angels.*

4803. *The part of Private Maggio in* From Here To Eternity. *Wallach bowed out to appear on Broadway in* Camino Real, *paving the way for Frank Sinatra's show business comeback.*

4804. *Nellybelle.*

4805. *Howard Johnson.*

4806. *In the 1990 film,* The Freshman.

4807. What two umbrella-carrying characters are featured in Walt Disney movies?

4808. What country music star appeared in three teen movies in 1960—*Sex Kittens Go To College*, *Platinum High School* and *College Confidential*?

4809. What actor served as Ronald Reagan's best man when he married Nancy Davis in 1952?

4810. How many motion pictures did Elizabeth Taylor and Richard Burton make together?

4811. What fictional character has been portrayed at various times by actors Humphrey Bogart, James Garner, Elliot Gould, Robert Mitchum, George Montgomery, Robert Montgomery and William Powell?

4812. In film and advertising slang, what do the letters SFX represent?

4813. What 1991 film role went to Kevin Costner after it was turned down by both Harrison Ford and Mel Gibson?

4814. What popular movie thriller was the first Hollywood film to include footage of a flushing toilet?

4815. What now-famous comedienne had a small role as nightclub hostess Texas Guinan in the 1961 Warren Beatty-Natalie Wood film *Splendor in the Grass*?

4816. What actress once gave her dimensions as 20-20-20?

4817. What actresses were the first mother and daughter to be nominated for Oscars in the same year?

4818. Before making it big in Hollywood, what famous actress provided the background singing for Andy Warhol's 1968 film *Lonesome Cowboys* and appeared as an extra in Warhol's 1971 movie *Trash*?

4807. *Mary Poppins, in the film of the same name; and Jiminy Cricket in* Pinocchio.

4808. *Conway Twitty.*

4809. *William Holden.*

4810. *10—*Cleopatra, The VIPs, The Sandpiper, Who's Afraid of Virginia Woolf?, The Comedians, The Taming of the Shrew, Dr. Faustus, Boom, Under Milk Wood, *and* Hammersmith Is Out.

4811. *Philip Marlowe, the hard-boiled private eye created by writer Raymond Chandler.*

4812. *"Sound effects."*

4813. *The part of New Orleans district attorney Jim Garrison in the docudrama* JFK.

4814. *Alfred Hitchcock's* Psycho, *in 1960. A long-standing taboo was violated when Janet Leigh was filmed flushing scraps of paper down a toilet.*

4815. *Phyllis Diller.*

4816. *Mia Farrow.*

4817. *Laura Dern was nominated for best actress and her mother, Diane Ladd, for best supporting actress in 1991—both for performances in* Rambling Rose. *Neither won.*

4818. *Sissy Spacek.*

4819. Why did Italian movie director Federico Fellini call his 1963 autobiographical film *8½?*

4820. What 1988 film ends with 763 names—the longest list of credits on record?

4821. To what famous actress did Winston Churchill propose marriage?

4822. When did Charlie Chaplin's 1952 film *Limelight* win an Oscar?

4823. In the 1985 film *Back to the Future* starring Michael J. Fox, what does Marty McFly's mother-to-be mistakenly think his name is?

4824. For the 1981 Oscar-winning movie *Chariots of Fire*, where was the race around the Great Court of Trinity College at Cambridge filmed?

4825. Who provided the voice of Mufasa, Simba's father, in the 1994 movie, *The Lion King?*

4826. After demanding top billing over Katherine Hepburn in the 1949 film *Adam's Rib*, what did Spencer Tracy reply when someone asked if he'd ever heard of "ladies first"?

4827. What was the name of the 1986 sequel to the 1979 film *Alien?*

4828. What famous Hollywood legend—named Carol Jane Peters at birth—took her stage name from a New York City drugstore?

4829. What father and daughter were originally scheduled to star in the 1973 film *Paper Moon* in the roles that went to Ryan O'Neal and his daughter, Tatum?

4830. In what movie did burly character actor Rod Steiger make his singing and dancing debut?

4831. What Oscar-winning film included scenes shot on the River Kwai in Thailand?

4819. *He considered it his No. 8½ directorial effort—having completed seven full-length and three short (or half-length) features.*

4820. Who Framed Roger Rabbit? *The credits take 6½ minutes and don't include Kathleen Turner, who asked not to be listed as the voice of Jessica Rabbit.*

4821. *Ethel Barrymore.*

4822. *The movie won the Oscar for Best Original Dramatic Score in 1972, when it was first screened in Los Angeles.*

4823. *Calvin Klein. The reason, she tells him, is, "It's written all over your underwear."*

4824. *At Eton College. The dons at Trinity refused to have anything to do with the movie.*

4825. *James Earl Jones.*

4826. *"This is a movie, not a lifeboat."*

4827. Aliens.

4828. *Carole Lombard. The drugstore was the Carroll, Lombardi Pharmacy on Lexington Avenue and 65th Street in Manhattan.*

4829. *Paul Newman and his daughter Nell Potts. Their deal was called off when John Huston bowed out as director and Peter Bogdanovich took over.*

4830. *In the 1955 movie musical* Oklahoma!, *in which he portrayed "Pore Jud" Fry.*

4831. The Deer Hunter. *The 1978 film won five Oscars—including one for Best Picture.* Bridge on the River Kwai, *the 1957 Oscar winner for Best Picture, was filmed in Ceylon.*

4832. What disclaimer appears with the opening credits of the 1954 film *The Caine Mutiny,* which featured Humphrey Bogart as Captain Queeg?

4833. What actor, in describing his craggy appearance, once said, "I resemble a rock quarry that got dynamited"?

4834. What Oscar-winning movie role was turned down by TV newscasters Walter Cronkite and John Chancellor before it was given to an actor?

4835. Why did filmmaker George Lucas file suit against President Ronald Reagan?

4836. By what professional name do we know the actor who was born Walter Palanuik?

4837. In what film besides *Yankee Doodle Dandy* did James Cagney play the legendary George M. Cohan?

4838. What is the closing line in the credits for the 1974 film *The Taking of Pelham One, Two, Three,* about a hijacked New York City subway train?

4839. For which of Jimmy Stewart's films did his father publicly chastise the actor for making a "dirty picture"?

4840. What movie starring Robert Redford was an adaptation of a Broadway play in which he also appeared?

4841. In what film did Marnie Nixon, who dubbed the singing for stars in a number of popular movie musicals, finally make her screen debut?

4842. Which was the only Alfred Hitchcock film to win an Academy Award for Best Picture?

4843. What was the literary source of the title of the 1961 Warren Beatty-Natalie Wood film *Splendor in the Grass?*

4844. Of the banks shown in the 1967 film Bonnie and Clyde, how many were actually robbed by the notorious outlaw couple?

4832. "There has never been a mutiny in the history of the United States Navy."

4833. Charles Bronson.

4834. The role of the crazed anchorman in Network, the 1976 film that starred Peter Finch and gave us the line, "I'm mad as hell and I'm not going to take it anymore."

4835. To get him to stop using the term Star Wars to describe his Strategic Defense Initiative, the outer space computer-controlled defense system.

4836. Jack Palance.

4837. The Seven Little Foys.

4838. "Made without any help whatsoever from the New York Transit Authority."

4839. Anatomy of a Murder. The actor's father found the 1959 film's frank treatment of rape offensive and took out an ad in his hometown paper urging people not to see it.

4840. Barefoot in the Park. Redford's co-star in the 1964 stage production of the Neil Simon play was Elizabeth Ashley; in the 1967 movie, Jane Fonda.

4841. The Sound of Music—in which she appears as Sister Sophia. She did the singing for Audrey Hepburn in My Fair Lady; Natalie Wood in West Side Story; and Deborah Kerr in The King and I.

4842. The romantic thriller Rebecca, his first American film, in 1940.

4843. William Wordsworth's Ode: Intimations of Immortality from Recollections of Early Childhood. It reads: "Though nothing can bring back the hour/Of splendor in the grass, of glory in the flower;/We will grieve not, rather find/Strength in what remains behind."

4844. Three. Although closed since the Depression, they were reopened briefly for the filming of the movie.

4845. What movie classic takes place in a town called Hadleyville?

4846. How many women appeared in Stanley Kubrick's 1964 film *Dr. Strangelove, or How I Learned to Stop Worrying and Love the Bomb?*

4847. In the 1977 film *Star Wars*, what name was originally planned for Luke Skywalker, the character played by Mark Hamill?

4848. In what Cary Grant film is a tombstone shown inscribed with his real name—Archibald Leach?

4849. Mae West once said she liked two kinds of men. What were they?

4850. Elizabeth Taylor starred in 10 movies with husband Richard Burton. How many did she appear in with hubby Eddie Fisher?

4851. How much did a Masai chief offer for actress Carrol Baker in 1964, when the average Masai maiden was valued at $200 and 12 cows?

4852. In what town did the Martian landing in Orson Welles' 1938 radio broadcast of *War of the Worlds* allegedly take place?

4853. What was the name of the ancient souped-up spacecraft captained by Han Solo in the film classic *Star Wars?*

4854. What 1959 film spectacular was nominated for 12 Oscars— and won all but one of them?

4855. Who was originally cast to play the role of T.E. Lawrence in *Lawrence of Arabia*, the Academy Award winner for Best Picture in 1962?

4856. In what Academy Award-winning 1967 film did a teenage Richard Dreyfuss make his movie debut in a one-line role?

4857. Which American actress had the longest screen career on record?

4858. What was the source of the hundreds of authentic-looking early 19th century tinware pieces used in the 1997 movie *Amistad?*

4845. High Noon, *starring Gary Cooper and Grace Kelly.*

4846. *Only one. Tracy Reed, daughter of British director Sir Carol Reed. She played a nubile Pentagon secretary.*

4847. *Luke Skykiller. The name was changed on the first day of filming.*

4848. *The black-comedy classic* Arsenic and Old Lace, *which was released in 1944.*

4849. *"Domestic and foreign."*

4850. *One.* Butterfield Eight, *in 1960—for which she won an Academy Award for Best Actress.*

4851. *He offered $750 along with 150 cows and 200 goats and sheep. She was in Kenya filming the movie* Mr. Moses.

4852. *Grovers Mill, New Jersey.*

4853. *The Millennium Falcon.*

4854. Ben-Hur. *The Oscar that got away was for Best Screenplay Based on Material from Another Medium.*

4855. *Marlon Brando. He had to bow out when the shooting schedule of* Mutiny on the Bounty *was extended by several months. The part went to a virtual unknown, Peter O'Toole.*

4856. The Graduate. *He appears in the rooming house scene. His breakthrough role in* American Graffiti *came six years later.*

4857. *Helen Hayes, whose career spanned 78 years. It started with her 1910 debut in* Jean and the Calico Doll, *when she was 10, and ended with her appearance in the 1988 religious docudrama* Divine Mercy, No Escape, *when she was 88.*

4858. *Old Sturbridge Village, a re-created 1830s New England community in Sturbridge, Massachusetts. The tinware was crafted in its tin shop.*

4859. What was the first black-and-white film to be converted to color electronically?

4860. For which performer did Hollywood greats Humphrey Bogart and Lauren Bacall name their daughter?

4861. What was the first name of Ensign Pulver—played by Jack Lemmon in the 1955 film, *Mr. Roberts* and by Robert Walker Jr. in the 1964 sequel *Ensign Pulver*?

4862. What is the name of the writer-director Chris Columbus's production company?

4863. What was actor Robert Redford doing when he first saw the vast alpine canyon in Park City, Utah, that he later bought and turned into an artists' retreat, ski resort and family compound?

4864. What serious actor worked as a lion tamer during a summer break form the Professional Children's Acting School in New York City?

4865. What 1951 movie classic inspired the pilot for a TV series that never made it, despite a cast that featured James Coburn and Glynis Johns?

4866. What replaced Charlie, the pet dog, when the 1961 movie *The Absent-Minded Professor* was remade as *Flubber* in 1997?

4867. What 1946 American film classic was denounced as Communist propaganda in an FBI memo because of its "rather obvious attempt to denounce bankers"?

4868. What high-flying actor named his son Jett?

4869. What popular actress wrote a magazine article entitled *The Alien Inside Me*?

4870. How much did actor Arnold Schwarzenegger pay for John F. Kennedy's set of golf clubs at a 1996 auction?

4871. What two films share the dubious distinction of having 11 Oscar nominations and no Oscar wins?

4859. Yankee Doodle Dandy, *the 1942 biopic of George M. Cohan with James Cagney in the title role.*

4860. *Leslie Howard. Their daughter's name is Leslie Howard Bogart. The couple's son, Stephen, was named for the character Bogie played in their first movie together,* To Have and Have Not.

4861. *Frank. Lemmon's portrayal won him an Oscar for Best Supporting Actor.*

4862. *1492 Films, Inc.*

4863. *Hunting mountain lions. At the time, Sundance, his 5000-acre spread in the Wasatch Range, was a sheep ranch.*

4864. *Christopher Walken, in 1961. His job was with the Tarryl Jacobs Circus.*

4865. The African Queen. *The pilot was aired as an episode of* The Dick Powell Show *in March 1962.*

4866. *Weebo, the computer.*

4867. It's A Wonderful Life, *starring Jimmy Stewart. The FBI memo said the film attacked bankers "by casting Lionel Barrymore as a 'Scrooge-type' so that he could be the most hated man in the picture. . . a common trick used by Communists."*

4868. *John Travolta, who's a licensed pilot.*

4869. *Sigourney Weaver, who starred as Ellen Ripley in the 1979 high-tech horror movie* Alien *and its sequels* —Aliens, Alien3 *and* Alien Resurrection. *Her article appeared in* Premiere *magazine.*

4870. *$772,500. Schwarzenegger is married to JFK's niece Maria Shriver.*

4871. The Turning Point *in 1977 and* The Color Purple *in 1985.*

4872. Who won a Best Actor Oscar for a role he also played on Broadway and in a weekly TV series?

4873. For what role did actress Jodie Foster have to undergo psychiatric evaluation by the California Labor Board?

4874. What celebrity bought the first Hummer manufactured for civilian use?

4875. What Hollywood legend played the accordion in a tearoom before he was offered a bit role in a Broadway play?

4876. What well-known actress, early in her career, appeared in a low-budget 3-D horror film as a young woman menaced by giant slugs?

4877. What did Lauren Hutton use to seal the gap between her front teeth early in her modeling career?

4878. What popular actor made an 18-second cameo appearance as a body-pierced, heavy-metal fan at a rock concert in the 1997 Billy Crystal-Robin Williams film comedy *Father's Day*?

4879. What highly acclaimed 1966 movie won five Oscars— including one for Best Cinematography for a black-and-white film?

4880. What did Marilyn Monroe do to create her sexy walk?

4881. Who coined the nickname "Tinsel Town" for Hollywood?

4882. What three John Ford films starring John Wayne featured the Seventh Cavalry?

4883. What are the names of the two cats in the animated 1955 Walt Disney film, *Lady and the Tramp*?

4884. What job did 7-foot 2-inch Peter Mayhew return to after playing the "Wookie" Chewbacca in the 1977 film *Star Wars*?

4885. How many names appeared above Elvis Presley's in the screen credits for his first film, the 1956 drama *Love Me Tender*?

4872. *Yul Brynner. The role, of course, was the King of Siam, whom Brynner portrayed on Broadway in the musical* The King and I *in 1951, in the hit movie of the same name in 1956, and in an unsuccessful TV version called* Anna and the King *in 1972. He continued to play the role in a series of revivals until his death in 1985.*

4873. *Iris, the teen prostitute in the 1976 film* Taxi Driver. *Because she was a minor, the board had to determine whether she was emotionally capable of handling the controversial role.*

4874. *Arnold Schwarzenegger, in 1992. The 6,300-pound, 7-foot-wide vehicle is the civilian version of the military Humvee.*

4875. *Jimmy Stewart, who played the accordion in the 1955 movie* The Man From Laramie.

4876. *Demi Moore. The film,* Parasite, *was advertised as "the first futuristic monster movie in 3-D" when it was released in 1982.*

4877. *Undertaker's wax or candle wax. She later had a dentist make a removable cap she could use as needed to hide the gap.*

4878. *Mel Gibson.*

4879. Who's Afraid of Virginia Woolf? *Starring Elizabeth Taylor (Best Actress), Richard Burton, Sandy Dennis (Best Supporting Actress) and George Segal. Its other Oscars were for Best Art Direction-Set Decoration (black-and-white film), and Best Costume Design (black-and-white film).*

4880. *She sawed off part of the heel of one shoe.*

4881. *Oscar Levant, the pianist, composer and cynical Hollywood wit, who observed, "Strip the phony tinsel off Hollywood, and you'll find the real tinsel underneath."*

4882. Fort Apache *(1948),* She Wore A Yellow Ribbon *(1949) and* Rio Grande *(1950).*

4883. *Si and Am. They were Siamese, of course.*

4884. *Hospital porter in London.*

4885. *Two. He got third billing, after Richard Egan and Debra Paget.*

4886. What was the name of the sly fox in the Disney film version of *Pinocchio*?

4887. What was the only movie about the Vietnam conflict to be filmed while the war was going on?

4888. What was the name of the baby in the 1987 film *Three Men and a Baby*?

4889. In the original script for the 1931 film *The Public Enemy*, what was James Cagney supposed to rub in Mae Clarke's face?

4890. What part did Robert De Niro play in his elementary school production of *The Wizard of Oz*?

4891. On what movie soundtrack did Gene Autry's 1939 rendition of Back in the Saddle Again go platinum for the second time?

4892. What special-interest magazine featured a photo of Demi Moore on its cover with a line promoting a story on her "secret passion"?

4893. What special clause, relating to clothes, did actor James Stewart have included in all his movie contracts?

4894. What Oscar-winning film featured a scene with an estimated 300,000 extras?

4895. What are the only two films to have received Oscars for Best Actor, Best Actress, Best Picture, Best Director, and Best Writing (Adaptation)?

4896. In the 1989 film hit *Field of Dreams*, what major flub was made by actor Ray Liotta in portraying baseball great Shoeless Joe Jackson?

4897. Who provides the voice for Yoda in the *Star Wars* series?

4886. *Worthington Foulfellow.*

4887. *The 1968 film* The Green Berets, *starring John Wayne.*

4888. *Mary.*

4889. *An omelette. In the famous scene Cagney ended up squashing a grapefruit in her face.*

4890. The Cowardly Lion. *De Niro was 10 at the time.*

4891. *The 1993 hit* Sleepless in Seattle.

4892. Cigar Aficianado, *in its fall 1996 issue. Moore's secret passion, the magazine reported, is cigar-smoking.*

4893. *The right to select the hats he wore on camera.*

4894. Gandhi. *The scene in the 1982 film was a recreation of the Indian leader's massive funeral in New Delhi 40 years ago today.*

4895. It Happened One Night, *in 1934, and* One Flew Over The Cuckoo's Nest, *in 1975.*

4896. *He batted righty—Jackson was a lefty.*

4897. *Frank Oz, also the voice of Muppets™ Cookie Monster, Fozzie Bear and Ms. Piggy.*

4898. Where did the clairvoyant in director Tim Burton's *Pee Wee's Big Adventure* tell Pee Wee he would find his bicycle?

4899. Who had a cameo playing the president of the United States in Mike Myers' psychedelic comedy, *Austin Powers: The Spy Who Shagged Me*?

4900. In the 1989 cult fairy tale *The Princess Bride*, for what did the initials R.O.U.S. stand?

4901. What movie heartthrob played the corpse in *The Big Chill*— but ended up on the cutting room floor?

4902. Who posed for *Cosmopolitan* magazine's first nude centerfold in April 1974?

4903. Until 1990, what was the only Western to have been awarded the Oscar for Best Picture?

Bonus Trivia

4904. Preston Foster, Joanne Woodward, Ernest Torrence, Olive Borden, Edward Sedgwick, Louise Fazenda, Ronald Colman and Burt Lancaster were the first stars in Hollywood's Walk of Fame, begun in 1958.

4905. Outlaw Jesse James has been portrayed on screen by many different actors, but the first person ever to play him in a movie was his own son, Jesse James Jr.—in *Jesse James Under the Black Flag* (1921) and *Jesse James as the Outlaw* (1921).

4906. It was escape artist Harry Houdini who gave the young vaudeville player, Joseph Keaton, the name by which he would be known throughout his long film career. Having seen the acrobatic youngster scramble and fall about in his parents' boisterous stage routine, Houdini re-christened him "Buster."

4898. *At the Alamo. In the basement.*

4899. *Tim Robbins.*

4900. *Rodents of Unusual Size.*

4901. *Kevin Costner.*

4902. *Burt Reynolds.*

4903. Cimarron, *in 1931. It would be nearly 60 years before another western-themed movie,* Dances with Wolves, *would win, in 1990. Two yeasr later Clint Eastwood's brooding wWestern,* The Unforgiven, *would also claim the award.*

4907. Lana Turner was not discovered at the now-defunct Schwab's Pharmacy in Hollywood, as movie legend has it. She was discovered across the street from Hollywood High in Top's Café by Billy Wilkerson of *The Hollywood Reporter*, in January, 1936.

4908. John Travolta's stand-in for *Saturday Night Fever* was Jeff Zinn. It was Zinn's legs that were shown walking down the street in the film's opening.

Miscellaneous

Questions

4909. In land surveying, how long—in feet—is a chain?

4910. What synthetic fabric, introduced in the 1970s, is made of Teflon?

4911. What shade results when the rhubarb plant is used in hair dye?

4912. How many square inches are there in an acre?

4913. According to the Greek philosopher Aristotle, what part of the body served as the seat of the emotions?

4914. What was the childhood nickname of Leslie Hornby, the English model and sometimes actress better known as Twiggy?

4915. How many sets of letters on the standard typewriter and computer keyboard are in alphabetical order —reading left to right, of course?

4916. How much water does a 10-gallon hat hold?

4917. What was the only wood used by famed London cabinetmaker Thomas Chippendale?

Answers

4909. *66 feet.*

4910. *Gore-Tex.*

4911. *Blond. Its principal active ingredient is chrysophanol.*

4912. *6,272,640. It's the number of square feet in an acre (43,560) times the number of square inches in a square foot (144).*

4913. *The liver.*

4914. *Sticks. It's the nickname Twiggy was derived from, given to her because of her gangling appearance.*

4915. *Three sets—F-G-H, J-K-L and O-P.*

4916. *³/₄ gallon—or 3 quarts.*

4917. *Mahogany.*

4918. What are the six fields of endeavor for which Nobel Prizes are awarded?

4919. In the early days of English law, why did grand juries sometimes write the word ignoramus on the back of indictments?

4920. What is a well-trained horse expected to do when given the command "gee"?

4921. Where on the grounds of the Playboy Mansion West did Hugh Hefner propose to his wife Kimberley?

4922. How many acres are there in a square mile?

4923. How large was the fund bequeathed in 1896 by Alfred Nobel to establish the annual Nobel Prizes?

4924. Who wrote the first known book on cosmetics, recommending face packs of barley-bean flour, eggs and mashed narcissus bulbs for smoother skin and warning against "powder too thickly applied, or ointments spread to excess"?

4925. Who referred to her famous son as "my golden Ziggy"?

4926. Approximately how many grains of sand does a quart-size pail hold?

4927. What is the fuel capacity—in gallons—of a Boeing 747 airliner?

4928. How many feet per minute does the standard escalator move?

4929. What philosophy was expounded by the American League for Physical Culture, established in 1929?

4930. What was the original name of the Girl Scouts?

4931. Charles E. Weller is best known for a single sentence he created. What is it?

4932. Who is credited with saying, "The bigger they are, the harder they fall"?

4918. *Physics, chemistry, physiology or medicine, literature, peace and economic science. Economic science was added in 1969.*

4919. *Ignoramus is Latin for "we do not know." Jurors wrote the word on indictments when they found insufficient evidence to indict.*

4920. *Turn to the right. The opposite command, "haw," means turn left.*

4921. *At the wishing well.*

4922. *640.*

4923. *$9.2 million.*

4924. *The Roman poet Ovid, in 10 A.D.*

4925. *Sigmund Freud's mother, Amalie Freud.*

4926. *8 million.*

4927. *57,285 gallons.*

4928. *120.*

4929. *Nudism.*

4930. *The Girl Guides.*

4931. *"Now is the time for all good men to come to the aid of their party." He invented it as a typing exercise.*

4932. *Heavyweight boxer Bob Fitzsimmons. He made the statement before fighting (and losing to) champion James J. Jeffries in 1902.*

4933. When Elizabeth Cochrane traveled around the world in less than 80 days in 1890, she used another name to conceal her identity. What was it?

4934. Identify the following: It was insured for $140,000; Sime Silverman, founder of *Variety* gave it its nickname; and it measured 2⅝ inches from head to tip.

4935. Who was Alexander the Great's teacher?

4936. Exactly how long is one year?

4937. Who was the first inductee into the National Trivia Hall of Fame?

4938. "Uphold the Right" (Maintiens le Droit) is the motto of what law enforcement agency?

4939. What do the initials, M.G., stand for on the famous British-made automobile?

4940. When were vitamins first described, and who is credited with their discovery?

4941. What is the origin of the $64 question?

4942. Canadian stagecoach-robber Bill Miner (the Gentleman Bandit), is credited for creating what classic line in a holdup?

4943. What are the only two letters that are not on a telephone dial?

4944. On what type of product would you find a message signed, "P. Loquesto Newman"?

4945. On what date will the twenty-first century begin?

4946. The most common hat size for men is 7⅛ what is the most common size for women?

4947. In earlier times, what building material did most Eskimos use to build their homes?

4933. *Nellie Bly.*

4934. *Jimmy Durante's nose.*

4935. *Aristotle.*

4936. *365 days, 5 hours, 48 minutes and 46 seconds.*

4937. *Robert L. Ripley, who was inducted in 1980 into the honorary Hall sponsored by* Trivia Unlimited *magazine of Lincoln, Neb.*

4938. *The Royal Canadian Mounted Police.*

4939. *Morris Garage.*

4940. *In 1912; F. G. Hopkins and Casmir Funk.*

4941. *It was the highest prize ever paid to a winner on radio's* Take it or Leave it.

4942. *"Hands up."*

4943. *Q and Z.*

4944. *Actor Paul Newman's line of food products.*

4945. *January 1, 2001. (Strictly speaking, January 1, 2000 will be the first day of the last year of the twentieth century.)*

4946. *22. Although both are measured in inches, men's hats are sized according to diameter and women's according to circumference.*

4947. *Sod. Igloos, made of ice, were generally built only as temporary shelters.*

4948. How is Eleanor Thornton, secretary to British Lord Montagu of Beaulieu in the early twentieth century, part of automotive history?

4949. Who has requested that her gravestone epitaph read, "Big deal! I'm used to dust"?

4950. In 1937, sewing machine heiress Daisy Singer Alexander put her will in a bottle and tossed it into the Thames River near London. Where and when did it wash up?

4951. Who was Grace Toof and how has she been immortalized?

4952. What was the first word that the blind Helen Keller learned in sign language from her teacher Annie Sullivan?

4953. Annie Oakley, in a demonstration of her incredible marksmanship, once shot at 5,000 pennies tossed into the air. How many did she hit with her rifle fire?

4954. What did comic genius Ernie Kovacs have installed in his California driveway to make maneuvering easier for visitors?

4955. In what year was January 1 first used to mark the beginning of the new year?

4956. What Census Bureau category do you fall into if you are classified as a POSSLQ?

4957. The four-leaf clover is considered lucky because of its rarity and symmetry. What about the even rarer five-leaf clover?

4958. What is the size of the standard credit card?

4959. What group's motto is "Blood and Fire"?

4960. What do the following crayon colors have in common—maize, raw umber, lemon yellow, blue gray, violet blue, green blue, orange red and orange yellow?

4961. What was the original use of crinoline—the stiff fabric most commonly associated with women's petticoats?

4948. *She was the inspiration for the Flying Lady statuette—known as "The Spirit of Ecstasy"—that graces the radiator of the Rolls Royce. The original was created for Lord Montagu's Silver Ghost by sculptor Charles Sykes in 1911.*

4949. *Writer-humorist-homemaker Erma Bombeck.*

4950. *On a beach in San Francisco, 12 years later. Under the terms of the will, the lucky beachcomber who found it inherited half of Daisy's $12 million estate.*

4951. *She's the woman that Graceland, Elvis Presley's estate in Memphis, Tennessee, is named after. Presley bought it from Ruth Brown, who had named it for her Aunt Grace.*

4952. *Water.*

4953. *4,777—for an average of almost 96 percent.*

4954. *An asphalt turntable, which made U-turns unnecessary.*

4955. *In 153 B.C., by the Romans. Previously, New Year's Day was in March.*

4956. *Person of Opposite Sex, Sharing Living Quarters.*

4957. *The superstitious consider it bad luck if kept—but good luck to both parties involved if given away immediately upon finding.*

4958. *3⅜ by 2⅛ inches.*

4959. *The Salvation Army's.*

4960. *They were the first colors ever dropped from the Crayola crayon line. They were replaced in 1990 with bolder colors—cerulean, dandelion, wild strawberry, vivid tangerine, fuchsia, teal blue, royal purple and jungle green.*

4961. *Men's collars.*

4962. Nineteenth century English physician Peter Mark Roget devised his famous thesaurus to help people find the right word. What equally useful tool did he develop for those searching for mathematical solutions?

4963. From what is rice paper made?

4964. What day is the middle day of the year—in non-leap years?

4965. Can you fill in the last word of this Victorian-era saying: "Horses sweat, men perspire, women . . ."?

4966. How much weight is saved when an airline doesn't paint an MD-11 jumbo jet?

4967. What did prospectors in ancient times use to collect grains of gold from streams?

4968. What was the average life span of a Stone Age cave dweller?

4969. What was used to erase lead pencil marks before rubber came into use?

4970. How many points are there on a Maltese cross?

4971. Why do federal park rangers working in the subtropical marshlands of south Florida wear snowshoes designed for use in subarctic climates?

4972. How many dust mites can a gram of dust hold?

4973. What inspired bareback rider Nelson Hower to introduce circus tights in 1828?

4974. What high-fashion clothing designer spent two years in medical school before deciding to find another career?

4975. What highly paid supermodel was valedictorian of her high school class and winner of a full college scholarship to study chemical engineering?

4976. An organization called SCROOGE was formed in 1979 in Charlottesville, Virginia. What does the acronym stand for?

4962. A special (log-log) slide rule.

4963. The pith—the inner part of the trunk—of a small tree native to swampy forests of southern China and Taiwan.

4964. July 2nd. There are 182 days before it, and 182 after.

4965. ". . .glow."`

4966. Almost 300 pounds.

4967. The fleece of sheep—unlike the '49ers and other prospectors who panned for gold.

4968. 18 years.

4969. Pieces of bread.

4970. Eight.

4971. The web-footed, wood-framed shoes keep them from sinking into the silty marshes.

4972. 500 (an ounce can hold 13,500).

4973. His regular costume was missing—so he performed in his long knit underwear. Hower and other performers with the Buckley and Wicks Show normally wore short jackets, knee breeches and stockings. When their costumes didn't arrive in time for a show, Hower improvised and changed circus fashions forever.

4974. Italian style-setter Giorgio Armani.

4975. Cindy Crawford. The college was Northwestern University. Crawford dropped out after just one semester to pursue a modeling career.

4976. Society to Curtail Ridiculous, Outrageous and Ostentatious Gift Exchanges.

4977. For what magazine did Hugh Hefner serve as circulation manager while he was raising money to launch *Playboy*?

4978. What article of clothing is named for James Brudenell, the British major general who led his men "into the valley of death" in the Crimean War's famous "Charge of the Light Brigade"?

4979. Prior to his death in 1999, John F. Kennedy, Jr. founded what politically-themed magazine?

4980. What was the cost of the first tour arranged by travel entrepreneur Thomas Cook in 1841?

4981. What problem did Leonardo da Vinci, Winston Churchill, Albert Einstein, Thomas Edison and General George Patton have in common?

4982. What would the Barnie Doll's measurements be if she were life-size?

4983. What did All Nippon Airways do in an effort to prevent its planes from sucking birds into their engines?

4984. Where did the phrase "Let George do it" originate?

4985. What is the "Newgate Calendar"?

4986. What foreign form of transportation was invented by American Baptist missionary Jonathan Goble in 1871?

4987. What was the chief source of the shiny material used in making artificial pearls before the advent of plastics?

4988. What is the centerfold feature called in *Playboar*, a magazine for swine breeders?

4989. What were the names of the two dogs launched into space aboard Russia's Sputnik 5 and later returned to earth, becoming the first animals recovered from orbit?

4990. What English earl had both a coat style and a furniture style named for him?

4977. Children's Activities *magazine.*

4978. *The cardigan sweater. Brudenell was the seventh earl of Cardigan.*

4979. George.

4980. *The equivalent of fourteen cents. It was a 48-mile round trip by British rail between Leicester and Loughborough for a temperance meeting.*

4981. *All were dyslexic.*

4982. 39-21-33.

4983. *It painted giant eyes on the engine intakes to discourage birds from approaching.*

4984. *With France's King Louis XII, who let his chief minister, Cardinal George d'Amboise, do it.*

4985. *The biographical record, first published in the late eighteenth century, of the most notorious criminals incarcerated at London's famous Newgate prison.*

4986. *The rickshaw. Goble, while serving as a missionary in Yokohama, had a Japanese carpenter build the rickshaw for his invalid wife.*

4987. *Fish scales.*

4988. *"Littermate of the Month."*

4989. *Belka and Strelka; they made their historic flight in 1960.*

4990. Philip Dormer Stanhope, the fourth earl of Chesterfield. The Chesterfield coat and sofa are named for him.

4991. Before the introduction of the hair dryer in 1920, what common household appliance was promoted for its hair-drying ability?

4992. Who was described in *Playboy* magazine as "Mary Poppins in Joan Collins' clothing"?

4993. How much hay was eaten daily by Jumbo, showman P. T. Barnum's famous 6½-ton elephant?

4994. What was the first living creature ever ejected from a supersonic aircraft?

4995. To whom did Mahatma Gandhi write for advice on diet and exercise?

4996. In 1964, a capsized freighter was refloated in Kuwait by filling its hull with polystyrene balls. Where did this idea originate?

4997. Where do these lines come from?
"I always voted at my party's call,
And never thought of thinking for myself at all."

4998. Why does the Bronx Zoo get blood daily from a local slaughterhouse?

4999. What famous Englishman's experiments with freezing meat in 1626 caused his death from exposure?

5000. What trade was Greek philosopher Socrates trained for?

5001. Who was billed as "The Human Mop" when he joined his family's comic acrobatic vaudeville act at age 3?

5002. What did Hyman Lipman do in 1858 that made life easier for students?

5003. Who went to New York City to launch her modeling career in 1966, after winning the Miss Rocket Tower beauty contest in California?

4991. The vacuum cleaner—which could be converted into a hair dryer by attaching a hose to the exhaust.

4992. Vanna White, of TV's Wheel of Fortune *fame.*

4993. Two hundred pounds.

4994. A bear, in 1962. It was parachuted from 35,000 feet to a safe landing on earth.

4995. Strongman Charles Atlas.

4996. In a 1949 Donald Duck comic, in which Donald and his nephews raised a yacht using ping pong balls.

4997. Gilbert and Sullivan's operetta, HMS Pinafore.

4998. To feed its vampire bats, part of its captive breeding collection of bats—the largest in the world.

4999. Sir Francis Bacon, philosopher, courtier, statesman, essayist.

5000. Stonecutting.

5001. Buster Keaton.

5002. He put pencil and eraser together.

5003. Cheryl Tiegs.

5004. How much did 16-year-old Edgar Bergen pay a woodcarver for Charlie McCarthy's head in 1925— and what size hat did it wear?

5005. The term "Siamese twins" originated with the birth of two brothers joined together at the chest. What were their names?

5006. What did Lizzie Borden, Napoleon, and Titian have in common?

5007. Gen. Tom Thumb, 3 feet 4 inches tall, was the first husband of Mercy Lavinia Bump, who measured 2 feet 8 inches. How tall was her second husband, Count Primo Magi?

5008. Who were actress-socialite Dina Merrill's super-rich parents?

5009. Who runs the Spirit Foundation, a charity dedicated to helping the aged, abused, and orphaned?

5010. In the words of the popular English nursery rhyme, "Who killed Cock Robin"—and how?

5011. By what name was Nobel Peace Prize winner Agnes Gonxha Bojaxhiu better known?

5012. How is Sir Benjamin Hall memorialized?

5013. Who was Apollos De Rivoire?

5014. Who was Pablo Ruiz?

5015. What reason did Yale University graduate student Edmund D. Looney give when he sought court permission in 1956 to change his name?

5016. What do the surnames Adler and Aguila have in common?

5017. What is the chief ingredient in the rich brown pigment we know as sepia?

5018. What was the response of England's White Chapel Foundry in 1970 when members of the Procrastinators Club of America demanded a refund for the Liberty Bell because it cracked in 1835?

5004. *Cost, $36; hat size, 5⅛.*

5005. *Chang and Eng, born in 1811.*

5006. *They were all redheads.*

5007. *Her equal at 2 feet 8 inches.*

5008. *Financier E. F. Hutton and cereal heiress Marjorie Merriweather Post.*

5009. *Yoko Ono.*

5010. *"I," said the sparrow, "with my bow and arrow."*

5011. *Mother Teresa, India's "saint of the gutter."*

5012. *His nickname—Big Ben—was adopted for the 13½-ton hour bell in the clock tower of the British Houses of Parliament in London. Hall was London's chief commissioner of works in 1859, when the bell was installed.*

5013. *The French Huguenot father of American patriot Paul Revere. Rivoire changed his name to Paul Revere after immigrating to the colonies as a boy, and later passed that name onto his son.*

5014. *Pablo Picasso. Born Pablo Ruiz, the great artist chose to use Picasso—his mother's less common surname.*

5015. *He claimed the name Looney would interfere with the practice of his chosen profession—psychiatry.*

5016. *Both mean eagle—Adler in German; águila in Spanish.*

5017. *The inky fluid secreted by the cuttlefish—which belongs to the genus Sepia.*

5018. *The British bell maker offered a full refund—but only if the defective product was returned in its original packaging.*

5019. What was the first man-made object to reach the moon?

5020. What is daredevil Evel Knievel's real first name?

5021. On board a ship, what times would be indicated by seven bells?

5022. What is the standard width between rails on North American and most European railroads?

5023. What do the letters stand for in the acronym CARE—the name of the relief organization established in 1945?

5024. Why wasn't 10-year-old Eric, the orangutan at Chicago's Lincoln Park Zoo, sent to China for stud duty as planned in 1984?

5025. What was the name of Hugh Hefner's all-black private jetliner?

5026. For what highly valued commodity did one early seventeenth-century Dutch farmer trade 4 loads of grain, 4 oxen, 12 sheep, 8 pigs, 2 tubs of butter, 100 pounds of cheese, 4 barrels of ale, 2 hogsheads of wine, a bed with bedding, a chest of clothes and a silver goblet?

5027. How thick is the gold leaf used for lettering and gilding?

5028. Where did the countdown used in rocket and spaceship launchings originate?

5029. What is the telephone area code for a cruise ship in the Atlantic Ocean?

5030. Left to right, what are the seven letters on the bottom row of the standard typewriter or computer keyboard?

5031. What is the color of the "black box" that houses an airplane's voice recorder?

5032. What did former president Richard Nixon, striptease artist Gypsy Rose Lee, opera impresario Rudolph Bing and French novelist Simone de Beauvoir have in common?

5019. *Luna 2, an unmanned Soviet spacecraft that crashed onto the lunar surface in September 1959.*

5020. *Robert.*

5021. *3:30, 7:30 and 11:30—both A.M. and P.M.*

5022. *4 feet 8½ inches—about the width of cart tracks in ancient Rome, where that was found to be the most efficient width for a loaded horse-drawn vehicle.*

5023. *Cooperative for American Relief Everywhere. When the group was first formed, the letters stood for Cooperative for American Remittances to Europe, and then Cooperative for American Remittances Everywhere.*

5024. *"He" unexpectedly gave birth to a baby—and was renamed Erica.*

5025. *"Big Bunny."*

5026. *A single tulip bulb.*

5027. *Approximately ¹/₂₀₀,₀₀₀ inch.*

5028. *In a silent German science fiction film,* Die Frau in Mond (The Girl in the Moon) *in 1928. Director Fritz Lang reversed the count to build suspense.*

5029. *871.*

5030. *z, x, c, v, b, n, m*

5031. *It's orange—so it can be more easily detected amid the debris of a plane crash.*

5032. *Their birthday—January 9.*

5033. In a famous New Year's Day column, newspaperman Westbrook Pegler repeated the same sentence 50 times. What was it?

5034. If we saw the emblem known as a fylfot decorating a Byzantine structure, what would we most likely call it?

5035. How did the inch-long 2-penny (or 2d) nail get its name?

5036. Approximately how many blades of grass are there in an acre of lawn?

5037. What did Aristotle believe was the main purpose of the human brain?

5038. In medieval days, how much did the average suit of armor weigh?

5039. In the children's rhyme that begins "Ding, Dong, Bell," who put Pussy in the well and who pulled her out?

5040. How big is a cord of wood?

5041. Who was the first person to walk untethered in space?

5042. What did movie star Mary Pickford use to christen the first Hollywood-to-San Francisco bus in the early 1920s?

5043. In a bid to calm manic and psychotic juveniles, what color did California's San Bernardino County Probation Department paint its detention cells?

5044. Who said, "The great question . . . which I have not been able to answer despite my 30 years in research into the feminine soul, is 'What does a woman want'?"

5045. What was the first hurricane named after a man?

5046. What great feat made Isaac Van Amburgh a circus headliner in the late 1830s?

5047. What incredible adventure did British seaman James Bartley survive while whale hunting in 1891?

5033. "I will never mix gin, beer, and whiskey again."

5034. A swastika. The Nazis adopted the ancient symbol as their emblem.

5035. It was the nail that was sold at the rate of 100 for 2 pennies, or pence, in Great Britain in the fifteenth century, when the sizing system for nails was first established. (The d in 2d is the British symbol for pence.)

5036. 564,537,600—according to the Lawn Institute.

5037. To cool the blood.

5038. Between 50 and 55 pounds.

5039. Little Johnny Green put her in; Little Tommy Stout got her out.

5040. It is 128 cubic feet and usually measures 4 feet high, 4 feet wide and 8 feet long.

5041. Navy Captain Bruce McCandless II, 164 miles above the earth, from the space shuttle Challenger on February 7, 1984.

5042. A bottle of grape juice. Prohibition made champagne taboo.

5043. Bubble-gum pink.

5044. Sigmund Freud.

5045. Bob, in July 1979. He put in a brief, blustery appearance on the Louisiana coast and then turned into an offshore breeze.

5046. He was the first animal trainer to put his head in a lion's mouth.

5047. He spent two days in a whale's stomach after being swallowed alive—and then lived another 35 years to tell about it.

5048. What was a 13.5-carat diamond used for on the Pioneer 2 space probe to Venus in 1978?

5049. Who was featured in the *Playboy* centerfold when the magazine made its debut in 1953?

5050. What did the R in Edward R. Murrow stand for?

5051. What is the source of the hair in most camel's hairbrushes?

5052. Several American zoos have put up signs indicating "The Most Dangerous Animal in the World." Where are they posted?

5053. What was the name of Smokey the Bear's mate?

5054. Where are the Islands of Langerhans?

5055. Why did the Smithsonian Institution develop a special perspiration and barnyard scent for one of their exhibitions?

5056. What unusual twosome spoke at ventriloquist Edgar Bergen's funeral in 1979?

5057. Why is the phrase "the quick brown fox jumps over a lazy dog" used to check typewriters?

5058. The highest surface wind speed ever recorded was at Mount Washington, New Hampshire, on April 24, 1934. What was it?

5059. What is the highest rating given a top quality diamond?

5060. What altitude does a vehicle have to exceed for its pilot and passengers to be officially recognized as spacemen?

5061. What did the Apollo 8 astronauts use to fasten down tools during weightlessness on their 1968 moon-orbiting voyage?

5062. In what kind of store are you most likely to find Chilean nylons and Australian bananas?

5063. What does a vamp have to do with a shoe?

5064. What did Shirley Temple, Enrico Caruso, Irving Berlin, and Gene Tunney have in common?

5048. *Instrument-viewing ports. It was the only substance that was both transparent to infrared light and also able to withstand the red-hot heat and tremendous pressure of the Venusian atmosphere.*

5049. *Marilyn Monroe.*

5050. *Roscoe.*

5051. *Squirrel tails.*

5052. *Next to full-length mirrors—for the viewing public.*

5053. *Goldie.*

5054. *In the human body—in the pancreas.*

5055. *To make their re-creation of a Maryland sharecropper's house more realistic.*

5056. *Muppet creator Jim Henson and Kermit the Frog.*

5057. *It's a pangram—it contains every letter in the alphabet at least once.*

5058. *It was 231 miles per hour. (Winds become hurricane force when they reach 74 miles per hour.)*

5059. *D-flawless.*

5060. *According to NASA 400,000 feet, or 75¾ miles, above the earth.*

5061. *Silly Putty.*

5062. *A fish store. They are species of shrimp.*

5063. *It's the upper front part of a shoe.*

5064. *When they married, their blue-blooded spouses were kicked out of the Social Register.*

5065. All told, how many children did Siamese twins Chang and Eng Bunker father?

5066. What is the maximum flight speed of a Boeing 747-300 jetliner?

5067. What was the greatest number of people ever carried in an airship?

5068. According to Aristotle, what determined whether a baby would turn out to be a girl or a boy?

5069. How many teaspoons are there in a cup?

5070. Why did local environmental officials spray-paint 108 pink plastic flamingos white and place them in groups around marshes in the Everglades?

5071. What was the symbolism behind flying a flag at half-mast as a sign of mourning when the custom was first introduced at sea in the seventeenth century?

5072. What are the names of the six Gummi Bears?

5073. How are the monkeys Mizaru, Kikazaru and Iwazaru better known to us?

5074. If all the water were drained from the body of an average 160-pound man, how much would the body weigh?

5075. What is the average life expectancy of a toilet?

5076. Which was the first Impressionist painting to be owned by the French government?

5077. How much does owning a typical dog cost over its average 11-year life span—not including the original purchase price?

5078. What famous medal depicts three naked men with their hands on each other's shoulders?

5079. What percentage of men are left-handed? How about women?

5065. *22. Chang had 10; Eng, 12.*

5066. *583 miles per hour.*

5067. *207. They were aboard the U.S. Navy's Akron in 1931. The trans-Atlantic record is 117—held by the ill-fated Hindenburg, which exploded in May 1937.*

5068. *Wind direction.*

5069. *48. There are 3 teaspoons to a tablespoon and 16 tablespoons to a cup.*

5070. *To attract snowy egrets, white ibis and wood storks. The plastic flamingos were much cheaper than white egret decoys.*

5071. *The top of the mast was left empty for the invisible flag of death.*

5072. *Gruffi, Cubbi, Tummi, Zummi, Sunni and Grammi.*

5073. *As See No Evil, Hear No Evil and Speak No Evil, respectively.*

5074. *64 pounds.*

5075. *50 years.*

5076. *Edouard Manet's* Olympia, *which was bought through public subscription in 1890, seven years after his death. It is still owned by the Louvre.*

5077. *An average of $14,600—with food ($4,020) the biggest expense, followed closely by veterinary costs ($3,930).*

5078. *The Nobel Peace Prize.*

5079. *10 percent of men; 8 percent of women.*

5080. How many seats are there on the standard 747 jumbo jet?

5081. What gem was once considered a charm against drunkenness?

5082. In the late 1920s, who arranged 200 golf balls in neat rows in the hollow of a fallen tree at a public golf course in Winnipeg, Canada?

5083. How many grooves are there on the edge of a quarter?

5084. How many letters are there in the Hawaiian alphabet?

5085. In writing Roman numerals what does $\bar{V}$ represent?

5086. What is the only fifteen-letter word in the English language that can be written without repeating a letter?

5087. What is the largest amount of American currency one can hold without having change for a dollar?

5080. *420.*

5081. *The amethyst—which gets its name from the Greek amethystos—which means "remedy for drunkenness."*

5082. *A gopher, in the mistaken belief that they were eggs and would make appetizing wintertime eating.*

5083. *119.*

5084. *Twelve: vowels A-E-I-O-U; consonants H-K-L-M-N-P-W.*

5085. *It represents 5,000. The bar is a multiplier, indicating 1,000 times the number below.*

5086. *Uncopyrightable.*

5087. *$1.19—three quarters, four dimes and four pennies.*